# China's Economy Amid New Challenges: Exploration of Chinese Economists

Editors in Chief: Prof. Jin Bei, Prof. Li Gang

经济科学出版社
Economic Science Press

Paths International Ltd

# Foreword

From the launching of reform and opening-up in 1978 to the dawn of the 21st century, China has been transformed from a self-enclosed, planned economy to a market-based one, and the country has integrated itself into the international community. China wishes to look beyond its border and engage in equal-footed dialogue with its partners and competitors. With China's rapid emergence and great achievements, other countries increasingly want to learn more about this "mysterious oriental country" and the miraculous changes taking place here. However, we have also found that abroad, the public, high-ranking officials and even media and academia may not have a clear picture of China. Chinese scholars' views on their country and beyond are not well understood by foreign scholars, not to mention people in the street, and overseas officials and scholars do not appreciate China's realities. Legitimate claims and well-intentioned expressions from China are often misunderstood or distorted by the media, and it seems that the world is unprepared for a changing China. China needs to know itself and the outside world, and the world needs to have a closer look at China as well. Research on the China phenomenon and its implications has become topical around the world. Hence, developing diversified channels and platforms of communication is necessary both in China and the outside world.

A possible way to meet this need is to express to the world Chinese scholars' opinions and research in a language that foreign readers, understand, particularly mainstream audiences and elites. That's why we launched the bio-monthly English journal *China Economist* in March 2006: to update the world about the latest outcomes of Chinese economics and management research and provide in-depth reports and statistical information about the current economic situation and events in China. There have been more than 400 articles published in this journal, and they have been well received internationally.

This book is a collection of some of the best articles published in 2012 on *China Economist*, and it represents top Chinese economists' major research outcomes and opinions on economic matters, status and trends from various perspectives. Some work with China's highest academic research institutes and policy consultation agencies, while others work with related agencies and universities. Hence, this book largely reflects the key concerns and efforts of economic research institutes, policy advisory agencies, regulatory policy research departments and universities on China's economy.

Since the 1980s, China has been increasingly seen as an economy of great vitality and appeal. Opening-up and robust growth in a country of such magnitude has shocked and worried the world, while China has become one of the developing countries most tolerant and least reserved toward economic globalization. The massive Chinese "dragon" is bringing about a fundamental transformation to the global economic landscape. What implications will such transformation have on China and beyond?

Indeed, rapid economic growth over the past three decades has transformed China and its people's lives. By economic size, China is already a major industrial producer and economic power. However, by per capita income or GDP, China is at most on the boundary between a low-income country and the lower tiers of a mid-income country. By current exchange rates, China is a low-income country. By purchasing power parity (PPP), China is only at the lower tiers of a mid-income country. China has one-fourth of the world's labor, but its GDP is far below the world average of 10%. Even if China becomes the largest exporter in the world, its export share would still be far below one-half the share of its population. In other words, China's output capacity and economic size make up a much smaller proportion than its population. China's per capita GDP is also below world average level. Premier Wen Jiabao has admitted that more than 100 million Chinese people are in desperate poverty. China's social security and basic welfare systems are still very weak. By any standard, China is not a developed and mature modernized country.

Chinese scholars wish to tell the world this truth: Although China has become the world's second largest economy, its GDP per capita is very low. China remains a developing country, and development is its top priority and the basis for all welfare programs. The rights of development are basic human rights upon which China cannot waiver. Development is the best gift China has to offer to the world. Meanwhile, Chinese scholars should also recognize that China must deepen reform and expand opening-up, balance efficiency with fair income distribution, use resources in more efficient, refined and clean ways, and challenge its enterprises to assume more social responsibilities. Only in this way can China complete its historic transition from a developing country to a mature, modernized country.

**Prof. JIN Bei (金碚) and Dr. LI Gang (李钢)**
February 15, 2013

# 序　言

从1978年中国开始改革开放到21世纪初，中国艰难地从封闭的计划经济脱胎出来，走过了向市场经济转轨的初级阶段，进入了经济全球化潮流汹涌的国际社会。在融入经济全球化的过程中，中国如饥似渴地希望了解世界，并越来越希望能够同国际合作者和竞争者进行平等的对话。而随着中国的迅速崛起和获得巨大的发展成就，其他国家也越来越希望能够了解这个“神秘的东方国度”以及在这个国度中发生的奇迹般的变化。但是，我们也发现，在国外，不仅普通民众，而且高层官员，甚至媒体和学界，对中国的认知与了解与中国对世界的了解十分不对称。中国学者对中国与世界问题的见解并没有被国外学者更不用说普通民众所了解；中国的现实状况与政策实施的客观条件并不被国外的官员与学者所认知；中国的正当利益诉求甚至善意表达往往被国际舆论所误解或曲解。面对中国的巨变，似乎全世界都准备不足。中国需要认识自己和世界，世界也需要深入了解中国。研究中国，发现中国现象的世界意义，成为一个国际性课题。因此，开拓更多的交流渠道和平台，有效地进行国际沟通和传播，是中国和世界共同的需要。

为了顺应这一需要，较可行的方式之一就是把中国学者有价值的观点与研究成果以国外读者能够读懂和了解的文字和表达方式，直接向世界传播，特别是要使主流和精英人群成为主要受众。因此，2006年3月，我们创办了英文双月期刊《中国经济学人》，向世界介绍中国经济学和管理学的最新研究进展，发表关于中国经济的学术论文和研究报告，提供关于中国当前经济形势及重大经济事件的深度报道和数据资料。迄今为止，该期刊已发表了近400多篇文章，受到广泛的关注，产生了很大的国际影响。

本书就是以《中国经济学人》2012年所发表的文章为主体，按照若干重要主题进行精选而编辑成书的。可以说，本书代表了中国顶级经济学家近年来对中国经济问题的重要研究成果和主要观点，从多角度透视了中国经济的现状与发展趋势。这些经济学家有的在中国最高学术研究机构和政策咨询机构工作，有的在相关部门工作，也有的在高校工作。因此，本书的内容在很大程度上反映了中国主要的经济研究机构、政策咨询机构、政府政策研究部门和高等院校在中国经济研究上所关注的主要问题和所进行的努力方向。

中国学者想告诉世界这个真正的事实：虽然中国经济总量已经居于世界第二，但人均收入仍旧很低；中国仍然是一个发展中国家。发展是中国的“第一要务”，发展是解决一切民生事业的基础，发展权是中国不可放弃的基本人权！而且，中国的发展是对世界最有利的贡献！同时，中国学者也认识到中国经济必须继续深化改革和扩大开放；中国社会必须更好地平衡效率和公平的关系；中国的产业必须更节约、更精致、更清洁；中国的企业必须承担起更多的社会责任；只有这样，才能实现从发展中国家向成熟的现代化国家转变的历史进步。

Prof. JIN Bei（金碚），Dr. LI Gang（李钢）

2013 年 2 月 15 日

# CONTENTS

## Part One: Macroeconomy



## Part Two: Institution & Mechanism

## Part Three: Government Policy



## Part Four: Industrial Development

# 目　录

## 第一篇　宏观经济



## 第二篇　体制机制

## 第三篇 政府政策



## 第四篇 产业发展

# Part One

# Macroeconomy

# Chapter 1

# "Middle-Income Trap" and "High-Income Wall": Challenges and Opportunities to China*

**Liu Shijin (刘世锦), Zhang Junkuo (张军扩), Hou Yongzhi (侯永志) and Liu Peilin (刘培林)**

**Development Research Center of the State Council, Beijing, China**

**Abstract:** The history of international industrialization shows that Latin American countries and former Soviet Union and Eastern European countries experienced siginificant drop in economic growth and fell into the middle-income trap when their per capita GDP reached 4,000 – 7,000 international dollar (based on the 1990 prices) as a result of long-term implemented import-oriented strategy and planned economic system. Fortunately, China adopted reform and opening-up policy beginning at a lower development phase and achieved sustained high-speed growth for more than thirty years. Currently, China has surpassed the phase which the above-mentioned countries fell into the middle-income trap. On the other side, experiences of successful runner-ups show that when per capita GDP reached 11,000 international dollar (based on the 1990 prices), economic growth speed will present regularly "natural drop". Without internal and external shocks, China's economy is expected to reach this level by 2015 and the potential growth rate will possibly drop significantly. In this regard, China's toughest challenges will be whether it can effectively prevent and solve the financial risks accumulated during high-speed growth and make a shift to innovation-driven growth model. Time is pressing for addressing the above challenges. A fundamental change in growth model depends on the intensification of reform, in particular, the promotion of an "participatory and facilitative reform" approach.

**Keywords:** middle income trap, high income wall, China's economic growth

China surpassed Japan in terms of GDP in 2010 to become the world's second largest economy, but in terms of per capita income it is still counted among middle-income countries. International experiences suggest that middle-income countries face a wide range of challenges including slowdowns in economic growth and intensified social conflicts. Some countries may fall into a so-called "middle-income trap" because of these factors, experiencing long-time stagnation.

As a major developing country, China faces certain development challenges that other middle-

---

* Corresponding author: lpl@drc.gov.cn.

This article is an outcome of the State Council Development Research Center's "Middle-Income Trap Research" project.

income countries do not. Will China fall into the middle-income trap that ensnared Latin America and other regions? How can we successfully navigate the middle-income phase to become a modern, high-income society? These are questions of common interest to people from various walks of life in both China and the international community. Correctly understanding and answering these questions can help us design and implement practical and forward-looking long-term development strategies in order to reduce or avoid mistakes, smoothly become a high-income country, and contribute to the stability and prosperity of the global economy.

This article, focusing on whether industrialization can be smoothly implemented, summarizes the practices of more than 30 major economies that, having a population of over 10 million, have experienced the industrialization process, while also categorizing the commonalities and differences between them by gathering extensive historical data. There are many data sources available for making international comparisons of economic growth①. In order to meet the needs for comparing different countries and different development stages, the data should at least meet two conditions: (1) they should be continuous and have a sufficiently long time span; and (2) they should avoid influence by factors such as exchange rates and prices, to make different countries and different stages comparable. Of these only *The World Economy: Historical Statistics* (Maddison, 2003) meets both conditions. Its principal unit is the international dollar in the G-K system, based on the 1990 prices. International dollar (Int $) is not an actual currency, but a notional pricing unit calculated using a specific method.

Based on theoretical analysis, we also compare current international practices, both the positive and the negative, with those of China. We believe that before the high-speed industrialization is over, the possibility for China falling into a middle-income trap similar to that of Latin American countries is low; China's toughest challenges will emerge after high-speed industrialization has concluded, testing whether we can effectively solve various structural conflicts and financial risks accumulated during industrialization and make a shift from growth driven by low-costs to growth driven by innovations in order to become a true high-income country. To cope with these challenges, we have to achieve substantial progress in shifting our growth model through "participatory and facilitative reform".

## I. A History of Industrialization

Looking at the history of global economy we see that although quite a few countries initiated industrialization and realized an early-stage economic take-off, there weren't many countries that were able to successfully cope with the risks and challenges in various phases of the process and eventually became the high-income countries. We have arranged the data by country into five categories based on the time economic take-off occurred, development strategies, economic systems and trajecto-

① The World Economy: Historical Statistics (Maddison), the International Historical Statistics (Palgrave MacMillan), the World Bank's WDI database, the IMF's WEO database, and the National Accounts of OECD Countries etc.

ries. These are:

(1) Countries that developed first and have always been at the frontiers of technological development such as the UK and U. S.

(2) Latin American countries and Southeast Asian countries similar to Latin American countries, which adopted an import-oriented strategy on a long-term basis and created growth miracles, but later fell into a middle-income trap.

(3) Former Soviet Union and Eastern European countries, which realized fast economic growth through planned economic models, but also fell into a middle-income trap.

(4) Latecomer European countries, which have successfully caught up with countries with cutting-edge countries.

(5) East Asian emerging industrialized economies, which have tapped their advantages as latecomers, realized concentrated growth, and achieved substantial progress in innovation-driven growth.

By analyzing the development process of these countries, we can accurately understand the nature and meaning of both the middle-income trap and high-income wall.

### (I) Countries that developed earliest such as the UK and U. S. are not currently experiencing fast economic growth, but have realized long-term and sustainable growth.

These countries initiated the industrial revolution, became the first to avoid the Malthusian trap and enter a stage of modern economic growth stage, and started a new era of sustainable growth in per capita income. They have always been at the frontier of the global technology, do not have many mature technical opportunities to choose from, and must invest a substantial amount of capital in high-risk innovation in order to invent new technologies continuously, create new products, and gestate new industries. As technological and business innovation involves high costs and high risks, such countries' growth is not very rapid. Through several rounds of innovating, however, they have realized sustainable and relatively steady growth. Although there have also been fluctuations in their growth due to economic cycles, except for major wars and great depressions, they have not suffered long-time stagnation. Their GDP growth rate has remained around 4% over a long period. Long-time and sustainable growth enabled these countries to pass through the middle-income stage and become the world's first high-income countries.

### (II) Latin American countries, and similar countries in Southeast Asia fell into the middle-income trap after a period of high-speed growth.

The concept of a "middle-income trap" was first formally proposed in "An East Asian Renaissance: Ideas for Economic Growth" published by the World Bank in 2007 (Gill and Kharas, 2007). The report points out that many economies quickly reach the middle-income level, but few countries can move beyond this stage because the policy and institutional changes required to move on are more complex and technically, politically and socially challenging. The report states that the fundamental reason for the fact that a country or region breaks out of an initial poverty trap but falls into the "middle-income trap" is that the development mechanism for a country to move from the middle-income level to the high-income level is fundamentally different from the mechanism for it to realize an initial take-off. By comparing the growth trajectories of countries that fell into a "middle-income trap" and those of catch-up countries that successfully reached the high-income status, we see that the speed of the former during the high-speed growth stage was slower than that of the latter. We believe that this may mean that the fundamental reason for Latin American countries' descent into a middle-income trap was not that their systems and policies failed to change to adapt to a high-income stage, but that the development strategies and systems they adopted at the beginning of the middle-income stage had serious defects.

Latin American countries and similar Southeast Asian countries are characterized by their latecomer advantage in technologies, and that many of them also have expansive and fertile lands as well as the rich deposits of high-grade mineral resources. Relying on these favorable natural conditions, these countries were able to realize a period of fast growth to catch up with developed countries, creating the Latin American miracle after World War II which attracted worldwide attention. But at the end of the 1970s, these countries' per capita GDPs were just Int $4000 – Int $5000—far behind that of the high-income countries when their industrialization process stalled and economic growth slowed dramatically, falling into a middle-income trap. For example, during 1950 – 1980, the annual GDP growth of Brazil, Argentina, and Mexico was 6.8%, 3.4%, and 6.5% respectively, but during 1981 – 2000, the figures fell to 2.2%, 1.7%, and 2.7%. Indonesia and the Philippines also realized a period of high-speed growth. During 1970 – 1980, Indonesia's annual GDP growth was 8%, and the Philippines's reached 6.6%. In the 10 years followed, Indonesia's growth fell to 5.5%, and the Philippines's fell to 1.6% (See figure 1). Meanwhile, because these countries didn't initiate fundamental reform of cripplingly unequal land systems,

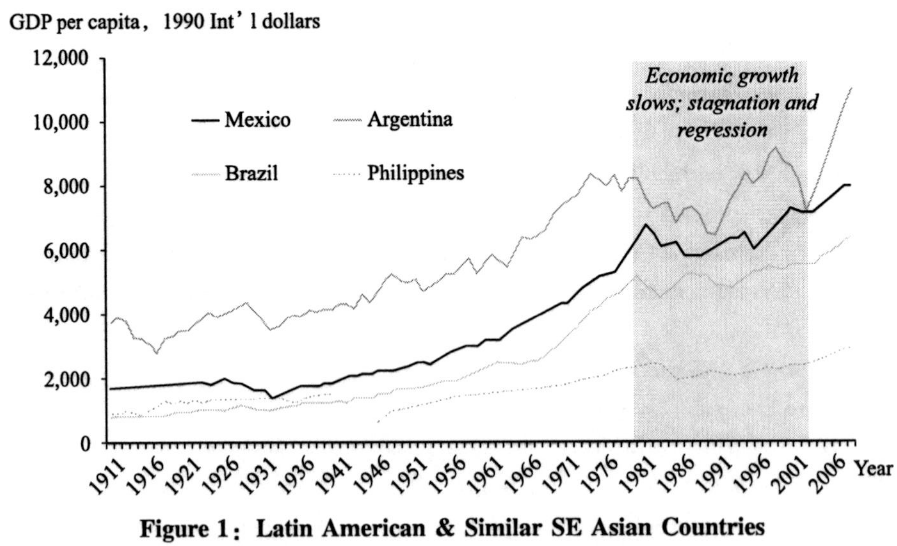


**Figure 1: Latin American & Similar SE Asian Countries**

Source: Macquarie Research, Bijiao, Maddison, September 2011.

many people without land and job flocked to cities. As a result, the urban population in such countries rose far higher than that of other countries at the same stage of development. Poverty became common in urban areas, and so-called "poverty-stricken urbanization" ensued.

**(III) Former Soviet Union and Eastern European countries, which achieved fast economic growth through planned economic models, also fell into a middle-income trap.**

The characteristics of former Soviet Union and Eastern European countries that allowed them to realize high-speed economic growth in the early-stage of industrialization was their advantage as the latecomers and the resource mobilization systems of a planned economy. When the per capita GDP of the former Soviet Union reached Int $5500 – Int $6500 during the mid – 1970s, however, the country's economic growth began to show serious fluctuation and obvious retraction; Eastern European countries also fell into economic stagnation roughly during the same period when their per capita GDP reached Int $4, 300 – 5, 800. From 1950 – 1975, the annual GDP growth rate of the former Soviet Union, Hungary, Romania, and Poland was 4.8%, 4.1%, 6.5%, and 4.6% respectively, while from 1976 – 2000, the figures for these countries fell to –0.6% (the combined amount of the member states following disintegration), 0.7%, –0.6%, and 1.5% respectively (See figure 2).

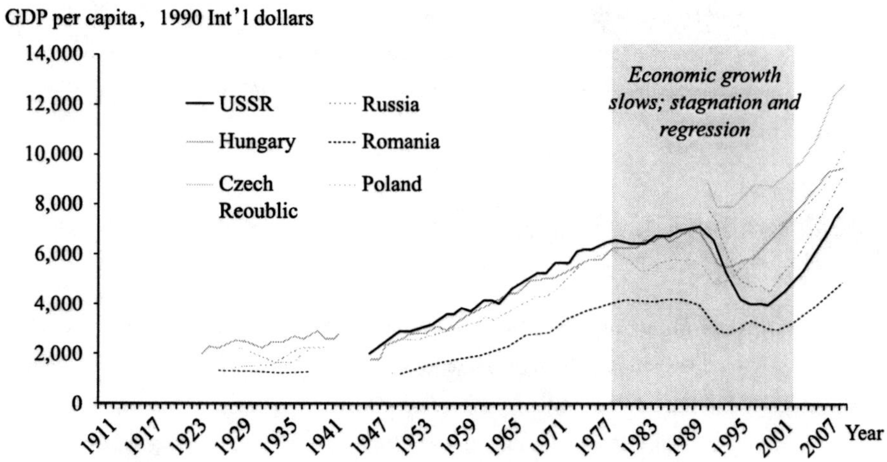


**Figure 2: Former Soviet Union & Eastern European Countries**

Source: Macquarie Research, Bijiao, Maddison, September 2011.

What we should point out is that falling into the middle-income trap doesn't mean that development stopped permanently. In fact, among the above-mentioned countries, some achieved decent performance after entering this century, and their economic growth accelerated.

**(IV) The latecomer European countries: successfully transformed into innovation-and service-driven economies following a "catch-up" period.**

Although European countries such as Germany, France, Italy, and Spain were traditionally capitalist, following World War II most of them still went through a process to catch up with countries on the frontiers of global technology and a period of high-speed growth, of which Germany was the most typical. They are characterized by having gone through a condensed rapid catch-up stage after World War II, relying on their advantages as technical latecomers and their strong human resources. When their per capita GDP reached Int $10, 500 at the end of the 1960s, their economic growth began to slow down, and they gradually approached the level of the most developed countries. Germany's annual GDP growth rate during 1947 – 1969 (when it was the Federal Republic of Germany) was 7.9%. After their per capita GDP reached Int $10, 440 in 1969, their economic growth slowed significantly: annual GDP growth rate was reduced to 3.1% from 1970 – 1979.

**(V) Emerging industrialized economies, which have tapped their advantages as technological latecomers, realized concentrated growth and achieved substantial progress in innovation driven growth.**

After the 1950s, several Asian economies including Japan, South Korea, Singapore, Hong Kong, and Chinese Taiwan realized continuous economic growth, gradually achieving high-income status. They are characterized by having fully tapped their latecomer advantage in mimicking global technology leaders at low cost to produce condensed high-speed growth for about 30 years. Having experienced reduced economic growth after per capita GDP reached about Int $10, 000; they went through a period of moderate growth, becoming stable high-income economies. During the process of shifting from high-speed growth to moderate growth, these economies also encountered several economic, social, and environmental crises, but managed to maintain sustainable growth during the moderate growth stage.

## II. Development Challenges

In 2009, Fatás and Mihov proposed the concept of "high-income wall", which refers to a per capita GDP threshold corresponding to high-income status, and have hypothesized that a country must meet a range of institutional conditions to overcome this threshold. ① We borrow this concept of a "high-income wall" to define the point when an economy meets the following criteria:

(1) Per capita GDP reached about Int $10000.

(2) Latecomer advantage no longer applied.

① Fatás and Mihov used a coordinates system to illustrate the high-income wall concept: the horizontal axis represents per capita GDP (in U. S. dollars) based on 2007 prices (calculated using the current year's exchange rate) and the wall, refers to a per capita GDP of $8, 000 – 13, 000; the vertical axis represents the institutional quality indicator issued by the World Bank in 2005 reflecting various social factors including political stability, government efficiency, legal system, corruption, and governance quality; countries are put into two categories based on whether their institutional quality indicator is above or below zero. Thus, the coordinate system is divided into four quadrants: for all countries with a per capita GDP of over $13, 000, the corresponding institutional quality indicator is very high (except for Saudi Arabia) and these countries are all concentrated in the upper right quadrant; for most countries with a per capita GDP under $8000, the corresponding institutional quality indicator is low, and these countries are concentrated in the lower left quadrant.

(3) Industrialization and urbanization characterized by the large-scale production and consumption of energy and heavy chemical products have concluded.

(4) Social production mainly aimed at meeting the basic consumption needs of the citizens concludes.

(5) Potential economic growth is significantly reduced, producing a range of difficulties, contradictions, and challenges.

Only by initiating institutional changes and policy adjustment to create new growth models, can countries effectively cope with these challenges and realize sustainable moderate growth. If these changes are unsuccessful, the economy will decline or stagnate. We describe countries which successfully realize this transformation as having "successfully overcome the high-income wall." ①

Analysis shows that the growth patterns and trajectories of countries that succumbed to a middle-income trap are similar to those that were able to get over the high-income wall. Both experience periods of compressed high-speed growth followed by reduced economic growth. Further analysis, however, reveals that the nature of these two types of reduced growth differ substantially (Figure 3).

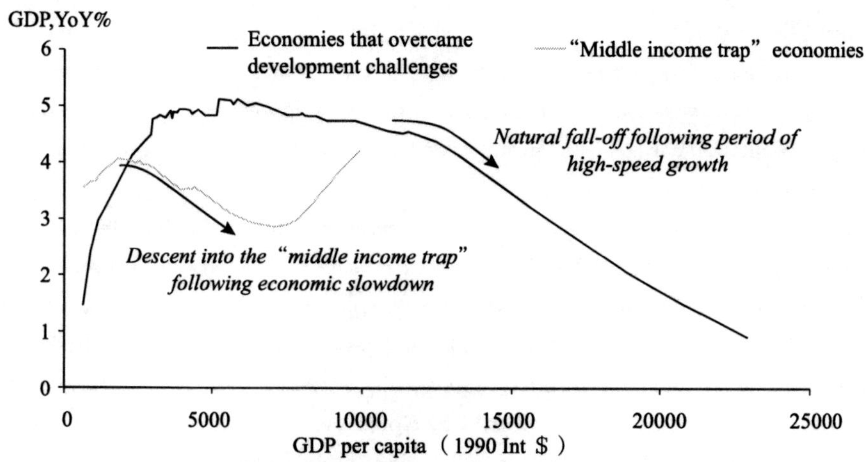


**Figure 3: The Middle Income Trap**

Source: Macquarie Research, Bijiao, Maddison, September 2011.

Firstly, reduced growth among countries that fell into a middle-income trap occurred when per capita GDP reached approximately Int $4000 – Int $7000, but countries that successfully navigated

---

① In 1987 the World Bank began to divide countries into four categories—low-income, middle-to-low-income, middle-to-high-income, and high-income. According to the World Bank's definition, Japan leapt over the wall around 1974. However, as the World Bank does not have an income classification standard for years prior to 1987, we cannot directly determine whether Japan became a high-income country at that time. To resolve this, we calculated Japan's income classification based on the method of the World Bank, and the results show that according to the World Bank's standard, Japan had already became a high-income country by 1974. The data for Korea also show that when the country went over the wall in 1994, it also became a high-income country according to the World Bank's standard.

their way over the wall did not start experiencing reduced growth until their per capita GDP reached Int $11000.

Secondly, the nature of, and reasons for the changes in growth were different. For countries that fell into a middle-income trap, reduced growth occurred in the middle stage of industrialization when the latecomer advantage had not yet completely dissipated. The fundamental reason for this lies in defects in the country's basic industrialization framework, and as a result, the industrialization process could not continue, hampering high-speed growth process. Among countries that successfully got over the wall, the latecomer advantage had basically disappeared by the time high-speed industrialization had naturally concluded.

From this we see that, on the one hand, falling into a middle-income trap during industrialization is not inevitable for latecomers, and if their strategies and policies are appropriate, such a fate can be avoided. On the other hand, reduced economic growth after successfully getting over the high-income wall can't be avoided. The fundamental reason is that when the development level of latecomer countries approaches that of frontier countries, in terms of supply, their ability to mimic the technologies at low cost is reduced, and the speed of their technological progress slowed down, such that the economic growth of latecomer countries approaches that of frontier countries; correspondingly, in terms of demand, the demand potential for large-scale construction during fast industrialization and urbanization disappears. Moreover, given the expanded size of economy, maintaining a constant growth speed requires new levels of scale that cannot be matched by demand.

We also need to point out that reduced growth experienced after falling into the middle-income trap or after getting over the wall differs from typical recession or depression during regular economic cycles. Recession and depression occurred when fundamentals do not change significantly, and it is possible to stimulate an economy out of recession and depression via policy policies. Reduced growth rate after falling into the middle-income trap is caused by major defects in a country's basic industrialization framework, and cannot be ameliorated by typical policy measures. Reduced growth rate after successfully getting over the high-income wall occurs when structural changes to the fundamentals of economic growth occur, and policy measures are ineffective in sustaining previous levels of growth.

## III. Factors and Strategies for Success

Whether or not a country's industrialization can be smoothly implemented depends on a series of dynamic factors and conditions. Here we propose a "Six-Factor Analytical Framework" for industrialization to summarize the experiences of countries that successfully achieved high-income stage as well as the lessons of countries that fell into a middle-income trap. This framework includes three basic component factors which account for the basic state of the industrialization process, and three basic influencing factors which have an important or even decisive influence on the direction and results of industrialization.

### (I) The Three Basic Component Factors of Industrialization and Their Interaction

The continuously expanding market space, the increasingly enhanced technological potential and accumulation of physical capital, as well as the continuously increasing participation rate of capital, especially human capital, are the three basic component factors of industrialization. These three factors interact with each other, continuously improve, and work together to drive the continuous development of industrialization.

Industrialization is a process by which the market space continuously expands, and the domestic consumption and investment market continuously expands and structurally upgrades. It is also a process by which related countries are deeply involved in international division of labor and obtain a growing international market share against a background of deepening economic globalization.

Industrialization is a process marked by technological progress, the release of technological potential, and a continuous increase of productivity. It is a process by which people continuously create new products and new technologies through the exploration of new fields of knowledge and expertise, to realize upgrades in industrial potential. Through innovation and the adoption of new technologies, the quality of material capital and human capital is improved, resulting in a continuous increase in productivity.

Industrialization is also a process marked by a gradually narrowing of rural-urban gap, a gradual increase in the participation of human capital, and continuous growth of income. During this process, the relative size of modern economic sectors continues to increase while the percentage of traditional sectors is gradually reduced, as they are reformed and upgraded on the basis of modern technologies and production methods. With the increased production level across the society, both depth and breadth of human capital participation are increased, the compensation level of workers and the income level of other production elements are also correspondingly raised, driving the expansion of the size of the consumption market.

Successful industrialization must strike a balance among above-mentioned three component factors. First of all, market capacity must match the size of dominant technology industries. A significant feature of industrialization is the use of economies of scale, including production economies of scale and market economies of scale. If the market's capacity is insufficient to support economies of scale brought about by industrial and technological development, a market gap will exist. Secondly, the quantity, and more importantly, the quality of human capital must be improved to match more advanced technologies. As industrialization moves forward, modern sectors making use of new technologies emerge one after another, and traditional sectors are reformed and improved through the adoption of new technologies. With the gradual application and adoption of new production styles and management methods, the quantity and quality of human capital must meet the requirements of technological progress and changes in production style, or there will be a shortage in the supply of human capital. Finally, income growth must match the expansion of market demand. The breadth and depth of the participation of human capital in the industrialization process determines levels of income growth and income distribution. Income growth is directly related to the expansion of market demand. If income growth can't reach the level required by the expansion of market demand, a gap in income growth results.

A successful implementation of industrialization balances the aforementioned three factors at certain level for an appropriately long period of time. Setback to the industrialization process is often seen in the form of a gap among the three factors. If such a gap persists and cannot be eliminated in time, the industrialization process would be interrupted or even reversed.

### (II) The Three Basic Influencing Factors and Their Roles

The historical experiences of industrialization shows that whether or not a dynamic balance can be reached between the three component factors is influenced by the following three basic factors.

(1) The initial conditions of a country, including natural conditions such as population, location, mineral resources, and natural environment, as well as non-natural conditions such as industrial foundation, transportation & communications, the surrounding international environment, education, research etc. Sound initial conditions favor the initiation and further progress of industrialization. However, it's not necessarily the case that these conditions must all be met to ensure optimal industrialization; likewise, meeting all these conditions does not necessarily mean that industrialization will be realized. Some countries with relatively poor initial conditions successfully realize industrialization by making up for their own shortcomings with appropriate systems, strategies and policies. In contrast, some countries with relatively good initial conditions encounter issues such as the so-called "resource curse" due to outdated systems or strategic or policy mistakes, and their industrialization process fails to start or stalls.

(2) The basic economic system of the country, including systems protecting property rights, the mechanisms of market competition, governance structure etc. A rigorous and effective property right protection provides incentives for various elements to participate in production activities and technological innovations. A competitive market system stimulates vital innovation among various parties, and drives the improvements in productivity. A unified market provides the scaling needed for industrial development based on dominant technologies. A high level of governance, including a synergistic relationship between government and market, as well as the provision of public services corresponding to a country's changing development can promote the expansion of market capacity, technological progress, the accumulation of physical and human capital, as well as the participation of various elements in the modern sectors. Of course, different industrialization stages have different requirements vis-à-vis the economic systems (Gilland Kharas, 2007; Rodrik, 2007).

(3) Government development strategies and policies play a critical role in industrialization. Different development strategies influence the design of development policies, and further determine market capacity, technological progress, and the accumulation and participation of human capital. For example, under an import-oriented strategy, domestic industries are protected. Although this is good for the development of industries during the initial stage, in the long run it is not good for technological innovation, but may contribute to the creation of interest groups, and limit human capitals participation in modern sectors. Under an import-oriented strategy, although domestic enter-

prises are able to receive subsidies, by participating competitively in international market, the energy of domestic enterprises is continuously enhanced, and market capacity from the perspective of domestic enterprises and industrial systems continuously expands, thus enabling more human capitals to participate in the industrialization process.

Whether a development strategy is good or bad is not absolute—the key is whether it can be adjusted and optimized in a timely fashion according to the changes in the domestic & international environments and conditions. During the initial stage of industrialization, many countries implemented an import-oriented strategy, but as their development stage progressed, some countries opted for an import-oriented strategy to smoothly drive industrialization while others adhered to the import-oriented strategy, hampering the industrialization process.

In sum, it is because of the differences in the arrangements of economic systems and the strategies of development, as well as different initial conditions, that the three basic factors-market spaces, technological potential, and the participation rate of the physical and human capitals-realized different dynamics, which in turn determines the performance of various countries during industrialization.

### (III) Typical Experiences of Countries that Have Successfully Industrialized

#### 1. Implement competitive supply policies, stimulate innovation and improve the efficiency of resource allocation.

Maintaining competition in supply is an important driver of efficiency improvements and technological innovation. Successful industrialized countries put great importance on creating a competitive business system, especially with respect to property rights protection, equal access, and anti-monopoly measures. They improve their systems on an ongoing basis, to encourage entrepreneurs to innovate actively and start businesses and also play a basic role in pricing mechanisms and resource allocation, in order to direct resources to places with higher efficiencies. For example, the UK established patent rights in 1623 to protect the rights to new inventions. The U. S. began to create a patent system shortly after announcing its independence, and Congress passed the *Patent Act* in 1790. In order to maintain market competition, the U. S. passed its first anti-trust law in 1890-*the Sherman Antitrust Act*, which effectively regulated market competition and maintained a competitive free enterprise system.

#### 2. Policies to promote economies of scale.

All the successful industrialized countries emphasize the expansion of market space. Domestically, a focus is put on breaking geographical, social and institutional restrictions, giving priority to the development of infrastructure while promoting the free flow and concentration of populations and other production elements so as to deepen industrial division and form a unified domestic market. For example, the UK abolished tariffs between England and Scotland in 1707 in order to unify the domestic market and from the late 18th century to the early 19th century also formed a domestic waterway transportation network connecting all major inland rivers and all major inland economic zones leading to overseas markets. This formed a basic structure for a unified internal market and connected all corners of the country to international markets. Yet another example is the U. S. 's historical emphasis on the development of railways-by 1888 the total length of its railway network was 26, 000 miles, longer than the combined railway network of Europe. Thanks to the excellent development of railways, transportation costs were dramatically reduced, enabling remote regions to be integrated into a unified domestic market, increasing domestic trade opportunities, promoting standards-based industrial production and expanding business size. This further triggered a revolution in business organization in the U. S. .

Externally, a country should continuously improve its position in the international division of labor according to dynamic changes in the comparative advantage afforded by its resource endowments. It is especially notable that during early economic development, developed capitalist countries often maintained a surplus in merchandise trade and current account for a long time. For example, during the 100 years period from 1870 – 1969, the merchandise trade account of the U. S. was in deficit for only 5 years, with all other years showing a surplus; during the 70 year period from 1900 – 1969, only 1935 saw a trade deficit, while all the other 69 years showed a surplus. This shows that actively exploring external markets and energetically developing international trade and investment is an important pillar for the continuous industrial improvement in developed countries.

### 3. Develop human capital.

Another important experience of developed countries is the emphasis put on the accumulation of human capital while removing institutional barriers, to enable people to smoothly participate in the modernization process. For example, during the 100-plus years after it became independent, the U. S. actively encouraged immigration, and abolished slavery after the Civil War. Germany became the first country in the world to implement compulsory education. In addition, successful countries also put great importance on maintaining mobility among social classes, to prevent an excessive income gap from occurring during the industrialization process, and, more importantly, to avoid the entrenchment of interests and multigenerational wealth. During the industrialization process of countries such as the UK and U. S. , there was a stage in which the gap in income distribution widened, but due to strong social mobility, solid economic growth was maintained.

### 4. Adjusting the role of the government.

During their high-speed growth phase of industrialization, the governments of successful countries and regions in East Asia participated significantly in resource distribution. However, as development progressed, the government played a more active role in encouraging business innovation, improving public services, and creating a favorable external environment; at the same time, they also gradually loosened government controls, introduced innovative management approaches, reduced government intervention, reformed the financial system, and simplified governmental organizations. The role of government in the market can be either increased or decreased; its function can be either expanded or contracted, as long as it plays a basic and decisive role in the market with regard to resource distribution, technological innovation and industrial progress, to drive growth in innovation. These are critical experiences of countries and regions that succeeded in getting over the wall.

## (IV) The Lessons of Countries that Fell into a Middle-income Trap.

### 1. Latin America: A long-term, rigid import-substitution strategy.

The implementation of an import-substitution strategy is not unique to Latin American countries. Except for the UK, almost all industrialized countries adopted an import-substitution strategy to some extent during the early stages of industrialization. However, no country has become a high-income country by relying on this strategy exclusively. There are many reasons that Latin American countries fell into a middle-income trap, such as the extremely unequal nature of the existing land system and the inability to solve income distribution issues for a long time, but the main reason has more to do with a long-term and rigid implementation of the import-substitution strategy.

In Latin American countries, the domestic market space was narrow and small, and protected industries were unable to realize economies of scale. Adoption of an import-substitution strategy also led to a lack of innovation among domestic industries. Industries under protection were hard-pressed to expand and couldn't create sufficient non-agricultural jobs. As a result, many laborers remained in traditional economic sectors for an extended period of time and lacked sustainable sources of income. This in turn further limited the expansion of domestic demand and market space. As land was highly concentrated in the hands of a small number of people, many landless farmers were forced to swarm into cities, but because they did not have any direct links to industrialization, they became marginalized.

Insufficient participation by the workforce and delayed reform of the land system caused a widening of the income gap. As a result, numerous people were unable to share the results of development, and wealth remained concentrated from one generation to another, triggering a range of serious social conflicts and problems.

On the other hand, using the import-substitution strategy, those sectors imported large quantities of capital goods and equipment. But it was difficult to accumulate large amounts of foreign currency via the export of primary products, so producers had to borrow significant sums of money from other countries, and as a result their countries' international income-expense balance sheet suffered. Furthermore, because the earnings of enterprises were low under an import-substitution regime, public revenue was insufficient, significantly reducing the ability of governments to engineer macro adjustment and control. With the growing level of debt, it became increasingly hard to seek long-term loans, so the countries had to seek large quantities of short-term loans, leading to increasingly serious instability at the macroeconomic level. After the 1970s, the international economic environment changed, short-term capital showed abnormal outflows, and the result was a debt crisis.

Generally speaking, countries in this category realized fast growth in the initial stages of industrialization through an import-substitution strategy by leveraging their advantage as latecomers in technology, and even created a short-lived "Latin American miracle" in the second half of the 20th century. However, it was the rigid implementation of this strategy that hindered conditions for further industrialization as countries were mired in a debt crisis during the 1980s when per capita GDP was just over Int $4, 000, and their economic and social development suffered long-term stagnation-they fell into a middle-income trap.

**2. The former Soviet bloc: long-term, rigid planned economic system.**

The former Soviet Union and Eastern European countries were able to quickly increase industrial growth within a short time by leveraging an exceptionally strong ability to mobilize resources under a planned economic system. They adopted a development strategy that "favored accumulation rather than consumption, and favored heavy industries rather than light industries," but distorted internal relations between sectors. A long-term accumulation of contradictions eventually led to the stagnation or even reduction of economic development.

These countries relied on their central government's planning authority to arrange production and consumption, resulting in a serious mismatch of resources. Under such a system, the private economy was basically eliminated, and it was difficult to establish a competitive business system. The market's ability to self-regulate was basically ignored, and natural pricing mechanisms did not play a significant role in resource allocation. Under a system in which production-supply-sales and human-financial-physical resources were arranged centrally, businesses didn't have effective incentives to improve their management and technologies and no reliable communication channel between the upper and lower levels of the economy existed. These conditions resulted in a low efficiency of resource allocation, a low quality of economic growth, and serious distortions in the economic structure.

The market in these countries was closed to the outside, and the market space was narrow and small. Influenced by Stalin's theory of the "two parallel world markets", the former Soviet Union's economy was forced into a semi-closed state. Foreign trade mainly took place among member states of the Council for Mutual Economic Assistance (Comecon), and such cooperation was in fact actually an extension of the Soviet Union's mandatory planned economic system. Therefore, there was no real international market driven by competition, and both businesses and their products had no real competitive edge. The economy that developed under such circumstances was basically supported by domestic demand and was detached from the development of the overall world economy, changes in international markets, and general scientific and technological progress. Governments continued to blindly provide investments in outdated projects, and returns on investment (ROI) naturally declined over time.

In these countries, human capital did not have sufficient opportunities to participate in the overall economy and the structure of the economy was seriously distorted. On the one hand, large numbers of people in the workforce were unable to move to non-agricultural sectors under the administrative restrictions of the collective farm system. Although the percentage of the industrial output as a function of total output continuously increased, because priority was given to the military industries, the resources and limited surplus available to agricultural and light-industrial sectors were forcefully taken away, and, as a result, light industry was underdeveloped while heavy industries were overdeveloped, leading to a continuous exacerbation of unemployment.

Generally speaking, the former Soviet Union and Eastern European countries realized high speed growth during a certain period by leveraging their ability to mobilize resources under a planned economic system. However, because of the rigid planned economic system that had been adopted for a long time, the overall economic structure was seriously unbalanced. Without changing the fundamental framework of the planned economic system, the strategy to shift social production to the intensive model proposed in the 1970s failed. Eventually, when per capita GDP reached about Int $6, 000, economic growth noticeably slowed, and these countries fell into a middle-income trap as well. It is worth noting that the dramatic reduction in growth did not occur after a drastic change in the governing structure of the former Soviet Union and Eastern Europe, but occurred when the planned economic system and the former Soviet Union's political & military hegemony were still very powerful. This shows that such reduced growth can be explained within the framework of our original system.

## IV. Around 2015, China's Growth will Naturally Slow

Drawing on the historical experiences and patterns of different types of industrialized countries regarding economic growth, we analyzed the historical process and future prospects of China's economic growth using three different but complementary methods. We expect that China's growth around 2015, plus or minus two years, will start to drop significantly.

The first method we employed involved the direct use of China's overall national economic data, with a look to the experiences of successful catch-up economies such as Japan, South Korea, and Germany, such as China's per capita GDP that reached Int $7, 864 in 2010. ① Assuming that China's GDP can maintain the high-speed growth momentum of the last 30 years during the next few years, and given the UN's forecast of China's population growth, by 2016, China's per capita GDP will reach Int $11, 608, a level roughly equivalent to that reached by previous successful catch-up economies when growth generally slowed. After 2016, given the experiences of successful catch-up economies, if the potential growth rate of China's economy is reduced by about 30% versus the previous high-speed growth period, GDP growth will be reduced by about 3 percentage points. Thus, it is expected that the GDP growth rate during the 12th Five-Year period will reach 9. 7% annually and this will be reduced to 6. 5% during the 13th Five-Year Plan (based on China's official statistical metrics).

The second method treats each provincial administrative region of China as a separate economy (which is reasonable considering that the populations of most of China's provincial administrative regions are close to that of a big or medium-sized country) and compares them appropriately with select international economies based on historical experiences and development patterns in order to predict changes within each. These results are then combined together to calculate China's national economic growth rate. China's three municipalities-Beijing, Tianjin, and Shanghai-are compared to two

① Due to differences in methodology, GDP growth rates released by China's National Bureau of Statistics need to be reduced and adjusted in order to make the data equivalent to the 1990 international dollar-based system used by Maddison.

city economies – Hong Kong and Singapore. Another 22 provinces are compared to successful catch-up economies such as Japan, South Korea, and Germany, and an appropriate adjustment is also made according to factors including per capita GDP, industrial structure, the level of urbanization, level of labor specialization, resource availability, and the level of reliance on exports. For the remaining six provinces where it is not appropriate to implement large-scale industrialization and urbanization due to natural geographic conditions, we look at the historical experiences of international economies that experienced high-speed growth, but didn't become high income economies.

The time required for each province to reach a level of development comparable to its international equivalent when its economic growth rate starts to drop is calculated using the current per capita GDP level of each province as a base, demographic projections, and the assumption that each province's total GDP will maintain an annual growth rate equivalent to the past 30 years; once this is determined, we assume that each province's total GDP growth rate will be reduced by about 30%. Finally, we put the data together to calculate the national economic growth rate. The results show that China's GDP growth will slow to less than 8% around 2014; annual GDP growth will drop to 8.2% in the 12th Five-Year Plan and 7.3% during in the 13th Five-Year Plan. ①

The third method predicts when China's economic growth rate will drop using relationships between the consumption (or production) of bulk commodities and per capita GDP, as a basis for comparison with the results obtained using the first two methods. The specific method employed was as follows:

(a) Five material indicators for 2009 were used as a base, including China's per capita electricity consumption (2742kwh/person), the number of automobiles per thousand people (48.7 units/thousand people), per capita accumulated steel & iron production (3.9t/person), per capita production of automobiles (10.3 units/thousand people), and per capital annual steel & iron production (0.5t/person).

(b) We assume that these indicators will continue to grow at a speed equivalent to their annual average over the past 10 years, in order to calculate when these indicators will reach a level comparable to that of economies such as Japan, South Korea, and Germany when GDP growth started to drop, and use this result to determine when China's GDP growth will begin to slow.

(c) Furthermore, we assume that a slowdown in China's growth will be on the order of 30%, as was the case with Japan, South Korea, and Germany. The results of our model are shown in Figure 4.

① There are two differences between the calculation results of the first method and the second method: the specific values of the growth rate predicted are different; and the inflection forms of the growth rate are different. In the first method, it's the stepped reduction; and in the second method, it's the smooth reduction. There are two reasons for this: One is the differences in the methods—the first method sees China as one economy, whereas the second calculates each province separately, and their mutual influence is set off to some extent, leading to the smooth drop of the national growth rate; the second is that the comparables selected are different—in the first method, all the regions of the country use the successful catch-up economies as the reference, whereas in the second method, comparables with a lower growth level are selected for some provinces in consideration of their natural geographic and resource conditions.

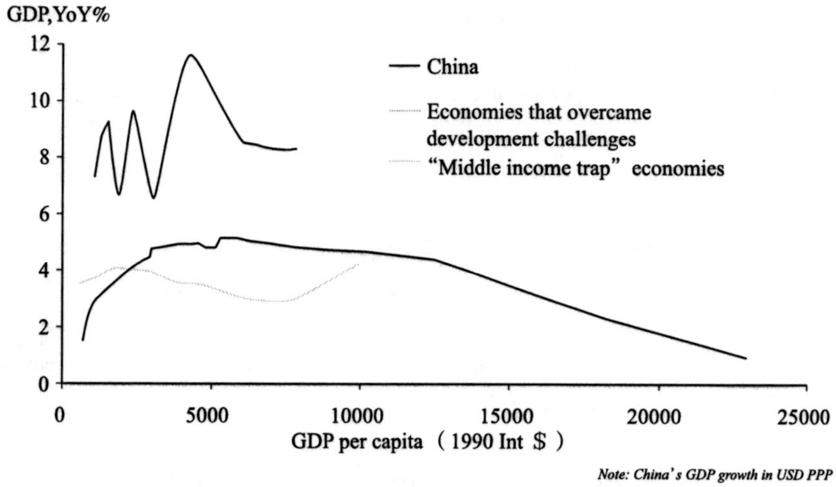


**Figure 4: The Middle Income Trap Is Unlikely**

Source: Macquarie Research, Bijiao, Maddison, September 2011.

The analytical results of the three methods show that if China's economic growth path approaches the historical patterns of successful catch-up economies, then it is very likely that China's potential economic growth will slow down by the end of the 12th Five-Year Plan, dropping substantially during the 13th Five-Year Plan.

**Table 1: China's Economic Inflection Point**

| Basis of calculation | GDP, average annual growth (%) | | | | GDP growth inflection point | |
|---|---|---|---|---|---|---|
| | 2001-05 | 2006-10 | 2011-15 | 2016-20 | Year | GDP per capita (1990 Int$) |
| National date | 9.8 | 11.2 | 9.7 | 6.5 | 2016 | 11, 608 |
| Provincial data | 9.8 | 11.2 | 8.2 | 7.3 | 2014 | 10, 680 |
| Electricity consumption | 9.8 | 11.2 | 9.0 | 7.2 | 2013 | 9, 853 |
| Automobile ownership | 9.8 | 11.2 | 9.4 | 7.0 | 2017 | 12, 967 |
| Steel production | 9.8 | 11.2 | 8.2 | 7.3 | 2017 | 12, 514 |
| Automobile production | 9.8 | 11.2 | 9.4 | 7.2 | 2017 | 12, 320 |
| Iron & steel production | 9.8 | 11.2 | 9.7 | 6.7 | 2013 | 10, 145 |
| Average | 9.8 | 11.2 | 9.1 | 7.1 | | 11, 441 |

Source: Macquarie Research, Bijiao, Maddison, September 2011

## V. Getting Over the Wall: The Real Challenges Faced by China's Economic Growth

By comprehensively analyzing relevant economic history and future prospects for China's industrialization, and comparing our findings with those of other comparable countries, we see that China may be able to avoid the middle-income trap encountered by Latin American countries as well as the former Soviet Union and Eastern European countries, but will face severe challenges after getting over the wall to become a high-income country. This is where China is unique, different from both Latin American countries and the former Soviet Union and Eastern European countries, as well as Germany, Japan, and South Korea.

### (I) The Middle Income Trap Is Unlikely

According to the analysis above, China's per capita GDP already reached Int \$7,864 in 2010, higher than the per capita GDP of Int \$4,000 achieved by Latin American countries and the per capita GDP of Int \$6,000 achieved by the former Soviet Union and Eastern European countries when they fell into a middle-income trap. Given its current growth momentum, after 3 – 5 years, China's per capita GDP will reach Int \$11,000, the level achieved by successful catch-up countries when they managed to leap over the wall. This means that unless there are major setbacks or unforeseen issues, the possibility of China falling into the kind of middle-income trap experienced by Latin American countries and the former Soviet Union and Eastern European countries is very small (See Figure 3).

Unlike Latin American countries, China already initiated an open, export-oriented development strategy when its per capita GDP was very low. ① Although China also adopted an import-substitution strategy on a long-term basis prior to its reform and opening up, it rapidly changed its development strategy and policy thereafter to adopt an open, export-oriented strategy. This expanded the market space for China's products, but also exposed China's enterprises to international competition while bringing many new technologies and management techniques to China. The high-speed growth of the export-oriented processing sector in coastal areas also effectively accelerated the development of China's urbanization.

Unlike the former Soviet Union and Eastern European countries, China launched market reforms when it was still at a relatively low level of development and its rapid industrialization has been accompanied by market reform. ② Proactive market reforms effectively promoted growth in general levels of wealth and the effective allocation of physical and human capital, allowing China to realize more than 30 years of condensed, rapid development even during the catch-up stage of its industrialization.

China's potential market space is substantial, and overall development conditions are good. China's population is the largest in the world-larger than the combined population of all current high-income countries, 4.3 times larger than the U.S., and 4.1 times higher the euro zone. In a sense, China is an entire "world" unto itself. When such a big population lives under the same system and the same market environment, the economies of scale it can produce are theoretically un-

① When free market reforms were initiated, China's per capita GDP was significantly lower than that of Latin American countries when the latter fell into a middle-income trap.

② China's per capita GDP at the time was significantly lower than the level of the former Soviet Union and Eastern European countries when they fell into a middle-income trap.

matched by any other country in the world. Through continuous reform and opening up, the mobility of China's products and other required elements are increasing, and levels of market integration are rising. What needs to be pointed out is that, though unbalanced domestic development itself is a shortcoming, objectively it constitutes a balance between the supply of required elements and industrial development, and increases the flexibility and sustainability of China's economic growth. In short, China's market advantage is not just bigger than that of Latin America and the former Soviet Union and Eastern European countries, but also to some extent it is bigger than that of cross border unified regional markets.

In terms of supply, China also has a unique advantage. First of all, China has a substantial, low-cost workforce that is increasingly well-educated and healthy, and is also diligent and disciplined. Secondly, China established a complete industrial system and national economic system during its era of central planning. The product designs as well as manufacturing and management experience accumulated during this period extended to private businesses initially, becoming critical sources for the latter's technical and management experience.

Following reforms, state-owned enterprises also have enjoyed bolstered technological prowess and expertise. Thirdly, the tradition of frugality enables China to maintain a high savings rate over a significantly long period of time as was the case in other successful catch-up countries, providing a deep pool of physical capital for industrialization.

What is especially important in China's case is the political system that is able to maintain political and social stability, focusing on properly handling tradeoffs between reform, development and stability. Following China's reforms in the 1980s, the focus of the Party and the government promptly shifted to economic development, a consensus was achieved across the Party's system and across the country, and people worked together to form a developmental synergy, avoiding the long-term social instability and political division of some countries that fell into a middle-income trap.

### (II) Scaling the Wall Is More Difficult

The natural drop that occurs in growth after per capita GDP reaches the "wall" level and the latecomer advantage disappears is virtually a law of nature. China's economic growth process will also follow this law, and it's hard to foresee any exception. In a sense, it is an important indicator of China's success in successfully completing its phase of high-speed economic growth. However, although China shares many similarities with high-income countries that have successfully gotten over the wall, there is some uncertainty as to whether or not it can successfully achieve the same feat and maintain a long period of steady growth at a new, reduced growth level after a drop in the current growth rate. Whether or not the current mode of growth can be adjusted to correspond with future changes in the growth environment will be key.

Historically, when economic growth began to slow, successful catch-up countries actively or passively adjusted their original growth model, gradually shifting to a model characterized by innovation as a key driver of growth. These countries fell into a growth pattern that was centered on private companies operating in areas where they had the strongest ability to innovate, particularly technology-intensive manufacturing sectors, through market competition. These countries further opened up their manufacturing and service industries, and encouraged and protected fair competition in the marketplace. They also established degree-based and vocational education systems as well as basic scientific and applied technical research systems that were innovation-friendly. Following their countries' high-speed growth, governments focused on encouraging businesses to innovate continuously and nurture new economic growth areas when facing changes in the market environment.

Against the background of an oil crisis, a drop in economic growth and the occurrence of several major environmental disasters, the Japanese government encouraged and guided businesses to develop energy efficient and environmentally-friendly products. This not only increased the efficiency of energy utilization, but also nurtured the country's auto industry, which later became one of the most competitive globally in terms of energy efficiency. Germany was also keen to encourage continuous innovation in one of its own traditionally strong sectors – the manufacturing industry. Many of Germany's big companies, the "centennial companies", are still very competitive today. Many SMEs in Germany own core technologies in numerous product fields, have majority market shares, and are known as the "invisible champions" . Although labor costs were very high, Germany had been the world's second largest garment export country until the 1990s. After the Asian financial crisis in 1997, South Korea set up a Knowledge Economy Ministry and a Bureau of Cultural Industry, passing both the "Special Law for Nurturing Innovative Enterprises" and the "Law for the Promotion of Cultural Industries" to energetically develop the knowledge intensive industries striving as needed in the shift from a manufacturing-oriented country to a design-and innovation-oriented country.

China's existing growth model shows some unique features which were absent from, or not as prominent in, the growth models of historically-successful high-income countries:

(1) As is the case in other countries, China adopts a governance model in which governments share authority at different administrative levels. Under China's existing financial system and performance evaluation system, financial resources available for local public services and employment opportunities are closely related to local production size and the economic growth in various regions has in fact become the most important and most measurable indicator for the selection and appointment of government officials. As such, local governments have a strong motivation to promote economic growth. On the other hand, under the existing system, local governments at various levels have significant authority to allocate resources and enormous economic influence (such as the authority to allocate land resources, the authority to loosen environmental regulatory requirements to reduce local investment costs etc. ). China's reforms enabled products and other required economic elements to move across regions in large scale, and participation in the global labor market as well as the formation and expansion of a unified domestic market enabled local governments at various levels to attract external resources to promote local economic development by improving the local investment environment. In essence, a particular level of local government is like an individual market competitor as local governments compete with each other for resources and the promotion of development. This phenomenon, which we refer to as a "local competitive" market economy may be one of the most prominent features of China's market economy, providing the basic motive force behind China's economic growth. At the same time, it also causes many problems, such as "bottom-line competition," over-

development, and the accumulation and concentration of financial risk.

(2) The role of mechanisms by which governments can concentrate resources to undertake large projects is prominent. Under the existing system, the government still possesses substantial power to directly control resources and indirectly intervene in their use, enabling it to mobilize and use many resources in a short time to achieve a certain strategic objective. Such a mechanism that allows resources to be concentrated in order to complete large projects has its own unique advantage in coping with emergencies as well as in implementing certain major initiatives, but if its use is inappropriately heavy-handed or misguided, the consequences can be serious. Additionally, how to improve the efficiency of resource allocation while adapting to the market economy remains an issue that must be addressed.

(3) State-owned enterprises still have a strong grip on the economy's most fundamental sectors. As reforms have progressed, SOEs have exited from many sectors, and the proportion of output by non-public enterprises and foreign-funded enterprises has obviously exceeded that of the public sector. However, the level of control by state-owned enterprises over areas such as energy, major infrastructure, and finance has not changed significantly and has even been enhanced in some areas. Some provincial level state-owned enterprises have returned to lead or control their respective industries following policies of administrative integration, prompting the complaint that "the state is moving forward while the people are moving backward". Over the years, the profitability of major state-owned enterprises has improved, and their equity and governance structure has also been improved to different degrees. However, if factors such as resource ownership and industrial monopoly are taken into account, whether or not substantial progress has been achieved in operating efficiency is still difficult to determine. Additionally, to what extent state-owned enterprises are up to the task of driving innovation remains to be seen.

(4) The level of market openness as well as general market competition still needs to be improved. Since its reforms, China has achieved substantial progress in opening up its market, market competition has become increasingly intense, and market order has gradually been improved. However, currently there is still a lack of access in many areas, and some industries, especially service industries, are still somewhat closed internally and externally, with market competition still thwarted by various factors. Some enterprises try to sway public policy to serve their own interests in order to obtain or consolidate their monopoly status. Some enterprises that have established an advantageous status during market competition also utilize their market dominating power to suppress or expel competitors through strategic actions. The credibility of the market as a whole is low, and the entire society consequently must bear significant transaction costs.

(5) The development of the legislative system is unable to meet the market economy's development needs. Since its reform and opening up, China has introduced and improved a number of basic laws relevant to the market economic system, such as *China's Corporation Law*, *Civil Law General Provisions*, *Criminal Law*, *Contract Law*, *Property Law*, and *Antimonopoly Law*, but we still have a long way to go in achieving a "market economy under the rule of law". The legal systems necessary for a market economy should be further improved and refined, but the most significant issue is

still the restriction of, and interference in, the laws by administrative powers, and laws that are on the books are often not followed.

(6) The accumulation and subsequent deferred elimination of financial risks. During the latest round of high-speed economic growth, due to institutional and mechanistic defects, some financial risks have been accumulated in the system, such as risks associated with local financing platforms, the risks associated with long-term loans, and the risks associated with the asset bubbles. If supported by high-speed growth, these risks may be gradually assimilated during later development (the so-called deferred elimination of risk). However, if economic growth naturally slows, the possibility that these risks suddenly emerge and wreak major macroeconomic havoc cannot be discounted.

(7) The issue of "half-way" urbanization remains. Since China's reform and opening up, many rural laborers have entered non-agricultural sectors and urban areas. However, under land policy, social security policy, and restrictions on migration, a significant percentage of migrant farmer workers cannot be truly integrated into cities and townships. Such a "half-way" urbanization not only hinders optimization of the workforce, but also limits increases in consumption demand and the improvement of the quality of human capital.

(8) The "vertical mobility" of society is impeded. Since China's market reforms, channels for obtaining an education, seeking a job away from home, and starting one's own business have been widened, and there have been increasing opportunities for people at various levels of society to realize self-development. However, channels that enable vertical mobility are still insufficiently open, and the impact of factors such as family background and social connections on employment and entrepreneurship is still present and even increasing in some aspects. The advent of the "Second-generation poor" and the "Second-generation rich" phenomena shows that there is a trend of entrenched social interests and fixed social classes. This situation, if it persists, will not only strangle China's vitality and creativity as a society, but also directly exert a negative influence on social stability.

Generally speaking, China's current growth model is effective as a model for high-speed growth and industrialization, and even has its unique advantages in some aspects. The dramatic structural changes that will accompany a drop in the country's economic growth rate shows that the fundamentals on which China's high-speed growth has been relying for more than 30 years will face major readjustments. If the current growth model continues to be maintained, as economic growth naturally slows, China's economy will face severe challenges in two respects.

First, the high liquidity and economies of scale accompanying high-speed growth have compensated for quite a few issues of low-efficiency in the market. However, once growth slows, a number of problems associated with low market efficiencies will come to the fore, including reduced profitability and revenues for businesses, a shrinkage in asset values, and a difficulty in recouping long-term loans.

Second, as China's level of development increases, several problems under the existing growth model such as limited market development, insufficient supply incentives, slow human capital accumulation, and limited channels for people to participate in modernization will become increasingly prominent. After the economy's low-cost advantage is gradually weakened, there is uncertainty as to whether or not a new, innovation-driven competitive advantage can be formed. Due to problems in these two aspects, China may face serious difficulties in getting over the impending high-income wall.

## VI. How China Can Scale the Wall

### (I) The Approaching High-income Wall Raises Clear and Urgent Need to Change the Economic Growth Model

Based on the above analysis, the growth of China's economy is slated to slow sometime in the next five years. After more than 30 years of high-speed growth, China's economy will very likely reach an upper bound to high-speed growth. The timeline for changing China's economic development model or growth model is thus clear.

Changing the current means of development (also known as the means of growth or growth model) has been proposed over and over again for about 20 years in China. A question that people often ask is: After such a long time, why hasn't it changed? Apart from sheer institutional inertia and the "perception" issue, one fundamental reason is that the existing growth model is to some extent well suited to the current stage of economic growth. Otherwise, how could we explain how we have achieved such remarkable results under a "bad" growth model? With 10% annual growth already achieved, policymakers are actually quite hard-pressed to change dramatically the current growth model.

However, once China's growth rate drops, the fundamentals previously maintaining high-speed growth will experience major changes and must be reconsidered. Changing the growth model or the means of development will therefore become inevitable. One important conclusion that can be drawn from this is that each development model is suited to a specific stage of development. In other words, the suitability of a particular development model is stage-specific. We should therefore view a specific development model historically. Another conclusion that can be drawn from this insight is that the approach of a natural drop in growth is necessary before changing the existing development model.

This conclusion stipulates that an active change to the development model is needed, and also presents an explicit deadline. This means that before a decline in growth, substantial progress should be made in shifting China's development model. However, to successfully realize such a transformation, an acceptance of the relevant challenges, clarity regarding the main problems to be solved, and the implementation of a roadmap or even a timetable for changing the model are all critical. The possibility of China falling into the kind of middle-income trap experienced by Latin American countries as well as the former Soviet Union and Eastern European countries is very small, but when getting over the "wall" to become a high-income society, we still face two possibilities:

One possibility is the successful prediction of the timetable for slowing growth, the adoption of concrete and effective measures to solve any major problems during the transition within a limited time, and the formation of new growth drivers while preventing and controlling risks. The growth rate will drop in the future, but the drop will not be big-from about 10% to about 7% for example-and we should also be able to avoid large fluctuations to achieve stable and high-quality growth at this new growth level over the long term, possibly 10 years or longer. Based on the experiences of successful catch-up countries, such a scenario is quite achievable.

Another possibility is that our current estimation for the high-speed growth is overly optimistic. For example, policymakers may think that "China's high-speed growth can last for another 30 years," and as a result do not pay attention to a possible drop in the future growth rate. Alternatively, policymakers might admit that the growth will drop, but may think that problems during the drop will not be serious, and that China will be able to enter its second stage of growth without incident. Yet another possibility is one where policymakers, although convinced that there will be major problems during the drop, take a "wait and see" attitude. In fact, the ability of our existing growth model to withstand the impact of a slowdown in growth rate is quite weak. From the second quarter of 2008 to the first quarter of 2009, for example, when year-to-year GDP growth was reduced from 10.7% to 6.5% due to the impact of the global financial crisis, year-to-year growth in government revenues and business profits dropped sharply from 31.4% and 22.4% to -8.3% and -37.1% respectively, and the number of non-agricultural jobs was also reduced by about 20 million. Once economic growth slows for not just one or two quarters but permanently, China may face a very difficult situation due to a lack of preparation, and the drop in growth may be big-perhaps by more than half-and trigger a certain degree of financial crisis or even social instability, making it difficult to get back onto a stable growth track.

### (II) The Obstacles to Successful Transformation

The first possibility we refer to as the "active transformation" scenario and the second as the "passive transformation" scenario. The cost of a "passive transformation" is very high, and the probability of failure is also very high. Obviously, we should strive for an active transformation and avoid a passive transformation. To this end, we should clearly define the main problems to be solved during China's growth transition as well as reform priorities to be addressed in order to solve these issues. To successfully realize the transformation of China's economic growth model, we should focus on solving two problems: (1) controlling risks and (2) promoting new sources of growth. Specifically, we should focus on addressing the important following questions:

(1) Can we effectively prevent and solve the financial risks accumulated during high-speed growth once growth slows? The experiences of Latin America, Southeast Asia and South Korea show that financial risks are a direct cause of economic stagnation and a centralized reflection of an intrinsic contradiction inherent in the economic growth model. For a long time, various risks in China's economy such as surplus production capacity and bad loans caused by clumsy policy have been solved through the high liquidity and economies of scale realizable in a high-speed growth regime, but potential risks associated with the local government's financing platforms, the expansion of bank loans, and asset price bubbles still exist.

(2) Can enterprises adapt to a slower growth environment, gradually changing their "speed-oriented" profit models? The high-speed growth of China's economy has compensated for problems

with enterprises' efficiency and operating profitability. For big enterprises, a financial support centre formed during a period of excessive liquidity allows for the realization of profitability through expansions in operating size; SMEs rely on fast-in-and-fast-out cash flows in goods trade, while running at high speeds in order to make a profit. The expansion of demand driven by high-speed growth as well as the optimistic expectations that are therefore created play an important role in the profitability of enterprises. Once the economic growth rate has dropped permanently, society's expectations and investment motivations will be reversed and the productivity and operations of enterprises will face a serious test. Especially during early drops in growth, a society's expectations will often be "excessively reversed," and the situation may be further exacerbated.

(3) Can China adjust its macroeconomic control objectives to correspond with a drop in the growth rate? If we are able to predict a permanent drop in economic growth, macroeconomic control objectives should be set accordingly, and China should not attempt to continue to maintain growth goals appropriate to high-speed growth environment. Otherwise, if growth goals exceed actual economic potential, problems such as excessive investment, surplus production capacity, asset bubbles, and inflation will emerge. In this regard, we should study and draw on the historical experiences of Japan: after the 1980s, Japan implemented an expansion-oriented macro-economic policy in an effort to restore previous high-speed growth, but ended up generating asset bubbles, and forcing its economy into a long-term recession.

(4) Can China nurture an adequate and effective market environment that will produce innovation-oriented enterprises and SMEs through competition, creating technology-and knowledge-intensive manufacturing and service industries possessing long-term international competitiveness? Industries formed under a regime of high-speed growth and inadequate competition are not motivated to innovate. Whether or not China can foster a market environment that promotes adequate competition, has effective incentives and is also innovation oriented; whether or not China can compel enterprises to shift from relying on specific economic inputs to relying on innovation; and whether or not China can produce a series of innovation-oriented enterprises and SMEs, in order to develop internationally competitive technology-and knowledge-intensive manufacturing and service industries remain the most fundamental challenges to such a transformation.

(5) Can China further liberate the market, loosening access restrictions to currently monopolized industries, especially the service industries, to provide space for substantial development within the service industries? Currently there are still many market access restrictions in industries such as telecommunications, railways, power generation & supply, petrochemicals, finance, education, healthcare, and culture and levels of monopolization remain high.

(6) Can China, based on current urban-rural integration efforts, accelerate the process by which farmers who have immigrated to cities become true "city residents", while promoting an optimized re-allocation of farmlands contracted by farmers while ensuring the latter's rights? The "countryside, farmer and agriculture" issue is central to China's industrialization and modernization process, and the most fundamental way to solve this issue is to let most farmers enter non-agricultural industries and cities while at the same time modernizing the production methods and lifestyles of

farmers remaining in the countryside. China should solve the most pressing issues that are currently encountered in urban-rural integration, which must include the elimination of de facto discrimination against farmers who have entered cities, enabling them to get the same public services as city residents; promotion of optimized allocation of rural production elements such as the lands contracted by the farmers, while at the same time ensuring the latter's rights, to enable farmers to get more income from their assets. This will help in narrowing the current income gap, and such measures are also vital to promoting the accumulation of human capital and improving the utilization rate of production elements such as land.

(7) Can China build the university research systems needed to establish an innovation-oriented society via reforms? Dynamic and creative universities and research systems are an important sign of a high-income, modern country, and form the basis of an innovation-oriented economy and society. Currently China's universities and research systems are still significantly government-dominated and bureaucratic, unable to meet the needs of an innovation-oriented society, and dramatic reforms must be implemented in order to achieve a breakthrough solution to this problem.

(8) Can China promote reform with respect to issues of employment, entrepreneurship and income distribution systems to enable the rapid growth of the middle class? The middle class usually possesses specialist knowledge and technical skills as well as a stable income and strong buying power, and they put particular stress on human capital development, moral standards and social responsibility. Therefore, the growth of the middle-class is fundamental to promoting innovation, driving up domestic demand, narrowing China's income gap, and ensuring the long-time peaceful stability for China's society. However, inadequate jobs, limited entrepreneurship opportunities, and inappropriate income distribution systems are not good for the expansion of the middle class, making it difficult to realize an "olive-shaped society".

(9) Can China create a modern financial system that satisfies development and innovation needs during periods of moderate growth while also effectively spreading and preventing risks? Optimizing resource allocation and spreading risks are the two functions of a modern financial system. Under the current modern financial system, a majority of China's financial resources flow to infrastructure and basic industries, real estate development, major enterprises, as well as local financing platforms etc, while support for entrepreneurship and innovation activities, especially innovation among SMEs, is inadequate. If China's financial system can't adapt to the rapid growth of the physical economy over the long term, we will face the problem of inefficiency and risky resource allocation on a long-term basis.

(10) Can the government shift from being growth-oriented to being public service-oriented? A growth-oriented government has been a key institutional factor during the previous 30 years of high-speed growth. However, now that China is entering a new developmental stage, growth-oriented governmental behaviors that have a negative impact on efficiency and innovation have become increasingly problematic. On the other hand, as China enters a new stage of development, the government will be required to play a leading role in improving people's livelihood and providing basic public services. Shifting from being growth-oriented to being public service-oriented logically becomes an

important milestone for overall change in government functions.

### (III) The Importance of "Participatory and Facilitative Reform"

Solving all of the aforementioned problems during an economic transformation will depend on substantial breakthroughs in the reform of related fields, including the reform of government functions, regulation of government behaviors, and the improvement of the government's performance evaluation system; continuing to implement strategic adjustments to SOEs, appropriately shrinking the purview of SOEs, and deepening reform in monopoly industries; accelerating the reform of fiscal, tax and financial systems, creating a complete and healthy risk prevention and control mechanism, and solving potential financial risks; and deepening reforms of product pricing, resource products and critical market elements, and improving pricing mechanisms to enable the market to play a basic role in resource allocation more effectively.

Drawing on the historical experiences and lessons of other countries that have undergone the industrialization process, and in conjunction with the prominent problems presently faced by China, we will introduce and elaborate on a concept that we call "participatory and facilitative reform".

By engaging in an in-depth analysis of the various problems that must be solved during China's economic transformation as discussed above, we find one critical clue—to fundamentally solve these problems, we have to rely on further increasing the scope of society's participation in industrialization and modernization. Currently there are two subjects in China receiving a very high level of attention that are also highly associated with the aforementioned transformational issues directly or indirectly: one is the narrowing of the current income distribution gap, and the other China's change to an innovation-driven society. It seems that these two subjects are independent of each other, or seemingly are not closely connected, but it is not hard to see through an in-depth analysis that they are actually the same subject in a sense. Although a serious income gap can be narrowed to some extent through redistribution policies, the most fundamental solution remains the improvement of primary distribution. The main reason for the widened income gap has to do with factors including the environment and conditions in which individuals grow up as well as certain regulatory arrangements and policies.

The fundamental solution to narrowing the income gap is to create roughly the same survival and development environment for all members of a society, especially members from different classes, and provide roughly the same opportunities for all individuals with respect to education, employment, entrepreneurship, and innovation; in other words, we need to create opportunities for all members of society to participate in industrialization and modernization to the greatest extent possible. As far as being innovation-oriented is concerned, at the end of the day we should fully tap the enthusiasm, especially the creativity, of all members of the society. A society with the enthusiasm and creativity of all of its members being fully tapped will also be a society with fast income growth and a small income gap. The historical experiences of successful catch-up countries such as Japan and South Korea have also proved that there is an intrinsic correlation between a narrowing of the income gap and an enhancing of a society's ability to innovate.

Therefore, as to how to solve important issues during the coming economic transformation, we should commit to and work hard to advance what we call "participatory and facilitative reform": working hard to seek breakthroughs in the reform of related fields with the aim of promoting the participation of all individuals in the industrialization and modernization process to a greater extent and at a higher level of quality. The key points of such a program can be summarized as follows: increasing participation opportunities, improving participation ability, and improving the regulations and policies that encourage entrepreneurship and innovation.

### (IV) Necessary Reforms

#### 1. Equal employment opportunities for all China should provide to as many members of its society as possible.

This begins with eliminating discrimination against migrant farmer workers. At the same time, the government must allow migrant farmer workers in cities as far as possible to become complete "city residents." We should allow all migrant workers and their family members who have been working in a city for a long time to obtain the residency status if they so choose, so that they may enjoy the same education, healthcare, housing, and social security services as enjoyed by other city residents. Secondly, we must put more importance on equal employment opportunities in order to terminate the "no connections, no employment" phenomenon that continues to be pervasive in Chinese society. We should create an open and transparent recruitment and hiring mechanism, and in particular we should work to eliminate the pernicious influence that social connections exert in determining employment in some public sectors. Finally, we must further open up the market, lowering access thresholds and encouraging self-employment, while refining the SME support system at the same time. We should further implement the "Thirty-six Regulations for the Non-public Sector," stimulating investment enthusiasm within the private sector and improve policy and service systems supporting the development of private enterprises and SMEs.

#### 2. Nurturing human capital.

China must improve its public service system to enable all individuals to have more opportunities to accumulate human capital. First, we should improve the healthcare system and the health of the general population by reforming the healthcare system and promoting the appropriate allocation of healthcare resources, enhance the development of the public healthcare service system, implement prevention-centered healthcare principles, accelerate the popularization of healthcare knowledge, advocate healthy lifestyles, and improve people's physical health. Second, we should provide equal opportunities for everybody to receive a decent education. China should strictly carry out its compulsory education law, promoting a balanced allocation of resources such as basic education resources, improving government financial aid and scholarships so as not to allow a child to leave school because of poverty, preventing inter-generation transfer of differences in competencies and skills. Third, China must upgrade current vocational education, especially the training for migrant farmer workers. We should promote the development of internship and training facilities as well as the training of full-time teachers for vocational education and encourage the training of high caliber professionals for continuously upgrading industries via various means including school-industry partnerships and on-demand training. At the same time the government must reform current methods for distributing government subsidies for vocational education, and adopt competitive mechanisms to improve the actual results of vocational education and the training of migrant farmer workers. Fourth, we must adopt specific poverty reduction policies for people beneath the poverty line. This means including people below the poverty line in universal social security systems including pension plans, healthcare insurance, and housing programs in order to help poor families improve their level of education and job skills through their own efforts and prevent a vicious cycle of fixed poverty.

### 3. Promote entrepreneurship and innovation.

China should create a improved system for the promotion of entrepreneurship and innovation, to provide as many opportunities as possible for members of society to engage in entrepreneurship and innovation. First, we must break up monopolies and encourage competition. For monopoly industries and sectors, on the one hand we should loosen access restrictions, support and promote fair competition among enterprises of various types of ownership; on the other hand, we should seek to break administrative monopolies, and encourage enterprises to increase their vitality and productivity through innovation in competition. Second, we must promote reform within universities and educational and research organizations. The government should seek to reverse the trend that research and educational organizations are becoming administrative and bureaucratic organizations to create conditions that allow professionals to dominate research and educational activities and research grant allocation as well as researcher selection and promotion. Third, we should create a modern financial system that supports innovation by encouraging and guiding financial institutions to accelerate the creation of a professional credit and loan management system including special incentives and an evaluation mechanism that supports innovation. We should actively promote financial innovations such as financing guaranteed by intellectual property, widen market-based financing channels for innovations in multiple sectors, actively explore the financing potential among multiple levels of the capital market, and introduce targeted regulatory policies. Fourth, we should deepen existing reforms to government function, and improve government services. For entrepreneurship and innovation, regulatory controls over industrial access should be loosened, and both application processes and approval procedures should be streamlined. Meanwhile, we should ensure the effective supply of common key technologies, and build an information exchange platform for innovation and entrepreneurship in order to provide support for entrepreneurs and innovators to optimize and combine production elements including funding, technology, and human resources. China must improve its legal environment and enhance existing protection for property rights, especially intellectual property rights. A system for protecting property rights can provide stable development expectations for entrepreneurs and innovators, stimulating investment enthusiasm, and motivating innovation. To this end, we should further improve our civil law system and property right protection system. In particular, we should create a complete system of IPR laws, enhance enforcement supervision, and improve enforcement results.

## References

1. Chen, Changsheng, and Xiaowei Xuan. 2010. "Abstraction and Summary of the General Rules from International Experiences Regarding the 'Middle-income Trap.'" The Development Re-

search Center of the State Council's Background Research Report.

2. Chen, Jianpeng. 2010. "Experiences & Lessons of the Former Soviet Union and Eastern European Countries in Economic Development." The Development Research Center of the State Council's Background Research Report.

3. Fang, Jin. 2010. "International Experiences of the Fast-growing Economies in Getting Over the 'Middle-income Trap' after World War II." The Development Research Center of the State Council's Background Research Report.

4. Fatás, A., Mihov, I. 2009. "The 4 I's of Economic Growth." Working Paper. INSEAD.

5. Gao, Shiji, and Xian Zhuo. 2010. "The Proposal of the 'Middle-income Trap' Concept and Review of Related Literature." The Development Research Center of the State Council's Background Research Report.

6. Gill, I., and Kharas, H. 2007. "An East Asian Renaissance: Ideas for Economic Growth." World Bank Publications.

7. Liu, Shijin, We Xu, and Peilin Liu. 2010. "Calculation of the Time Window for the Turning Point of Economic Growth." The Development Research Center of the State Council's Background Research Report.

8. Liu, Yunzhong, and Jianwu He. 2010. "The Impact of the Reduced Economic Growth in China on Some Economic Indicators." The Development Research Center of the State Council's Background Research Report.

9. Maddison, A. 2003. *The World Economy: Historical Statistics*, OECD, Paris.

10. Mitchell, B. R. 2007. *International Historical Statistics* (Sixth Edition). New York: Palgrave MacMillan.

11. Rodrik, D. 2007. *One Economics, Many Recipes: Globalization, Institutions, and Economic Growth.* Princeton, NJ: Princeton University Press.

12. Wang, Xiaoming. 2010a. "Lessons and Inspirations from Typical Countries Falling in the 'Middle-income Trap' -The Case Study of the Latin American Countries." The Development Research Center of the State Council's Background Research Report.

13. Wang, Xiaoming. 2010b. "Lessons and Inspirations from Typical Countries Falling in the 'Middle-income Trap' -The Case Study of the Four Southeast Asian Countries." The Development Research Center of the State Council's Background Research Report.

14. Yuan, Dongming. 2010. "Main Experiences of the Latecomer Developed European Countries in Coping with the 'Middle-income Trap.'" The Development Research Center of the State Council's Background Research Report.

15. Zhang, Junkuo, and Yongzhi Hou. 2010. "China's Challenges in Development and the Favorable Conditions in Getting Over the Middle-income Stage." The Development Research Center of the State Council's Background Research Report.

16. Zhang, Liping. 2010. "Performance of UK and the U. S. in Handling the 'Middle-income Trap.'" The Development Research Center of the State Council's Background Research Report.

# Chapter 2

# Don't Overlook GDP and Investment: An Analysis of China's Current Economic Trend

**Liu Shucheng** (刘树成)

**Economic Research Institute, Chinese Academy of Social Sciences, Beijing, China**

**Abstract**: In this paper, we first examine various causes of China's unexpected low economic growth rate since the beginning of 2012. Particularly, we propose the possibility of one tendency masking the other tendency. That is, there is a tendency of neglecting and downplaying GDP while making fewer efforts to develop economy in some regions that oppose GDP worship and irrational pursuit of and competition for GDP, which deserves our full attention. We further propose in this paper that the decline of China's potential economic growth rate should keep a gradual process and the government should favor consumption while not overlooking investment, given that a certain amount of moderate investment will remain the key impetus to China's economic growth over a certain period in the future.

**Keywords**: economic trend, macro control, periodic fluctuation, stabilizing growth

## I. China's Current Economic Trend: Fluctuating at an Unexpected Low Level

Since the beginning of 2012, China's economy has faced increasing pressure from a noticeably slowing economic growth rate beyond public expectation. As shown by the quarter-on-quarter GDP growth rate, the growth in the first quarter of 2012 has followed the trend of decline in the four quarters of the previous year (with a growth rate of 9.7%, 9.5%, 9.1% and 8.9%, respectively) and further reduced to 8.1%, which is below the general public expectation of 8.4% or 8.5%. The figure marks the minimum growth over the past 12 quarters since the recovery of China's economy beginning in the second quarter of 2009 in the aftermath of global financial crisis. It is also among the six rare quarterly growth rates that are below 8.1% over the past 12 years since 2000 (see Figure 1, the other five quarterly growth rates below 8.1% are 7.3% in the fourth quarter of 2000, 7.7% in the second quarter of 2001, 7.8% in the third quarter of 2001, 7.4% in the fourth quarter of 2008 and 6.6% in the first quarter of 2009).

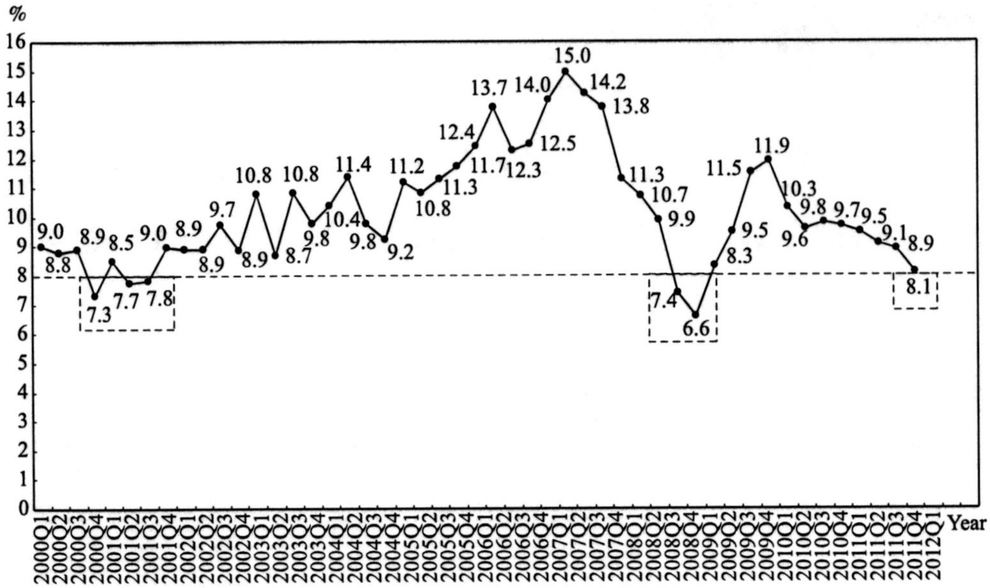

**Figure 1: Quarter-on-quarter GDP Growth Rate**
**(the first quarter of 2000 to that of 2012)**

Source: website of National Bureau of Statistics; all previous press conferences hosted by National Bureau of Statistics on the quarterly national economy.

The month-on-month growth rate of added value of China's large-scale industrial enterprises in 2012 has followed the trend of decline since July 2011 and further reduced to 9.3% in April, which is also below the general public expectation of a growth rate of 12.2%. The figure marks the lowest growth rate over the past 35 months since the rise of growth rate of domestic industrial added value in the aftermath of global financial crisis. It is also among the 14 rare month-on-month growth rates that are below 10% over the 148 months since January of 2000 (see Figure 2, the other 13 months with a growth rate below 10% are July, September to December of 2001 and October of 2008 to May of 2009). The month-on-month growth rate of large-scale industrial added value this May, despite a slight increase by 0.3 percentage point than that in April to 9.6%, is still fluctuating at a low level below 10%.

In response to the unexpected decline of China's economic growth since this year, we should neither overreact to the situation by proposing loose macro control policy or embracing the once popular theories of China's economic collapse, economic crisis, the hard landing of China's economy and the economic stagflation; nor should we overlook the status quo, which requires us to carefully examine various possible causes of the noticeable decline of economic growth rate and take various measures accordingly to avoid the sharp fluctuation of economic growth and ensure the rapid and stable economic development over a long period.

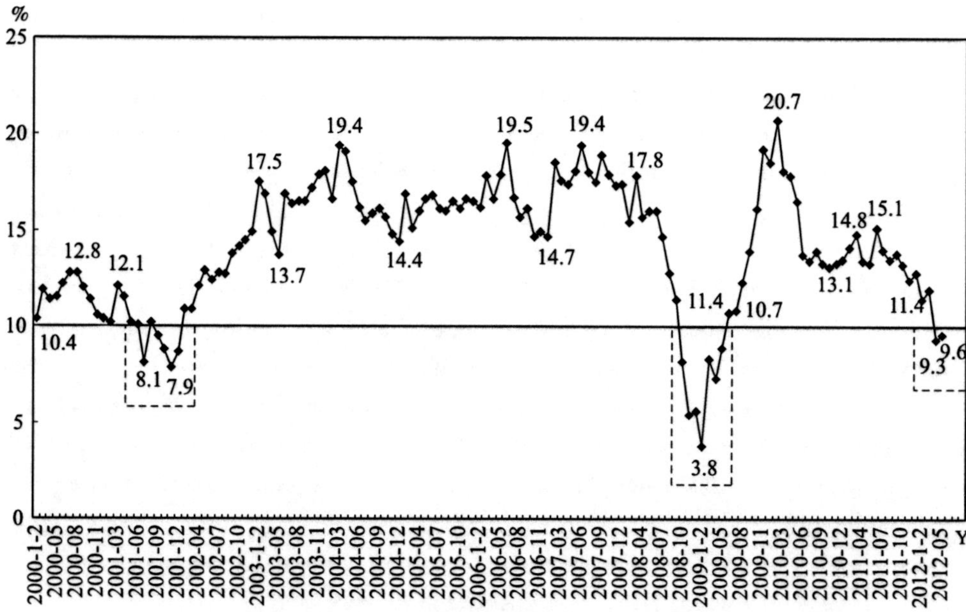


**Figure 2: Month-on-month Growth Rate of Industrial Added Value (January and February of 2000 to May 2012)**

Source: website of National Bureau of Statistics.

## II. Cause Analysis: Paying Attention to the Possibility of One Tendency Masking the Other

The further decline of economic growth is caused by various factors. Based on the existing studies in the academic circle, we find out the following seven major factors:

First, active macro control;

Second, active transformation of economic development mode and acceleration of restructuring;

Third, a depressed overseas demand and export market, and the lasting impact of global financial crisis;

Fourth, insufficient domestic consumption and weak demand for investment;

Fifth, intensifying restriction of natural resources, environment and labor force, as well as the decline of potential economic growth rate;

Sixth, difficulty in business management, increase of various costs, shortage of capital, weak market demand and decrease of profits;

Seventh, lasting decline of economic growth rate.

All of the above factors account for the decline. Here we want to suggest the possible eighth cause of one tendency masking the other. There is a tendency of overlooking and downplaying GDP while making fewer efforts to develop economy in some regions that oppose the irrational pursuit of and competition for GDP, which deserves our full attention.

The historical experience since the reform and opening-up shows that the second year of each five-year plan, which coincides with the reelection of leadership at all levels and fits what we call "the year of double impetus", usually sees a tendency of increasingly heated economic growth. Since the reform and opening-up from the Sixth Five-Year Plan (1981 - 1985) to the Eleventh Five-Year Plan (2006 - 2010), there have been six cases of "the year of double impetus", namely, the year of 1982, 1987, 1992, 1997, 2002 and 2007 (see Figure 3 for the GDP growth rate of each year). Of the six cases, there are three cases of heated or overheated economic growth (11.6% in 1987, 14.2% in 1992 and 14.2% in 2007), two cases of recovery of economic growth (the growth rate in 1982 climbed from 5.2% in the previous year to 9.1% whereas that in 2002 climbed from 8.3% in the previous year to 9.1%), and only one case of decline of economic growth (the growth rate in 1997 reduced to 9.3% from 10% in the previous year). This year happens to fit the so-called "year of double impetus". While historical practice tells us that we should take efforts to prevent overheated economic growth, the reality is exactly the opposite for there has been a sharp decline in economic growth, which, like in the case in 1997, could be attributed to the impact of Asian Financial Crisis and weak domestic demand. But we should also pay attention to the before mentioned problem of one tendency masking the other.

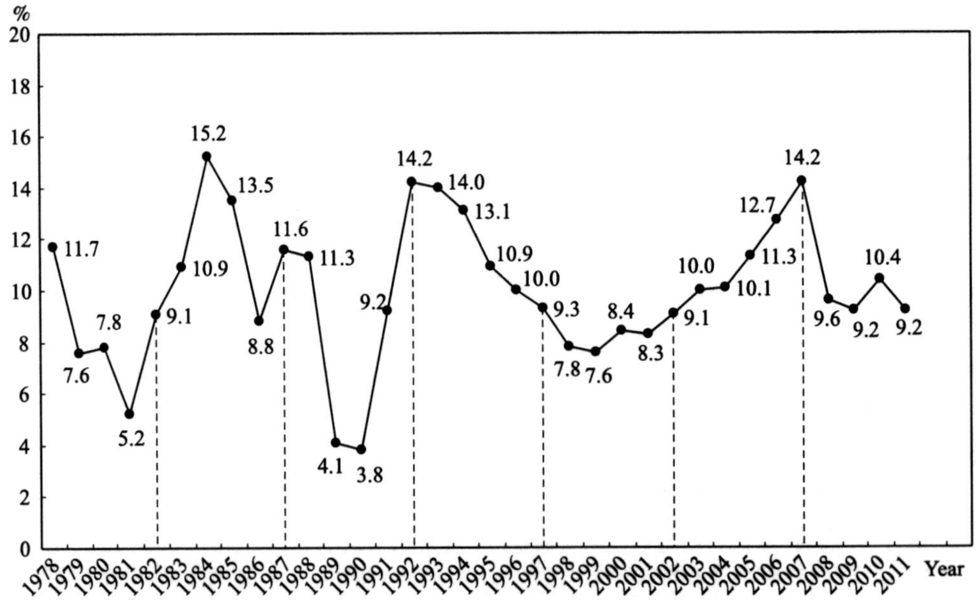


**Figure 3: China's GDP Growth Rate (1978 - 2011)**

Source: *China Statistical Abstract* 2012, China Statistics Press, 2012.

Why we should not overlook GDP? GDP is the added value of products and services of all permanent units in a country (or a region) over a certain period. The production of material goods and relevant producer and consumer services makes up the base for a real economy that the society relies on to ensure a stable development. However, the GDP growth rate should not be too high in a real economy. Since the founding of People's Republic of China in 1949, our domestic economic growth has undergone a couple cases of "sharp fluctuation" whose crux is "sharp increase," for the excessively high economic growth rate will soon cause the problem of "four highs", that is, high energy consumption, high consumption of material goods, high pollution and high inflation rate, which will soon disturb the various balances indispensible for the normal operation of the economy and result in the subsequent "sharp decrease" of economic growth rate. However, while it is appropriate to oppose GDP worship and the irrational pursuit of and competition for GDP, we should also understand that an excessively low GDP growth rate over a certain period will on the other hand cause a series of problems. First, it will bring difficulty to residents' income increase and daily living, given that GDP is the material base for improving people's living standard. While making the GDP "cake" bigger does not necessarily mean that it can be divided fairly, it would be more difficult to distribute "the cake" fairly if we do not make "it" big enough. Second, an excessively low GDP growth rate will affect financial revenue, whose sharp decrease will subsequently affect economic restructuring, development of social undertakings and achievement of social security based on financial support. Third, an excessively low GDP growth rate will affect the macro environment of a business, for slow GDP growth indicates a weak market demand, which will affect production and sales of a business as well as the increase of job opportunities. Overall, an excessively high economic growth rate will deteriorate economic structure, so will an excessively low growth rate. In the former case, the trend can not last long, nor can it in the latter case. So it is crucial to maintain a certain and moderate economic growth rate.

The "stable growth" with a moderate growth rate does not simply mean that we should loosen macro control policy and resume "rapid growth", GDP worship or irrational pursuit of GDP, but that new and higher requirements should be put on governments at all levels under the new circumstances. In one word, "stable growth" should be combined with transforming economic growth mode, adjusting economic structure, controlling the commodity prices, promoting reform and benefiting people's well-being to achieve scientific development.

So what should be the proper economic growth rate? This involves the understanding of potential economic growth rate.

## III. The Decline of Potential Economic Growth Rate Should Keep a Gradual Process

Some scholars correctly point out that China's economy has entered a new stage characterized by the decline of potential economic growth rate after developing at a double-digit growth rate over the past thirty years since the reform and opening-up. Here gives rise to three issues.

### (I) Whether the Decline of Potential Growth Rate Is a Sudden or a Gradual Process

Some scholars argue that China's potential economic growth rate will noticeably reduce to a lower level from a high rate of 10% to a medium rate between 6% and 7% over 2013 to 2017. However, experience in the global context suggests that cases of the decline of potential economic growth rate vary in different countries with different geographical size, population size and natural resources as well as different external and internal environments.

Case One: The decline of potential growth rate is a sudden process in some countries. For example, Japan has undergone four stages in the aftermath of WWII (see Figure 4):

(1) The country saw an annual GDP growth rate of 7.2% over the seven years from 1953 to 1959 (in which 1952 is the base year).

(2) Its annual GDP growth rate increased to 9.7% over the 14 years from 1960 to 1973 (in which 1959 is the base year).

(3) Its annual GDP growth rate noticeably reduced to 4.1% over the 18 years from 1974 to 1991 (in which 1973 is the base year).

(4) Its annual GDP growth rate further reduced remarkably to 0.7% over the 20 years from 1992 to 2011 (in which 1991 is the base year).

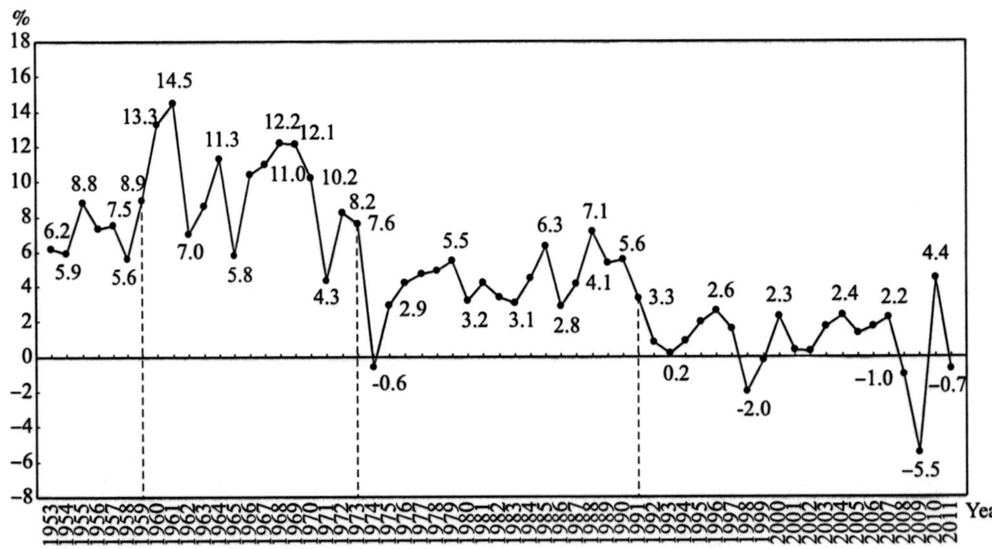


**Figure 4: Japan's GDP Growth Rate (1953 – 2011)**

Source: IMF's *International Financial Statistics Yearbook*, 1983, 1993; IMF's Database, Apr. 2012.

Case Two: Some countries have seen a relatively gradual decline of potential growth rate. For example, South Korea has also undergone four stages in the aftermath of WWII (see Figure 5):

(a) The country saw an annual GDP growth rate of 3.9% over the nine years from 1954 to 1962 (in which 1953 is the base year).

(b) Its annual GDP growth rate increased to 9.5% over the 17 years from 1963 to 1979 (in which 1962 is the base year). During the period, there are five years whose GDP growth rates peaked to a range of 11% to 14%.

(c) Its annual GDP growth rate slightly reduced by 1.3 percentage points to 8.2% over the 18 years from 1980 to 1997 (in which 1979 is the base year). During the period, there are four years whose GDP growth rates peaked to a range of 11% to 12%.

(d) Its annual GDP growth noticeably reduced to 4.2% over the 14 years from 1998 to 2011 (in which 1997 is the base year).

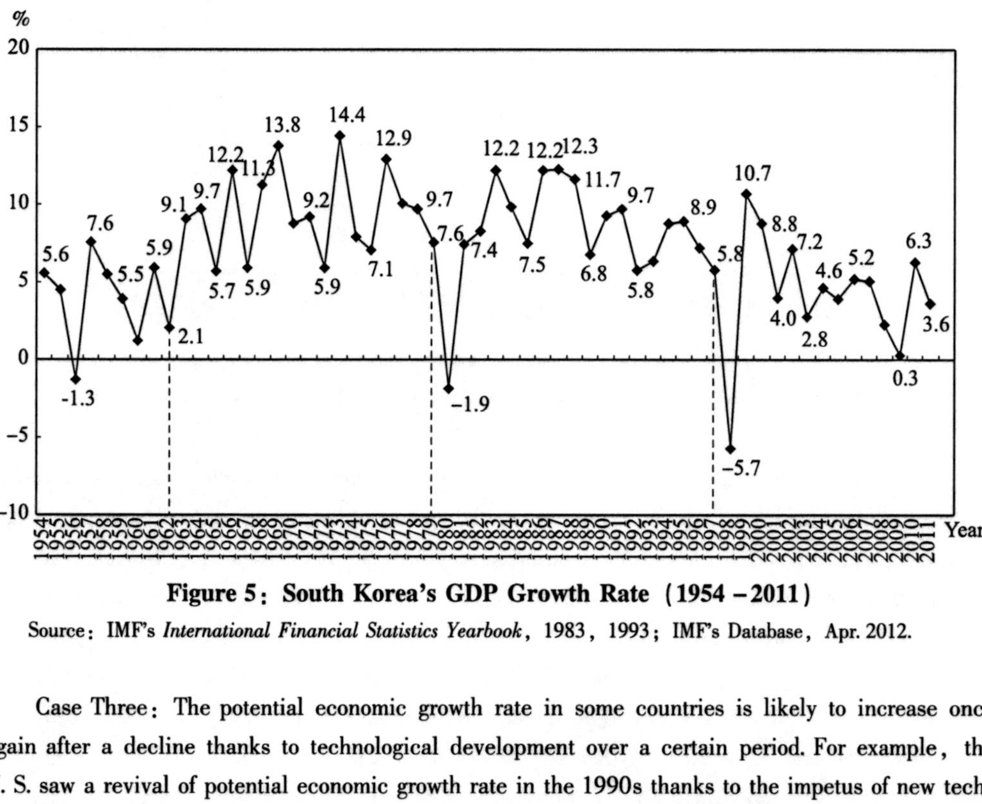


**Figure 5: South Korea's GDP Growth Rate (1954 – 2011)**

Source: IMF's *International Financial Statistics Yearbook*, 1983, 1993; IMF's Database, Apr. 2012.

Case Three: The potential economic growth rate in some countries is likely to increase once again after a decline thanks to technological development over a certain period. For example, the U. S. saw a revival of potential economic growth rate in the 1990s thanks to the impetus of new technological revolution characterized by IT industry. The country has also undergone four stages in the aftermath of WWII (see Figure 6):

(a) It saw an annual GDP growth rate of 3.45% over the 21 years from 1953 to 1973 (in which 1952 is the base year).

(b) Its annual GDP growth rate reduced to 2.65% over the 19 years from 1974 to 1992 (in which 1973 is the base year).

(c) Its annual GDP growth rate again increased to 3.5% over the 8 years from 1993 to 2000 (in which 1992 is the base year).

(d) Its annual GDP growth again reduced to 1.57% over the 11 years from 2001 to 2011 (in which 2000 is the base year).

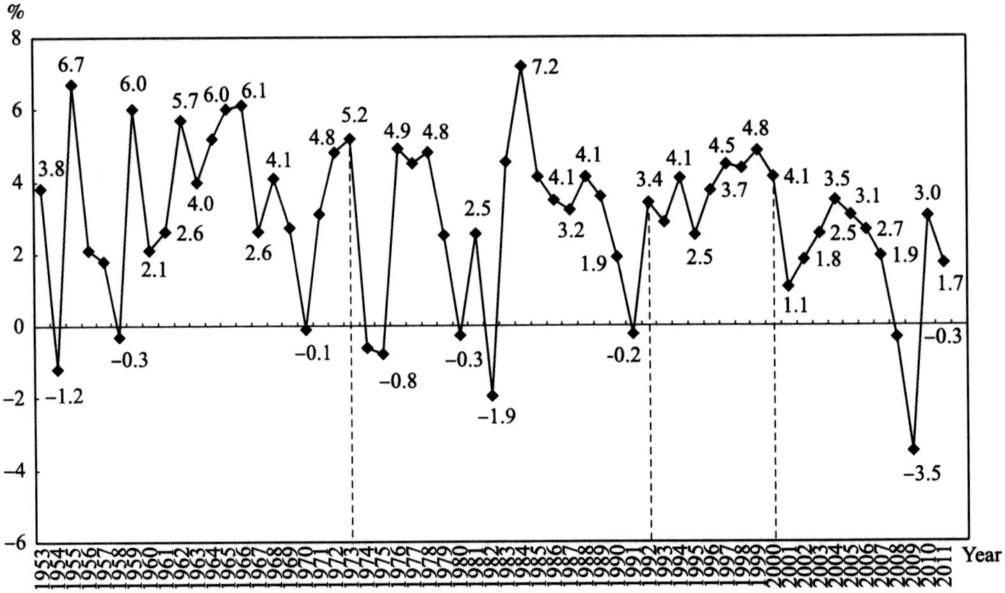

**Figure 6: the U. S. 's GDP Growth Rate (1953 – 2011)**

Source: IMF's *International Financial Statistics Yearbook*, 1985, 1997; IMF's Database, Apr. 2012.

It is hard to calculate the precise potential economic growth rate in each period. The practical macro control also depends more on experience. In the decline of potential economic growth rate, the excessively rapid and sharp decrease of real economic growth rate is likely to cause economic and social instability. Meanwhile, the whole society (governments, enterprises and individuals) requires a gradual adaptation to the decline of potential economic growth rate. So in order to avoid economic and social instability, macro control should focus on slowing the decrease of economic growth rate to a gradual process in stages, for example, by first reducing high rate (10%) to medium and high rate (above 8% and below 10%), then to medium rate (7% to 9%), and further reducing to medium and low rate (6% to 8%) and eventually to low rate (below 5%). Though real economy will not run in a way that strictly follows our subjective will, we can still try our best to make the decline of economic growth rate as gently as possible, especially given that China is a country with a vast territory and a large population which sees a flexible domestic demand and gradually further development of industrialization and urbanization. Such conditions are favorable for achieving a smooth decline of potential economic growth rate.

## (II) The Control of Upper and Lower Limits of Potential Economic Growth Rate in Decline Should Not Necessarily Be Symmetrical

Our research group has calculated the results of pro-filter potential GDP growth rates by applying HP filter method based on the GDP growth indexes over 1978 to 2009. The results show that the pro-filter potential growth rates in general fall into the range of 8% (lower limit) to 12% (upper limit) over the past 30 years since the reform and opening-up. It is necessary to reduce both upper and lower limits by 2 percentage points in the case of decreasing potential economic growth rate. In the recent period, the macro control should reduce the upper limit of growth rate by 2 percentage points to 10% while keeping the lower limit temporarily at 8%, given that China's previous economic growth rate is easy to exceed 10%. The practical experience proves that an economic growth rate above 10% will result in excessively rapid or overheated economic development which is not sustainable. Considering China's existing intensifying restrictions of natural resources, energy and environment, we should first reduce the upper limit of its economic growth rate to 10% or below.

The practical experience over the years also suggests that an economic growth rate of 8% is the base line of China's current economic development. If the growth rate is below 8%, it will severely impede production of business as well as employment in urban and rural areas and thus result in a negative growth of national fiscal revenue. Two of the cases are the fourth quarter of 2008 and the first quarter of 2009, in which China's GDP growth rates respectively reduced to 7.6% and 6.6% due to the impact of global financial crisis. The GDP growth rate in the first quarter of this year reduced to 8.1%, which immediately brought pressure to the whole society and further caused crisis in business management and public revenue. In the "Report on the Work of the Government" published this March, it sets the expected goal of GDP growth rate at 7.5% which is lower than the previous 8% over the years, mainly for the purpose of shifting the focus of whole society to transforming economic development mode while improving the quality and efficiency of economic growth. However, in practical macro control, it is nevertheless appropriate to set 8% as the lower limit of moderate growth range.

In practical macro control, when economic growth rate exceeds 10%, the government should implement moderate tight fiscal policy. When economic growth rate is below 8%, it should implement moderate loose fiscal policy. when economic growth rate fluctuates closely around 9% and the economy is running smoothly, the government can implement neutral fiscal policy. While China's previous macro control often focuses on limiting the "peak" of economic growth rate to avoid "sharp increase", it should pay more attention in the future to the "valley" of economic growth rate to avoid "sharp decrease" in the decline of potential economic growth rate.

### (III) It Is Not Necessarily the Case that Economic Growth Rate Is Decreasing Year by Year in the Decline of Potential Economic Growth Rate

In the decline of potential economic growth rate, it does not fall linearly in terms of annual economic growth rate. In other words, the growth rate does not decrease year by year and there are still fluctuations between the years. Many foreign and domestic economic institutes have predicted that China's economic growth rate in 2012 will be lower than that in 2011 and the growth rate in 2013 will be a little higher than that in 2012. For example, International Monetary Fund (IMF) predicted that China's economic growth rate will reduce to 8.2% in 2012 and increase to 8.8% in 2013; Asian Development Bank predicted that China's economic growth rate will reduce to 8.5%

in 2012 and increase to 8. 7% in 2013; The World Bank first predicted that China' economic growth rate will reduce to 8. 4% in 2012 and further reduce to 8. 3% in 2013 in its estimation released in the November of 2011. However, in its latest estimation released this April, the World Bank predicted that China's economic growth rate will reduce to 8. 2% in 2012 and increase to 8. 6% in 2013.

In order to answer why China's economic growth rate in 2013 is likely to be a little higher than that in 2012, here we briefly review the process of China's macro control shifting the focus from "guaranteeing growth" to "stabilizing the commodity prices" and to the recent "stabilizing growth" since 2008 with the impact of the worst global financial crisis in a century. During the two and a half years period from the second half of 2008 to 2010, the macro control focused on "guaranteeing growth" in order to stop the noticeable decline of economic growth rate and promote economic stability and revival. China has adopted positive fiscal policy and moderately loose monetary policy while implementing "a package of" stimulus plans. By the second quarter of 2009, China has effectively stopped the sharp drop of economic growth and becomes the first country in the world to realize the overall economic revival characterized by a "V-shape" trajectory. Its economic growth rate in 2008 is 9. 2%, which is only 0. 4 percentage point lower than that in the previous year. In 2010, the economic growth rate increases to 10. 4%. With the economic revival and the extraordinary increase of monetary loans, China's commodity prices have started a new round of rise month by month since the January of 2010, breaking the growth rate of 3%, 4% and 5% successively. By the November of 2010, the growth rate of consumer price has risen to 5. 1% compared with the previous month (see Figure 7). Against such background, the Central Economic Working Conference held in the December of 2010 proposed to focus more on "stabilizing the overall price" and stressed that the government is "determined to prevent irrational launch of projects at the start of the twelfth five-year plan" and "to control the head gate of mobility". Thanks to the efforts of "stabilizing the commodity prices", the growth rate of commodity prices declined month by month after rising to the peak of 6. 5% in July 2011 and reduced to 4. 1% by that December. Accordingly, the economic growth rate in 2011 reduced by 1. 2 percentage points to 9. 2% from that in the previous year. The growth rate of commodity prices in 2012 keeps declining and falls to 3% by May, which leaves room for preventing the excessive decline of economic growth rate and making a slight adjustment to moderately loose macro control. By this May, given a noticeable decrease in such economic indicators as the growth rates of industrial production, investment in fixed assets, as well as import and export, the government has further proposed that macro control should "focus more on stabilizing growth". As a result, a series of relevant measures have been released to expand domestic demand, stimulate consumption, encourage investment, promote the implementation of planned projects during "the twelfth five-year plan", make structural tax reduction, reduce deposited reserve ratio as well as deposit and loan rates. Compared with "a package of" stimulus plans during 2008 to 2010, the plans in 2012 are not as intensive as before. If there is no severe and unexpected impact on the external and internal economic environments, China is likely to see a slight increase of economic growth rate in the second half of this year whereas the growth rate of next year is expected to slightly exceed that of this year.

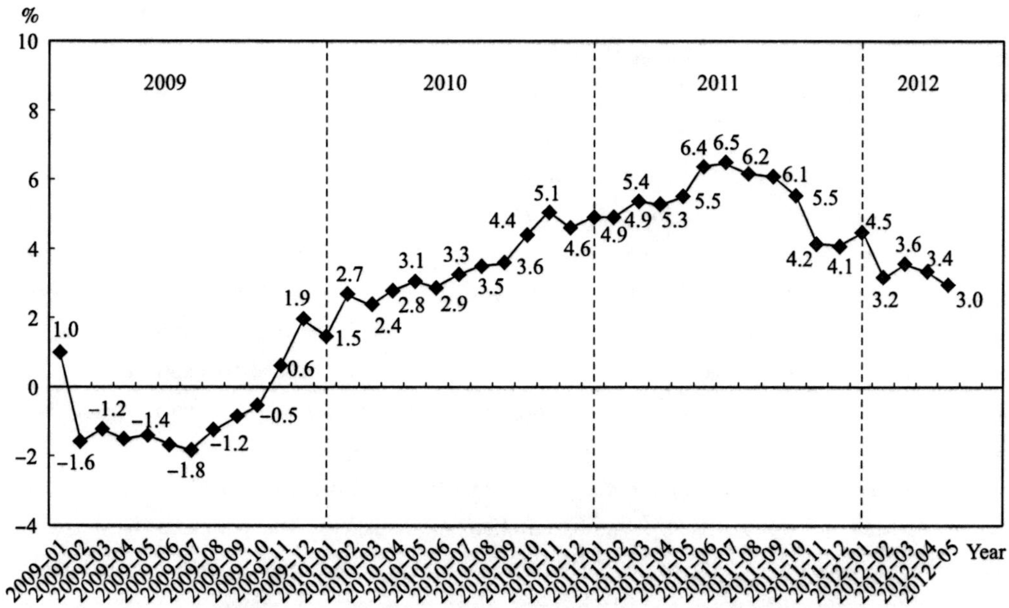


**Figure 7: Month-on-month Growth Rate of Household Consumption Price (January 2009 to May 2012)**

Source: website of National Bureau of Statistics.

The fluctuation of annual economic growth rate suggests that China has entered a new round of economic cycle since 2010 (the eleventh round). By the end of this year, the cycle will have lasted for three years. The economic growth rate of 2010 and 2011 is 10.4% and 9.2% respectively while that of 2012 is expected to be 8.5%. The new round of cycle will neither follow the ninth round characterized by "two plus seven", that is, two years of rising growth rate plus seven years of steadily declining growth rate, nor will it follow the tenth round characterized by "eight plus two", that is, eight years of steadily rising growth rate plus two years of declining growth rate. The current cycle is likely to follow a new trajectory characterized by a "zigzag-shape" gradual rise and decline.

## Ⅳ. Impetus of Domestic Demand: Favoring Consumption While Not Overlooking Investment

Accompanied by the before mentioned tendency of overlooking GDP is the tendency of overlooking investment in fixed assets.

Some scholars suggest that China's rapid economic growth rate since the reform and opening-up is mainly spurred by investment, a growth mode that is not sustainable and must be changed. On one hand, it is fair to say that China's rapid economic growth "over the recent decade" is mainly spurred by investment and such growth mode needs to be changed, for statistics shows that demand for investment over the recent decade (except for 2005) has been contributing more to the GDP growth than demand for consumption. On the other hand, it would distort the reality to say that China's rapid economic growth "since the reform and opening-up" has always been stimulated by investment. A look at the statistics on the contribution of demand for consumption, investment and net export to GDP growth reveals that consumption has contributed more than investment over the first 23 years from 1979 to 2001 excepted for 1993, 1994 and 1995; only over the recent decade from 2002 to 2011 (except for 2005) does investment contribute more than consumption. Meanwhile, statistics shows that only ten of the 33 years from 1979 to 2011 see a net export contribution rate of over 15% to GDP growth whereas there are only seven years in which net export contributes to a GDP growth rate by over two percentage points. Calculating GDP by the expenditure approach, we find out that external demand does not play a leading role in stimulating China's economic growth since the reform and opening-up.

That investment has been contributing more to GDP growth than consumption over the recent decade is mainly a result of fast growing urbanization. The impact is clearly seen in the decreasing proportion of consumption in the overall GDP calculated by the expenditure approach (consumption rate) and the increasing proportion of investment (investment rate). In Figure 8, three curves are drawn to explain China's consumption rate, investment rate and urbanization rate during 1952 to 2011. As it illustrates, urbanization rate showed a noticeable upward tendency during 2001 to 2011 and had a strong negative correlation with consumption rate while a strong positive correlation with investment rate. There are four different views in the academic circle regarding the correlation between urbanization and consumption.

(1) Positive Correlation. It argues that the rising urbanization rate can effectively stimulate the demand for consumption (Liu Yirong, 2005). The public has reached a common view of advocating promoting consumption by means of urbanization.

(2) Zero Correlation. It argues that China's rising urbanization rate has almost zero contribution to the increase of consumption rate (Fan Jianping, Xiang Shujian, 1999).

(3) Negative Correlation. It argues that the rising urbanization rate instead results in the decrease of consumption rate. There are also two different judgments among scholars who hold this view. One judgment argues that such negative correlation "violates the common practice" and is "abnormal" (Wang, Cheng, 2003). The other view argues that such negative correlation is absolutely "normal" (Liu, 2007) and points out China is undergoing fast growing urbanization, which will on one hand stimulate "consumption" (the impact of urbanization on absolute level of consumption), yet on the other hand cause the decrease of "consumption rate" (the impact of urbanization on relative level of consumption). It is because the rise of urbanization rate will stimulate both consumption and investment, of which the latter benefits more. As a result, the proportion of consumption in the overall GDP calculated by expenditure approach will see a relative decrease whereas that of investment will see a relative increase (Liu, 2007, Chen, 2010). The before mentioned view of "positive correlation" indeed discusses the relation between urbanization and investment rather than that between urbanization and investment rate. Yet the before mentioned view that "negative correla-

tion" "violates the common practice" actually confuses the two different concepts of consumption and consumption rate.

(4) U-shape Correlation, that is, first negative correlation and then positive correlation. The view argues that the rising urbanization rate will reduce consumption rate in the earlier period of urbanization but stimulate it in the later period. Accordingly, consumption rate has an "inverted U-shape" correlation with investment rate, that is, the rise of urbanization will stimulate investment rate in the earlier period but reduce it in the later period (Chen, 2010).

There are more complicated cases in real economy regarding the relations between urbanization rate, consumption rate and investment rate. In Figure 8, it shows that the relations can be divided into seven stages from 1953 to 2011.

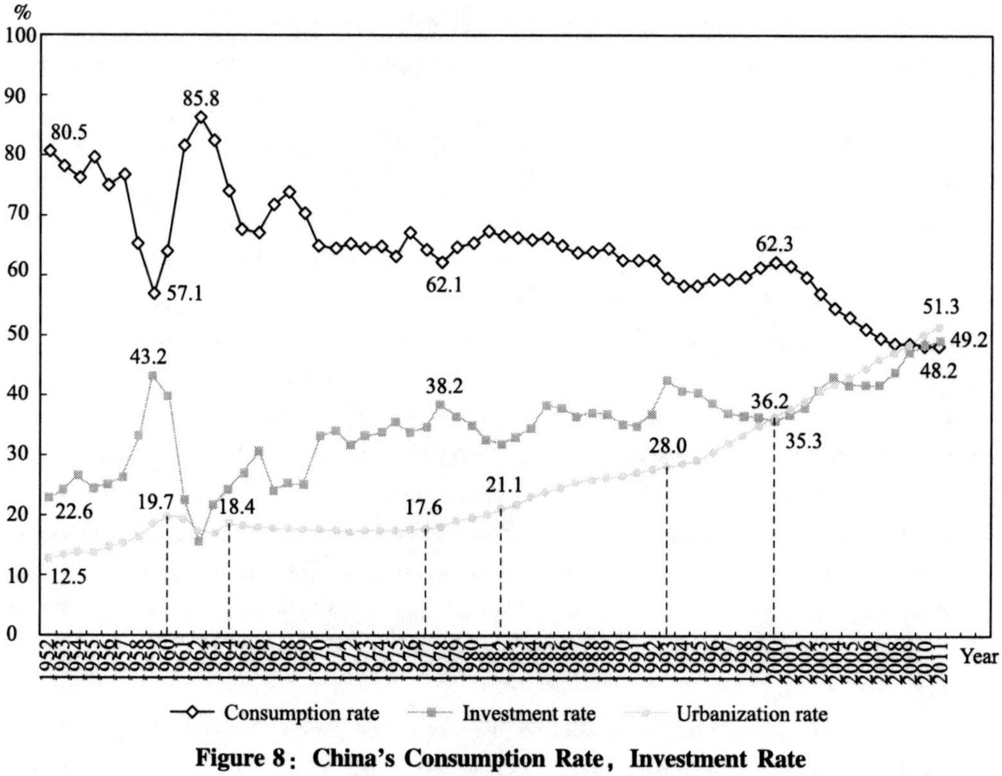


**Figure 8: China's Consumption Rate, Investment Rate and Urbanization Rate (1952 – 2011)**

Source: *Historical Data of China's Gross Domestic Product* 1952 – 1995, Dongbei University of Finance and Economics Press, 1997; *China Statistical Abstract* 2012, China Statistics Press, 2012; *China Statistical Yearbook* over the years.

(1) The eight years from 1953 to 1960 are the initial stage of urbanization since the founding of New China, in which the average annual urbanization rate increased by 0.9 percentage point whereas the average annual consumption rate reduced by 2.06 percentage points and the average annual investment rate increased by 2.11 percentage points. Urbanization rate has a high and low nega-

tive correlation with consumption rate, with a correlation coefficiency of -88%, while it has a strong same-direction increasing positive correlation with investment rate, with a correlation coefficiency as high as 93% (see Table 1).

(2) The four years of economic restructuring from 1961 to 1964 in the aftermath of "Great Leap Forward" are characterized by decreasing urbanization rate, increasing consumption rate and decreasing investment rate. Urbanization rate has a low and high negative correlation with consumption rate, with a correlation coefficiency of -41%, while it has a same-direction decreasing positive correlation with investment rate, with a correlation coefficiency of 51%.

(3) The thirteen years from 1965 to 1977 over "the Cultural Revolution" are a special period characterized by decreasing urbanization rate (numerous "Educated Youth" went to the mountains and the countryside), decreasing consumption rate and increasing investment rate. Urbanization rate has a same-direction decreasing positive correlation with consumption rate, with a correlation coefficiency of 67%, while it has a low and high negative correlation with investment rate, with a correlation of -56%.

(4) The five years from 1978 to 1982 of restructuring at the beginning of the reform and opening-up are characterized by increasing urbanization rate, increasing consumption rate and decreasing investment rate. Urbanization rate has a same-direction increasing positive correlation with consumption rate, with a correlation of 90%, while it has a high and low negative correlation with investment rate, with a correlation of -98%.

(5) The eleven years from 1983 to 1993 are characterized by increasing urbanization rate, decreasing consumption rate and increasing investment rate. Urbanization rate has a high and low negative correlation with consumption rate, with a correlation of -90%, while it has a same-direction positive correlation with investment rate, with a correlation coefficiency of 55%.

(6) The seven years from 1994 to 2000 are a period of dealing with overheated economy during 1992 to 1993 and the impact of subsequent Asian financial crisis. It is characterized by increasing urbanization rate, increasing consumption rate and decreasing investment rate. Urbanization rate has a same-direction increasing positive correlation with consumption rate, with a correlation coefficient of 95%, while it has a high and low negative correlation with investment rate, with a correlation of -96%.

(7) The eleven years from 2001 to 2011 are a period of fast growing urbanization. With an average annual urbanization rate increasing by 1.37 percentage points, it witnesses the fastest increase of urbanization rate since the founding of New China. The average annual consumption rate has decreased by 1.28 percentage points whereas the average annual investment rate has increased by 1.26 percentage points. Urbanization rate has a high and low negative correlation with consumption rate, with a correlation coefficiency of -95%, while it has a strong positive correlation with investment rate like the case in the early period of New China, with a correlation as high as 94% (see Table 1).

Taken as a whole, urbanization rate has a negative correlation with consumption rate and a positive correlation with investment rate in all of the three periods from 1953 to 2011 since the founding of New China, from 1953 to 1977 before the reform and opening-up, and from 1978 to 2011 during the reform and opening-up (see Table 1).

**Table 1: Fluctuations of Urbanization Rate, Consumption Rate and Investment Rate and Correlation Coefficients**

| Period | Average annual fluctuation of urbanization rate (percentage point) | Average annual fluctuation of consumption rate (percentage point) | Average annual fluctuation of investment rate (percentage point) | Correlation coefficients of urbanization rate and consumption rate (%) | Correlation coefficients of urbanization rate and investment rate (%) |
|---|---|---|---|---|---|
| (1) 1953 - 1960 | 0.90 | -2.06 | 2.11 | -88 | 93 |
| (2) 1961 - 1964 | -0.33 | 2.55 | -3.85 | -41 | 51 |
| (3) 1965 - 1977 | -0.06 | -0.76 | 0.78 | 67 | -56 |
| (4) 1978 - 1982 | 0.71 | 0.44 | -0.48 | 90 | -98 |
| (5) 1983 - 1993 | 0.62 | -0.65 | 0.97 | -90 | 55 |
| (6) 1994 - 2000 | 1.10 | 0.43 | -1.04 | 95 | -96 |
| (7) 2001 - 2011 | 1.37 | -1.28 | 1.26 | -95 | 94 |
| (8) 1953 - 2011 | 0.66 | -0.55 | 0.45 | -82 | 76 |
| (9) 1953 - 1977 | 0.20 | -0.65 | 0.47 | -46 | 37 |
| (10) 1978 - 2011 | 0.98 | -0.47 | 0.32 | -92 | 80 |

Over the recent decade, investment has been contributing more to China's economic growth than consumption, which is mainly a result of fast growing urbanization with some inevitability. Yet such growth mode is unsustainable given its excessively high investment rate and excessively low consumption rate. China saw an urbanization rate of 51.3% in 2011 and will still undergone a long period of urbanization in its future economic development, which is the characteristic of a certain development stage. In a certain period in the future, though the urbanization rate may not rise as fast as it did in the previous ten years, the country will still be in the middle stage of urbanization. Urbanization, especially the improvement of its quality, requires a certain amount of moderate investment. Meanwhile, it requires investment to transform development mode, adjust economic structure and benefit people's well-being. For example, (1) enterprises should promote technological innovation and improvement, replace equipments, improve product quality and increase benefits, (2) developing strategic emerging industries, (3) dealing with energy-saving and emission reduction to protect environment, (4) developing modern agriculture, (5) promoting infrastructure construction of social undertakings such as science, education, culture and public health, (6) promoting projects that benefit people's well-being such as government subsidized housing. We should focus on improving the structure and efficiency of investment and expanding the sources of investment funds to give full play to the fundamental role of market in distributing resources and take full advantage of non-government investment. The goal of "where the money comes, where it goes" puts higher requirements for our economic working. In short, we should adhere to the principle of expanding domestic demand, especially demand for consumption and direct economic growth to rely harmoniously on consumption, investment and export. We should favor consumption while not overlooking investment, given that certain amount of moderate investment will remain a key impetus to China's economic development over a certain period in the future.

## References

1. Chen, Changbing. 2010. "Study on Relations between Urbanization, Investment Rate and Consumption Rate." *Economic Perspectives*, (9).

2. Chen, Jiagui, and Yang Li, ed. 2011. *Analysis and Prediction of China's Economic Situation in* 2012. Beijing: Social Sciences Academic Press.

3. Chen, Jiagui, and Yang Li, ed. 2011. *Analysis of China's Economic Prospects—Report in Spring* 2012. Beijing: Social Sciences Academic Press.

4. Fan, Jianping, and Shujian Xiang. 1999. "Impact on Household Consumption Rate of China's Urban-rural Dual Social Structure." *Management World*, (9).

5. Liu, Shijin. 2011. "Decrease in Growth Rate and Transformation of Development Mode." *Economic Perspectives*, (5).

6. Liu, Shucheng. 2009. "Retrospection and Outlook of New China's Economic Growth Curve over 60 Years—A Further Discussion of the New Round of Economic Cycle." *Economic Perspectives*, (10).

7. Liu, Shucheng. 2011. "Analysis of China's Economic Growth and Fluctuation in 2011 and 'the Twelfth Five-year' Period." *Economic Perspectives*, (7).

8. Liu, Yirong. 2005. "Accelerating Urbanization is the Lasting Impetus to Consumption Growth." *Consumer Economics*, (4).

9. Liu, Yirong. 2007. "Empirical Study of Relation between China's Urbanization Rate and Consumption Rate." *Consumer Economics*, (6).

10. Wang, Fei, Chunlin Cheng. 2003. "Impact of Urbanization on China's Household Consumption Rate." *Gansu Agriculture*, (11).

11. Research Group of Macro Economic Control, Economic Research Institute, The Chinese Academy of Social Sciences, 2010. "Analysis of Macro Control in 'the Eleventh Five-year Plan' and Prospects for 'the Twelfth Five-year Plan'." *Economic Perspectives*, (2).

# Chapter 3

# How Long Can China's Economy Keep Growing?*

**Zhang Jun** (张军)

**China Center for Economic Studies, Fudan University, Shanghai, China**

**Abstract**: Since 2010, there has been renewed discussion on China's economic future. After 30 years of breakneck economic growth, China's position in the world economy is more important than ever and people must understand how China's economic dominance will change the world economy. Some economists who are bearish about China's future believe that China's growth engine will lose fire in the next two or three years. To address their predictions about China's future, the author will address three themes: (1) Why did China manage to grow so rapidly? (2) How long will China keep growing? (3) Can China's economy keep growing in the future? By analyzing the theory of inadequate consumer demand in China and by evaluating the general patterns of China's basic advantages in education, technology and human capital and industrial upgrading, the author explicitly argue why it is unlikely for China to fall into the "middle-income trap."

**Keywords**: economic growth, convergence hypothesis, capital accumulation, technology progress, China

Since 2010, there has been renewed international enthusiasm on the discussion about China's economic future. Why does the Western world give so much attention to China's economic future? For one thing, China's economy has grown in magnitude and significance and is poised to exert significant changes to the world economy that cannot be overlooked. For another thing, pessimism about China also holds sway in some circles. Mr. Huang Haizhou, a senior economist at the International Monetary Fund, he personally feels during his recent trip to the Wall Street that many investment bankers are not optimistic about China's economic prospects and very seriously so. According to Huang, these hedge funds may have come to realize that it could be profitable to badmouth China. Indeed, many other famous economists have been predicting the fall of Chinese econo-

---

* Corresponding author: junzh_2000@fudan.edu.cn.

This paper is a transcript based on the speech made by Professor Zhang at *China In-depth Lecture* held by the Advanced Institute of Social Sciences, Fudan University, March 15, 2012. This script has been reviewed by the speaker.

my. One is the Nobel laureate in economics Paul Krugman, who has been forecasting the recession of Asia as a whole for 20 years. Another is Nouriel Roubini who is with New York University's Stern Business School. Both argue that China's economy will run into big problems and lose its momentum in two to three years. In contrast, optimistic views about China's economy attract no attention and are even unpopular. This is a strange phenomenon.

Over the past three years, I have had more time than anyone else to interpret, observe and reflect on China's economy, which gives me an opportunity to share with you my thought on the future prospects of China's economy. However, it is indeed a tough job to predict how long China's economy can keep growing, and I will only briefly discuss my reflections before turning to you for comments. Tonight I would like to address three minor topics: first, how did China manage to grow so rapidly in the past? Second, how long can China keep growing in the future? Lastly, I would like to talk with you about the conditions required for China's economy to keep growing in the future and whether these conditions will be satisfied.

## I. Why Did China Grow So Rapidly?

China's economic output by current year prices has reached about RMB50 trillion, which is approaching half of the US's economic output, and it is growing very rapidly. By nominal terms, the size of China's economy basically doubled every five years, and even if by comparative prices, its GDP was able to double every seven years. China's GDP aggregate surpassed that of the UK in 2005, that of Germany in 2007 and that of Japan just across the threshold of 2010 to become the second largest economy in the world. By current growth rate, if China grows faster than the US by 3.5 to 4 percentage points, China's GDP aggregate will be equal to or even surpass the US level around 2020.

It is interesting to discuss the connotations of speed. The famous economic historian who passed away not long ago, Professor Angus Maddison, discovered from the recovered data of early economic history of the Western world that per capita incomes changed very slowly in the Western world before the 18th century and that it took more than 1400 years for per capita incomes to be doubled. It was not until the Industrial Revolution that many Western countries saw a real increase in their economic growth rates and per capita income growth by 2% –3%. After World War II, some economies mainly in East Asia began to grow dramatically. Take the Four East Asian Tigers for instance, these economies maintained a growth rate of 7% –8%. In this way, their per capita income could double in ten years. The phenomenon of rapid economic growth is in fact not in the distant history and occurred just half a century ago.

In order to interpret these phenomena of rapid growth, economists have proposed a simple yet important concept, which is the "convergence hypothesis." According to this concept, a relatively backward economy is likely to achieve a higher growth rate than rich nations. But what makes this possible? First, less developed economies have a smaller denominator and thus it is easy to achieve higher growth rates for them. Second, more importantly, less developed economies can emulate the systems, technologies and way of production from advanced economies and narrow their gaps with the latter. Having no forerunners to catch up with, frontier countries thus experience slower growth rate.

This hypothesis is highly important. At the very least, it helps us understand what makes it possible for economic catch-ups to happen today, and these catch-ups have indeed reaped very positive results. However, what the convergence theory did not specify is the prerequisite conditions for such convergence to occur. It failed to address a fundamental issue, i. e. what a country should do to complete this catch-up process. In fact, we must seek and read research literature on developmental economics or growth economics about why some economies have become so successful. It should be noted that the World Bank published an influential research report called *East Asian Miracle* in 1993, which systematically reviews the question why economies of East Asia are able to achieve rapid and sustained growth. Controversial as it may be, this report provides important reference for us to shed light on the conditions for economic convergence to take place.

Economists discovered that a country must have rapid capital accumulation in order to achieve economic development. In other words, they cannot consume all their incomes otherwise there would be no accumulation and no development to talk about. Here, I would like to quote from Arthur Lewis, a Nobel laureate in economics of 1979, and this paragraph appears in his influential thesis known as *Economic Development under Unlimited Supply of Labor*:

> [T] he central problem in the theory of economic development is to understand the process by which a community which was previously saving and investing 4 or 5 per cent of its national income or less, converts itself into an economy where voluntary saving is running at about 12 or 15 per cent of its national income or more, This is the central problem because the central fact of economic development is rapid capital accumulation (including knowledge and skills with capital).

Arthur made it clear that the most central issue for economic development is rapid capital accumulation and the fact that a country must significantly increase the proportion of saving to national income. National income cannot be exhausted. For countries struggling with the European debt crisis, the reason for their economic recession is first of all due to the fact that their income level is already high and growth momentum is depleted. Besides, the national savings of these countries are already low and revenues are all spent on social security and other spending. Some countries have even had to raise debts for government spending and social welfare expenditure. This is a big problem. For those very poor countries such as African countries, their economic development has been sluggish. But why? A few years ago, I attended a conference on economic development in Cairo to discuss what Africa can learn from East Asia. For over half a century after the World War II, the World Bank has attempted all kinds of growth models in African yet none of the models has succeeded, and a key reason is the excessively low savings rate.

After the 1960s, Hong Kong, Taiwan, Singapore and South Korea have achieved economic growth, but one thing they have in common is high savings rate. Why are East Asians savers and why are Africans not? This is a big theoretical question and economists have failed to provide a convincing and simple answer until this day. But culturally, the East Asians attach great importance to the wealth and happiness of their children and always hold a forward-looking view.

How to achieve capital accumulation in a relatively short span of time? The former USSR managed to have rapid capital accumulation and countries that used to practice planned economy also had fairly good accumulation rates, but their economic development faltered after a short-lived period of rapid growth. I think the reason is due to the lack of technology progress. Only high accumulation is not enough. Without technology progress, the marginal return to capital will diminish, so that growth becomes unsustainable. In fact, for developing countries or relatively backward countries, it is very important to ensure that capital accumulation is supported by sufficient technology progress.

China has maintained a fairly high investment rate over the past 20 years (yet even so, China's savings rate still exceeds investment rate in most years) and the result is rapid increase of capital stock. According to my calculations, over the past 20 years, China's capital stock increased by an annual average of about 12%, which is higher than the growth rate of the first ten years after China launched its reform and opening-up program. Therefore, capital output ratio increased rapidly after the 1990s, which coincides with the most rapid growth of China's GDP.

It needs to be noted that China's capital accumulation is accompanied by technology progress, which is very different from the former USSR. In China, technology progress largely derived from trade. China witnessed rapid growth of trade over the past 20 years mainly through foreign direct investments (FDI) in China that expedited technology progress. Import plays an even more important role than export to China's economic development, given that relative to consumer goods for export, most of China's imports are capital goods and intermediate goods that contain elements of foreign technology. Absorption and imitation of foreign technology through trade enabled China to achieve the process of technology localization and upgrade. This is a basic pattern of China's technology progress.

Whether capital accumulation has been accompanied by technology progress can be assessed using the simplest method of growth accounting. The basic principle of growth is to look at how much the weighted growth rate of input factors deviates from the growth rate of output. Their delta is referred to as growth rate of "total factor productivity (TFP)." Growth accounting of the former USSR indicates that its TFP was good before 1965 yet became very negative afterwards until its disintegration. Research on the Four East Asian Tigers using the same approach indicates that TFP growth rate is positive. This is an essential difference. Despite high accumulation of both the former USSR and South Korea, their respective growth mechanisms were totally different.

Studies so far have all identified that China has maintained fairly positive TFP growth rate during the process of rapid capital accumulation, which averages 3% – 4% on an annual basis and contributes to 35% – 40% of GDP growth. Even in comparison with the East Asian economies, this is fairly good performance. We believe that this is understandable, considering that with the process of capital accumulation over the past 20 years, China experienced a process of market openness, competition, trade expansion and foreign direct investment. All these achievements have enabled China to maintain a fairly good speed of technology progress. This answers the question about why China's economy can grow this fast. I think China has not only increased its speed of capital accumulation and investment rate, but significantly improved its investment efficiency and technology progress.

## II. How Long Can China Keep Growing?

All of us are interested about how long China's economy can keep growing. Frankly speaking, economists have not come up with any method to predict future economic growth. However, the convergence theory can still help us think about the answer to this question. Observed from the perspective of convergence, we need to discuss briefly the gaps between China's and U. S. 's economies. The greater the gaps, the greater the potential to catch-up; whereas the smaller the gaps, the slower it takes for China to catch up with the United States. In other words, the higher per capita incomes, the slower will be the growth.

In 2003, Goldman Sachs made a bold prediction that China's economic output cannot overtake that of the US until 2041. That is to say, it would take 38 years for China to surpass the United States to be the largest economy in the world. By today's standard, this estimate tends to be conservative. Nevertheless, when China's per capita GDP just exceeded USD1, 000 in 2003, Goldman Sachs also predicted that China's economic growth rate would decline from 10% to 5%. By today's standard, this assumption significantly underestimates the capabilities of China's economic growth.

After China overtook Japan to become the second largest economy in the world in 2010, there appeared multiple versions of forecast about when China could overtake the United States, and most of these forecasts are based on the convergence hypothesis. For instance, one hypothesis presumes that China's economy will grow 8% over the next 10 to 15 years, the U. S. economy will grow at 2% and Renminbi's exchange rate to the US dollar will appreciate by 3%. In addition, we presume that CPI will be less than 5% in China and less than 2% in the United States. In this way, we can estimate that China can reach the same economic output as the United States before 2020. If China's economy maintains a growth rate of 8. 5% in the first five years of the next decade before growth drops to 7% in the latter five years, the average growth rate of China's economy over the next ten years will be 7. 75%. If the United States grows by 3% over the first five years and 2% in the second five years, the U. S. average growth rate over the next ten years will be 2. 5%. If Renminbi appreciates by 3% against the U. S. dollar on an annual basis, China will catch up with the United States by 2019. This is the approach of forecast adopted by the Chinese Academy of Social Sciences and British *Economist* by the end of 2010.

In the beginning of 2011, the IMF also published a forecast on China's economic catch-up with the United States based on purchasing power parity (PPP). According to the PPP conversion of the IMF, China's GDP aggregate should be twice the calculation result using official exchange rate and reach USD 11. 2 trillion or so, while the US GDP has no change and still stands at USD 15. 2 trillion. According to the IMF estimation, after four years, which is 2016, China's GDP aggregate will reach the level of USD19 trillion and the US GDP will reach USD 18. 8 trillion. In this way, it would take just five years for China to catch up with the United States. It can be calculated that the share of China's economic output in the world economy would be 18% of the world total. Following this logic, by 2020, China's economic output by PPP would represent 25% of the world economy. This reminds me of a statistic recovered by the famous economic historian Professor Maddison: in 1820, China's economy accounted for 28. 7% of the world. After 200 years, by 2020, China's economy will return to this point. What a cycle!

By the end of last year, the Peterson Institute for International Economics published a book written by senior research fellow Arvind Subramanian called *Eclipse: Living in the Shadow of China's Economic Dominance*. By the estimation of "economic dominance index" calculated by him, China's economy is already the No. 1 in the world, not after five years, but now. Besides, he is very optimistic about the prospects of China's economy.

To date, very few people are opposed to the forecast that China's economy will surpass that of the United States by 2020, so for the time being we take this as a high probability event. What I would like to discuss with you is that after 2020, how long will China continue to grow as the largest economy in the world?

Even if China's economy is on a par with the United States around 2020, China's per capita income will still be very low and account for merely one fourth the US level, which is equivalent to the per capita GDP gap between Shanghai and the United States today. By today's standard of the World Bank, measured by USD 15, 000, China will still be in the range between a middle-income and high-income country by 2020, which is still below the income level of the Four East Asian Tigers. According to the convergence hypothesis, China still has room to grow rapidly. But where will this potential come from and how long will rapid growth be sustained? Frankly speaking, these questions are not easy to answer. Let us look into the statistics here.

First, as an upper-middle-income country, China still has great investment potential in the future. By the end of 2010, China's capital stock was roughly two times that of GDP at RMB 93. 3 trillion, or USD13. 8 trillion. The US capital stock was USD 44. 7 trillion by the end of 2010, which is three times higher than China's. On per capita terms, China's capital stock was only USD 10, 000 in 2010, which is less than 10% that of the United States and less than 20% that of South Korea.

Even with the great achievements of infrastructure, China still has great gaps with the U. S. Take railway for instance, according to central planning, China's railway mileage will reach 120, 000 kilometers by 2015, which is a bit more than half of the U. S. level of 220, 000 kilometers. Most of China's existing railways with the length of 90, 000 kilometers are in the eastern region and the mileage of 50, 000 kilometers in China's central and western regions is expected to complete by 2015. China has accelerated the construction of highway over the past 20 years, but the density of highways remains below the average level of OECD members and only represents 70% of their level. Highway density is even lower in the interior regions of China. As for urban rail transit, there are almost 100 cities with population above five million, yet 80% of these cities have no subways and 90% of existing subways are concentrated in the eastern region. In this sense, even after 2020, China will still enjoy enormous potential for investment and great room for economic improvement. This is important. Even if China enters upper-middle-income level, there still exists tremendous room for "catch-up" between China's interior provinces. Great gaps exist in the per capita stock between eastern, central and western regions. In 2009, the per capita GDP and per capita capital stock of 11 coastal provinces and municipalities were almost twice as high as those of 20 interior provinces and municipality. If per capita GDP is USD12, 000 in the coastal region and USD6, 000 in the interior region, presuming that growth rate is 9% in interior regions and 5% in the coastal region, it will take about 20 years to converge with the level of coastal region.

It is possible that China's economic growth will slow after 2020 but will not stay too low (such as 5%). I believe that it is totally possible for China's economic growth to stay at 6% –7% in the next 10 years. This is not only because of international precedents, e. g. East Asian economies all experienced sustained and rapid growth after their per capita incomes reached a middle and high level, but more importantly, China's great regional gaps have created massive room for investment and productivity improvement.

Why am I so confident about China's economic growth over the next 20 years? In addition to the above analyses, this can be deduced from observations on the tendencies of certain parameters. First, let us look at the tendencies of China's employment structure. There is one common characteristic to all economies that have successfully achieved industrialization, i. e. in the process of growth gravity transferring from agriculture to modern industries and services, labor will move from agriculture to manufacturing and services. The process of change in employment structure is an important hallmark of economic development and China is no exception. Over the past 30 years, the share of labor force employed in manufacturing and services increased significantly, and the share of agricultural labor force declined by 30%, or one percentage point each year. Today, the value added by agriculture accounts for about 10% of GDP, and this ratio will continue to nudge downwards. According to some studies, this figure will decline to 5% –7%, which is near the level of developed countries. This means that in China's future economic development, still fewer people will be employed in agriculture. By the reduction of one percentage point per year, it still takes at least 20 years for the share of agricultural labor force to drop from current level of 30% to less than 10%, which is close to the share of agricultural value added in GDP.

Similar conclusions can be drawn from another parameter, which is China's urbanization rate. According to the National Bureau of Statistics, China's urbanization rate exceeded 50% last year, which means that urban population exceeded agricultural population for the first time in China. It took 30 years for urbanization rate to increase from a bit more than 20% to the current level of 50%, which means one percentage point each year or more than 10 million people becoming city dwellers per year. Following this tendency, it will take another 20 years for China's urbanization rate to reach the average level of 70% for high-income countries. Therefore, I believe that even if China becomes the largest economy by 2020, it will take at least 10 years thereafter to transform its economic and employment structures to maintain a fairly high growth rate.

## III. Can China's Economy Keep Growing in the Future?

To some extent, the above discussions only dwelled on the necessary rather than sufficient conditions for China's sustained and rapid growth in the future. Everybody is interested in whether it is possible for China to keep growing in the future. In particular, whether China is able to release and maintain exuberant domestic demand to support its sustained economic growth; will China successfully achieve industrial upgrade through breakthroughs in cutting-edge technologies? For these questions, I may only briefly express some of my views today. First, I will touch upon the tendencies in the evolution of domestic demand, especially the evolution of consumer demand and savings rate. On the other hand, I will talk about technology progress and future industrial upgrade. Given that both questions relate to the "middle-income trap", my discussions will also help address the question as why it is unlikely for China to be stranded in the "middle-income trap".

First, conditions to maintain rapid growth in the future. I mention this because a very popular view recently is "insufficient domestic demand," particularly the lack of consumption. Based on the assessment of insufficient demand, most people believe that shrinking consumption has deprived China of its momentum and growth will lose steam.

Frankly speaking, for me, the shrinking share of consumption has always been a mystery. Statistically, the growth of China's household spending is not slow, given that the nominal growth rate of retail sales volume of social consumer goods exceeded 17% and households have dramatically increased their spending on housing, education, financial intermediary services, healthcare and pension. Even deducting price factor, there is not much difference between the growth rate of consumption and the growth rate of GDP. Recently, Professor Subramanian mentioned that if you compare the per capita consumption growth rates between China and major economies in Asia, you will notice that in similar stages of high growth rates, the Chinese mainland's per capita consumption grows much faster compared with Japan, Hong Kong SAR, Singapore, South Korea and Taiwan. So, I don't understand why the share of consumption in GDP kept falling over the past 10 years. Judging by official statistics, household spending on housing and services is likely to be seriously underestimated. For instance, with housing privatization reaching 90%, even the National Bureau of Statistics (NBS) admitted that the estimation of "virtual rents" lacks reliable history information. Besides, the NBS estimation using official statistics on social security, healthcare, finance and insurance also underestimates actual household spending on education, healthcare and financial intermediate services.

It is understandable that compared with developed countries, the share of China's total consumer spending in GDP remains low. The reason is that China is in the stage of rapid growth and high accumulation and each year a greater portion of GDP is spent on infrastructure construction in order to increase per capita capital stock and labor productivity. Indeed, even if we believe that the share of consumption is on the decline, it doesn't mean any reduction in the absolute value. In this sense, it is not necessary to be pessimistic about the release of China's future consumer demand.

I am confident that the share of consumption, regardless of any fluctuations in the past, will continue to grow in the future. First, as China's per capita income grows, the structural upgrade of consumption becomes inevitable. Second, the process of urbanization will continuously release potentials for the housing market. Thirdly, increasingly equal access to public goods such as education, healthcare and social security will induce further growth of spending on services. Lastly, as the affordable housing system improves, the consumer spending of low-income groups will increase sharply as a result.

The conclusion that consumption will represent an increasing share can also be deduced from the future development of national savings rate. The Four Asian Tigers and Japan have experienced the shift from the increase to the reduction of savings rate, and this is largely due to changing demographics. The reason is that demographic dividend will increase national savings rate, and vice versa. According to the research and forecast on China's demographic transition, it is impossible for China to maintain such a high level of national savings rate in the coming 20 years. According to the Sixth National Census, China's fertility rate is already very low and similar to the level of developed countries. On average, a Chinese woman gives birth to 1.6 children. Besides, China has 177.6 million people above 60 years old and is rapidly entering an ageing society just like other East Asian economies. With the process of ageing society, national savings rate will decline. Following the forecast approach of the United Nations, the proportion of Chinese savers (people aged between 35 and 54) peaked around 2010. This means that the highest national savings rate will be registered around these years and the savings rate will inevitably fall thereafter.

As an ageing society becomes a reality, China's household savings rate will decline and the current level of 30% will be impossible to sustain. Not only will household savings rate decline but an aging populace will force the government to use a greater portion of its revenue on social security, pension and healthcare instead of economic development. This will inevitably reduce public savings rate and increase the share of public spending. Observed from this perspective, China's economy will only have another 15 to 20 years of golden age for capital construction and capital formation, which is critical to the convergence of China's economy with high-income countries. Judging by international experience, I think that after this period, it is unlikely for China's economic growth rate to exceed 5%. By then, consumer demand will play a more important role.

Technological and industrial upgrade is an important phenomenon of economic growth. Future economic growth and the increase of per capita income from USD 5,000 to USD 15,000 and even USD 20,000 to USD 30,000 must rely on the sustained upgrade of technologies and industries. Most people are pessimistic and worry about China's capabilities of technological and industrial upgrade. They have this concern because they are not happy about the current situation: technology progress in China over the past 30 years still derived from technology transfer associated with trade and foreign direct investment (FDI) and indigenous R&D and innovation capabilities were lacking. Although China has already becomes a major trading nation, the value added by our exports remains limited. But the problem is that given the great gaps between China and advanced economies in terms of technology innovation and industrial structure, can we conclude that China can maintain a vigorous momentum of technology innovation and industrial upgrade? I don't think so. A correct approach is to observe whether China has embarked on the right path of technology progress and industrial upgrade and whether China's path has followed general empirical laws.

According to the international experience of economic development, there is a significant positive correlation between technological and industrial upgrade and the increase of per capita income. Over the past 30 years, China's industrial structure has been significantly transformed. Even in the area of trade, great changes are taking place in the composition and technological complexity of export products. In 2006, Professor Dani Rodrik of Harvard University found that the composition of China's export products is almost identical to that of France. Judging by the technological complexity of export products, China's per capita income should be three times higher than the statistics today. Indeed, for countries with similar types of export products, their per capita GDP levels are significantly higher than China's. According to a study by Yang et al. in 2009, since the 1980s, there has been a significant improvement in the technological composition of China's export products. In 2010, Amiti and Freund found through a study on the composition of China's export products between 1992 and 2005 that the share of agricultural products and textile apparels in China's export has significantly fallen, while the share of computers and other electronic products in China's export has dramatically increased. In 2010, Wang and Wei compared the types of China's export products with those of developed countries and found that the categories of products G3 countries exported but China did not dropped from 101 categories in 1996 to 83 categories in 2005, accounting for 2.44% and 1.97% of all categories respectively.

There is no denying that the increase of technology content and complexity in China's exports would be overestimated due to the high proportion of processing trade. But we must be aware that the share of processing trade has been on the decline over the years. More importantly, technology progress and trade are closely related to each other. The division of labor between developed countries and emerging market economies has already shifted towards vertical division of labor. Against this backdrop, technology progress no longer takes place within individual countries. In this sense, it is consistent with empirical experience for China to introduce and absorb the technologies of multinational firms through technology importation, particularly trade and investment before developing indigenous capabilities of innovation. Even in the area of processing trade, although it seems that China is using or absorbing the technologies from other countries but this is no easy job. A country cannot achieve technology progress simply through the transfer of technologies from other countries. Multiple empirical studies have found that for the transfer of foreign technology to have a positive spillover effect and expedite the achievement of technology localization, a country must have a solid foundation of research and development and learning capabilities. With rapid advances of education and accumulation of human capital, China obviously has an edge here.

Recently, we have estimated the export value added ratio of more than 100 manufacturing sectors, i. e. the share of domestic value added in export value, using the customs trade data and industrial census data of 2008 and calculated the industry-weighted domestic value added ratio of China's export products in 2008 to be 67.78%. In order to understand what this ratio means, we have referred to a report on the changes of trade patterns published by the World Trade Organization (WTO) in 2011 under a collaborative study between the WTO and Japan's Asia Research Institute (IDE-JETRO). Using the data of Asia Input and Output sheets of 2008 covering nine countries and regions (Japan, Indonesia, South Korea, Taiwan, Thailand, Malaysia, the Philippines, Singapore and the Chinese mainland) formulated using IDE-JETRO, this report has estimated the average value of trade-weighted domestic value added ratios of export products for nine economies to be 72%. Of which, the domestic value added ratio of export products is 42% for Singapore, 53% for Taiwan, 63% for South Korea and 65% for Thailand. This ratio is 63% for the Chinese mainland, which is fairly close to our estimation result. It is higher compared with Singapore and Taiwan and similar to the level of South Korea and Thailand. This indicates that the Chinese mainland is not lagging behind major economies of Asia in terms of technology content and value added of its export products. China has achieved much headway in terms of technology progress and structural upgrade of manufacturing industry. In addition, the report mentioned that the US and Japan are quite close to each other in terms of their domestic value added ratios of export products in 2008, which are both around 85%. The message is that relative to advanced industrialized economies, emerging industrialized economies and emerging market economies have lower export value added ratios, which is normal. This means that the Chinese mainland and other East Asian economies still have potential for technology progress and industrial upgrade, particularly in terms of increasing the value added ratios of capital-intensive industries with sophisticated technologies and reducing the share of processing trade.

From a national perspective, over the past 10 years, China has implemented strategies on technology development and indigenous innovation with a top-down approach, which greatly enhanced China's capabilities of technology research and development. This is of great significance to China's technological and industrial upgrade in the coming 20 years. According to the experience of OECD, it takes a rather long period of time for the share of R&D investment in GDP to reach 1% but this process will accelerate after crossing the threshold of 1%. This phenomenon is referred to by economists as "technology take-off." Defined by the standard where R&D investment represents 1% of GDP, China is already in the stage of technology take-off. Today, China's R&D investment accounts for 1.7% of its GDP and this figure is poised to reach 2%. Currently, the growth rate of China's R&D investment is roughly 6%, which is among the highest and more or less the same with South Korea and Singapore. According to the estimation of the State Council's *Mid-& Long-term Technology Development Planning* (2006 – 2020) released in 2006, by 2020, the share of R&D spending in GDP in China will increase from current 1.7% to 2.5% and the share of imported technologies will reduce from today's 50% to 30%. The *Planning* also predicts that the share of value added of China's emerging strategic industries will jump from current 3% to more than 15%. China has already made much progress in the technology upgrade and indigenous R&D in communication sector. A few years ago, some technical standards developed by China's communication and information authorities have already aroused great attention and even protest from multinational firms. This indicates that China is getting close to acquiring indigenous capabilities for the research and innovation of frontier technologies.

Considering the basic advantages in education, technology and human capital, as long as China continues to practice open trade policies, participate in global vertical division of labor, assimilate foreign technologies and increase its spending on indigenous research and development, I am convinced that China will be able to move up the technology ladder very swiftly, continuously upgrade its industries and acquire an edge in frontier technologies.

## References


1. Amiti, Mary, and Caroline Freund. 2010. "The Anatomy of China's Export Growth." Chapter 1 in Robert C. Feenstra and Shang-Jin Wei, eds., *China's Growing Role in World Trade*. Chicago: The University of Chicago Press.

2. IDE-JETRO, and WTO. 2011. *Trade Patterns and Global Value Chain: From Trade in Goods to Trade in Tasks*. Geneva: World Trade Organization.

3. Lewis, S. A. 1954. "Economic Development with Unlimited Supplies of Labor." *The Manchester School*, Vol. 22: 139 – 191.

4. Maddison, Angus. 2007. *Contours of the World Economy*, 1 – 2030 *AD: Essays in Macro-Economic History*. New York: Oxford University Press.

5. Rodrik, Dani. 2006. "What's so Special about China's Exports?" *China and World Economy*, 14 (5): 1 – 19.

6. Subramanian, Arvind. 2011. *Eclipse: Living in the Shadow of China's Economic Dominance*. Washington, DC: Peterson Institute for International economics.

7. Wang, Zhi, and Shang-jin Wei. 2010. "What Accounts for the Rising Sophistication of China's Exports?" Chapter 2 in Robert C. Feenstra and Shang-Jin Wei, eds., *China's Growing Role in World Trade*. Chicago: The University of Chicago Press.

8. World Bank. 1993. *The East Asian Miracle: Economic Growth and Public Policy*. New York: Oxford University Press.

9. Yang, Rudai, Yang Yao, and Ye Zhang. 2009. "Upgrading Technology in China's Exports." Chapter 9 in Arthur Sweetman and Jun Zhang, eds., *Economic Transitions with Chinese Characteristics: Thirty Years of Reform and Opening Up*. Montreal: McGill-Queens University Press.

# Chapter 4

# How China Can Avoid the "Middle-Income Trap"

**Ma Xiaohe (马晓河)**

**Academy of Macroeconomic Research, China's National Development and Reform Commission (NDRC), Beijing, China**

**Abstract:** After decades of sustained effort, many low-income countries have successfully made the transition to middle-income status following World War II. However, when trying to make a further transition from middle-to high-income status, many of these countries are still relying on the same strategies. This has stalled the upward progress of some countries which are now hovering beneath the $10, 000 per capita income ceiling. These countries are now stuck in the "middle-income trap" . Only a few countries have managed to avoid this trap and grow into high-income countries. In 2010, China entered what the World Development Bank Report of 2010 labeled as the upper-middle-income threshold with a GDP per capita of $4, 396. ① China's current momentum will likely carry it through sustained growth in the foreseeable future, but it remains unsure whether China will escape the middle-income trap and grow into a high-income country. The answer lies in China's ability to restructure its industrial and social structure.

**Keywords:** middle-income trap, economic restructuring

## I. China Needs to Restructure its Economy and Adjust its Demand Structure

### (I) China Faces Dual Pressures to Transform Its Economic Structure

China currently faces intensifying competition from both the high and low end of the global supply chain—a "high-end squeeze" and a "low-end squeeze. " Before the global financial crisis, the world economy could be roughly divided into three categories: developed consumption economies

① In the 2010 World Development Report published by the World Bank, countries with gross national income (GNI) per capita of $975 or below are low-income countries, $976 - $3, 855 are lower middle-income countries, $3, 856 - $11, 905 are upper middle income countries and above $11, 906 are high-income countries. World Bank: World Development Report 2010, Tsinghua University Press, June 2010.

such as the United States and European countries; developing production economies such as China and India; and resource-producing countries such as Russia, Brazil, Australia, Canada, and Middle Eastern countries. Developed countries supported deficit spending with financial expansion while exporting high-tech products and importing a large amount of labor-intensive products. Their savings rates were low, and residents relied on credit consumption. Developing countries' economic growth was export-oriented, with domestic production far exceeding domestic demand. However, this supply-demand dynamic broke down after the financial crisis as governments cut fiscal expenditure and residents reduced consumption. With the demand for its labor-intensive products falling, China faced great challenges.

The global market is undergoing two profound changes in the wake of the financial crisis. For one, the U. S. , Europe, Japan, and other developed economies have implemented re-industrialization policies aiming to restore national advantages. These economies have specifically promoted industries such as new energy, biofuel, information technology, and aerospace technology in an effort to boost high-tech exports. In March 2010 the U. S. government announced a plan to double exports within five years through a focus on emerging industries and high-tech products. This increased competition has led to a "high-end squeeze" effect on China's own emerging industries.

On the opposite end of the spectrum, cheaper land resources and lower labor costs have made Honduras, Vietnam, Bangladesh, India, Sri Lanka, Ethiopia, and other developing countries competitive with China on the low-tech, labor-intensive end of the industrial spectrum. This has resulted in a "low-end squeeze" on China's economy.

China has two ways of coping with these two competitive pressures: first, it must foster a vibrant domestic consumer market by adjusting its domestic demand structure; second, it must promote structural transformation from export to demand-oriented industries at the low, middle, and high end of the industrial ladder. Neither solution will be easy to implement.

### (II) China's Difficulties in Adjusting Demand Structure

The key to the first solution lies in expanding domestic demand, raising domestic consumption as a portion of GDP. To do this, China must increase income levels for both urban and rural residents, and especially for middle & low-income residents. To form a "consumer society" based around a strong middle-class, China must adjust its income distribution structure. This will involve reducing the amount of income allocated to the government, enterprises and high-income groups while raising the proportion going to middle & low-income groups. But doing this will require two significant breaks with history.

First, China's national income distribution dynamics have consistently put the middle and lower classes at a disadvantage while the government and enterprises have taken the lion's share of national income. From 1995 to 2010, in non-budgetary revenue, China's government income ratio rose from 24.25% to 30.48%. Over the same period, the income ratio for enterprises rose from 9.88% to 15.82%. For residents, however, the figure dropped from 65.87% to 53.35 % (see Table 1). After the 2008 global financial crisis, this pattern intensified. From 2008 to 2010, national fiscal revenue increased from 6.133 trillion yuan to 8.308 trillion yuan, a nominal growth rate of 35.5%. Profits for industrial enterprises with annual business incomes above five million yuan increased by 27.1%[①] while, over the same period, the nominal growth rates of urban and rural residential incomes were 21.1% and 24.3%, respectively.[②]

**Table 1: Changes in China's Income Distribution Structure**

| Year | Disposable income according to fund flow statements (100 million yuan) | | | Governmental non-budgetary revenue | Adjusted disposable income (100 million yuan) | | | Distribution (% of national income) | | |
|---|---|---|---|---|---|---|---|---|---|---|
| | Government | Enterprises | Residents | | Government | Enterprises | Residents | Government | Enterprises | Residents |
| 1992 | 5064.9 | 3560.3 | 18090.3 | 2177.6 | 7242.5 | 1757.8 | 17715.3 | 27.11 | 6.58 | 66.31 |
| 1995 | 9504.6 | 9618.8 | 38491.2 | 4480.4 | 13985 | 5695.4 | 37981.2 | 24.25 | 9.88 | 65.87 |
| 2000 | 17352.9 | 13895.5 | 57562.7 | 8312.2 | 25665 | 6997.2 | 56498.5 | 28.79 | 7.85 | 63.37 |
| 2005 | 38251.3 | 37307.4 | 110609.5 | 13822.3 | 52073.5 | 27447.9 | 110100.5 | 27.46 | 14.48 | 58.06 |
| 2007 | 63084.4 | 48298.5 | 150816.3 | 20908.5 | 83993.0 | 35147.1 | 150230.4 | 31.18 | 13.05 | 55.77 |
| 2008 | 67977.4 | 69002.7 | 182429.5 | 21822.5 | 89800 | 54065.3 | 181861.1 | 27.57 | 16.6 | 55.83 |
| 2009 | 75191.7 | 75249 | 196478.8 | 25519.9 | 100711.5 | 61873.7 | 195925.3 | 28.09 | 17.26 | 54.65 |
| 2010 | 95056.6 | 81310 | 227513.7 | 36152.7 | 131209.3 | 67297.3 | 226973.7 | 30.84 | 15.82 | 53.35 |

Note: Governmental non-budgetary revenue includes income outside of the system, such as revenue from local government land transfers and rural non-tax revenues.

Sources: Chang Xinghua, Li Wei, Research on China's Income Distribution, Social Issue Research Center of Macroeconomic Research Institute of the NDRC.

When enjoying high revenue growth, government and enterprises tend to invest more, whereas when current expenditures are less than current income then the government and enterprises will naturally increase savings. From 1998 to 2010, the savings deposits of financial and governmental bodies in China increased by a factor of 25.4, rising from 347.08 billion yuan to 9.163 trillion yuan. As a proportion of total social savings deposits, this reflects an increase from 3.63% to 12.76%. Corporate deposits increased by a factor of 6.53, from 3.248 trillion yuan to 24.449 trillion yuan, or from 33.95% to 34.04%. Despite a substantial increase, the proportion of household savings deposits in total social savings dropped from 55.8% to 42.22% in the same twelve-year window.[③] This disproportionate increase in savings from the government and enterprises has further increased their ability to spend on investment, exacerbating the problem of medium & long-term investment overcapacity.

The second historical point to consider here is that national income consistently tilts toward

① In 2009, the producer price index for China's industrial products was 94.6%.

② The profits for industrial enterprises shown here is for January to November, 2010.

③ Calculation based on the *China Statistical Yearbook* 1999 and the *China Statistical Abstract* 2011.

high-income groups. According to sample data from the National Bureau of Statistics, incomes for high-income groups increased by 264.3% between 2000 and 2009. Over the same time period, incomes for middle & upper-middle-income groups rose by 174.7 – 209.7% and those for low-income groups rose by 142.8%. ① The proportion of national income earned by low-income groups, who account for 20% of the total population, dropped from 11.11% to 8.78%, while that of the middle & upper-middle groups, who account for 40% of the total population, dropped from 34.35% to 31.48%. In contrast, the proportion of national income earned by the 20% of the population who comprise the high-income group rose from 31.86% to 38.4%. In 2009, this top 20% earned nearly two-fifths of all urban revenue (see Table 2).

**Table 2: Proportions of Urban Residential Income for Different Income Groups Change over Time**

| Type of household | Proportion of surveyed households (%) | 2008/2000 (%) | Proportion of income in 2000 (%) | Proportion of income in 2009 (%) |
|---|---|---|---|---|
| Low-income | 20 | 1.94 | 11.11 | 8.78 |
| Medium-low-income | 20 | 2.21 | 15.46 | 13.81 |
| Middle-income | 20 | 2.37 | 18.89 | 17.67 |
| Upper-middle-income | 20 | 2.57 | 22.68 | 22.99 |
| High-income | 20 | 3.07 | 31.86 | 38.4 |

Source: The *China Statistical Yearbooks* for 2001 and 2010.

The situation in rural areas is similar to that in urban areas. In 2009, the top 40% of earners in rural areas earned 63.02% of the total revenue, while the bottom 60% earned only 36.98% (see Table 3). ② The income polarization seen here is a major obstacle for establishing a strong middle class. Only 12.1% of China's population belongs to the middle class according to the Institute of Sociology at the Chinese Academy of Social Sciences. ③ However, after deducting the lower-middle class, only 38.8% of the population in China can be considered as middle-class. ④ International experience suggests that the middle class must become the majority in order for a society to transit from production-oriented to consumption-oriented. This is because middle & low-income groups prefer

① Source: *China Statistical Abstract* 2006 and 2011.

② Source: China Statistical Yearbook 2001 and 2010. Proportions of different urban and rural income groups in the total income are the proportions between the arithmetic products of surveyed households in different groups and income per capita and total income of the surveyed households.

③ Asian Development Bank (ADB) 's defines middle-class as those who spend \$2 – \$20 per person per day.

④ Li Peilin, Zhang Yi. The Size, Identity and Social Attitude of China's Middle Class. According to estimates based on income, education, and work status, in 2005 China's core and semi-core middle class accounted for 12.1% of the total population and 25.4% of the urban population. Source: Society, 2008.2.

The Asian Development Bank (ADB) stated that China's middle class has exceeded 800 million by the standard of daily spending of \$2 according to the *Guangzhou Daily*, August 30, 2010. According to ADB estimates, in 2008 817 million Chinese people spent \$2 – \$20 daily. After removing the lower-middle class of 303 million, China actually had 515 million middle-class residents, or 38.8% of the total population.

spending to saving, while the opposite is true for high-income groups. Increasing the incomes of high-income groups will only lead to more savings; it is only when low-income groups become middle-income groups that can China successfully stimulate consumption growth.

**Table 3: Proportions of Urban Residential Income for Different Income Groups**

| Type of household | Proportion of surveyed households (%) | Proportion of income in 2009 (%) |
|---|---|---|
| Low-income | 20 | 6.67 |
| Medium-low income | 20 | 12.77 |
| Middle-income | 20 | 17.54 |
| Upper-middle income | 20 | 23.33 |
| High-income | 20 | 39.69 |

Source: *The China Statistical Yearbook*, 2010.

A consensus has been reached in China that it is necessary to increase middle & low-income group incomes by adjusting the existing income distribution structure. However, institutional arrangements and distribution channels have hampered the flow of income to these residents in four ways. First, the financial and administrative power given to the central and local governments is enormous. Local governments in particular seize revenues for themselves at the expense of urban and rural residents. Second, China has so far failed to respond to rampant tax evasion in high-income groups. Third, local governments favor enterprises over individuals as these governments have single-mindedly pursued higher GDP figures and fiscal revenues. This has led to abuses of power and public resources. A flawed legal system and rubber-stamp trade unions have failed to protect workers' rights and have actually contributed to wage stagnation and low worker welfare. Fourth, China's social security system is not conducive to increasing these income levels. In China, residents mainly rely on family members for social security because the official social security system has low coverage and offers minimal benefits. One of the reasons that Chinese savings rates are so high is that much money is put aside for precautionary purposes. This can only be reversed when a sound nationwide social security system is put in place that the people trust.

After years of trying, China has now established basic social security systems covering child birth, pension, sickness, disability and unemployment. However, the system in its current state is flawed and cannot fix the complex problem at hand. Developed regions, mainly cities, enjoy better social security benefits while needy groups in rural areas and medium & small-sized towns receive fewer and poorer benefits. The rate of coverage in general is far too low as well. ① The government quite

① Take basic pension insurance and basic medical insurance as an example. In 2008, 218.91 million people participated in the urban basic pension insurance system, accounting for 36% of the urban population; in the 2nd half of 2009, the rural basic pension insurance pilot project was launched, covering 13% of the population by year's end; in 2008, 199.96 million people participated in the urban basic medical insurance system, accounting for 33% of the urban population; in 2008, although the new rural cooperative medical system covered almost all farmers, the level of the medical care for farmers was still low.

simply does not invest enough into social security. In Western Europe and Nordic countries, 50% of fiscal expenditures go to social security. This figure is about 30% in the U. S.. In China, however, this figure was below 16.16% in 2009. ①If these problems are not addressed and policy barriers are not removed, then China will continue to be hampered by an inadequate, ineffectual social security system.

In adjusting its demand structure and expand consumption, China currently faces problems caused by systematic barriers and flawed policies. Only by speeding up systematic reforms and restructuring related policies can China hope to unleash suppressed consumer demand and establish a consumer society.

## II. Difficulties in Adjusting China's Industrial Structure

Although China has reached the upper-middle per capita income threshold, its industrial structure still closely resembles low-income countries where manufacturing is the basis of society and supply always exceeds demand (see Table 4). China needs to move away from this model, and it must overcome four challenges if it is to do so.

**Table 4: International Comparison of Industrial Structure (2008) (%)**

| | Primary | Secondary | Services |
|---|---|---|---|
| Low-income countries | 25 | 29 | 46 |
| Lower-middle-income countries | 14 | 41 | 45 |
| Middle-income countries | 10 | 37 | 53 |
| Upper-middle-income countries | 6 | 33 | 61 |
| High-income countries | 1 | 26 | 73 |
| China (2010) | 10.2 | 46.9 | 43.0 |

Note: China's industrial structure refers to the proportions of the primary, secondary and tertiary industry in national GDP.

Source: The World Bank: *World Bank Development Report* 2008. Data for China is from the *China Statistical Abstract* 2011.

### (I) Efforts to Modernize Agriculture Lag Behind

In order to maximize income from limited arable land, China's farmers continuously increase material inputs. This leads to greater production costs, falling yields, and little progress towards agricultural modernization. Under the current tax system, local governments are not willing to assume

① According to the *China Statistical Yearbook for* 2010, the Chinese government invested 760.668 billion yuan in social security and employment, 72.597 billion yuan in affordable housing building and 399.419 billion yuan in health care in 2009. These expenditures combined accounted for 16.16% of total fiscal expenditure. The majority of health care support was not ultimately spent on real public health protection.

the responsibility of modernizing the agricultural industry. When the central government's investment in agricultural falls short, then agricultural modernization is bound to stagnate. Simply stated, China and its 1.3 billion inhabitants will have great difficulties escaping the middle-income trap without agricultural modernization, and current systems are not well positioned to bring about this surely needed adjustment.

### (II) A big but Weak Manufacturing Sector

Over the three decades of China's pro-market reform, China has formed a huge manufacturing capacity based around low costs and large scale. China has also long lingered among the bottom rungs of the value chain in global manufacturing. Most of China's industries involve processing and assembling, which puts them right in the middle of the "smiling curve."① These industries do not enjoy comparative advantages in high-value-added sectors like R&D, patents, technical standard setting, and brand development. Industries on either end of the "smiling curve" have higher profit margins than those in the middle, which only earn merger fees from processing and assembly. China is stuck in its current position because it has yet to establish a worldwide production system and marketing network. Chinese enterprises looking to increase their added value and profits often seem to have few choices beyond expanding scale and squeezing wages for workers. However, even these options are being adversely affected by shrinking demand from the U.S. and Europe, rising labor costs, and the appreciation of the RMB.

Furthermore, China cannot rely on technological innovation to move it up the supply chain if it continues to underfund R&D and suffer from under-trained personnel. China's total manufacturing output accounts for 14% of the world total, while its R&D input only accounts for 0.3% of the world total. The proportion of scientists and engineers working in R&D is much lower than that of the U.S., Japan or South Korea. For example, 80% of technology and equipment used in China's oil refining industry is imported. Due to inadequate domestic innovation, the value-added for China's manufacturing sector is only 26.6%. This figure is 23, 22, and 12 percentage points below that of the United States, Japan and Germany respectively. This leads to China handing over a large amount of revenue to foreign countries.

### (III) China's Service Industry Is Weak and Imbalanced

The pervading urban-rural divide in China makes it very difficult for rural residents to permanently relocate to cities. International experience shows that when a country's urbanization rate cannot exceed 60% and the service sector cannot account for over 60% of a country's economy then it is difficult for that country to join the high-income club. China's manufacturing sector is generally limit-

① Modern industrial value chain studies have shown that the profits created by different enterprises in the industry chain show a "U" shape, hence the term the "smiling curve." One end of this curve involves R&D and design, including the development of technical standards. The other end involves brand, sales and services. Processing and production are in the middle of the curve. Companies at both ends of the curve have high profit margins, while the processing enterprises in the middle section tend to have low profitability. Thus, technology is the core of business competitiveness and overall national strength, and developing technical standards signifies the height of global technology innovation. Developing technical standards is an important benchmark for measuring the innovation capacity of enterprises and countries. The "smile curve" was first put forward by Taiwan's Acer Group Chairman Stan Shih.

ed to assembly, which restricts the development of service industries such as telecommunications, finance, insurance, information consultation, R&D, tourism, journalism, publishing, and television broadcasting. China's service industries are all hampered by the role that China's manufacturing sector plays in the global economy.

### (IV) Energy-intensive Industries Skirt Pollution Costs Caused by Their Growth

China's recent economic growth has been fuelled by cheap labor, cheap resources, low pollution costs, and a low exchange rate. Energy consumption provides a good example: From 2000 to 2010, overall energy consumption rose from 1.455 billion to 3.25 billion tons of standard coal, an increase of 123.3%. Within this figure, industrial energy consumption grew from 1.038 billion tons to 2.192 billion tons, an increase of 111.2%. Of that 2.192 billion tons, consumption by eight[①] major industrial sectors accounted for 70%. This has led to a small number of people benefitting from industrial growth and an overwhelming majority of people being left to bear the new burden of pollution. Extensive and difficult institutional reforms are needed to realign incentives and correct the current course of energy consumption in China.

## III. Strategies for Escaping the Middle-income Trap

Making the leap from middle-income to high-income status requires new strategies and ways of thinking. What worked to move an economy from low to middle-income status will likely not work again. China needs to actively and comprehensively readjust its growth strategies in order to make this difficult transition and avoid being perennially stuck in the middle-income trap.

### (I) Cultivating An "Olive-shaped" Society

China should work to develop an "olive-shaped" society where the middle-class outnumbers both the high & lower-classes. China quite simply needs to increase the size of its middle class. In Japan and South Korea, the middle-class accounted for more than 70% of the population before those countries gained high-income status based on per capita income. China has a long way to go in this regard.

Policymakers should also work to accelerate urbanization. The urbanization rate generally exceeds 70% before a country attains high-income status. China's current urbanization rate is currently 49.68%, which includes 220 million migrant workers who have not settled permanently in the cities. In order to absorb over-capacity in industry, China must accelerate urbanization, promote service sector development, and encourage farmers to settle in the cities. Urbanization creates demand while industrialization creates supply. The urbanization of farmers will bring massive consumption to

① Namely textiles, paper and paper products, petroleum processing, chemical materials and chemical products, non-metallic mineral products, ferrous metal smelting and rolling processing, non-ferrous metal smelting and rolling processing, and fabricated metal products.

the cities and create huge demand for urban infrastructure and services. Within five to ten years, China's urbanization process should be focusing on the development of small and medium-sized cities and towns. Those cities and towns should be striving to improve their infrastructure and public services in order to enhance their attractiveness to rural residents and migrant workers.

Third, China should strive to enhance consumption capacity in less developed, rural areas. Urban residents alone cannot absorb China's massive industrial production capacity. China should work to raise consumption in rural areas in the following ways: increase government investment in public infrastructure; encourage inland regions to make themselves more attractive to industries looking to relocate from developed coastal areas; increase transfer payments to rural regions; and improve social security systems in rural regions to lessen concerns related to education, medical care, and pensions.

### (II) Transforming China's Industrial Structure

There are three ways in which China can work to transform its industrial structure to help keep it out of the middle-income trap. The first is a well-developed services sector. This would help China optimize industrial structures and create the conditions necessary for the establishment of a consumer society. In high-income economies, the service sector is generally above 60%, even exceeding 70% in the U. S.. To better foster service industry growth, China's policymakers should create a favorable environment for financial services, modern logistics, high-tech services and high-end business services. Entry restrictions to monopolized service sectors should be removed, and private enterprises should be encouraged to enter the telecommunications, railway, aviation, finance, education, medical and cultural industries. This will lead to a healthier, more diverse services market. In order to assist urbanization, China should try to integrate rural and urban services. All levels of government should have the same enthusiasm for developing business services, travel services, housekeeping services and cultural services for both urban and rural residents.

The second is for China to climb the international supply chain, increasing outputs of high value-added goods. In developing its consumer goods industry, advanced technologies should be adopted to transform existing industries by improving product quality and developing independent brands. In the equipment manufacturing industry, efforts should be taken towards the localization of core components and basic manufacturing processes.

Third, China should develop strategic new industries, changing the paradigm from "made in China" to "created in China." This is essential if China is to transit from prioritizing heavy industry to more profitable industries with higher value-added opportunities. These new industries should be knowledge and technology intensive and have relatively small carbon footprints. China should apply Joseph A. Schumpeter's theory of "creative destruction"① to innovate industrial structure. This will involve mobilizing social resources to develop a new, efficient generation of emerging industries such as information technology, biotechnology, high-end equipment manufacturing, and new-energy ve-

① Tang Min, Yu Jiantuo, etc., Michael Spencer Talks about China's Economic Transformation, study reference for China Development Research Foundation, 2010, No. 8.

hicles. China should reconstruct its national innovation system, develop supporting tax, finance and market access policies, and strengthen enterprises' technological innovation capabilities. It would also be prudent to set up a special fund for the development of strategic new industries and the implementation of key industrial demonstration projects with the goal of making major breakthroughs in core technologies within three to five years.

Lastly, China must restructure its supply and demand dynamics for energy. In order to move away from its current high-carbon-emission development path, a new energy revolution is needed. China should promote energy-efficient and low-carbon technologies. It should provide funding as well as technical and institutional assistance for low-carbon growth initiatives. It should decrease the importance of fossil fuels as an energy source and encourage investment in sustainable energy sources such as biomass, wind, solar, and geothermal energy. China must also eliminate counterproductive production in major industries by leveraging economic and legal tools such as carbon emission standards and tax policy.

## References


1. Charcoln Industry Research Dept. 2010. Abstract of Japan's Economic History: Rapid Growth Era of 1955 – 1980, April 2010. http://www.charcoln.com/referrence_201004jp.htm.

2. Comprehensive Department of National Development and Reform Commission. 2004. "International Comparison of the Rate of Consumption." *China Economic Herald*, no. 16.

3. Guo, Jinlong. 2000. *International Comparison of the Transformation of Economic Growth Modes*, China Development Press.

4. Guo, Kesha, and Yanzhong Wang. 1999. *Trends and Policy Research of China's Industrial Structure Change*, Economic Management Press.

5. Li Peilin, and Yi Zhang. 2008. "The Size, Identity and Social Attitude of China's Middle Class." *Society*, no. 2.

6. Li, Jianwei. 2007. "International Comparison of the Evolution Characteristics of Investment Rate and Consumption Rate." *China Finance*, no. 8.

7. Lin, Chonggeng, and Michael Spencer. 2011. *Medium and Long-term Development and Transition of Chinese Economy*, CITIC Publishing House.

8. Liu, Shijin, Junkui Zhang, Yongzhi Hou, and Peilin Liu. 2011. "Trap or Wall-Real Challenges and Strategic Choice for China's Economy." *Comparison*, no. 3, 2011.

9. Ma, Xiaohe, etc. 2009. *China's Industrial Structure Change and the Policy Evolution*, China Planning Press.

10. Ma, Yan. 2009. "Adjustment and China's Countermeasures for the Middle-income Trap." *Economic Perspectives*.

11. Madison, Angus. 2009. *Millennium World Economic Statistics*, Peking University Press.

12. Song, Jiawu. 2010. "Beware of the Middle-income Trap." *China Development Observation*, 2010 (9).

13. Tang, Min, Jiantuo Yu, etc. 2010. "Michael Spencer Talks about China's Economic

Transformation." *Study reference for China Development Research Foundation*, no. 8.

14. Xiao, Wei, and Zhaohui Lan. 2010. "China Faces A Passive Industrial Upgrading." *China Business*, July 2010.

15. Zhang, Sai. 1996. *International Statistical Yearbook*. China Statistics Press.

16. Zheng, Bingwen. 2009. "The Phenomenon of Poverty Rate Climbing with Economic Growth and Poverty Reduction Effects of Social Security in Latin U. S.: An International Perspective." *Latin American Studies* (Supplement of February 2009 version).

# Part Two
# Institution & Mechanism

# Chapter 5

# The Contribution of Marketization to China's Economic Growth*

**Fan Gang[1] (樊纲), Wang Xiaolu[1] (王小鲁) and Ma Guangrong[2] (马光荣)**

[1]National Economic Research Institute, China Reform Foundation, Beijing, China[2] Duke University, USA

**Abstract**: Market-oriented economic transition since 1978 has led to remarkable economic development in China. In this study, we use the National Economic Research Institute (NERI) Index of marketization and a panel data model to investigate the quantitative contributions of marketization to China's total factor productivity (TFP) and economic growth. Our results indicate that marketization contributed 1.45 percentage points on average to China's annual economic growth rate during the period from 1997 to 2007 and accounted for 39.2% of the increase in TFP. Marketization significantly improved resource allocation. However, economic transition in China has not yet been completed and sustainability of future growth will depend on further market-oriented reforms.

**Keywords**: marketization, economic transition, growth, Total Factor Productivity

## I. Introduction

In 2010, as a result of 30 years of economic expansion China overtook Japan to become the world's second largest economy, outranked only by the United States. Rapid economic development has lifted hundreds of millions of people from poverty as well as improved living standards.

China's market-oriented reforms have played a pivotal role in making these achievements possible. Yet, to date there still lacks quantitative study on contribution of marketization to economic growth and productivity changes, due to the lack of a general indicator to measure the achievement of market-oriented reform. This process is a systematic transformation of the country's overall economic, social and legal systems other than only a few regulational changes. Due to limited information,

* Corresponding author: wangxiaolu@neri.org.cn.

previous empirical studies often employed one or a few proxy variables, such as the development of the private economy and economic openness, to represent the process of marketization. These studies, while meaningful, are insufficient to reflect the full impact of market-oriented reform on economic development. In order to measure such impact, a better indicator is needed.

This paper employs the NERI Index of Marketization, which was developed by the National Economic Research Institute of China Reform Foundation, to measure the impact of market-oriented reform on economic development at the provincial level. Our findings indicate that between 1997 and 2007, market-oriented reform contributed an average of 1.45 percentage points to annual economic growth rate. The process of marketization significantly improved resource allocation, which contributed 39% to total factor productivity (TFP).

This paper is structured as follows. Part 2 surveys the existing literature on marketization and economic growth. Part 3 explains the econometric models and data that we employed, as well as reviews the process of marketization in China's provinces (including autonomous regions and municipalities) between 1997 and 2007. Part 4 presents the regression results and analysis, and decomposes different factors' contribution to economic growth via growth accounting. Part 5 is the conclusion and policy recommendations.

## II. Literature Review

Both growth theory and cross-country empirical studies suggest that international disparities in economic growth performance are largely due to differences in TFP. There are two main sources for TFP increases. One source is technical progress that results from R&D activities or technology transfer. The other source is efficiency gains from improved resource allocation, i. e., shifts of capital or labor from low productivity companies, sectors or regions to those with high productivity. If reallocation of these factors is impeded by policy or certain institutional conditions, then efficiency losses will occur and productivity will be reduced.

Based on the disparities among corporate technology capabilities, Hsieh and Klenow (2009) proposed that if China's resource allocation efficiency reached the level enjoyed by the United States, China's TFP would increase by 30% to 50%. In developed market economies with higher allocation efficiency, increases in TFP mainly resulted from technical progress. However, for China and other transitional economies, their market-oriented reform that promotes resource allocation efficiency may be the major source to bring about productivity gains.

The impact of market-oriented reforms on economic growth has been one of the biggest areas of interests for studies on transition economics since the early 1990s (Roland, 2000). Starting with the economic transitions of Eastern Europe and the former USSR following the collapse of the Berlin Wall, Western economists began to study the impact of reform policies on economic growth in transition economies, particularly pay attention to the drastic and discontinuous pattern of the institutional change (North, 1990).

The key to such research, however, is the ability to identify systematic indicators to measure the transition process. The European Bank for Reconstruction and Development (EBRD) 's annual *Transition Report* provides representative indices for various aspects of reforms, such as price liberalization, corporate reform, privatization, foreign exchange and trade liberalization, competition policies, reform of financial institutions, and so on, in 27 transition economies. ① However, with assessment difficulties, measurement problems, differences in research approaches, as well as the differences in countries' transition paths, previous studies have failed to reach consistent conclusions (see Babetskii and Campos, 2007). Some earlier studies such as Havrylyshyn *et al.* (1998), using EBRD transition indices, and De Melo *et al.* (1997), using self-invented transition indices, both concluded that market-oriented reform significantly contributed to economic development. However, these were not corroborated by subsequent studies. According to the results of empirical research by Falccetti *et al.* (2002), the effect of reform on economic growth is not robust, depending on the selection of sample countries and periods. Fidrmuc (2001) also found that, although economic transition had a positive effect on economic growth before 1995, the impact was insignificant for the period between 1996 and 2000.

As to the samples, all of the studies above were conducted on Eastern European and the former USSR countries. For a long time, mainstream international economists gave insufficient attention to China's different transitional path. Only in the past decade, China's economic achievements and transition experiences started catching the attention of the international economics community. Nevertheless, researches on the effect of China's marketization on economic growth have been limited.

In China, many studies have been carried out on the relationship between China's economic growth and its marketization. However, due to lack of systematic measurement, these studies offered limited quantitative analysis on the overall contribution of marketization to growth, and only touched certain aspects of China's reform. Among them, Jefferson *et al.* (1992) identified that China's private industrial sector made significant contributions to industrial productivity. Cai Fang and Wang (1999) discovered that the developments in the labor market had a positive effect on the inter-sector reallocation of labor and led to increased TFP. Wang (1999, 2000) further disclosed that labor reallocation between rural and urban areas driven by pro-market reforms was an important source of growth and productivity gains during the reform period and further led to the reallocation of capital, which in turn amplified the positive effect of labor reallocation. In a more recent study, Wang, Fan and Liu (2009), through a time-series growth analysis over the past 50 years, confirmed that marketization contributed substantively to economic growth during the reform period. However, due to lack of long-term and comprehensive indicators, the study used the share of non-state-owned enterprises in the economy as a proxy of marketization. As a result, the contribution of marketization to economic growth appeared underestimated, with less than one percentage point across all periods.

Some cross-region studies have examined the effects of human capital (Yao, Zhang, 2008),

---

① The 27 transition economies are all located in Eastern Europe and the former USSR. When rating various reforms, EBRD used a score system from 1 to 4, with 1 meaning no reform at all and 4 meaning complete marketization.

R&D (Wu, 2008), financial development (Shen, Zhang, 2004; Lin and Sun, 2008), local government incentives (Zhang, Gong, 2005; Xu, 2007) and infrastructure (Liu, 2010). Most of these studies treated market-oriented transition as a control variable, which is commonly represented by one (or two) indicator (s) such as the shares of state owned enterprises or non-state enterprises in employment, investment or output. These proxies measure only one aspect of market-oriented reforms and are actually incapable of reflecting the full picture.

Our present study uses the NERI (stands for National Economic Research Institute) Index of Marketization at the provincial level to estimate the contribution of marketization to economic growth. The Chinese mainland has 31 provincial level administrative regions, many of which are comparable to medium-sized countries in terms of population and economy. The levels of marketization vary substantially across regions. These conditions assist our current study. Start from 2001, NERI has issued six reports for annual marketization indexes for China's 31 provinces (including autonomy regions and five municipalities that administratively at the provincial level), see Fan Gang and Wang Xiaolu (2001); Fan Gang, Wang and Zhu (2003, 2004, 2007, 2010). NERI Index of Marketization spans 13 years from 1997 – 2009. These indices make it possible to conduct a more comprehensive study on the regional differences in China's marketization process and to examine its impact on economic growth in a relatively long period.

In terms of research framework, international transition studies focus mainly on the measurement of economic freedom and pay little attention to the development of market systems. In NERI Index of Marketization, we see marketization as a systematic, and gradual, process of institutional development. We therefore measure the progress of marketization from five aspects, including the relationship between government and market, development of the non-state (private) sector, development of product markets, development of factor markets, and the development of market intermediaries as well as the market-friendly legal environment. This system is constructed on the basis of objective statistics or survey data. We believe that such a system can provide rich information on the process of marketization, and helpful for analyzing the effect of marketization on economic growth.

While the NERI Index makes the cross province comparison possible, progress of marketization in each province over time can also be identified. The Index provides panel data sets to catch regional differences, over time changes, and measures these by sub-indices in five aspects and 23 basic indicators.

## III. Model and Data

### (I) A Growth Model for Empirical Study

For empirical study on economic growth, the Cobb-Douglas production function remains a commonly used functional form for its analytical convenience. In Lucas (1998) model, human capital, as an important production factor, is defined as effective labor that is determined by both the quantity and educational level of the labor force, i. e., the quality of labor. In order to distinguish the two effects, our study divides the Lucas-defined human capital into two variables: the size of labor force and its educational level, in a Cobb-Douglas production function:

$$Y_{it} = A_{it}K_{it}^{\alpha}L_{it}^{\beta}E_{it}^{\gamma} \tag{1}$$

where $Y_{it}$, $K_{it}$, $L_{it}$ and $E_{it}$ respectively denote GDP, fixed capital stock, labor force, and average schooling year of labor force of province i in year t. $\alpha$, $\beta$ and $\gamma$ are the output elasticities of physical capital, labor force and year of schooling, respectively. Ait represents TFP, which comes from two major sources: the technological progress, and efficiency gains from both improvement in resource allocation and changes in the incentive mechanism at the firm level, as a result of market-oriented reforms. Our previous studies found that technological progress, marketization, urbanization, economic openness, the spillover effect of human capital and infrastructure all contributed positively to productivity growth (Wang Xiaolu, Fan Gang, Liu Peng, 2009). Some of these effects are national in nature and cannot be well caught at the provincial level. Factors that are found in our preliminary studies to have significant effects on TFP growth at the provincial level are technological progress, marketization, and improvements in infrastructure. Thus, TFP in this study is defined as:

$$A_{it} = Ae^{(\rho MI_{it} + \delta \ln Tech_{it} + \theta Tran_{it} + \lambda_i + u_{it})} \tag{2}$$

where $MI_{it}$ is the marketization index of province $i$ in year $t$. ln $Tech_{it}$ is the stock of research capital in logarithm form, which stock is an accumulation of R&D inputs, calculated using the Perpetual Inventory Method. $Tran_{it}$ is the infrastructure condition in province $i$, and is measured by the ratio of standard transport route length to the provincial population. Standard route length is converted from length of railway and highway of different grades based on their transportation capacity. $\lambda_i$ denotes the fixed effect of provinces and is intended to capture province-specific productivity factors that do not change over time.① $\varepsilon_{it}$ is the random disturbance term.

Substituting $A_{it}$ in equation (1) by equation (2) and taking logarithm on both sides, we arrive at the following econometric model:

$$\ln Y_{it} = \ln A + \alpha \ln K_{it} + \beta \ln L_{it} + \gamma \ln E_{it} + \rho M_{it} + \delta \ln Tech_{it} + \theta Tran_{it} + \lambda_i + \varepsilon_{it} \tag{3}$$

## (II) Description of Variables and Data

### 1. The NERI Index of Marketization.

Market-oriented reform involves transition of the economic, social and legal systems. The NERI Index of Marketization is composed of the five aspect-indices stated above, with each index consisting of a few sub indices or base indices. There are 23 base indices that form this index system, all of which are based on quantitative indicators from statistics or survey data at the firm level.

As for the calculation of base indices, we define the maximum and minimum values of an original indicator by province in the benchmark year to be 10 and 0 (reversing 0 to 10 for negative-effect indicators), respectively. For other provinces, their scores are determined between 10 and 0, by their value of the original indicator relative to the maximum and minimum values. Several base indices form a higher level of sub-indices or aspect indices. Five aspect indices form the general index of

① Our subsequent Hausman test supported the fixed effect rather than the random effect model.

marketization, which reflects the relative position of a province in marketization in the benchmark year. ①

The NERI marketization index indicates the relative process of marketization, but it does not denote how far a province is from a pure market economy. So far, no economic theory can depict a hundred-percent market economy. Nor does it exist in reality. However, the relative progress of marketization is observable. The Index is designed to compare relative achievement of marketization across provinces and measure their temporal changes. The multi-angle analysis, together with the horizontal and vertical comparability and measurement using objective indicators, constitute the distinctive features of the NERI index. Another advantage of the NERI index is that it avoids the subjective judgment that exists in some international studies. A few indicators used in NERI Index are assessments collected from corporate executives, but the survey includes extensive samples, thus minimizing the impact of random errors.

The NERI Index suggests that provincial marketization made remarkable progress between 1997 and 2007. The average score of NERI Index by province was 4.01 for 1997 and increased to 7.50 in 2007. The marketization process was slow between 1997 and 2001, during which time the average score only increased by 0.15 points each year. The marketization pace accelerated between 2002 and 2007 with an average annual increase of 0.48 points, suggesting that China's WTO accession in 2001 might have played a positive role in promoting China's marketization.

However, the marketization process varied greatly across provinces. In 1997, the scores of Guangdong, Zhejiang and Fujian, the top three provinces in marketization according to the Index, were 6.29, 6.17, and 5.43, respectively, while those of Qinghai, Ningxia and Xinjiang, which ranked the lowest, were only 1.29, 1.69, and 1.77, respectively. In 2007, scores of the top three, Shanghai, Zhejiang and Guangdong, were 11.71, 11.39 and 11.04, respectively, while Tibet, Qinghai and Gansu received the lowest scores at 4.25, 4.64, and 5.31, respectively. Standard deviation of provincial scores kept widening after 1999, which indicates growing disparities in the inter-provincial marketization process. Nevertheless, provinces with both high and low level of marketization all experienced appreciable progress in this period.

The five aspects of marketization all improved between 1997 and 2007. Rapid progress has been made in development of the private sector, development of market intermediaries and the legal environment, and development of product markets, whose average scores increased by 4.78, 4.00, and 3.85 points, respectively. However, the development of factor markets, and the government-market relationship, was slow in progress and the scores only went up by 2.95 points and 2.39 points (Figure 1). In terms of government-market relationship in particular, the progress stalled over the past few years. These facts indicate that China's factor market reform is lagging behind, and there is still too much unnecessary government intervention.

---

① More details about the calculation method can be found in *China Marketization Indices* 2011 (Fan Gang, Wang Xiaolu, Zhu Hengpeng, 2011).

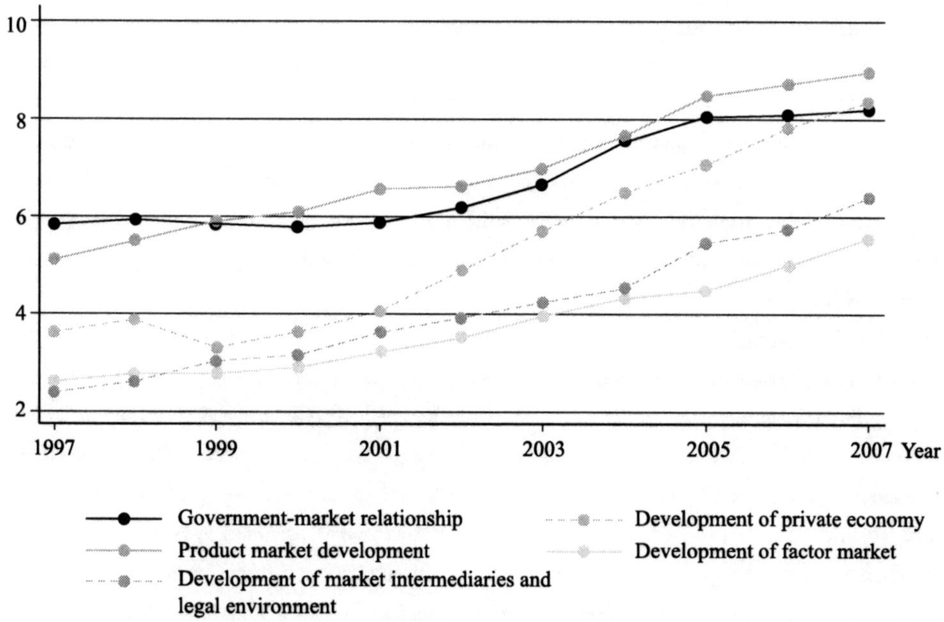


**Figure 1: Changing Scores of the Five Aspect Indices (1997 – 2007)**

Figure 2 illustrates the relations between marketization and GDP growth. GDP statistics are from *China Statistical Yearbook* (National Bureau of Statistics, or NBS, various years). As Figure 2 shows, there is a significant positive relationship between GDP growth and the marketization process indicated by the NERI Index.

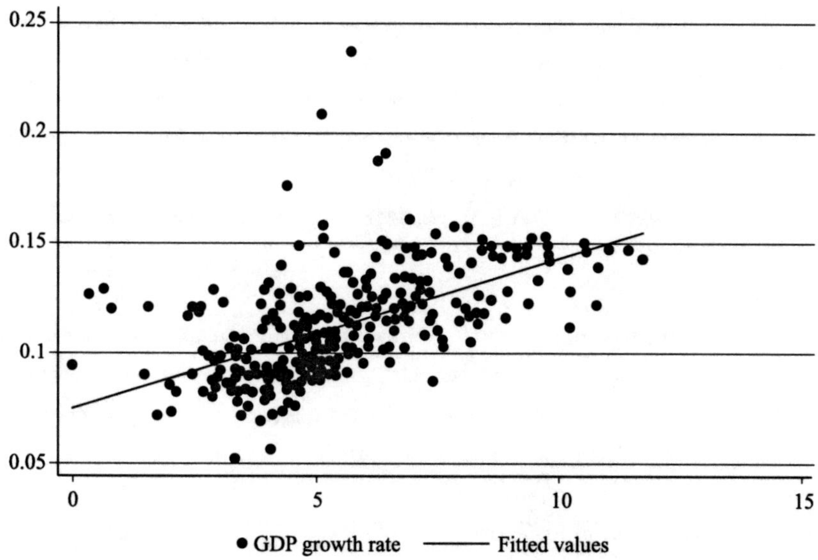


**Figure 2: Provincial GDP Growth and Marketization Indices (1997 – 2007)**

**2. Years of Schooling of Labor Force.**

It is calculated from the annual numbers of graduates from primary, secondary and tertiary educational institutions in the past 56 years and the national census data. Schooling years of graduates from the tertiary, senior secondary, junior secondary and primary levels were taken as 16 years, 12 years, 9 years, and 6 years, respectively. We find that the number of workers changed slowly between 1997 and 2007, from 698 million to 770 million and representing an increase of 10.3%. Larger increases are seen in workers' year of schooling, up from 6.98 years to 8.18 years and representing an increase of 17.2%.

**3. Capital Stock.**

Using the perpetual inventory method and taking 1952 as the base period, we calculated capital stock using fixed asset investment data over the past 56 years (data from NBS). The initial capital stock is assumed to be 10 times of the value of fixed asset investment in 1952. The method used by Wang Xiaolu, Fan Gang and Liu Peng (2009) is adopted for depreciation, whereby the depreciation rate is set at 5% for the period between 1952 and 1977 and is assumed to be under stable acceleration during the reform period (1978 – 2007) to ultimately reach 8%. Because no statistics are available on price deflator for fixed asset investment before 1991, they are replaced by the commodities retail price index. Between 1997 and 2007, China's fixed capital stock experienced an annual growth rate of 14%, much higher than the GDP growth rate.

**4. Research Capital.**

We use the provincial stock of research capital to measure technological progress. This stock is an accumulated aggregation of spending on research and development, on importing foreign technology, and on domestic technology acquisition, using the perpetual inventory method. All statistics are taken from *China Statistical Yearbooks on Science and Technology*. Due to incomplete statistics for years before 1996, we adopt Wu Yanbin (2008)'s assumption and use 1996 as the base period. In conformity with existing literature, we set the rate of research capital depreciation at 15%. Between 1997 and 2007, provincial research capital stock on average increased by 3.48 times, indicating relative rapid technological progress. However, considerable differences exist in the research capital growth rates across provinces. Over a period of eleven years, the technology capital inventory of Yunnan only grew by 18.49% and Gansu by 26.34%, whereas in Hainan and Fujian it grew by 5.88 and 5.35 times, respectively.

**5. Infrastructure.**

Even though many types of infrastructure are involved, only limited statistics are available for some of them. The most important, and measurable, infrastructure is the route length of highway and railways. In order to make the statistics comparable, we convert the length of different grades of highways into standard length, which is equivalent to grade-II highways according to their transportation capacity. We then combine railway length and standard highway length into standard route length using a conversion factor of 14.7. Between 1997 and 2007, China's standard route length per 10,000 people nearly doubled, up from 9.73km to 17.19km. However, the growth rate differed considerably across provinces. For instance, in Jilin province it only increased by 26.37% over ten years, while it increased by 270.94% in Chongqing during the same period.

## IV. Regression Results

### (I) Effects of Marketization on Economic Growth

Table 1 demonstrates the regression results of equation (3).

**Table 1: Marketization Index and Economic Growth**

| | Dependent variable: LnY | | | | |
|---|---|---|---|---|---|
| | (1) | (2) | (3) | (4) | (5) |
| Periods | 1997 - 2007 | 1997 - 2007 | 1999 - 2007 | 1999 - 2002 | 2003 - 2007 |
| LnK | 0.513*** (23.49) | 0.548*** (25.11) | 0.499*** (20.28) | 0.639*** (14.24) | 0.481*** (17.52) |
| LnL | 0.272*** (4.358) | 0.399*** (13.52) | 0.357*** (5.755) | -0.0607 (-0.497) | 0.349*** (4.865) |
| LnE | 0.405*** (5.556) | 0.420*** (5.826) | 0.314*** (3.723) | 0.0668 (0.843) | 0.312*** (3.554) |
| MI | 0.0416*** (8.334) | 0.0356*** (7.606) | 0.0404*** (7.508) | 0.0232*** (4.544) | 0.0610*** (7.096) |
| Lntech | 0.0861*** (4.941) | 0.0792*** (4.661) | 0.0840*** (4.333) | 0.0932*** (2.917) | 0.0575*** (2.754) |
| Tran | 0.00481*** (3.546) | 0.00197* (1.665) | 0.00574*** (4.205) | 0.00410** (2.503) | 0.00202* (1.734) |
| Constant | -0.910** (-2.088) | -2.023*** (-8.967) | -1.210*** (-2.699) | 1.164 (1.416) | -0.662 (-1.261) |
| Model | Fixed effect | Random effect | Fixed effect | Fixed effect | Fixed effect |
| Observations | 330 | 330 | 270 | 120 | 150 |
| $R^2$ | 0.984 | | 0.985 | 0.970 | 0.988 |

Note: *, ** and *** respectively denote a significance level of 10%, 5% and 1%.

The first and second columns of Table 1 show the regression results for fixed effect and random effect using full samples. Hausman test reject the null hypothesis (random effect) and thus the fixed effect results are accepted. Based on regression (1), the output elasticity of physical capital, labor and schooling year is 0.51, 0.27 and 0.41 respectively. The coefficient of Marketization index (MI) is 0.042, which shows that with other conditions unchanged, an increase in the score of marketization index by one point leads to 4.2% of GDP growth.

Because certain sub-indices are not available for 1997 and 1998, the third column of Table 1 documents fixed effect regression results from samples between 1999 and 2007. The result shows that the coefficient for marketization index is 0.0404, almost identical to that in the first column.

In the fourth and fifth columns of Table 1, growth effects of marketization between the periods of 1999 – 2002 and 2003 – 2007 are compared. Results indicate that marketization index is 0.023 for the former period and 0.061 for the latter period. This implies an increasing, rather than diminishes effect of marketization on growth.

Based on the regression results in the first column of Table 1 derived from growth accounting, Table 2 shows the decomposition of provincial economic growth between 1997 and 2007. It indicates that physical capital, labor quantity, educational level and TFP contribute 6.83, 0.37, 0.64 and 3.70 percentage points, respectively, to economic growth. Evidently, capital still plays an important role in economic growth. Among the factors that determine TFP, marketization, technological progress and infrastructure contribute 1.45, 1.08 and 0.40 percentage points, respectively, to economic growth, and the remaining unobservable factor contributes 0.77 percentage points. Market-oriented reform remains the most important factor of TFP growth. ①

**Table 2: Growth Accounting (1997 – 2007)**

| Region | Contribution (percentage point) | Contribution (%) |
|---|---|---|
| GDP growth rate | 11.54 | 100 |
| Factor contribution | 7.84 | 67.92 |
| TFP contribution | 3.70 | 32.08 |
| Contribution factor decomposition | | |
| Capital | 6.83 | 59.22 |
| Labor | 0.37 | 3.17 |
| Education | 0.64 | 5.53 |
| Marketization | 1.45 | 12.58 |
| Technology | 1.08 | 9.35 |
| Infrastructure | 0.40 | 3.44 |
| Unobserved factors | 0.77 | 6.70 |

## (II) Effects of Five Aspects of Marketization on Growth

In order to examine whether the various aspects of marketization have different effects on economic growth, we replaced the general marketization index in equation (3) with five separate mar-

① These results are consistent with the growth accounting results using time series data at the national level in directions (see Wang Xiaolu, Fan Gang, Liu Peng, 2009), yet the magnitudes of contribution differ for the following reasons: 1) statistical inconsistency exists between provincial GDP growth rates and national GDP growth rate, as the average of former usually higher than the latter by 2 – 3 percentage points due to differences in methodology and data source between them; 2) the previous time series analysis adopted proxy variables due to the unavailability of long-term marketization variables, which does not reflect the full picture; 3) model specification differences, including certain variables used in the previous models are unavailable at the provincial level. Based on the second reason, we believe that this study gives more reliable estimates on the contribution of marketization. Further analysis may be necessary to properly examine the differences caused by other reasons.

ketization indices. Table 3 shows the regression results. The first column conducts regression using the full samples between 1997 and 2007. Except for factor market development, the other four aspect indices all have a significant impact on economic growth. In terms of the magnitude of the coefficient, improvement in government-market relationship has the strongest impact on economic growth. The development of market intermediaries and legal environment, and development of product market also has significantly affected market development. Development of the private sector is also significant, although with a lower coefficient.

The second column of Table 3 reports the results excluding the years of 1997 and 1998. The results are similar to the results in the first column.

The third and fourth columns of Table 3 show the results of regression for the two periods of 1999 – 2002 and 2003 – 2007. These results indicate that the coefficient of factor market development is insignificant for the former period, but positive and significant for the latter period. Development of product market, and development of market intermediaries and legal environment, also have a higher contribution to growth in latter period.

**Table 3: Aspects of China's Inter-provincial Marketization and Economic Growth**

| | Dependent variable: LnY | | | |
|---|---|---|---|---|
| | (1) | (2) | (3) | (4) |
| periods | 1997 – 2007 | 1999 – 2007 | 1997 – 2002 | 2003 – 2007 |
| LnK | 0.502*** (22.39) | 0.507*** (20.74) | 0.666*** (14.61) | 0.499*** (16.33) |
| LnL | 0.261*** (4.229) | 0.318*** (5.276) | –0.132 (–1.055) | 0.341*** (4.556) |
| LnE | 0.417*** (5.780) | 0.381*** (4.627) | 0.0790 (1.000) | 0.312*** (3.413) |
| MI_1 Government – market relationship | 0.0203*** (5.269) | 0.0271*** (6.032) | 0.0131** (2.115) | 0.00733 (1.329) |
| MI_2 Development of private sector | 0.00636* (1.912) | 0.00376 (1.128) | 0.0106** (2.078) | 0.00673 (1.480) |
| MI_3 Development of product markets | 0.0107*** (2.903) | 0.00827** (2.377) | 0.00158 (0.382) | 0.0161*** (4.256) |
| MI_4 Development of factor markets | –0.000518 (–0.148) | –0.000180 (–0.0461) | –0.00588 (–1.111) | 0.0133*** (2.966) |
| MI_5 Development of market intermediaries and legal environment | 0.0123*** (4.540) | 0.0122*** (4.177) | 0.00806* (1.788) | 0.0143*** (4.244) |
| Lntech | 0.0792*** (4.474) | 0.0620*** (3.214) | 0.0779** (2.366) | 0.0553*** (2.624) |
| Tran | 0.00421*** (3.037) | 0.00433*** (3.198) | 0.00191 (0.995) | 0.00175 (1.459) |

Continued

| | Dependent variable: LnY | | | |
|---|---|---|---|---|
| | (1) | (2) | (3) | (4) |
| Constant item | -0.718<br>(-1.607) | -0.884**<br>(-1.975) | 1.645*<br>(1.961) | -0.696<br>(-1.293) |
| Model | Fixed effect | Fixed effect | Fixed effect | Fixed effect |
| Observed value | 330 | 270 | 120 | 150 |
| R square | 0.985 | 0.987 | 0.973 | 0.988 |

Note: all regressions use fixed effect model. *, ** and *** respectively denote a significance level of 10%, 5% and 1%.

## V. Conclusions

Using the NERI Index of Marketization, this paper presents a quantitative analysis of the role of market-oriented reform in China's economic growth and TFP changes. Our results indicate that for the period between 1997 and 2007, market-oriented reforms contributed 1.45 percentage points on average to China's economic growth rate, accounting for 39.2% of TFP growth. Contribution of marketization may be even greater because the acceleration of factor input growth, technology and infrastructure changes are also relate to the reform. This implies that China has embarked on the right path of transition from a planned economy to a market economy. Marketization has been the primary cause for acceleration of China's economic growth and TFP changes during the reform period.

Although there have been remarkable achievements, the process of China's marketization has not complete. Marketization has made crucial progress in some parts of China, particularly in the eastern coastal areas, but in some less developed areas, market mechanism is still underdeveloped. In terms of the reform process in different fields, development of the product market has made major achievements, yet the factor markets are still underdeveloped. The government-market relationship had limited improvement over the past few years and even regressed in certain areas. The government sector reform has been lagging behind, and the size of government keeps expanding. These problems may negatively affect future economic growth.

With consideration of the above, future reforms are recommended to focus on the following areas:

First, reform of the factor markets should be carried out to improve the institutional framework for capital and land markets. Market-based pricing mechanism should be established, and transactions should be made transparent. The urban household registration system should also be reformed to promote rural-urban labor mobility and population migration.

Second, entry barriers of monopolistic sectors should be reduced, and both market competition and public monitoring mechanisms should be enhanced in those sectors. Resource tax and the SOE dividend distribution systems should also be reformed to make better use of monopolistic profits.

Third, excessive government intervention should be further reduced and discriminative policy treatment in terms of bank credit, interest rate and market access should be eliminated.

Lastly, government sector reform should be carried out to promote a transparent, uncorrupt, and efficient government.

## References

1. Cai, Fang, and Dewen Wang. 1999. "China's Economic Growth: Labor, Human Capital and Employment," in Wang Xiaolu and Fan Gang (eds) *Sustainability of China's Economic Growth: Cross-century Review and Prospects* Wang Xiaolu, Fan Gang, Economic Science Press, Beijing.

2. Fan, Gang, and Xiaolu Wang. 2001. *NERI Index of Marketization of China by Province* (2000), Economic Science Press.

3. Fan, Gang, Xiaolu Wang, and Hengpeng Zhu, various years, *NERI Index of Marketization of China by Province*, Economic Science Press.

4. Fan, Gang, Xiaolu Wang, and Hengpeng Zhu. 2003. "Marketization Index of China by Regions." *Economic Research*, no. 3: 9 – 19.

5. Li, Fuqiang, Zhiqing Dong, and Linhui Wang. 2008. "Categorized Experiences of Institutional Drive, Factor Contribution and China's Economic Growth Momentums." *Economic Research*, no. 4: 53 – 65.

6. Justin, Yifu Lin, and Xifang Sun. 2008. "Banking Sector Structure and Economic Growth." *Economic Research*, 9th Issue: 31 – 45.

7. Liu, Ruiming, and Lei Shi. 2010. "Double Efficiency Loss of State-owned Enterprises and Economic Growth." *Economic Research*, no. 1: 127 – 137.

8. Liu, Yong. 2010. "Transport Infrastructure Investment, Regional Economic Growth and Spatial Spillover Effect." *China Industrial Economy*, no. 12.

9. Man, Yanyun, and Xinye Zheng. 2010. "Should China Cut Taxes and Which Taxes." *First Financial Daily.*

10. Shen, Kunrong. 2004. "Financial Development and China's Economic Growth-Empirical Study Based on Regional Dynamic Data." *Management World*, no. 7.

11. Wang, Feng, Zongyi Zhang, and Jijun Tang. 2008. "Corporate Marketization, Opening-up and Conditional Convergence of China's Economic Growth Conditions." *World Economy*, no. 6.

12. Wang, Xiaolu. 1999. "China's Rural Industrialization and Economic Growth." *Reform*, no. 5: 97 – 106.

13. Wang, Xiaolu. 2000. "Sustainability of China's Economic Growth and Institutional Reform." *Economic Research*, no. 5: 3 – 15.

14. Wang, Xiaolu, Gang Fan, and Peng Liu. 2009. "Changing Economic Growth Pattern and Growth Sustainability in China." *Economic Research*, no. 1: 4 – 16.

15. Wu, Yanbin. 2008. "Indigenous R&D, Technology Import and Productivity." *Economic Research*, no. 8: 51 – 64.

16. Xu, Xianxiang, Xianbin Wang, and Yuan Shu. 2007. "Local Officials and Economic Growth." *Economic Research*, no. 9: 18 – 31.

17. Yao, Xianguo, and Haifeng Zhang. 2008. "Disparities of Education, Human Capital and Regional Economic Disparity." *Economic Research*, no. 5.

18. Zhang, Man, and Liutang Gong. 2005. "Tax Division, Fiscal Decentralization and China's Economic Growth." *Economics* (Quarterly), Volume 5, no. 1.

# Chapter 6

# China's Marketization since WTO Accession*

**Li Xiaoxi (李晓西)**

**School of Economics and Resource Management, Beijing Normal University, Beijing, China**

**Abstract**: After joining the World Trade Organization (WTO), China has intensified market-oriented reforms in the renminbi exchange rate, foreign trade, utilization of foreign funds, and foreign-related economic laws etc. In terms of ownership structure, a move from state-owned asset management system policies toward non-publicly-owned enterprises has been undertaken. In addition, China has proactively reformed the government administration system.

**Keywords**: WTO, China, reform and opening-up

The *Protocol on the Accession of the People's Republic of China* took effect on December 11th, 2001, and China officially became the 143rd member state of the WTO. This began a new era for China's reforms that brought far-reaching influences on all aspects of the economy and society. Through honoring its WTO committeements, China has intensified its market-oriented reforms, and has steadily improved marketization in all aspects of its socialist market economic system.

## I. A New Era of Market Reforms

Since its entry into the WTO, China has integrated well into the world multilateral economic and trade systems. The country has begun the groundwork for a socialist market economic system, successfully survived the global financial crisis, and maintained rapid economic growth. Meanwhile, it has transitioned from promoting internal economic balance to balance far beyond, from being an enforcer to creator of international rules, and shifting from shouldering responsibility merely as a developing country to being committed as an established economic power.

---

* Corresponding author: lxx62205058@263.net.

By 2010, China's economic aggregate surpassed Japan to rank second in the world and foreign trade volume exceeded USD2.9 trillion placing it third in that category. Facts show that after joining the WTO, China created a successful paradigm for emerging economies to assimilate into open global economic systems.

In the wake of the third technological revolution of the 21st century, the world economy witnessed accelerated growth in the service sector. In China, the service trade is constantly increasing its share of economic growth. As of 2009, out of over 160 service trade sectors as classified by the WTO, China had opened 104 sectors, or 62.5%, close to the average for member states of 108. Among them, 54 sectors allow single proprietorship and 23 allow foreign funds-holding joint ventures.

The WTO accession has also improved China's trade environment, and governmental behaviors have been better disciplined with international rules widely applied. Despite China's entry into the WTO, some European countries and the U.S. still consider China a "non-market economy" and adopt discriminative anti-dumping policies and non-tariff barriers. Since 2001, the School of Economics and Resource Management of Beijing Normal University has carried out a project to measure the marketization level of China. After eight consecutive years of measurement, a series of "*Report* [*s*] *on China's Market Economic Development*" were drafted. According to these reports, the level of marketization for the eight years from 2001 to 2008, as measured by five areas of criterion and 33 indicators, is 64.26%, 64.76%, 67.07%, 70.53%, 76.03%, 75.19%, 76.19% and 76.40%, respectively. From these figures, China's market economic development stages and characteristics are generalized.

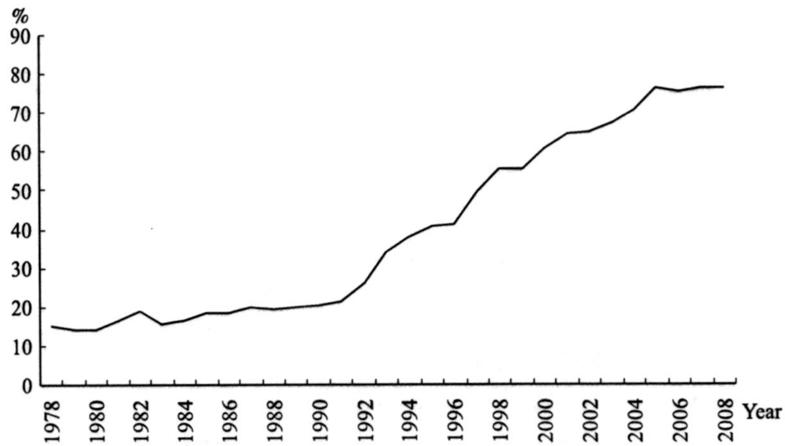


**Figure 1: Trend of the Marketization Index after Market Reforms**

By the end of 2010, China has approved the establishment of 710,000 foreign-owned enterprises and utilized USD1,051.2 billion foreign funds, ranking first among developing countries. Foreign-owned enterprises have become an important part of China's economy. Disputes as witnessed in the last century on whether China should utilize foreign funds or the amount of utilization are now less prominent due to a shift in academicians' focus to issues of how to deal with foreign funds and improve the quality of China's utilization of foreign funds in the context of globalization.

A milestone in China's opening-up after WTO attainment lies in the transition from stressing "introduction of foreign funds" to attaching equal importance to "going-global." As a basic state policy in the new era of market reforms, the "going-global" strategy encourages enterprises to go-global through direct investment, undertaking foreign contracted projects, or cooperating with foreign countries in labor services. Broadly speaking, channels of investing abroad also include economic and technological assistance to foreign countries, export, and utilization of foreign funds abroad, etc. In the *Blueprint for the 10th Five-Year Plan* (2001 – 2005) released in 2001, the "going-global" strategy is listed together with foreign trade and utilization of foreign funds as one of the three major pillars for development of an open economy.

In foreign exchange administration China has transitioned to a balanced management in order to bring the role of interest and exchange rates into play in a market-oriented economy. Furthermore, the country has advanced renminbi convertibility under the capital account, and focused on preventing and mitigating global financial crisis and promoting the balance of international payments. In addition, since integration into the global economy in 2001, China's renminbi exchange rate formation mechanisms have been brought under reform. There are two key points in reforming the renminbi foreign exchange regime. First, a market-oriented exchange rate formation mechanism that meets the requirements of China's economic development should be established. Second, the reform should minimize the risks of macro-economic fluctuations brought about by exchange rate adjustments, especially in speculation of the renminbi or output fluctuations in the short run.

On July 21st, 2005, the People's Bank of China announced that China would adopt a managed floating exchange rate regime based on supply and demand in the market and adjusted in relation to a bundle of currencies. Moreover, China explicitly proposed that renminbi exchange rate reform should proceed in a self-initiated, controllable and gradual manner. Accordingly, the market plays a more prominent role in forming more elastic and effective exchange rates and promotes a balance in international payments.

The managed floating exchange rate regime aims to stabilize the renminbi exchange rate at a reasonable and balanced level. Actually, since exchange rate reform was initiated in 2005, the renminbi has appreciated by over 20%. The renminbi central parity rate dropped below 8.0 in July 2006, below 7.0 in April 2008 and stood at 6.6 in January 2011. Entering the year 2000, the global economy was at a low water mark, with growth in some Western developed economies having stalled or receded. China not only maintained rapid economic growth but also withstood the global financial crisis successfully. To protect their interests and reverse their trade deficits, developed countries like Japan and the U. S. persistently placed pressure on the renminbi. In June 2011, China's central bank again released the approach of reforming the exchange rate, reiterating that China should follow a market-based regime to be adjusted in relation to a bundle of currencies which can reflect the exchange rate more accurately. Accordingly, the government regulates and maintains the renminbi exchange rate at a reasonable equilibrium level. Managed fluctuation of the renminbi exchange rate serves a fundamental need of the economy: macro-economic control and balance of international payments. Nonetheless, exchange rate reform should be carried out in a gradual manner to allow time for the restructuring of enterprises and to mitigate the impact of a floating renminbi. Of special note is that close attention should also be paid to supervision and management of short-term speculative capital lest large-scale flows of hot money disrupt the domestic financial system.

China's entry into the WTO provided a broader space to participate in international economic affairs. In the 21st century, regional economic cooperation, mainly in the form of free trade agreements, flourished as an important way for countries to facilitate trade investment. The China-ASEAN Free Trade Area (CAFTA), established in 2002, represents China's accelerated pace of regional economic cooperation. In the report of the 17th National Congress of Communist Party of China, it was officially proposed to proactively implement the free-trade-area strategy. So far, only a rudimentary framework has been created, but the aim is to establish new regional economic cooperation organizations.

Progress has been made in building foreign-related economic laws, rules and regulations. In accordance with WTO rules, between 1999 and 2002 China streamlined over 2,300 articles of laws and regulations. Many laws and regulations governing the import and export of goods were abolished or revised. Additionally, the country unveiled the *Regulations Governing Import and Export of Goods* as well as supporting regulations for ten departments, covering all aspects of the import-and-export administration system. According to the notice released by the central government in September 2001, local governments at all levels also sorted out over 190,000 articles of laws, rules and policies based on the principles of alignment, non-discrimination and transparency. In July 2004, China released the revised *Foreign Trade Law*, which changed the foreign trade examination and approval system into the registration system and initially established a three-level legal framework for foreign trade administration. Further, steps have been taken to improve laws and regulations protecting intellectual property rights. Aligned, non-discriminatory and transparent foreign-related economic laws, rules and regulations can better serve the socialist market economy and balance the relationship between domestic and foreign economic subjects. China has taken the initiative in formulating new international trade conventions to fulfill its commitment as a large WTO member state. During 2003 – 2004, China ratified approximately 74 treaties and agreements with foreign countries as well as seven additional treaties ratified in 2009.

## II. Improvement in Ownership Structure①

Over the last decade, China has reformed the state-owned asset administration system and unveiled policies supporting non-publicly-owned enterprises. In the report of the 16th National Congress

① Corporate data and analysis are mainly extracted from "Marketization of Enterprises", a paper by Gao Minghua and Du Wencui and incorporated as Chapter II of the Report on China's Market Economic Development in 2010.

of Communist Party of China, it was pointed out that except for in a few areas, China should proactively develop the shareholding system and a mixed-ownership economy. This shift represented a new philosophy for China's economic reforms.

Established in 2003, the State-owned Assets Supervision Commission began the task of transforming the state-owned asset management system. Marketization of state-owned enterprises (SOEs) is manifested in four aspects: market-oriented reform, diversification of property rights, marketization and disciplining of operational behavior, and establishment of the withdrawal mechanism. The purpose of marketization is to make an SOE an autonomous legal entity operating and competing in the market independently, assuming sole responsibility for its profits and losses, and seeking self-development and self-reliance. Under the precondition of state ownership, the central and local governments perform duties as an investor on behalf of the state, enjoy both the owner's equity and obligations, and manage state assets in conjunction with management of personnel and affairs. Under this system, the property right of large SOEs becomes diversified, which improves the withdrawal mechanism and increases SOE profits. The *Property Law of the People's Republic of China*, passed in March 2007, specifies the investor and the owner of equity. According to the Property Law, for enterprises invested in by the state, the State Council and local governments perform duties as the investor on behalf of the state and enjoy the investor's equities pursuant to laws and administrative regulations. Here, the concept of "enterprises invested by the state" is replaced by "SOEs," defining clearer the relationship between the state and SOEs and marking a milestone of reform of SOEs.

Diversification in the property rights of SOEs is an important part of China's economic marketization. For example, the main orientation in the restructuring of SOEs is to build a limited liability company or a company limited by shares (including Sino-foreign joint ventures and joint ventures with Hong Kong, Macao & Taiwan). Restructuring enables SOEs to be free from administrative intervention and to be run in accordance with market rules.

The standardized governance organization of the parent company of large state-owned corporations also exemplifies marketization of enterprises. Table 1 shows the percentage of large state-owned corporations whose parent company has established a board of shareholders, board of directors and board of supervisors.

**Table 1: Restructuring of the Parent Company of Large State-owned Corporations during 2007 – 2008**

| Year and item / Registration type of the parent company | 2007 | | 2008 | |
|---|---|---|---|---|
| | Number | Percentage in the total number of state-owned corporations (%) | Number | Percentage in the total number of state-owned corporations (%) |
| The total number of corporations | 2,926 | | 2,971 | |
| The total number of large state-owned corporations* | 1,315 | 100 (44.94) | 1,293 | 100 (43.52) |

Continued

| Registration type of the parent company \ Year and item | 2007 | | 2008 | |
|---|---|---|---|---|
| | Number | Percentage in the total number of state-owned corporations (%) | Number | Percentage in the total number of state-owned corporations (%) |
| The number of un-restructured large state-owned corporations | 304 | 23.12 | 305 | 23.59 |
| The number of restructured large state-owned corporations ** | 1,011 | 76.88 (100) | 988 | 76.41 (100) |
| In which: wholly state-owned company ** | 662 | (65.48) | 646 | (65.38) |
| Absolutely-controlled and relatively-controlled SOEs ** | 349 | (34.52) | 342 | (34.62) |

Source: Compiled and computed based on 2007 – 2008 data from State Statistics Bureau: *Large Corporations of China* (2008 – 2009), Beijing, China Statistics Press.

Note: The figure in brackets in the line marked in * refers to the percentage in all large corporations. The figure in brackets in the line marked in ** refers to the percentage in restructured large state-owned corporations.

**Table 2: Establishment of Governance Organization in the Parent Company of Large State-owned Corporations during 2007 – 2008**

| Year and item | 2007 | | 2008 | |
|---|---|---|---|---|
| Type of the parent company of establishment of governance organization | Number | Percentage in the total number of restructured state-owned corporations (%) | Number | Percentage in the total number of restructured state-owned corporations (%) |
| The total number of restructured state-owned corporations | 1,011 | 100 | 988 | 100 |
| Already established the board of shareholders * | 315 | 80.98 | 313 | 91.52 |
| Already established the board of directors | 956 | 94.56 | 942 | 95.34 |
| Already established the board of supervisors | 808 | 79.92 | 799 | 80.87 |
| Wholly state-owned company | 622 | 100 | 646 | 100 |
| Already established the board of shareholders | 40 | 6.04 | 52 | 8.05 |
| Already established the board of directors | 613 | 92.60 | 605 | 93.65 |

Continued

| Year and item | 2007 | | 2008 | |
|---|---|---|---|---|
| Type of the parent company of establishment of governance organization | Number | Percentage in the total number of restructured state-owned corporations (%) | Number | Percentage in the total number of restructured state-owned corporations (%) |
| Already established the board of directors | 478 | 72.21 | 481 | 74.46 |
| Absolutely-controlled and relatively-controlled SOE | 389 | 100 | 342 | 100 |
| Already established the board of shareholders | 315 | 80.98 | 313 | 91.52 |
| Already established the board of directors | 343 | 88.17 | 337 | 98.54 |
| Already established the board of directors | 330 | 84.83 | 318 | 92.98 |

Source: compiled and computed based on 2007 – 2008 data from State Statistics Bureau: *Large Corporations of China* (2008 – 2009), Beijing, China Statistics Press.

* : According to the *Company Law*, wholly state-owned companies do not establish a board of shareholders, although there are some exceptions. Data here on the number/percentage of companies with a board of shareholders excludes wholly state-owned companies.

With regard to policies supporting non-publicly-owned enterprises, the most influential strategy arrangement is *Several Opinions of the State Council on Encouraging, Supporting and Guiding Development of Non-publicly Owned Economy like Individual and Private Economy* formulated by the State Council in 2005. It explicitly set out 36 key policies to develop a non-publicly-owned corporate economy. Driven by these policies, the non-publicly-owned economy developed rapidly into a new growth engine. Specifically, in the non-public sector, the numbers of companies became bigger, registration funds increased, employment grew, the economic aggregate enlarged, technical advance accelerated, corporate governance improved, the threshold for market access was lowered, foreign trade expanded, and economic returns and tax proportion increased.

The Chinese Government's efforts to advance marketization of enterprises in order to adapt to WTO rules can also be reflected in policies released in 2007. In that year, the China Securities Regulatory Commission released *Administrative Measures on Information Disclosure by Listed Companies*, the State Assets Administration Committee released the *Notice on Further Building Central Government-led Companies' Corporate Legal Consultant System Centering around the General Legal Consultant*, and the Ministry of Finance and Ministry of Science and Technology released *Interim Measures for the Administration of Guidance Funds for Promoting Venture Capital Investments in Small and Medium-Sized Technology Enterprises*. The 5th meeting of the 10th National People's Congress (NPC) passed the *Property Law of the People's Republic of China* and the 29th meeting of the Standing Committee of the NPC passed the *Anti-monopoly Law of the People's Republic of China*. These policies were very significant in establishing a mature market and improving the investment environment. Of special note is the proposition, as stated at the 17th National Congress of the Communist Party of China in October 2007, about "developing a mixed-ownership economy based on the modern property right system" and "an environment for the economy of all ownerships to compete on an equal basis and to promote each other."

By the end of 2008, the number of enterprises in the country totaled 9.7 million, 99% of which were small and medium-sized enterprises (SMEs). SMEs contributed over 60% of GDP, over 50% of tax revenue, 70% of import and export trade and 80% of urban employment opportunities. They also absorbed 50% of lay-offs from SOEs, 70% of incremental employed people and more than 70% of migrant worker employment. In terms of independent innovation, SMEs owned 60% of patents, 74% of technological innovations and 82% of newly-developed products. Subsequently SMEs occupied a great share of the whole national economy. ①

In 2008, the ratios of the number of private enterprises and their registered funds among the primary, secondary and tertiary industries were 2.05 : 30.82 : 67.13 and 1.96 : 36.71 : 61.33, respectively. Apparently, the tertiary industry was the focus of development for private enterprises. In 2008, the number of private enterprises and their registered funds increased by 19.25% and 25.03% versus 2007, respectively. See Table 3.

**Table 3: The Number and Percentage of Private Enterprises in Three Industries during 2007 – 2008**

| Industry \ Year | 2007 | | 2008 | | Growth rate in 2008 | |
|---|---|---|---|---|---|---|
| | The number of private enterprises | Registered funds (RMB trillion) | The number of private enterprises | Registered funds (RMB trillion) | The number of private enterprises (%) | Registered funds (%) |
| Total | 5,513,100 (100) | 9.39 (100) | 6,574,200 (100) | 11.74 (100) | 19.25 | 25.03 |
| Primary | 115,600 (2.10) | 0.18 (1.91) | 135,100 (2.05) | 0.23 (1.96) | 16.87 | 27.78 |
| Secondary | 1,814,300 (32.91) | 3.52 (37.49) | 2,026,300 (30.82) | 4.31 (36.71) | 11.68 | 22.44 |
| Tertiary | 3,583,200 (64.99) | 5.69 (60.60) | 4,412,800 (67.13) | 7.20 (61.33) | 23.15 | 26.54 |

Note: The figure in brackets refers to the percentage.

Source: Compiled and computed based on 2007 – 2008 data from *Yearbook of China Industrial and Commercial Administration* (2008 – 2009), Beijing, China Industry and Commerce Press.

① China Enterprise Confederation and China Entrepreneur Association: Report on Development of China's Small and Medium-sized Enterprises 2008 – 2009, Beijing, China Economy Publishing House.

The development of high-tech industries reflects the scientific advance and international competitiveness of a country. Furthermore, expansion of non-SOEs in this industry is a key element measuring development of the non-state-owned sector of the country. See Table 4.

**Table 4: Aggregate and Percentage of Non-SOEs in the High-tech Industry during 2007 – 2008**

| Year | | 2007 | 2008 |
|---|---|---|---|
| The number of enterprises | The total number of non-SOEs | 19, 700 | 24, 074 |
| | Percentage in the total number of enterprises in the high-tech industry (%) | 91. 56 | 93. 25 |
| | Percentage of foreign-funded enterprises in the total number of enterprises in the high-tech industry (%) | 37. 31 | 36. 01 |
| The number of workers | The total number of workers at non-SOEs | 7, 231, 813 | 8, 201, 230 |
| | Percentage in the total number of workers in the high-tech industry (%) | 85. 79 | 86. 81 |
| | Percentage of workers at foreign-funded enterprises in the total number of workers in the high-tech industry (%) | 60. 49 | 60. 20 |
| Total output | Total output of non-SOEs (RMB billion) | 1, 011. 803 | 5, 060. 059 |
| | Percentage in total output of the high-tech industry (%) | 8. 782 | 8. 864 |
| | Percentage of total output of foreign-funded enterprises in total output of the high-tech industry (%) | 6. 269 | 7. 025 |
| Profit and tax | Total profit and tax of non-SOEs (RMB100 million) | 2, 89. 01 | 3, 44. 844 |
| | Percentage in total profit and tax of the high-tech industry (%) | 86. 19 | 85. 70 |
| | Percentage of profit and tax of foreign-funded enterprises in total profit and tax of the high-tech industry (%) | 55. 95 | 52. 94 |

Source: Compiled and computed based on 2007 – 2008 data from State Statistics Bureau, National Development and Reform Committee and Ministry of Science and Technology: *Statistical Yearbook of China High-tech Industry* (2008 – 2009), Beijing, China Statistics Press.

Note: Small-sized industrial enterprises below the designated size from the nuclear fuel processing industry, the information chemical product manufacturing industry and other high-tech industries are excluded here.

In 2010, the State Council unveiled *Opinions of the State Council on Encouraging and Guiding Healthy Development of Private Investment*. Incorporating 36 measures to advance China's marketization, it proposed that China broaden the scope of private investment and encourage and guide private funds to invest in basic industries and infrastructures, utilities, policy-related house construction, social undertakings, financial services, trade circulation and national defense industries. It also proposed to guide restructuring or alliance of private capital and encourage them to participate in reforming SOEs and to push independent innovation and transition of private enterprise, encourage and guide private enterprises to participate in international competition, create a favorable environment for private investment and strengthen service to and disciplining of private investment. In October 2011, the State Council again unveiled nine measures to support small and micro-sized enterprises, adding to care for non-SOEs.

## III. Reform of the Government Administrative System

China's entry into the WTO also exerted significant influence on the government administration system. First, it pointed out a clearer direction for transformation of government functions, namely that government administration should cater to the market economy. The WTO has 142 member states, over 120 of which are market economies and ten are transitioning towards a market economy. WTO principles, agreements and treaties are all based on the market economic system. This directly increased government's determination to reduce administrative examination and approval. Consequently, all items for examination and approval without legal basis or which ought not to be directly presided over by the government should be cancelled.

Over the same period, local governments cleaned up and cut items for approval through four rounds of reform. Up to 1, 992 items for administrative approval have been cancelled or adjusted by all competent authorities, accounting for over 50% of the original 4, 100 items. For example, through nine clean-ups, Chengdu City of Sichuan Province cut over 90% of such items from 1, 166 to 107, and nearly four-fifths of items for non-administrative license examination and approval from 1, 006 to 210. More local governments have begun establishing government affairs centers and administrative service centers offering "one-stop" administrative examination and approval services and are promoting online examination and approval.

Entry into the WTO made social management more transparent. The Chinese Government has taken several measures to improve policy transparency, such as distributing government bulletins free of charge in many areas. Meanwhile, the Government has established relevant institutions to enhance communication with the WTO in order to improve transparency in foreign affairs. For example, China's WTO Notification and Enquiry Center under the Ministry of Foreign Trade and Economic Cooperation was responsible for explaining and disseminating China's foreign trade policies and measures to the outside world.

Enterprises that previously were governed unjustly are now treated equally. Further, previous direct government intervention has been replaced by indirect administration. Over the last decade, the Chinese government has strived to promote the WTO's non-discriminatory principles. Not only WTO member states but also their enterprises should be treated equally in terms of market access, trade conditions and trade dispute resolution. The government has endeavored to break industrial monopolies and encourage competition while cultivating and regulating social intermediaries which organize social governance and maintain a sound environment for market competition. From 2008, China's authorities in industry and commerce have strived to improve government administration from three aspects, including carrying out administration based on laws and policies, standardizing administration and streamlining procedures. Also, permanent mechanisms for market regulation have been established, including "enterprises credit category supervision," "Hotline 12315 for consumer complaints and reports," "access and withdrawal of goods" and "registration of individually-owned business by hierarchs and category."

A clearer boundary between the function of government and laws has been established after entry into the WTO. Over the last decade, the Chinese Government has endeavored to reduce administrative intervention and standardize government behaviors in strict accordance with law. In 2007, the State Council released the *Regulations on Disclosure of Government Information*, an important step in building a law-based government. This has led to improving government transparency, safeguarding the public's right to information, building a positive government administration style, and preventing corruption. The government's administrative power was briefly reinforced during the recent period of global financial crisis, but less government intervention is now an overall orientation. An important driving force here is marketization. Meanwhile, China has strived to ensure transparency, consistency and continuity between legislation and the enforcement of laws.

After entry into the WTO, more consideration has been given to international practices and interaction between domestic and overseas economies when macro-economic policies are formulated. Over the last decade, the Chinese Government has aligned itself with international practices in terms of statistics approach and data use, a matter concerning the government's public trust. Meanwhile, it also proactively established various bilateral or multilateral mechanisms for communication with the outside world.

Generally speaking, the function of the Chinese government has not been diluted after entry into the WTO. The country has been transformed from a planned economy to a market economy. However, although administrative powers in the area of administering the operation of enterprises have weakened, the administration of public policies has strengthened. Demands on government administration have increased rather than diminished, but the requirement on the administration approach has changed. Even though there is improvement still to be made, entry into the WTO has improved the government administration system, which in turn has smoothed the progress of China's integration into the WTO.

It took 15 years of negotiations, but it has been proven that China made a wise choice in joining the WTO. China is building a society ruled by law and is increasing its economic and political stability. It is an event of great and far reaching implications.

## References

1. Chen, Zongsheng *et al.* 2009. "Research on Essence and Feature of China's Economic Development Miracle Based on the Analysis of Route Evolution since Reform and Opening-up." *Journal of Finance and Economics* (5).

2. Chi, Fulin. 2010. *The Second Reform: China's Road to a Powerful Nation in the Next* 30 *Years*. Beijing: China Economic Publishing House.

3. Fan, Gang *et al.* 2007. *China's Market Index-Progress of Marketization in Different Areas*. Beijing. Economic Science Press.

4. Fan, Hengshan. 2006. "Progress and Key Tasks of China's Reform on Administrative System." *Review of Economic Research* (74).

5. Jiang, Xiaojuan. 2007. "A New Era of China's Pro-Market Reform: Integrate into the Global Economy in a Balanced Way." In *Forward Position in Economics* (6).

6. Li Xiaoxi, ed. 2011. *Research Report on China's Economy and Resource Management* 2011: *China's Economic Transformation*. Beijing: Encyclopedia of China Publishing House.

7. Li Xiaoxi *et al.* 2008. *Thirtieth Anniversary of China's Pro-market Reform: Marketization*. Chongqing. Chongqing University Press.

8. Li Xiaoxi *et al.* 2010. *The Effects of Global Financial Crisis on China's Economic Growth and Employment*. Beijing: Science Press.

9. Li Xiaoxi. 2008. "Advancing Chinese Market Reform and Some Consideration." *Reform* (4).

10. Li Xiaoxi. 2009. China's Marketization Progress. Beijing. People's Publishing House.

11. Li Xiaoxi. 2010. *Review of China's* 30 *Years of Prof-market Reform*. Beijing: Beijing Normal University Press.

12. Lu, Zhongyuan. 2006. *Reflections during the Reform Era*. Beijing. People's Publishing House.

13. School of Economics and Resource Management. 2010. *Report of China's Market Economy Development*. Beijing: Beijing Normal University Press.

14. Wu, Jinglian. 2008. *Collection of Wu Jinglian's Works on Reform*. Beijing. China Development Press.

15. Zhang, Zhuoyuan. 2009. 60 *Years of China's Economics*. Beijing: China Social Sciences Press.

Chapter 7

# Shifting to a Market-Based Wage-Setting Mechanism for Low-Skilled Labor: Macroeconomic Effects*

**Yang Ruilong (杨瑞龙) and Yang Jidong (杨继东)**

**The Academic Group in Renmin University of China for *Analyzing and Forecasting on China's Macroeconomy*①, Beijing, China**

**Abstract**: After the emergence of a severe labor shortage in 2004, wage levels for rural migrant workers (hereafter referred to as "migrant workers") ceased their long time stagnation and began to rise rapidly. This rise can be attributed to various factors, such as demographics, business cycles, policy, and China's economic structure. As the wage-setting mechanism for migrant workers changes from traditional minimum wage to negotiated pricing rules subject to the reservation wage, China's economy indicates that it is embracing a new era of rapid wage increases. Changes in China's income distribution will bring opportunities to the turning point of Kuznets "Inverted-U" Curve, and allow China to narrow its significant income gap. These changes will transform China's economic growth model from one that is export and investment-dependent to one that is driven by domestic consumption.

**Keywords**: low-skilled labor, wage-setting mechanism, income distribution

## I. Introduction

After the emergence of a severe labor shortage in 2004, wages levels for migrant workers, which had been consistently steady, began to trend upward rapidly. Later, as the financial crisis hindered global economic growth, China's economy recovered quickly, and its low-skilled labor market simultaneously underwent a structural change. As labor shortages began to replace an over-supply of migrant workers, wage levels were pushed up. More than twenty local governments raised

* Corresponding author: yangjidong2001@163.com.

① Interim result of "Structural Basis for Sustainable Domestic Demand and Policy Study on Macroeconomics" supported by Projects of the National Social Science Foundation of China.

minimum wage by approximately 20%, and private and foreign-funded companies raised wages by as much as 40%①. In early 2011, labor shortages became even more severe, and firms in China's central and western regions and eastern one began to compete over migrant workers. This paper attempts to answer the following questions: How should we interpret these wage hikes? Are they temporary? What will be the impact on China's economy?

## II. China's Low-skilled Labor Market Is Shifting from Overall Surplus to Structural Surplus

The eruption of labor shortage not only signifies the turning point of China's low-skilled labor market from overall surplus to structural surplus, more importantly, it announces the transformation of wage-setting mechanism in China's low-skilled labor market.

### (I) Migrant Worker Wages and the Financial Crisis

Migrant worker wages began rising in 2004 and have risen for the past six years, with their annual growth rate surpassing 12.4%. Even during the financial crisis, wages continued to rise by 10% annually. Under China's urban-rural dual employment structure, migrant worker wages grew faster than urban workers': between 2001 and 2005, the growth rate reached 64%②. Figure 1 depicts the growth rate of actual wages in manufacturing industries since 1985. After 2000, wage growth stayed at approximately 10%.

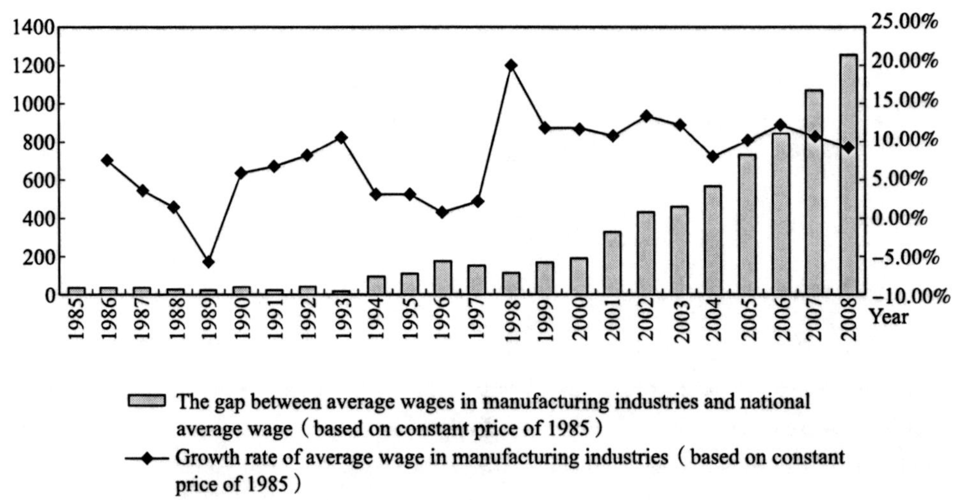


**Figure 1: Growth Rate of Average Wages in Manufacturing Industries**

---

① Without special remarks, all the data in this paper comes from National Bureau of Statistics, OECD database and Institute of Economic Research of Renmin University of China.

② Refer to the sub-report of China's Macroeconomic Analysis and Forecast (third season of 2010) conducted by Renmin University of China.

### (Ⅱ) Labor Supply and Demand

In March of 2010, the number of employed migrant workers increased by 3.5% from the previous year. Between January and March of 2010, hiring in industrial enterprises grew by 2.9%, while the demand-supply ratio for labor in urban areas reached 103%, higher than the average level of 95%. At the same time, labor shortages appeared in coastal and certain inland regions (Figure 2). Regional statistics also showed that the labor demand-supply ratio in China's eastern, western, and central regions all surpassed 95%, becoming the highest ratios in history. Furthermore, according to the National Bureau of Statistics' *Monitoring Survey Report on Migrant Workers (2009)*, the number of migrant workers working outside of their hometowns fell 8.9% in eastern regions, especially in the Pearl River Delta, and had fallen by 22.5% compared with 2008.

**Figure 2: Employment in Urban Areas**

### (Ⅲ) Demographic Changes

Although working-age labor still makes up a large proportion of China's total population, the growth rate of the labor pool has slowed significantly in recent years. According to predictions by the U.N., China's gross dependency ratio will have hit its historical low in 2010; afterwards, it will begin to climb, and the proportion of working-age labor in the general population will start to decline (Figure 3).

### (Ⅳ) Worsening Labor Disputes

Private and foreign-funded companies have raised recruitment wage levels for migrant workers, as have local governments at various levels. We see evidence of labor disputes in the following examples: (1) workers in China's north and south striking over suicides at Foxconn, China's largest

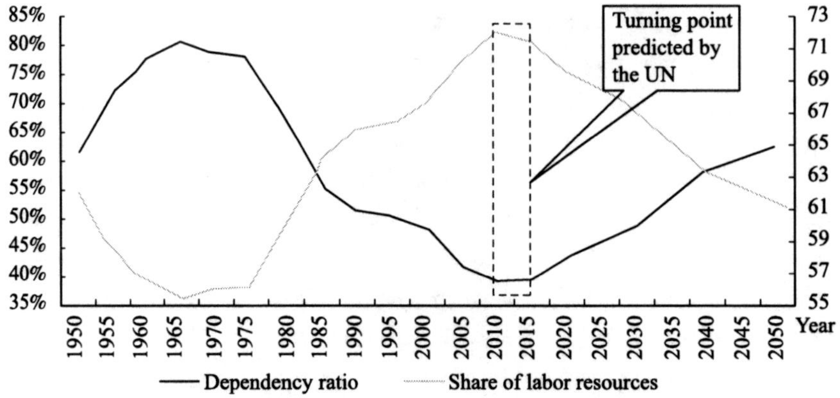


**Figure 3: China's Population Structure**

employer in the manufacturing sector; (2) more than twenty local governments' raising minimum wages by as much as 20%, exceeding annual nominal GDP growth for the first time; and (3) private and foreign-funded companies beginning to raise wages for migrant workers by as much as 40%. See Figure 4.

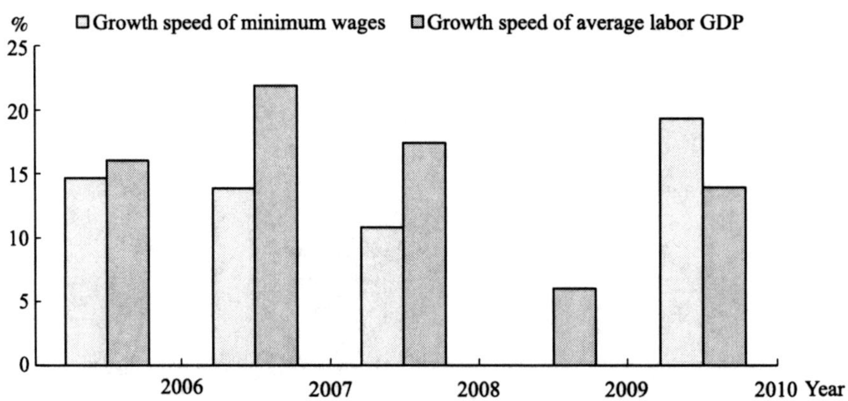


**Figure 4: Minimum Wage and Nominal GDP: Growth Rates**

The most striking evidence of labor disputes are the growing number of cases and workers involved. According to the Labor Statistics Yearbook of 1996, China heard 48,121 labor dispute cases in 1996, which involved 189,120 workers. In 2008 these numbers rose to 693,465 cases and 1,214,328 workers, 14.4 and 6.4 times the number of disputes and workers, respectively, as in 1996. See Figure 5.

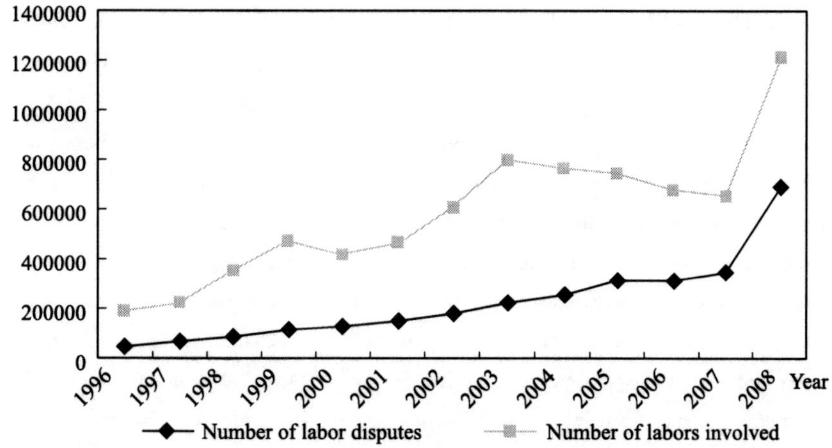


**Figure 5: Labor Dispute Cases and Number of Workers Involved**

## III. Changes in China's Wage-setting Mechanism

The round of wage hikes that began in 2004 not only signifies a structural turning point for China's low-skilled labor market but also heralds a shift of the wage-setting mechanism.

### (I) Reservation Wage Pressure

Reservation wage has risen in tandem with China's economic development and has pushed up the price of low-skilled labor. Reservation wage rises for farmers who stay in rural areas for the following reasons: first, rural reform has put agricultural income on a steady upward trajectory. Under the household contract land system, farming income is equal to per capita agricultural output within a family. When there is surplus labor, marginal productivity is low; however, per capita output increases when surplus labor is transferred to non-agricultural industries. While the government previously suppressed the rise of agricultural income by levying agricultural taxes and forcing down grain prices, recent measures such as the abolition of China's 2600-year-old agricultural tax in 2006, grain subsidies, and a minimum grain price policy have enabled farmers' per capita income to rise. Moreover, we foresee that China will continue to carry out rural reforms in order to sustain the momentum of agricultural income growth.

Second, as resources become constrained, rising resource prices will drive up living costs in urban areas, transportation fare and transferred costs. One survey found that the three primary expenses for migrant workers were food, clothing, and transportation and communication expenses, with food expenses making up two thirds of total expenses. Between 2003 and 2008, food prices have risen by 48%, with an average annual increase of 10%, which in turn drove up the cost of living in cities and, in turn, the reservation wage.

### (II) The End of Unlimited Elasticity of Rural Labor Supply

Currently, China's agricultural labor force is roughly 300 million, while China's employment rate has reached 40% which means that there is still significant surplus labor in the agricultural sector. Despite a steady stream of laborers leaving the agricultural sector for other industries, grain output jumped from 430 million tons in 2003 to 530 million tons in 2008.

It should be noted that the existence of surplus labor does not mean that China's labor supply curve is of unlimited elasticity, as described by the Lewisian Dual Economic Structure Theory. This theory traditionally assumes that due to extremely low income in agricultural sectors, the opportunity cost for rural surplus labor to work in industrial sector is essentially zero. Hence, as long as wages in the industrial sector surpass reservation wage and transfer cost in the agricultural sector, rural surplus labor will flood into cities. In fact, the opportunity cost for farmers working away from their hometowns has been increasing, especially under the dual urban-rural economic system. In essence, workers who migrate to cities but leave family in rural areas cannot assist in the intra-household division of labor, and family utility loss becomes increasingly evident.

According to Gary S. Becker's theory on the intra-household division of labor, individual's labor supply depends not only on the cost-benefit analysis of the labor market; more importantly, it depends also on needs within the household. Even if an individual can earn higher wages by working in a distant city, as long as the wage does not cover the loss of utility, the individual will choose to remain at home. In the early days of China's market reforms, the stay-at-home labor force in rural areas was large, and removing labor from the agriculture sector did not cause significant intra-household utility loss. Continued migration of workers, however, is unsustainable, as home labor would be quickly depleted. Domestic labor undertakes crucial roles in the household, including assisting with farm work, caring for aging parents, raising children, or safeguarding the house.

Currently, it is estimated that there are 250 million rural households and 300 million agricultural laborers in China. This means that on average, only 1.2 domestic laborers per household. If workers continue to migrate from rural to urban areas, many rural households would have no labor left at home. It is important to bear in mind that the precondition of addressing these constraints, however, is improvement in a household's economic situation. After the implementation of rural reforms in recent years, agricultural income and rural life have improved significantly, and farmers are less motivated to leave rural areas to look for work. From 1999 to 2008, net per capita income for rural households increased from 2,210 yuan to 4,761 yuan; calculated by comparable price, net per capita income grew 68%. If we assume 3.2 income earners per household, annual per household rural income would have reached 15,000 yuan by 2008[①].

For workers engaged in agriculture, the above changes mean that the urban labor is no longer without opportunity cost. In order to increase labor supply in urban areas, therefore, the industrial sector must compensate for such a loss of family utility with an incentive of higher wages. Thus, even if rural areas have abundant surplus labor, demand from the industrial sector will push up wages, twisting the labor supply curve into an upward and inelastic line.

① Refer to Ding Shouhai. 2010. "Rising wages and the labor surplus-reflections on the emergence of the Lewis turning point," China's Macroeconomic Analysis and Forecast Subreport (third quarter, 2010), Renmin University of China.

## (Ⅲ) The Industrial Sector Matures

As China established itself as a world leader in manufacturing, labor conditions have shifted from oversupply to structural shortages. As industrialization accelerates, furthermore, wages will increase. In 2010, the labor demand-supply ratio in western, eastern and central China surpassed 0.95, hitting an historical high. Wages will continue to rise for the following reasons: first, tremendous employment pressure forces China to accelerate its industrialization. Employment and industrial expansion are inexplicably linked in China's development model. Secondly, the resulting labor demand will drive the shift of China's wage setting mechanism from survival wages to market negotiated wages. In addition, as China may still be considered to be transitioning between the first and second phases of industrialization, pillar industries will shift from heavy manufacturing and chemical industries to higher value-added industries. This, in turn, extends the industrial chain, increases the output ratio of intermediate inputs, and diversifies the tiered production structure.

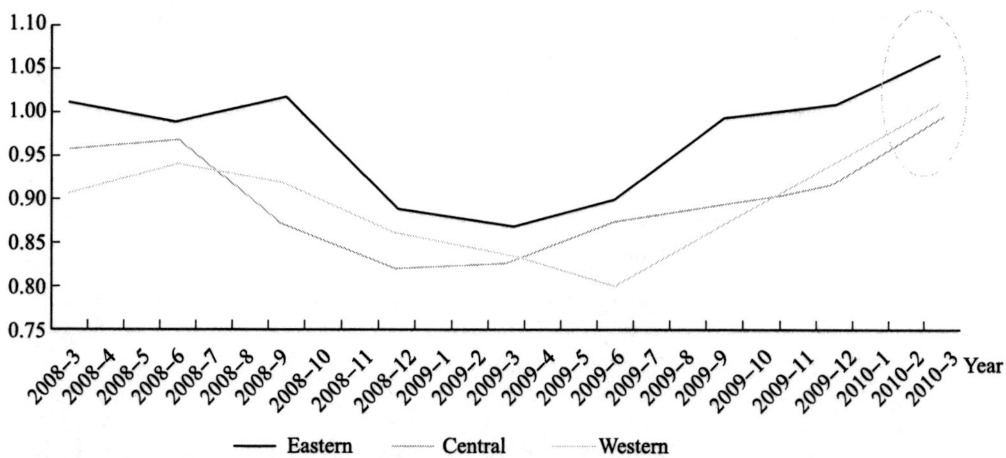


**Figure 6: Demand-supply Ratio of Labor in Various Cities**

## (Ⅳ) Heavy Industry, Chemicals, and Processing

When China's heavy industries, chemical industries, and processing industries reach their peak, wages, which were long suppressed, will begin to rise to market level. Factor price equalization theorem states that competition will force convergence of the relative prices of two identical production factors in the same market. In general, developed countries are rich in skilled labor, whereas low-skilled labor is relatively scarce. In developing countries, however, the opposite is true. In the global marketplace, developed countries enjoy comparative advantages in high-tech industries while developing countries enjoy comparative advantages in industries that employ low-skilled labor. Global trade strengthens demand for skilled labor in developed countries and, similarly, for low-skilled labor in developing countries. Wage increases for both skilled and low-skilled labor are reflected in labor factor pricing.

Figure 7 depicts changes in relative wages for skilled and unskilled workers in China and the

U. S. from 1998 to 2008. In the U. S. , free trade has driven down demand for low-skilled labor and, as a result, wages. In 1998, the average wage of a low-skilled laborer in the U. S. was 65% of the average wage for a skilled laborer. This figure dropped to 58% in 2008.

In contrast to the U. S. , wages of low-skilled labor in China form a U-shaped curve. From 1998 to 2003, the average wage ratio of China's low-skilled laborers to its skilled labor dropped from 71% to 64%, which to some extent reflected excessive depressed wages. After 2003, demand for low-skilled labor increased in tandem with the expansion of heavy industries (processing, chemical manufacturing), and this ratio rose from 64% in 2003 to 72% in 2008, an obvious "recovery".

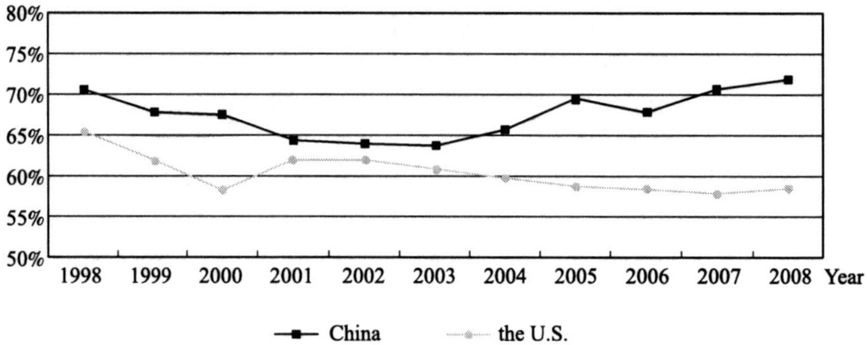


**Figure 7: Relative Wages for Skilled and Unskilled Workers in China and the U. S. , 1998 – 2008**

Note: Relative wage is calculated using the ratio of average wages in low-skilled industries to that in skilled industries. For industrial skill levels, please refer to OECD (2007). Data on the U. S. comes from the US Bureau of Economic Analysis, while China's data is calculated from the *China Labor Statistics Yearbook*.

## IV. Rising Migrant Wages, the Market Mechanism, and Resource Allocation

Rising wages for low-skilled laborers will lead to changes in wages for middle and high-end labor and will eventually strengthen the role of the market in determining factor pricing and resource allocation. As factor prices become market-based, the market mechanism will expand, creating new sources of growth in the Chinese market.

### (I) Income Distribution and the Industrial Structure

The rising price of labor in China, triggered by a rise in migrant worker wages, has led to changes in China's income distribution, spurring the rapid growth (doubling) of market-oriented income and accelerating the income-consumption curve. These kinds of reforms will inevitably cause China to shift from an economic situation in which wages account for a small proportion of GDP and consumption trails that of similar countries.

Despite a significant rise in real wages (10%), the proportion of total wages within China's

GDP is still declining. The constraint of income on consumption impedes China's transition from an export-driven economy to one driven by domestic consumption. When per capita GDP exceeds $3000, an economy is said to have entered the era of industrial consumption. In 2011, China's per capita GDP broke the threshold of $4000; according to traditional development models, demand for service industries in China will begin to accelerate. As the wage setting mechanism for migrant workers shifts to become more market-based, these effects will snowball.

### (II) Domestic Consumption

Urban residents' consumption has remained low, which has the effect of stifling economic growth. Rising labor income will increase urban residents' purchasing power and encourage migrant workers to settle in cities, thus accelerating the urbanization process and domestic consumption. In 2009, urban consumption expenses accounted for 35.6% of GDP, lower than average levels in low-income countries. Figure 8 reveals that since the implementation of pro-market reforms, consumption has contributed only slightly to economic growth. After 2000, in particular, consumption's contribution to economic growth dropped significantly.

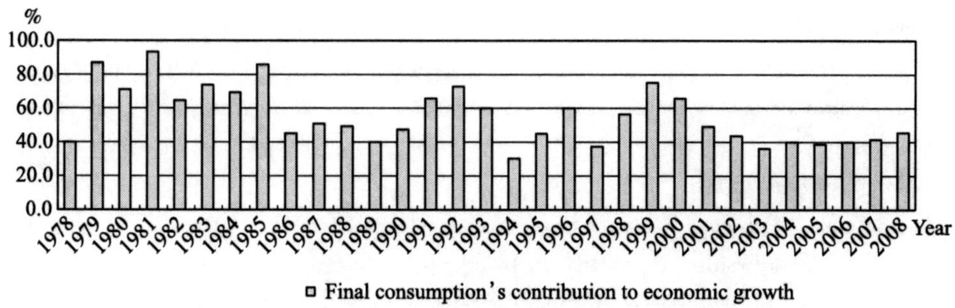


**Figure 8: Domestic Consumption and Economic Growth**

### (III) The Geography of Industry

China's economic development is marked with significant regional disparities, which are reflected in different wage levels among different regions. As shown in Figure 9, between 1996 and 2008, the annual average wage of eastern regions was strikingly higher than in central and western regions. Between 1996 and 2008, average manufacturing wages in the eastern region were, on average, 29.8% higher than in the western region, and 40.8% higher than in the central region. Even if regional economic disparities are taken into account, labor cost still varies substantially among regions. In 2008, for example, Beijing, Shanghai, and Fujian had relatively high labor costs while inland provinces such as Henan and Anhui had relatively low labor costs.

Transformation of the wage setting mechanism will squeeze out industries in China's eastern regions, causing industrial relocation to central and western regions. In fact, per capita wages in eastern and western regions have already been polarized due to labor supply issues: by 2009, per capita wages in China's eastern region were almost 30% higher than in central and western regions,

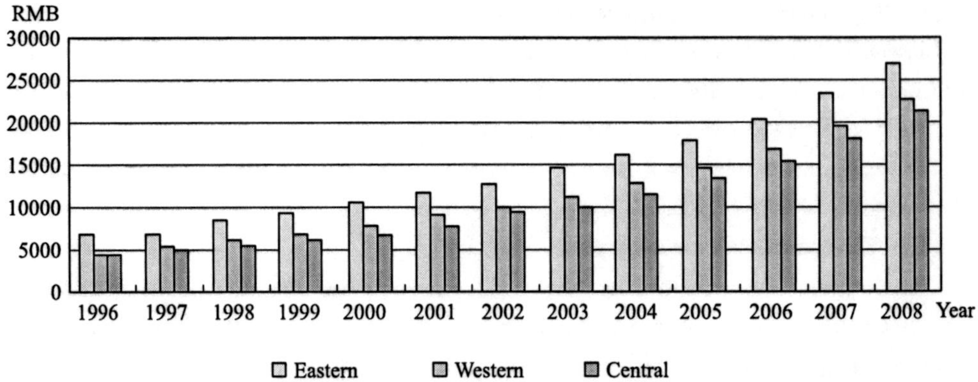


**Figure 9: Average Manufacturing Sector Wages Among Different Regions (1996-2008)**

while land prices were 40% higher. This directly resulted in the relocation of labor-intensive industries to western regions. In addition, worsening labor disputes in the east have also driven capital to flee to central and western regions. Notably, most inbound foreign capital in 2009 flowed to central and western regions.

Finally, in addition to per capita wage disparities among the eastern, central, and western regions, the unit labor cost in the eastern region was higher than in the central and western regions (2001 figures).

### (IV) Urbanization

The difficulty of economic restructuring lies in the lack of intrinsic drivers for market-oriented restructuring. In other words, under the dual economic structure, factor pricing failed to marketize. Economic growth is a process of lifting per capita income by restructuring production and employment. Transformation of the wage-setting mechanism promotes the market mechanism and upgrades the industrial structure. As China continues to shift away from manufacturing and heavy industry, the market will play a major role in resource allocation. In addition, as urbanization is positively correlated with urban per capita consumption, to the extent that the transformation of China's wage-shifting mechanism increases opportunities to shift from agricultural to industrial sectors, urbanization will accelerate.

## V. Conclusion and Policy Implications

The emergence of a migrant labor shortage in recent years not only signifies a structural turning point in China's low-skilled labor market, but, more importantly, it augurs the shift of the wage-setting mechanism from traditional survival-wage pricing rules to market-negotiated pricing subject to the reservation wage. Urbanization, industrialization, and institutional reform will inevitably push up compensatory wages, the reservation wage, and production efficiency. China's economy will embrace a new era, marked not only by rapid wage increase but also by the following characteristics:

First, profound changes in labor relations will usher in changes in income distribution—an opportunity to take advantage of the Kuznets reverse U curve inflection point. These changes also provide the opportunity to shrink income disparity and shift China's development model away from one that relies heavily on exports and investment to one driven by domestic demand and consumption.

Second, regional structural change will lead to the formation of a new dynamic between industry and agriculture, and by proxy, city and countryside.

Third, changes in factor price will begin to upgrade the industrial structure. China will begin to push value-added manufacturing while pushing forward industrialization, and climbing to a higher position on the global value and supply chains.

Fourth, profound changes in labor relations and rising wages will accelerate urbanization.

Fifth, rising wages and complementary policies will accelerate China's investment in human capital, which in turn will drive China's economic growth.

Based on our analysis, rising wages will drive the adoption of policies and market practices that ultimately promote China's economic growth. In order to further capitalize on the advantages brought about by rising wages, we offer the following policy suggestions:

First, promoting the adoption of the market mechanism in the low-skilled labor market (as well as for factor pricing in general) should be the core of future economic restructuring. Policies should leverage this pricing mechanism. Markets, in turn, should take the lead in equitable resource allocation, industrial upgrading, and innovation.

Second, to consolidate *the Labor Law*, policies should promote collective wage bargaining. In addition, government and industry should pay closer attention to labor disputes and provide training to migrant workers.

Third, the coexistence of surplus labor and rising wages calls for appropriate intervention from the government to prevent this market mechanism from singlehandedly suppressing employment. At present, government intervention is reflected mainly in industrial intervention and policy direction at the micro level. When migrant wages begin to accelerate rapidly and the market mechanism begins determining wages, the government should intervene to prevent wage pressure in the medium-and high-wage labor markets, as well as to cultivate and establish market mechanisms across industry.

## References

1. Arthur, Lewis. 1988. Dual Economy Theory (translated edition), Beijing Economic College Publishing House.

2. Cai, Fang. 2007. "The Turning Point of China's Economy and Its Challenges on Development and Reform." *China Social Sciences*, no. 3.

3. Cai, Fang. 2007. "Development of China's Labor Market and Changes in Employment." *Economic Research*, no. 7.

4. Ding, Shouhai. 2010. "Wage Rise against Labor Surplus-Comment on the Arriving of Lewisian Turning Point." China's Macroeconomic Analysis and Forecast Sub-report, Renmin University of China.

5. Hu, Jingbei. 1994. "Explanation on the Rise in Wages During Economic Growth." *Economic Research*, no. 3.

6. Han, Jun, Cui Chuanyi, and Aiai Fan. 2007. "Micro-survey on Rural Surplus Labor," Published on *Report on China's Population and Labor*, edited by Cai Fang, Social Sciences Publishing House.

7. John, C. H. Fei, John Fei, and Gustav Ranis. 2004. *Growth and Development from An Evolutionary Perspective* (translated edition), The Commercial Press.

8. Sun, Jiuwen, and Anjun Hu. 2010. "Inter-regional Industrial Transfer in the Context of Remuneration Increase," China's Macroeconomic Analysis and Forecast Sub-report, Renmin University of China.

9. Wang, Jiangui, and Shouhai Ding. 2005. "How Many Surplus Labors Remained in China's Agriculture?" *China Social Science*, no. 5.

# Chapter 8

# Regulation or Property Rights: The Effect of China's Coal Mine Shutdown Policy on Work Safety*

**Bai Chong-en (白重恩), Wang Xin (王鑫)**
**and Zhong Xiao-han (钟笑寒)**

**School of Economics and Management, Tsinghua University, Beijing, China**

**Abstract**: Since 1999, shutdown policy has been one of the most important industrial policies in China's coal mining industry. There have been many controversies surrounding this policy and its effect on coal mine safety. This paper summarizes, analyzes and tests two contradicting views of the effects of shutdown policy on the mortality rate of township-and-village coal mines. One view, the regulative view, believes that shutdown policy induces firms to increase safety input, thus decreasing mortality. The opposing view, the property rights view, argues that shutdown policy disturbs property rights stability and actually increases mortality. We built a simple theoretical model to analyze these contrasting rationales. The model uses the difference-in-difference method and provincial panel data from 1995 to 2005 to empirically test the policy's effects. Our findings are that shutdown policy significantly decreases output while also increasing mortality in township-and-village coal mines. This result is consistent with the property rights view.
**Keywords**: regulation, property rights, shutdown policy, coal mine safety, difference-in-difference

## I. Background

Beginning in 1998, the Chinese government implemented a series of industrial policies to force out small coal mines (mainly township-and-village coal mines)①, i. e. shutdown policy. Between 1999 and 2005, more than half of China's small coal mines have been closed under this policy. The

---

* Supported by: Key Project of National Social Science Foundation (10Zd&007); Research Project of Economic Development and Structure supported by Center for China in the World Economy, Tsinghua University.

① A small coal mine is one with annual output less than 300,000 tons and town or village ownership (Wang Fuqin, 2006). We do not differentiate small coal mines and township-and-village coal mines in the following analysis.

combined capacity of the closed mines exceeds a quarter of China's annual output①. The policy's extended duration, wide coverage, and strict enforcement have made it unprecedented in the coal industry and even across industries. The government has moved for ubiquitous application of this policy to address several problems within the coal industry: excessive capacity, unclear property rights, work safety, resource conservation and environmental protection. Shutdown policy is also meant to lay a solid foundation for the sustainable development of China's coal industry.

Has shutdown policy achieved its target? How has it affected the coal industry, especially those township-and-village coal mines it is meant to target? Of particular significance-is the policy effective in limiting mining accidents? Shutdown policy has stirred up a great deal of debate among scholars, policy-makers and stake-holders. Academically, this debate reflects a confrontation between regulative and property rights economics②.

Supporters of regulative economics argue that allowing a large number of private enterprises to develop public resources will inevitably lead to the tragedy of the commons. The government is therefore responsible for stepping in to regulate behavior and prevent this misuse of the country's natural resources. People supporting this view tend to blame weak regulation for mining accidents. Partially to blame in this equation are the high costs of regulation, especially information costs, as well as corruption among the local officialdom among other reasons.

Among the regulative view's supporters, Liu (2006) believes that mining accidents can be and have been effectively reduced by the responsible regulative bodies seeking out and punishing unsafe mining behaviors. However, the instinct of local governments to protect vested interests and collusion between regulative officials and mining owners has led to many accidents. Lin et al. (2008) argue that, without safety control measures and the proper administration of strict regulations, safety will not be prioritized. Given the costs and benefits of employing proper safety procedures combined with coal mining enterprises' preference for high risk, it is unrealistic to expect mine operators to behave safely absent proper oversight. This problem can be addressed by government ex-ante regulation and ex-post culpability assignment.

By estimating a VAR (Vector Auto-regression) model, Xiao et al. (2008) find that China's coal mine safety regulation is effective in the long-term but insignificant in the short-term. Xiao et al. conclude that this was due to perverse thinking on the part of coal miners, who deprioritize their own safety due to an increased investment in safety by their employer. Guo (2007) argues that an influx of rural migrant labor coupled with too few professionals and inadequate training has led to a drop in the quality of employees in the coal mining industry. This quality gap prevents safety from im-

① According to Caijing Magazine (2004), 33, 200 small coal mines were shut down in the first year of implementing the policy (1999), decreasing total capacity by 300 million tons compared to peak level in May 1995 by one fifth of annual output. These numbers were reported elsewhere as 31, 200 and 253 million tons (Lin Di et al., 2000). According to Li Yizhong, former Minister of the State Administration of Work Safety, in June 2006, "currently, there are 17, 000 small coal mines in China, a significant drop compared with the 61, 000 operational coal mines before implementing shutdown policy."

② Classic regulatory economic literature includes Spulber (1989) and Laffont and Tirole (1993). Classic literature on property rights economics in Chinese includes Ronald H. Coase, Armen A. Alchian, and Douglass C. North (1994).

proving. Guo concludes that the government should strengthen regulations in the labor market to combat this-regulations such as market entry permission, training, and labor unionization. Tao et al. (2007) find that enterprises which encounter mining accidents tend to be characterized by non-state ownership and incomplete certification as a result of rent-seeking behavior by the government. Collusion between enterprises and local officials wherein local officials become shareholders is particularly to blame. By coopting the very officials in charge of regulation, dangerous mines manage to continue operation.

Contrary to the regulative view is the property rights view. Supporters of this view stress that unclear property rights are the root of the problem, even while they acknowledge that the tragedy of the commons may come into play. That is to say, enterprises whose property rights are clearly defined will proceed with efficient investment, including necessary safety precautions and responsible resource exploitation. Clear property rights reduce the need for government regulation as incentives are properly aligned. Property rights advocates believe that shutdown policy may discourage enterprise investment, encouraging short-term and serious rent-seeking behaviors and actually inducing more accidents. Qian (2004) believes that township-and-village coal mines are motivated to reduce mine accidents out of benign self-interest. Shutdown reduces the returns on safety investment for a mine operator, thus inducing more accidents in the short-term. Tang and Guo (2006) also believe that inadequate safety investment is the major cause of mine accidents, and that such short-term behaviors come from the current property rights regime.

Zhong (2011) discovered a clear negative correlation between output and mortality based on data from China's coal industry spanning nearly ten years. He also proved a negative effect of exogenous shock of output (supply) on mortality, therefore indirectly validating the property rights view. Tan and Tang (2004) built a decision-making model for enterprises engaged in exhaustible resource exploitation. They argue that excessive property rights distortions, especially the separation of ownership and management rights, is the fundamental reason for China's frequent mine accidents.

Since reform and opening, Chinese government policy on the coal industry has swung back and forth between strengthening regulation and strengthening property rights. Before and after the implementation of shutdown policy, the government rolled out a series of regulative measures for township-and-village coal mines. The most typical regulations are the so-called four licenses (a mining permit, coal production license, business license and owner qualification certificate), to which was later added a fifth (the safety output license). The state also promulgated and revised the *Mineral Resources Law* and other laws that give private enterprises the rights to resources and, to some extent, allow property rights to operate properly (Liu Can, 2009; Caijing Magazine, 2002)

However, Chinese law stipulates that the state has the ownership of mineral and other natural resources while private enterprises have only "limited" rights of use. In this context, state regulative policies run counter to property rights protection. Excessive regulation and heavy-handed policies have affected miners' expectations with respect to the stability of their mining rights, which make the conflict between regulation and property rights even more significant.

This paper analyzes these two schools of thought using both theoretical and empirical means.

The theoretical model constructed in this paper shows that shutdown policy may reduce mortality through regulation and also increase mortality through its effect on property rights. Only by adopting and strictly adhering to a moderate regulative regime can shutdown policy have positive effects.

In our empirical research, we look at panel data in different provinces for key state-owned coal mines and for township-and-village coal mines from 1995 to 2005. Our goal is to test the effect of shutdown policy on township-and-village mine output and mortality by using the difference-in-difference method. Results show that shutdown policy has significantly reduced the output of township-and-village coal mines, suggesting that the policy has effectively cut overcapacity. However, results also show that the policy has clearly raised mortality for township-and-village coal mines, especially in the short term. This is more consistent with the property rights view, and also suggests that shutdown policy may not just fail to achieve its safety objectives but actually run counter to them.

The rest of paper is structured as follows: Section II elaborates on the regulative effect and property rights effect of shutdown policy using a simplified theoretical model and establishes a hypothesis for testing; Section III introduces our empirical model and data and presents empirical test results; Section IV carries out several robustness tests; and lastly are conclusions and policy suggestions.

## II. Theory and Hypothesis

We call outcomes following from the regulative view the regulative effect and outcomes following from the property rights view the property rights effect. This paper focuses on enterprises' safety inputs, mortalities and outputs. We separately analyze these two effects and then combine the two to consider how enterprises respond to shutdown policy. Next, we consider extending the model to analyze the price effect of shutdown policy.

### (I) Basic Model

The basic model is based on Bojas' (2000) firm behavior model on dangerous work. This basic model considers endogenous firm safety input and then mortality is determined by firm safety input. Workers earn compensation wages. ①, and then a township-and-village coal mines' maximum profit can be defined as:

$$\operatorname*{Max}_{w,\,L,\,Y,\,s}\ pY-(w+s)L$$

Meeting the following requirements:

$$Y=F(L) \tag{1}$$

$$U(w,\ m)\geqslant U_0 \tag{2}$$

$$m=m(s) \tag{3}$$

Here $p$ stands for coal price (exogenous), $Y$ for output, $w$ for worker's wages, $s$ for safety in-

① The model also implies the following assumptions: workers' labor input differentiates in quantity but not in quality or initiative (Xiao Zhixing *et al*, 2008; Guo Chaoxian, 2007); all township enterprises are homogeneous, which stresses the average impact of the policy, ignoring adverse (or positive) selection effects.

put per unit worker[①], $L$ for labor input, and $m$ for mortality per worker (per unit labor time). $U_0$ denotes workers' reservation utility (exogenous). Constraint (1) denotes output function, condition (2) denotes workers' reservation utility (i. e., differentials of compensating wages), and condition (3) is the determined pattern of mortality.

In addition, the output function satisfies the following standard assumptions:

$$F'(L)>0,\ F''(L)<0,\ F(0)=0,\ F'(0)=\infty,\ F'(\infty)=0$$

Workers' utility function is quasi-concave, and utility increases with wages but decreases with mortality:

$$\frac{\partial U(w,\ m)}{\partial w}>0,\ \frac{\partial U(w,\ m)}{\partial m}<0$$

Mortality decreases with safety input with decreasing marginal effects:

$$\frac{\mathrm{d}m}{\mathrm{d}s}<0,\ \frac{\mathrm{d}^2 m}{\mathrm{d}s^2}>0。$$

## (II) The Regulative Effect

The regulative effect refers to the successful promotion of safety inputs by the threat of shutdown of coal mines. Assuming that the regulative effect prompts enterprises to provide safety input required by the government $s=\bar{s}$[②], maximum profits for an enterprise can be described as:

$$\underset{w,\ L,\ Y}{\mathrm{Max}}\, pY-(w+\bar{s})L \qquad (4)$$

This can be solved with two steps. First, solve for the minimum cost (average labor):

$$AC_L(\bar{s})\equiv \underset{w}{\mathrm{Min}}AC_L=w+\bar{s} \qquad (5)$$

Meeting above constraints (2) and (3) to arrive at the following conclusions (verification process omitted):

Proposition 1 (regulative effect): mortality decreases and labor cost increases given higher regulation ($\bar{s}$) (i. e. $AC_L'(\bar{s})>0$).

Second step: consider maximum firm profits. According to the above equation, marginal costs rise in tandem with labor costs. When regulation rises, the output of township-and-village coal mines falls under market equilibrium. To summarize the regulative effect on output and mortality, we propose the following hypotheses:

Hypothesis 1 (regulative effect): Shutdown policy leads to a decrease in both output and mortality in township-and-village coal mines.

## (III) The Property Rights Effect

Unstable property rights induced by shutdown policy are referred to as the property rights effect. We assume that safety inputs should be decided before operation (while wages and output can be decided during operation). We further assume shutdown probability as $1-\theta$, $\theta\in(0,\ 1)$ (as-

① Here we assume that safety input has no "Scale Effect", which means that the output $Y$ won't affect the relationship between $m$ and $s$. If safety input has "Scale Effect", it is obvious that the firms have more incentive to increase safety input. However, the analysis and result as follows won't change no matter whether safety input has "Scale Effect" or not.

② Here we implicitly assume that an enterprise's optimal safety input is smaller than the level called for by safety regulations. This is a precondition for shutdown policy even existing in the first place.

suming that it costs for the enterprise to supervise safety inputs, so shutdown probability is less than one), thus enterprise profit maximization is:

$$\underset{Y,L,w,s}{\text{Max}}\ \theta(pY - wL) - sL \tag{6}$$

Fulfill constraints (2) and (3). The key assumption of the objective function is that safety input has already been completed before wage expenditures, therefore safety input must be made regardless of shutdown. This assumption highlights the impact of unstable property rights. The above maximization problem can therefore become:

$$\text{Max}\ pY - AC_L L \tag{7}$$

Wherein $AC_L$ is the resolution of following labor cost minimization equation:

$$AC_L(\theta) \equiv \underset{w,s}{\text{Min}} AC_L = w + \frac{s}{\theta} \tag{8}$$

Again, fulfill constraints (2) and (3). We are focusing on the effect of property rights stability (i. e. $\theta$, or shutdown probability $1-\theta$). We then arrive at the following proposition:

Proposition 2 (property rights effect): A higher probability of being shutdown (or lower property rights stability) will lead to less safety inputs and result in a higher mortality rate and higher labor costs (i. e. $AC_L'(\theta) < 0$).

For the verification process please refer to Zhong (2011), Part 1 of Proposition 2①. Intuitively, when the probability of being shut down rises, an enterprise's return on safety inputs decrease compared with wage expenditures. This induces enterprises to meet workers' reservation utilities by cutting safety inputs and increasing wages.

Similarly, rising labor costs will push up marginal costs, leading to diminished total output for township-and-village coal mines. We therefore develop the below hypotheses.

Hypothesis 2 (property rights effect): Shutdown policy has resulted in increased mortality and decreased output in township-and-village coal mines.

### (Ⅳ) Regulation or Property Rights: The Enterprise's Countermeasures

We have analyzed via two slightly different models the possible regulative effect and property rights effect brought about by shutdown policy. We will combine these two models in the following analysis. We assume the existence of safety policy standards that dictate when and if an enterprise is shutdown: an enterprise should meet safety input $\bar{s}$ to avoid being shut down, otherwise there will be a shutdown with probability $1-\theta$②③. Shutdown policy is defined as the government's efforts to simultaneously raise regulative level $\bar{s}$ and shutdown probability $1-\theta$. $AC_L(\bar{s})$ denotes the labor cost when an enterprise chooses to invest in complying with safety regulation $\bar{s}$ (and thus face zero probability of being shutdown), while $AC_L(\theta)$ refers to the labor cost when an enterprise chooses to evade safety regulations (and thus face probability of shutdown$1-\theta$). In the latter scenario, safety

① According to Zhong (2011), safety input is called effective safety input and denoted by $\bar{s}$.

② More generally, we can assume that shutdown probability decreases with increase in safety input; however, this will increase complexity in analysis without changing the qualitative conclusion.

③ If there isn't any threatening policy prior to the shutdown policy, we can order $\bar{s}=0$, $\theta=1$.

input $s$ is endogenous. We then arrive at the following propositions:

Proposition 3 (shutdown policy effect): When shutdown policy increases regulation level to $\bar{s}$ and shutdown probability to $1-\theta$, two situations materialize: (i) when $AC_L(\bar{s}) > AC_L(\theta)$, shutdown policy leads to fewer safety inputs and higher mortality; (ii) when $AC_L(\bar{s}) < AC_L(\theta)$, shutdown policy leads to greater safety inputs and lower mortality.

The verification process for Proposition 3 is omitted①.

Different application of shutdown policy may lead to different mortality rates: If regulation is excessively strict but the probability of being shut down is low, then enterprises will work to evade regulation and higher mortality results in line with the property rights effect. But if the opposite is true and the probability of shutdown is high, enterprises will comply with regulation, mortality declines, and the regulative effect is prominent. Although both outcomes start with shutdown policy, the results are mutually exclusive and only one can truly work. This conclusion is of theoretical significance as we work to isolate and analyze the two effects.

Two special cases merit consideration. The first is when the probability of shutdown $(1-\theta)$ is not correlated to safety input $(s)$② . In this case, only the property rights effect will come into play and shutdown policy will inevitably lead to higher mortality. Another extreme case involves extremely strict and strong safety regulations so that, if an enterprise fails to meet regulations, the probability of shutdown is 1. In this scenario, the regulative effect will be the only observable effect, enterprises will choose to meet safety regulations, and mortality will decrease (or remain the same if it is already very low).

### (V) The Price Effect

The above analysis ignores the price effect, another likely by product of shutdown policy. The shutdown policy leads to a smaller number of coal mines operating in the market, thus reducing supply and raising coal prices. Facing higher coal prices, the remaining coal enterprises (state-owned coal mines and township-and-village coal mines that are still operational) will increase output.

How does the price effect impact mortality in township-and-village coal mines? In the analysis and models above, the price effect does not alter mortality because mortality depends only on safety inputs and safety inputs are not dependent on output. To include the price effect in our analysis we need to extend the above model to include the direct impact of output on mortality. Therefore we modify equation (3) to:

$$m = m(s, Y) \tag{3'}$$

Fulfill the following requirements:

$$\frac{\partial m(s, Y)}{\partial s} < 0, \quad \frac{\partial m(s, Y)}{\partial Y} > 0, \quad \frac{\partial^2 m(s, Y)}{\partial s^2} > 0, \quad \frac{\partial^2 m(s, Y)}{\partial Y^2} > 0, \quad \frac{\partial^2 m(s, Y)}{\partial s \partial Y} < 0$$

---

① Refer to: Bai Chongen et al. 2011. "Regulation and Property Rights: Analysis on Shutdown Policy's Effect on Coal Mine Safety." *China Soft Science*, No. 10, P. 16.

② Reasons may be originated from the multipurpose of the shutdown policy, not limited to safety issues (for example, heavy pollution, neighboring to state-owned coal mines etc). In addition, mines in the same region or even in the neighboring regions will be implicated in rectification once there is mine accident (Caijing Magazine, 2010)

In this situation, mortality decreases as safety inputs increase and with diminishing marginal returns; mortality increases with increased output and with increasing marginal returns. The cross effect of safety input and output on mortality is negative, indicating that the negative effect of output on mortality decreases with higher safety input, and the positive effect of safety inputs on mortality rises with rising output. Our conclusions, therefore, are as stated below.

Proposition 4 (output and mortality): As output increases, the safety inputs will increase, however, the change of mortality per unit of output is not clear. ① (For the verification process, please refer to Zhong (2011), Part 1 of Proposition 1.)

Now let us relate this back to enterprise profit maximization. The rising prices that result from shutdown policy will induce those mines still operational to increase output, and mortality may either increase or decrease as a result. Synthesizing this analysis brings us to the following hypothesis:

Hypothesis 3 (price effect): Shutdown policy's effect on mortality in township-and-village coal mines is uncertain, but shutdown policy will result in lower output overall.

## III. Empirical Testing

### (I) Empirical Strategy and Quantitative Equations

Though all three schools of thought argue that shutdown policy reduces the overall output of township-and-village coal mines, verifying the effect of shutdown policy on output cannot verify which effect itself is at play. Rather, verifying the effect of shutdown policy on output is a kind of precursor to a more complete understanding of shutdown policy. The three different predictions stemming from the three different effects differ on their interpretation of shutdown policy's effect on mortality: the regulative effect expects a decline in mortality; the property rights effect expects a rise in mortality; and the price effect is indeterminate on mortality. Given how vague the price effect is, we attempt to use demand control variables to better isolate the price effect's impact on mortality. ②.

We apply the difference-in-difference method for analysis. Specifically, we order township-and-village coal mines as the experimental group, and key state-owned coal mines as the control group③. The equation is as follows:

$$Y_{ijt} = \beta_0 + \beta_1 \cdot Sector_j + \beta_2 \cdot Policy_{jt} + (\gamma_1 + \gamma_2 \cdot Sector_j) \cdot X_{it} + year_t + prov_i + \varepsilon_{ijt} \qquad (9)$$

① It should be noted that the model introduced for unit labor mortality and the final proposition itself uses per unit output mortality. It can be proved that the probability of an increase in per unit output leading to a jump in mortality per unit of output is greater than the probability of an increase in per unit output leading to a jump in mortality per unit of labor. . Even if per unit labor mortality remains unchanged with output, as output per labor diminishes, unit output mortality still rises with output (refer to Zhong, 2011, Appendix 1, A3).

② For a single enterprise, there is no difference between a rise in the coal price due to shutdown policy and a rise in coal price due to demand, therefore the effect of the demand variable and the price effect are the same.

③ There is also a category of local (non-key) state-owned coal mines, the size and ownership of which is between these two. The market share and output of these firms is very small and therefore not considered in this paper (see Figure 1).

Within this equation, subscript $i$ denotes province, $j$ denotes type of enterprise (key state-owned coal mine or township-and-village coal mine), and $t$ denotes the year. Explained variable $Y$ denotes output (logit) and mortality. $Sector_j$ denotes dummy variables relating to enterprise type①. $Policy_{jt}$ measures the effect of shutdown policy and is the core variable in this paper②. $X$ represents other control variables. We used several control variables to describe demand and supply; the demand side control variables include regional GDP, the proportion of value-added coming from heavy industry in the value-added of the secondary industry (referred to as the proportion of heavy industry), traffic mileage (waterways, roads and railway), and the average winter temperature. Supply side control variables include rainfall and farming incomes. Variable $prov_i$ and $year_t$ measure the fixed effects of province and year, controlling for the effect of a given province given time and national macroeconomic fluctuations, respectively. Regional GDP and farming income adopt the CPI index to eliminate inflation in different regions. In addition, except for average temperature (possibly negative) and dummy variables, the values of all variables were processed as logarithms③.

### (Ⅱ) Data and Descriptive Accounting

We use inter-provincial panel data between 1995 and 2005. Coal output and mortality rates are sourced from the *China Coal Industry Yearbook*. 1995 is the first year where a death toll across different kinds of coal mines in China is available, while 2006 is the last year where coal mine deaths were thusly recorded④. We have made some amendments to the available statistics as they are not consistent across different years (for details, refer to Zhong (2011), Appendix). The mortality variable denotes death toll per million tons of coal, which can be obtained through dividing coal output by the total number of deaths⑤. Data for value-added in heavy industry is sourced from the *China Industrial Economics Statistical Yearbook*⑥, and other control variable data is all sourced from the *China Statistical Yearbook*.

Figure 1 shows the output of various types of coal mining enterprises before and after 1998. There is a substantial decline in the output of township-and-village coal mines after 1998 which gradually picked up after 2001. The output of key state-owned coal mines has been rising steadily.

---

① $Sector_j = 1$, if $j$ = township coal mines, otherwise $Sector_j = 0$.

② $Policy_{jt} = 1$, if and only if $t > 1998$ and $j$ = township coal mines.

③ This paper does not introduce coal price as an explanatory variable for two reasons: first, the price of coal is endogenous, and regression in this paper can be viewed as a reduced form of supply and demand. Second, the regional price of coal is not available.

④ Mortality by region but not by type and mortality by type but not by region are both available until 2006. After that, mortality rates by region or type across the country are no longer available.

⑤ Mortality per million tons of coal is a universally recognized index in the coal industry. In China, this index is obtained by dividing total output by the death toll rather than through sampling. The defect of this index is that it is vulnerable to the double error in death toll and output. However, no alternative statistical indicators are available.

⑥ Since the *China Industrial Statistical Yearbook* was not published in 1996, 1999, 2000, and 2005, and the 2001 edition did not have data on the value-added for heavy industry, value-added data for heavy industry by province in 1995, 1996, 1998, 2000 and 2004 are not available. However, this data can be estimated through data smoothing with data from 1994 – 1997, 1997 – 2001, and 2003 – 2005.

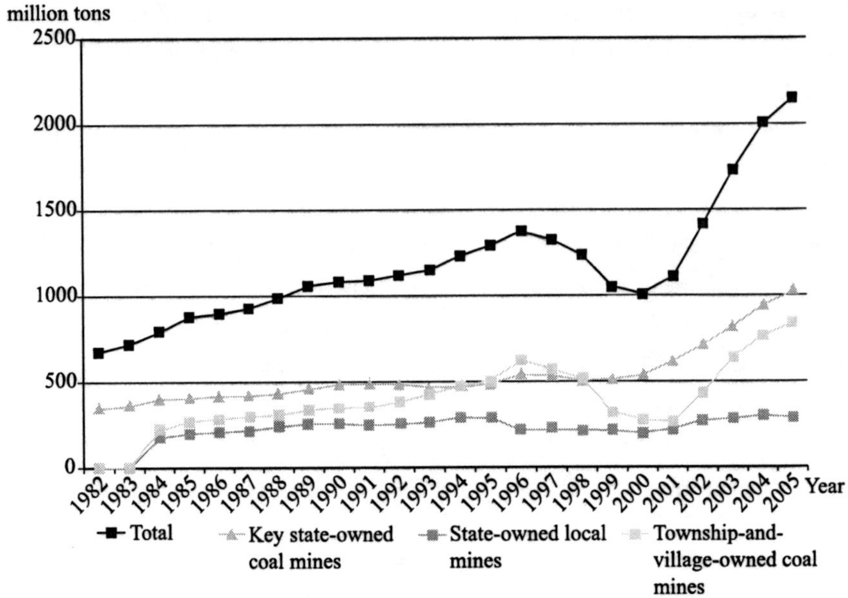


**Figure 1: The Output of Coal Mines of Various Types**

Figure 2 shows the mortality of different types of coal mines before and after 1998①. There is an observable increase in township-and-village coal mine mortality after the implementation of shutdown policy. Though this trend reversed itself, mortality remains high on average compared with levels before shutdown policy was implemented. This result intuitively suggests that the property rights effect ought to prevail (See Table 1).

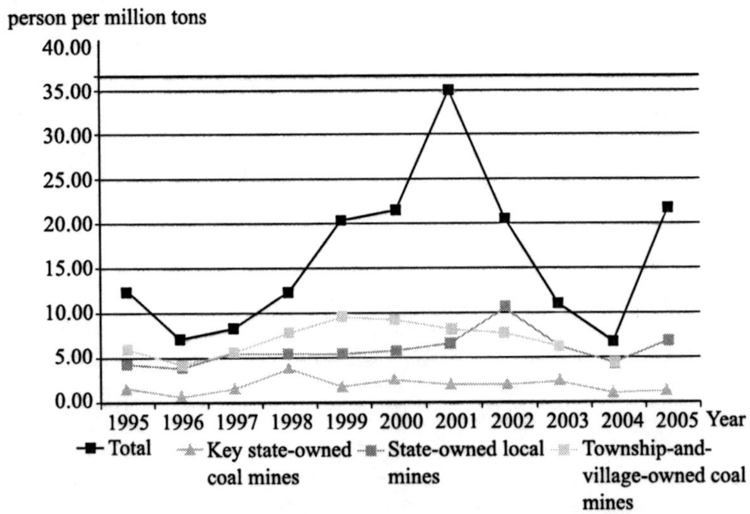


**Figure 2: The Output of Coal Mines of Various Types**

① In order to eliminate systematic errors, mortality in this paper is calculated by the average mortality of all provinces.

**Table 1: Statistics for Major Variables**

| Variables | Unit | Observation value | Average value | Variance | Minimum | Maximum |
|---|---|---|---|---|---|---|
| Total output | Ten thousand tons | 294 | 5, 296. 07 | 7, 372. 75 | 51. 00 | 55, 416. 00 |
| Output of key state-owned coal mines | Ten thousand tons | 239 | 2, 992. 30 | 3, 802. 70 | 42. 00 | 25, 621. 00 |
| Output of township-and-village coal mines | Ten thousand tons | 287 | 1, 973. 21 | 3, 106. 81 | 1. 00 | 21, 252. 00 |
| Output of township-and-village coal mines (amended) | Ten thousand tons | 287 | 2, 372. 01 | 3, 552. 52 | 2. 04 | 23, 417. 37 |
| Total mortality | Person/one million tons | 294 | 7. 54 | 7. 13 | 0. 27 | 57. 24 |
| Mortality of key state-owned coal mines | Person/one million tons | 238 | 2. 57 | 4. 31 | 0. 00 | 50. 60 |
| Mortality of township-and-village coal mines | Person/one million tons | 287 | 16. 51 | 33. 02 | 0. 00 | 400. 00 |
| Mortality of township-and-village coal mines (amended) | Person/one million tons | 287 | 12. 28 | 23. 21 | 0. 00 | 302. 51 |
| GDP | 100 million yuan (current prices) | 590 | 3, 380. 63 | 3, 013. 01 | 165. 31 | 20, 213. 57 |
| Regional CPI | 100 by year 1995 | 594 | 110. 96 | 5. 90 | 100 | 130. 30 |
| Proportion of heavy industry | Expressed as a decimal | 590 | 0. 48 | 0. 16 | 0. 20 | 0. 87 |
| Power consumption | 100 million kilowatt-hours | 588 | 529. 89 | 397. 39 | 69. 02 | 2, 673. 56 |
| Value-added of major coal consumption industries | 100 million (current prices) | 590 | 338. 29 | 388. 26 | 16. 73 | 2, 850. 66 |
| Thermal power | 100 million kilowatt-hours | 590 | 437. 31 | 385. 45 | 17. 85 | 2, 117. 34 |
| Steel output | Ten thousand tons | 590 | 562. 66 | 764. 82 | 1. 08 | 6, 591. 12 |
| Cement output | Ten thousand tons | 590 | 2, 456. 96 | 2, 199. 84 | 63. 80 | 14, 425. 85 |
| The average winter temperature | Degrees Celsius | 594 | 3. 68 | 7. 69 | - 15. 43 | 17. 17 |
| Farm incomes | Yuan (Current prices) | 588 | 1, 331. 13 | 339. 23 | 723. 16 | 2, 382. 98 |

Continued

| Variables | Unit | Observation value | Average value | Variance | Minimum | Maximum |
|---|---|---|---|---|---|---|
| Rainfall | Average annual mm | 594 | 862. 79 | 495. 92 | 74. 90 | 2, 678. 90 |
| Railway mileage | Kilometer | 590 | 2, 354. 16 | 1, 284. 25 | 219. 00 | 6, 337. 30 |
| Waterways mileage | Kilometer | 524 | 4, 650. 18 | 5, 393. 84 | 26. 00 | 24, 793. 00 |
| Highway mileage | Kilometer | 590 | 54, 215. 11 | 27, 893. 47 | 8, 554. 00 | 167, 638. 00 |

Note: Total output and total mortality in the table is for key state-owned coal mines and township-and-village coal mines as well as state-owned local coal mines.

### (III) Results

#### 1. Shutdown Policy's Effect on Coal Output.

We begin by testing shutdown policy's effect on coal output using equation (9) with results shown in Table 2A. Column (1) shows results without any control variables, which demonstrates that the coefficient of the interaction variable of policy-time dummy variable and enterprise dummy variable are negative. Column (2) has added provincial fixed effects, and with this addition results becomes significantly negative (−0. 464), with output declining by $| e^{-0.464} - 1 | * 100\% = 37.1\%$①. Column (3) has added other control variables, and the shutdown policy (cross-term) coefficient and significance are not affected. Among the control variables, GDP is seen to significantly affect coal output, wherein the elasticity is slightly larger than 1②, while other control variables are shown to be insignificant. Column (4) adds the cross-term for other control variables and also the enterprise dummy variable after considering different reactions to demand and supply between state-owned and township-and-village coal mines. The effect of shutdown policy thus becomes more evident and township-and-village coal mines' output is extended to $| e^{-0.659} - 1 | * 100\% = 48.3\%$. We therefore conclude that shutdown policy reduced output in township-and-village coal mines.

**Table 2: Shutdown Policy's Effect on Output and Mortality**

Table 2A: Shutdown policy's effect on output

| Explained variable / Explanatory variables | Log (Output) | | | |
|---|---|---|---|---|
| | (1) | (2) | (3) | (4) |
| Enterprise category dummy variables | −0. 077<br>(0. 108) | −0. 063<br>(0. 106) | −0. 096<br>(0. 120) | −22. 077***<br>(2. 695) |

① The value is too large, and changes in the variable's logit are not similar to the percentage shown here. The variable's percentage change in the following sections is also adjusted using this method.

② Due to limited space, detailed results for the control variable are not listed in Table 2. If necessary, readers may request these from the author.

Continued

Table 2A: Shutdown policy's effect on output

| Explained variable<br>Explanatory variables | Log (Output) | | | |
|---|---|---|---|---|
| | (1) | (2) | (3) | (4) |
| Policy time dummy variables × enterprise category dummy variables | -0.462***<br>(0.133) | -0.464***<br>(0.130) | -0.475***<br>(0.147) | -0.659***<br>(0.114) |
| Demand variables' effect on key state-owned coal mines [Prob > F] | | | | [0.000]*** |
| Demand variables' effect on township-and-village coal mines [Prob > F] | | | | [0.000]*** |
| Control variable | NO | NO | YES | YES |
| Cross-term of control variables | NO | NO | NO | YES |
| Year fixed effect | YES | YES | YES | YES |
| Province fixed effect | NO | YES | YES | YES |
| Sample number | 526 | 526 | 464 | 464 |
| $R^2$ | 0.1706 | 0.1706 | 0.1902 | 0.6471 |
| Prob > F | 0.0000 | 0.0000 | 0.0000 | 0.0000 |

Table 2B: Shutdown policy's effect on mortality

| Explained variable<br>Explanatory variables | Mortality | | | |
|---|---|---|---|---|
| | (1) | (2) | (3) | (4) |
| Enterprise category dummy variables | 7.864**<br>(3.562) | 6.677**<br>(3.346) | 6.471*<br>(3.846) | -132.749<br>(125.262) |
| Policy time dummy variables × enterprise category dummy variables | 9.485**<br>(4.448) | 10.933***<br>(4.105) | 12.694***<br>(4.722) | 13.025**<br>(5.315) |
| Demand variables' effect on key state-owned coal mines [Prob > F] | | | | [0.202] |
| Demand variables' effect on township-and-village coal mines [Prob > F] | | | | [0.446] |
| Control variable | NO | NO | YES | YES |
| Cross-term of control variables | NO | NO | NO | YES |
| Year fixed effect | YES | YES | YES | YES |
| Province fixed effect | NO | YES | YES | YES |
| Sample number | 525 | 525 | 463 | 463 |
| $R^2$ | 0.0919 | 0.1253 | 0.1395 | 0.2080 |
| Prob > F | 0.0000 | 0.0000 | 0.0000 | 0.0000 |

Note: Figures in brackets are the standard deviations of statistics. *, ** and *** indicate significance at 10%, 5% and 1%, respectively. Except for the proportion of heavy industry, average winter temperature and the dummy variable, control variables are logarithmic. R-squared value is amended $R^2$ for the non-fixed effect model and within $R^2$ for the fixed effect model.

Among all the control variables, the response of key state-owned coal mines' to GDP is significantly positive, while the response from township-and-village coal mines is not. However, the responses to changes in the proportion of heavy industry are the reverse. The joint significances of the demand variable (described by GDP, the proportion of heavy industry and the average winter temperature) on key state-owned coal mines and township-and-village coal mines are both high. (Refer to Table 2A.)

**2. Shutdown Policy's Effect on Mortality.**

As shown in Table 2B, shutdown policy has a significant positive effect on mortality if one does not add in control variables, regardless of whether or not one considers province fixed effects. Specifically, shutdown policy raised mortality in township-and-village coal mines by approximately 10 persons per million tons of coal (Table 2B, column (1), (2)). After adding in the control variable in column (3), shutdown policy's cross-term effect has changed slightly (12.694 persons per million tons), and all control variables are shown to be insignificant. Adding in control variables in column (4) and considering the different responses of township-and-village and key state-owned coal mines makes shutdown policy's effect is even bigger (13.025 persons per million tons), and significance falls slightly. Our final conclusion is that shutdown policy does increase mortality①.

As stated previously, we want to estimate the price effect of shutdown policy by estimating the demand variable's effect on mortality. According to the regression results in column (4) of Table 2B, only GDP has a positive effect on township-and-village coal mine mortality at a 10% significance level. We also jointly tested the GDP coefficient and the proportion of heavy and average winter temperature, the effects of which were not significant (refer to Table 2B). Compared with regression analysis on output, the price effect brought about significant output growth. Theses two findings suggest that output growth may affect mortality but not significantly, further supporting the property rights effect.

**3. Quantitative Estimates on Policy Effect.**

Based on the above findings, we can now estimate the effect of shutdown policy on total mortality in the coal industry. For results, please refer to Table 3. We also intentionally neglected the third category of enterprise, state-owned local (non-key) coal mines. Total mortality in both kinds of coal mine that we examined depend on the output ratio. Line 1 in Table 3 describes the situation prior to shutdown policy. The output ratio of township-and-village coal mines here is more than half, and its mortality is higher than key state-owned coal mines. Therefore, when mortality remains constant and the output ratio of coal falls significantly, overall industrial mortality will fall sharply.

① Considering the heterogeneous nature of the enterprises involved, the property rights effect and regulative effect may have different dynamics for different enterprises. Empirical studies prove that the former is more significant overall.

**Table 3: Shutdown Policy's Effect on Overall Mortality in the Coal Industry**

| Time | Output ratio | | Mortality | | Total mortality |
|---|---|---|---|---|---|
| | State-owned coal mines | Township-and-village coal mines | State-owned coal mines | Township-and-village coal mines | |
| Prior to shutdown policy (1995 – 1998 average value) | | | | | |
| Actual value | 0. 4825 | 0. 5175 | 1. 3147 | 7. 8416 | 4. 6922 |
| After shutdown policy (1999 – 2005 average value) | | | | | |
| Estimate using output changes | 0. 6429 | 0. 3571 | 1. 3147 | 7. 8416 | 3. 6456 |
| Estimate also considering mortality changes | 0. 6429 | 0. 3571 | 1. 3147 | 20. 8666 | 8. 2971 |
| Actual value | 0. 5948 | 0. 4052 | 1. 1154 | 8. 7382 | 4. 2044 |

As shown in Line 2, shutdown policy caused the output ratio of township-and-village coal mines to fall to 36% (according to column (4), Table 2A)①, and, if mortality remains constant, overall mortality in the industry will fall by 1. 0 person per million tons (or 22%).

However, shutdown policy actually raised mortality in township-and-village coal mines. First, we assume that mortality remained constant in state-owned coal mines. Given this, the 13. 0 people per million ton jump in mortality for township-and-village coal mines (Table 2B, column (4)) pushes up total mortality by 3. 6 people per million tons (an increase of 77%) (Table 3, Line 3). The bottom line lists the facts after implementation of shutdown policy: township-and-village coal mines' actual output is higher than the target set when shutdown policy was implemented, but lower than the level prior to the policy. However, township-and-village coal mines' mortality increases only slightly (due to factors other than shutdown policy). This combined with a slight fall in mortality in state-owned coal mines mean that final overall mortality is equivalent to the level prior to the implementation of shutdown policy②.

## IV. Robustness Test

### (I) Short-term and Long-term Effects of Shutdown Policy

In addition to the main regression, we applied regression analysis to samples of various intervals and estimated the short-term and long-term effects of shutdown policy. 1995 – 1998 was used as the pre-policy interval. 1999 – 2002 was taken as the short-term interval following implementation,

① The output ratio of township and state-owned coal mines were 51. 75% and 48. 25%, respectively. After shutdown policy, the former fell by 48. 2% and reached 51. 75% * (1 – 48. 2%)/[51. 75% * (1 – 48. 2%) + 48. 25%] = 35. 71%.

② We estimate that the confidence interval for 95% of shutdown policy is (2. 6, 23. 5). Therefore township coal mine mortality after the policy should be within (10. 4, 31. 3), close to the actual final rate of 8. 7. Additionally, considering that $R^2$ for the regressed mortality is only 0. 21, there should be reasons beyond the model's explanation that affect total mortality.

and 2002 – 2005 was taken to represent long-term effects①. For regression results of shutdown policy on output, short-term mortality, and long-term mortality, please refer to Table 4.

In the short-term, both the extent and significance of shutdown policy on output and mortality for township-and-village coal mines are larger than overall regression results. In the long-term, there is a significant drop in output, but the policy itself is shown to have an insignificant (but positive) effect on this change. Therefore, the short-term negative effect of shutdown policy on mortality is stronger than the long-term one. These results may suggest that shutdown policy highlights a transition in the regulative effect from motivating the protection of interests to motivating actual safety.

**Table 4: Short-term and Long-term Effects of Shutdown Policy on Output and Mortality (simplified)**

| Explained variable / Explanatory variables | Log (Output) | | Mortality | |
|---|---|---|---|---|
| | Short-term (1) | Long-term (2) | Short-term (3) | Long-term (4) |
| Policy time dummy variables × enterprise category dummy variables | −0.704*** (0.104) | −0.598*** (0.154) | 15.214*** (5.427) | 8.304 (6.139) |
| Demand variable's effect on key state-owned coal mines [Prob > F] | [0.140] | [0.000]*** | [0.615] | [0.440] |
| Demand variable's effect on township-and-village coal mines [Prob > F] | [0.000]*** | [0.000]*** | [0.765] | [0.775] |
| Control variable | YES | YES | YES | YES |
| Cross – term of control variables | YES | YES | YES | YES |
| Year fixed effect | YES | YES | YES | YES |
| Province fixed effect | YES | YES | YES | YES |

Note: Figures in brackets are the standards of these various statistics. *, ** and *** indicate significance at 10%, 5% and 1%, respectively.

## (II) The Effect of Adjusted Coal Output Data on Results

After the 2005 Economic Census, the National Bureau of Statistics (NBS) adjusted coal output data for recent years given a high likelihood of serious data manipulation (China Macroeconomic Information Network, 2006). The *China Statistical Yearbook of* 2006 adopted this adjusted data. The latest version (2010) has adjusted coal output data starting in 1998. Figure 3 shows a comparison between the two adjustments and the original data.

① Given that the time interval is similar both before and after policy implementation, the interval surrounding 2002 is repeatedly used for short-term and long-term analysis.

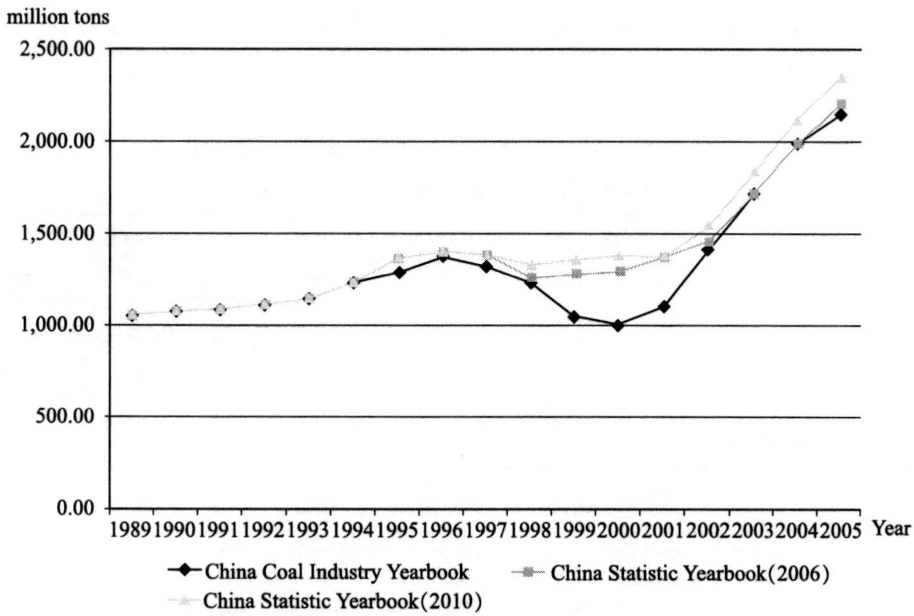


**Figure 3: Coal Output Data of Various Calibers**

Source: *China Statistic Yearbook* (2006 - 2010).

The adjusted data may affect our estimates. It is foreseeable that relatively more manipulation exists in township-and-village coal mines, and the shutdown policy's effect on output may therefore have been overstated. It is not clear how the adjusted data affects mortality caused by shutdown policy. However, if the manipulated output corresponds to a higher mortality rate, then the above estimation would underestimate shutdown policy's (positive) effect on mortality. Conversely, if the manipulation corresponds to a lower mortality rate, then the shutdown policy's effect on coal mining deaths has been overestimated①. We assume that all manipulated output comes from township-and-village coal mines. Also, the new data relates to output figures② rather than mortality figures. Findings based on this data should therefore be taken as a base level for the negative effects of output and the positive effects of mortality caused by shutdown policy.

According to Table 5, the significance of shutdown policy's effect on output has not been obviously affected by the new data. However, estimates for short-term effects and overall effects have dropped because of this data. Mortality has been heavily affected, though short-term results are still

① Another possible cause of data manipulation is to count the output of small coal mines on key state-owned coal mines and local state-owned coal mines. This would underestimate the output of small coal mines and overestimate the negative effects of shutdown policy on output; furthermore, if statistics on mortality do not include this "transfer", then this will lead to overestimated mortality of small coal mines. Such a scenario would adversely affect our findings. However, due to data limitations, we can not estimate the impact of this possibility. We appreciate an anonymous source for having indicated this situation.

② Given that the amended output data, divided both by province and by enterprise type, was not provided in the *China Statistical Yearbook*, we allocate the gap to township coal mines according to the proportion of provincial coal mine output.

significant①. To sum up, even considering the impact of the false reporting, our main regression's findings remain valid.

**Table 5: Estimates of Shutdown Policy's Effect Prior to and After Output Amendment (simplified)**

| | Output | | | Mortality | | |
|---|---|---|---|---|---|---|
| | Overall | Short-term | Long-term | Overall | Short-term | Long-term |
| Original data | −0.659*** | −0.704*** | −0.598*** | 13.025** | 15.214*** | 8.304 |
| Amended data according to the *China Statistical Yearbook* (2006) | −0.285** | −0.246** | −0.646*** | 4.819 | 5.510* | 8.073 |
| Amended data according to the *China Statistical Yearbook* (2010) | −0.214* | −0.183* | −0.527*** | 3.770 | 4.460# | 5.888 |

Note: The coefficient here is policy time dummy variable × enterprise type dummy variable. #, *, **, and ** denote significance at 15%, 10%, 5% and 1%, respectively. All control variables have been controlled for, and year fixed effects and province fixed effects have also been added.

## V. Findings and Policy Implications

China's reforms have always been progressive, fixing problems and correcting inefficiencies gradually over time. Defects in property rights and inappropriate management systems are likely to cause property rights instability across industries, particularly in the coal industry.

This paper has sought to analyze shutdown policy through both a regulative effect and property rights effect lens. Theoretical analysis has found that, when the regulative effect is true, shutdown policy forces small coal mines to pursue higher resource utilization, better environmental protection, and better safety standards. This leads to lower mortality. But if regulative costs are too onerous and become unaffordable for township-and-village enterprises, smaller mine operators may choose to evade safety protocols. In this scenario, the property rights effect will come into play and shutdown policy will lead to increased mortality and exacerbated predatory exploitation of workers. Empirical analysis finds that shutdown policy has played a significant role in reducing township-and-village enterprise coal output, which at least proves that the policy is not insignificant or a "dead letter." However, the policy is shown to have an undesired impact on mortality, especially in the short term. Our conclusion is that the property rights effect will play a dominant role in this equation at least part of the time.

Ongoing coal industry reform is, in a way, an extension of shutdown policy by promoting merg-

① For data amended based on the *China Statistical Yearbook of* 2010, short-term results are significant at 15%.

ers and reorganization of state-owned coal mines through the closing of smaller mines. This paper hopes to provide valuable reference material for ongoing coal industry reform in the following ways.

First is the issue of how to respect and protect private property rights during reform. Problems have certainly emerged due to property rights disputes in the past, and it is important that this topic be given due consideration (Caijing Magazine, 2010). Second, despite the trend in China of "the state sector expanding and the private sector retreating", the existence of private small and medium-sized coal mines is still desirable given the geographical distribution of China's coal resources (Wang Fu Qin, 2006; Caijing Magazine, 2010). A stable property rights regime is necessary for efficient, safe investment, regardless of industry or enterprise type. If China can continue to leverage the positive aspects of the regulative effect while fixing its system of property rights, then reform can still hope to be entirely beneficial①.

## References

1. Borjas, G. J. 2000. *Labor Economics*, 2nd edition. McGraw-Hill.

2. Cao, Haidong. 2010. "Resource-based Development: the Lesson of Shanxi." *Caijing Magazine*, 273: 66 – 69.

3. *Caijing*. 2002. "Times of Emergency: Mining Industry." *Caijing Magazine*, 51: 45 – 48.

4. *Caijing*. 2010. "The Reform of Mining Industry." *Caijing Magazine*, 257: 48 – 64.

5. Guo, Chaoxian. 2007. "Research on Coal Mine Enterprise Safety Production in China: From Perspective of Troop and Quality of Labor Force." *China Industrial Economy*, 10: 103 – 110.

6. State Administration of Coal Mine Safety. *China Coal Industry Yearbook*, Beijing: China Coal Industry Publishing House.

7. National Bureau of Statistics of China. *China Industry Economy Statistical Yearbook*, Beijing: China Statistics Press.

8. National Bureau of Statistics of China. *China Statistical Yearbook*, Beijing: China Statistics Press.

9. Laffont J-J, and J. Tirole. 1993. *A Theory of Incentives in Procurement and Regulation.* Cambridge: M. I. T. Press.

10. Coadse, R. , A. ALchain, D. North, etc. 1994. *Property Rights and Institutional Change*, Shanghai: Shanghai People Publishing House.

11. Li, Yizhong. 2006. "Correct the Vague Understanding and Deepen the Rectification and Shutting Down Policy." http: //www. chinasafety. gov. cn/.

12. Li, Shixiang, and Qiaosheng Wu. 2005. "The Setup of Return Model of Coal Demanding

① Suggested policies include educating workers on safety and emphasizing the role of unions, thereby increasing the cost of ignoring worker safety. Other policy ideas include levying resource and environmental taxes, giving greater compensation to work-related injuries and death, and strengthening law enforcement (in a more nuanced way than simply shutting down coal mines). Other ideas include encouraging inventions that help improve efficiency and safety for small coal mines and reforming state-owned coal mines so as to improve their market competitiveness.

Function and the Forecast of Coal Demand." *China Coal*, 6: 17 – 19.

13. Lin, Boqiang, Weixian Wei, and Pidong Li. 2007. "China's Long-run Coal Demand: Impacts and Policy Choice." *Economic Research Journal*, 2: 48 – 58.

14. Lin, Di, and Zongshou Jia. 2000. "Shutting Down Coal-mine and Lower the Output: the Foggy Future." *Coal Enterprise Management*, 5: 5 – 10.

15. Lin, Hanchuan, Hao Wang, and Li Wang. 2008. "Safety Regulation, Responsibility Rules and Coal-mine Safety." *China Industrial Economics*, 6: 17 – 24.

16. Liu, Can, etc. 2009. *Research on Building the Property System of China's Nature Resource*, Sichuan: Southwestern University of Finance and Economics Press.

17. Liu, Qiongzhi. 2006. "Game Theory Analysis on Coal-mine Accident and the Government Control Policy Choices." *Economic Review*, 5: 59 – 63.

18. Qian, Yongkun, Hong Xie, and Jianbo Xu. 2004. "The Relationship between Safety Input and Economy Benefit: the Case of China's Township and Village Coal Mine." *Quantitative & Technical Economics*, 8: 40 – 45.

19. Spulber, D. F. 1989. *Regulation and Markets*, Cambridge: M. I. T. Press, 1989.

20. Shi, Dong, and Weina Li. 2004. "Looking for the Origin of Coal Mine Tragedy." *Caijing*, 123: 25 – 39.

21. Tan, Manyi, and Xiaowo Tang. 2004. "Property Right Distortion: the Further Thought to Mine Tragedy." *Journal of China Coal Society*, 12: 756 – 759.

22. Tang, Lingxiao, and Xibao Guo. 2006. "Causes and Countermeasures Against Frequent Occurrence of Coal-mining Accidents in China Today: Based on the Standpoints of Safety Inputs." *China Industrial Economy*, 12: 53 – 59.

23. Tao, Changqi, and Jing-ong Liu. 2007. "Economics Analysis of Coal Mine Enterprise's Production." *The Journal of Quantitative & Technical Economics*, 2: 124 – 135.

24. Wang, Fuqin. 2006. "Development Problems and Policy Analysis of Small Coal Mines in China." *Journal of China University of Geosciences (Social Sciences Edition)*, 11: 61 – 67.

25. Xiao, Xingzhi, Yingfei Qi, and Hongjuan Li. 2008. "An Empirical Study on Effects of Coal Mine Safety Regulation in China." *China Industrial Economics*, 5: 67 – 76.

26. Ye, Guoxing, Pidong Li, and Shuai Chen. 2008. "China's Coal Demand: Comparison and Forecast." *Statistics and Decision*, 4: 97 – 98.

27. China Macroeconomic Information Network. 2006. The Analysis of China's Coal Output. http://www.hdcmr.com/article/jzqb/09/01/7708.html.

28. Zhong, Xiaohan. 2011. "On the Negative Correlation between Mortality and Output: Effects of Shutdown Policy in China's Coal Industry." *Journal of Economics*, 5: 67 – 103.

# Chapter 9

# A Modeling Analysis of Local Governments Competing in Offering Subsidies to Attract Investment: the Cause of Industrial Overcapacity*

**Jiang Feitao (江飞涛)[1], Geng Qiang (耿强)[2], Lv Daguo (吕大国) and Li Xiaoping (李晓萍)[4]**

[1]Institute of Industrial Economics of Chinese Academy of Social Sciences (CASS), Beijing, China

[2]School of Business, Nanjing University; Institute of Industrial Economics of CASS, Beijing, China

[3]School of Business, Nanjing University Nanjing, China

[4]School of Business, Sun Yat-sen University, Guangzhou, China

**Abstract**: Although championed by academia and policy-makers, the theory of "wave phenomenon" is a questionable explanation for overcapacity. First, enterprises do not necessarily share the same expectation for future demand of a promising industry. Second, in its model, overcapacity is explained as a deviation from equilibrium under the incomplete information hypothesis, which is in fact nothing but normal in a market economy. The prime reason for overcapacity resides in the fact that local governments are engaged in a subsidy competition to attract investment. We endeavor to illustrate the following via modeling: the subsidy effect produced by local government's offering of cheaper land and matching loans results in less investment from companies. Under this circumstance, enterprises channel a disproportionate amount of funding to building production capacity, which overloads the entire industry. To address the problem, re-

---

* Corresponding author: gengq@ nju. edu. cn.

This paper is sponsored by the Chinese National Social Science Foundation Project "Industrial Overcapacity, Redundant Construction in the Transitioning China: Formation and Management" (grant 09AZD017), the Chinese National Social Science Foundation Project "Overcapacity Management and Reform of the Financing System" (grant 09AJY002), the Chinese National Social Science Foundation Project "Restructuring and Revitalization Planning of Key Industries in China" (grant 10zd&026), the Chinese National Social Science Foundation Project "A New Industrialized Path: Industrial Restructuring and Upgrading" (grant 06&ZD002), MOE Project of Key Research Institute of Humanities and Social Sciences in Universities "Financial Innovation, Capital Market and Regional Economic Growth" (grant 10JJD790027); Nanjing University "985" Project of Humanities and Social Sciences "Improving indigenous innovation capability in China" (grant NJU985FW01)

forms are needed in land property, environmental protection policies, and financial and fiscal systems.

**Keywords**: overcapacity, investment subsidy, cost externalization, risk externalization.

## I. Introduction

Since the 1980s, economic decision-makers have struggled with the problems of unnecessary construction, excessive competition, gratuitous investment and excess capacity. These problems are seen as a major threat to industrial organization, business profitability and financial security. Large amounts of resources will thus be squandered. Consequently, environmental and resource constraints will be more prominent, as will structural imbalances, creating a more complex atmosphere for China to achieve sustainable, balanced and sound economic growth. Given its gravity, overcapacity has long been the focus of scholars and government officials. In attempts to explain its occurrence, there have been two divergent research proposals. One is based on the theory of market failure; the other is founded on the belief that institutional flaws in a transition economy have distorted the behavior of market participants. Accordingly, there have been two types of policy prescriptions. As policymakers have primarily sided with the market failure explanation, they largely relied on administrative measures. These included market access approval, project approval, land use approval, credit verification, sector-specific guidance and mandatory clearance. Redundant construction, overcapacity and market failure have become the justifications for the government to implement extensive microeconomic intervention (Jiang & Li 2010).

However, the studies based on market failure theory are perplexing. Jiang and Cao (2009) argued that there are fundamental flaws in the market failure approach which attributes overcapacity to low market concentration and excessive entry. Lin (2009) and Lin, Wu and Xing (2010) have attempted to illustrate the causal relation between "wave phenomenon" and overcapacity. They believe that there is readily an accurate, positive consensus on the prospect of a certain new industry in developing countries and that the consensus will lead to a wave of investment in this industry. This theory has had overarching influence since its publication; however, few people seem to notice its fundamental weakness in market failure theory. As evidenced by the outcome of capacity management policies in China, direct microeconomic intervention cannot stem overcapacity and have caused strong side effects (Jiang & Chen, 2007; Cao & Jiang, 2010).

Studies of institutional flaws in a transition economy that distort the behavior of market participants are insufficient. Several studies have noted that subsidy competition between regions has been the main reason behind overcapacity (Li, 2005; Guo & Jia, 2006; Tao, 2007; etc.), but none of them elaborated on the micro-mechanism as to why subsidy competition led to overcapacity. Therefore, further study is needed to explain overcapacity from the perspective of institutional distortions and regional competition and to establish a theoretical model for the micro-mechanism. The aim of this study is to enrich existing examinations and devise a specific model to elaborate on the micro-mechanism of the overcapacity under the circumstance of regional subsidy competition.

## II. Literature Review

### (I) Market Failure: Approach and Shortcomings

Market failure approach to overcapacity originated in the economic cycle theory from socialist political economics. Earlier studies attributed redundant construction to the assumption that investment decisions under the background of mass production were made in a decentralized and disordered manner. Later, most scholars based their studies on industrial organization theory and interpreted redundant construction and excessive competition as market failures. In this regard, there are four typical observations: First, redundant construction is caused by low market concentration. Second, redundant construction occurs because of low entry barriers and high exit barriers. Third, excessive competition or redundant construction is caused by excessive entry.

Lastly, redundant construction and excessive competition can be explained by the fact that enterprises preserve excess capacity to maintain price collusion across the industry. Jiang and Cao (2009) discussed the four observations respectively and pointed out there are fundamental flaws in the theoretical opinion.

In recent years, the "wave phenomenon" has been an influential explanation for overcapacity and is attributed to special market failures in developing countries (Lin, 2007; Lin, Wu & Xing, 2010). In this approach, enterprises in a developing country share a common understanding on the prospect of a certain new industry, particularly on its future demand. Such consensus will trigger a wave of investment and eventually overcapacity in the industry. But the theoretical hypothesis is flawed. First and foremost, the "wave phenomenon" hypothesis is groundless. Based on the existent situation in China, there is currently no common understanding among enterprises or government authorities on the prospect of a new industry. Projections about a given industry often vary greatly①. Moreover, accurate universal projection on the future path of an industry does not exist, particularly in terms of industry-wide improvements and aggregated demand. For example, there exists a huge discrepancy between projected demand and real demand in industries such as automobiles, steel and aluminum. In addition, incomplete information on the part of market participants may result in "overcapacity", which is normal in a market economy. The imbalances between supply and demand will be recognized and corrected through market mechanisms which have the ability to spread market information; the market will direct itself towards equilibrium.

### (II) Institutional Distortion Approach and Shortcomings

Kornai (Chinese version, 1986, 2007) illustrated in his work the "thirst for investment" that existed in the classical socialist economy and the transition economy. This observation can be seen as the first attempt to explain the distorted behavior of market participants from the perspective

① Take the example of the steel and auto industry; there has been ongoing debate about the demand volume when the steel industry is on the path of rapid growth and opinions are divided greatly. The same takes place in the aluminum and auto industry.

of institutional shortcomings in a transition economy. Kornai's ground-breaking work offered a new perspective on the mechanism of overcapacity. Some Chinese scholars (Zhang & Ma 1999; Yang 2006; Pi 2008) followed Kornai's approach and focused on the institutional problems of the transitional economy to explain redundant construction. Their work incorporated the real situation of China's transition and extended Kornai's findings to some extent. Although these studies provided food for thought, some of their shortcomings require further discussion (Jiang & Cao 2009).

Since the end of 1990s, a number of scholars noticed dramatic changes that had taken place along with the transition and believed that the improper intervention of the local governments was the root cause for redundant construction. Guo and Jiang (2006), Zhou (2004), China Center for Economic Research at Peking University (2004), Li and Zhong (2004), and Li (2005) believed that excessive focus on economic growth and investment inflow, which are key pillars of an official performance evaluation system, have shaped the decision-making of local government, and that under an imperfect market economy, local governments artificially intervened in the allocation of rare resources to meet their objectives. With these constraints, local governments offered several types of preferential treatment to investors, such as free land, tax credits, and lower power tariffs. Since investment cost was far lower than social cost, enterprises invested disproportionately in building production capacity. The research of Zhou, Li and Guo (2006) seems to imply that regional competition for investment is the main reason behind overcapacity. They have different focuses—either analyzing the behavior of local governments or exploring the impact of overcapacity on the macroeconomic level. What is missing from their equations is how the subsidy competition among regions has distorted the behavior of investors and caused overcapacity.

### (Ⅲ) Research on Subsidy Competition

Regional subsidy competition between areas is the main reason behind overcapacity in China; it should also be the main approach for studies of the formation of overcapacity. Most existing studies about subsidy competition center on the neo international economics and can be divided into two categories. Category 1 is based on strategic trade theory and explores the effect of export subsidy competition. Helpman and Krugman (1989) analyzed the interplay between the strategies undertaken by two countries and developed a two-stage game model. In their model, both countries offered subsidies to domestic exporters and competed to provide more attractive subsidies. The welfare effect generated by such subsidy intervention was analyzed in the model. Helpman and Krugman's study is expanded by Neary and Leathy (2000). Category 2 is centered on the governments' subsidy competition to attract foreign direct investment (FDI). Bond and Samuelson (1986), and Doyle and van Wijnbergen (1984) evaluated the effect of tax competition, particularly tax exemption, on FDI inflow. Barros and Cabral (2000) used modeling and analyzed the subsidy competition between two countries to win FDI from a third country, and compared the welfare effects of competitive, zero, and first-best subsidies. Facundo Albornoz *et al.* (2009) developed a three-stage game to analyze governmental competition for investment from multinational corporations and evaluated the welfare effects of such competition. Parcero (2007) developed a two-stage game model that included the central government, two regions and a multinational, and analyzed how regional competition influenced the welfare of the whole country and what was the best policy option for state government.

In China, local governments constantly rival each other for both domestic and foreign investment. Subsidy competition between regions is all the more ferocious and ubiquitous. In fact, constraints and behavioral patterns of local governments exhibit a major departure from the hypotheses in existing literature. The previous studies failed to consider the effect of regional subsidy competition on production capacity investment and on utilization rate. Although international economics provides us with the basic principles that can serve as the basis for the study, it does not offer a readily available theoretical framework.

## III. Formation of Overcapacity and Relevant Institutional Flaws

After fiscal decentralization reform, local state corporatism began to emerge in China. This means local governments directly intervened in the economy and took on corporate management roles, and governments, the Party and subordinate corporations formed conglomerate-like interest communities. During economic transition, local state corporations first consisted of the Party, the government and local SOEs; later, private enterprises joined in. Local state corporations, formed by these players, constituted the micro-institutional basis of economic reform in China. Generally, local jurisdictions, which showed signs of local state corporatism, considered the following as externalities: macro-economic stability, fair income distribution and environmental spillover effects. They would also attempt to garner outside investment, financial resources, higher-level government subsidies or special preferences (Qian & Roland, 1998; Jin, 2005; Li, 2005). In addition, the promotion system of local officials resembled a competition (Zhou, 2004); because higher positions are always limited, such contests by nature are a zero-sum game. The promotion of one inevitably reduces the chance of another. Hence, fierce political rivalry would easily turn into a race for economic expansion and political gains, with no regard for social economic cost and gains (Zhou, 2007).

Under the current transitional economic system, land transfer rights are ambiguously defined and the banks have soft budgetary constraints; so there is no market price for land and credit, creating great opportunities for arbitrage to local governments and investors (China Center for Economic Research at Peking University, 2004). Driven by an evaluation system focused on GDP growth and investment, government officials tend to take advantage of institutional loopholes. These are highlighted by ambiguous land transfer rights and soft budgetary constraints of banks, thus leading to a strong holding of land, credit and other rare resources. Their purpose is to ensure that local government objectives are reached (Li, 2005). Further, the ambiguities of environmental property rights and the defects of the environmental protection mechanism allow many local governments to tolerate environmental pollution and disruption in return for investment.

Local governments in China have a strong motivation to attract investment and propel economic growth. Ambiguous land transfer rights allow them to offer enterprises huge subsidies and crucial collaterals required for financing. Soft budgetary constraints on the banking sector make it possible for them to help local enterprises transfer financing and risk costs. In addition, because of ambiguous environmental property rights and defects of the environmental protection mechanism, they tend to lure investment and solidify local capital at the expense of the environment. These factors greatly reduce the individual cost to investors, which becomes far less than the social cost, and investors gain huge external benefits from social wealth transfer. This is a type of subsidy competition, changing the incentive mix and distorting the investment behavior of corporations. The subsidy competition, common in many places, has led to a general distortion in investment.

Investment subsidies seriously distort corporate capacity expansion and competition (Manfred Neumann, 2003), and cost externalization inevitably leads to excess capacity. Government subsidies consist of the following types: direct transfer payment, tax exemption, below-market land sales, government guarantees for enterprises and capital injections into state-controlled corporations, etc. When private equity investors are absent and the conditions remain unchanged, it would be considered as subsidy if the government chooses to increase its equity. In the mid-1970s to early 1990s, member states of the European Community rushed to subsidize their steel companies and help expand their market shares. This resulted in huge excess capacity in the steel industry and social welfare loss. In China, local governments mainly provide investment subsidies to local companies and companies with outside investment through favorable land policies, tax reduction and exemption. Before tax system reform, tax reduction and exemption were the prevalent practices; after the reform, offering cheap or free land replaced the tax tools as the most common approach for providing investment subsidies. Because of the large investment subsidies companies would gain extra benefits by accepting local market entry. This greatly distorts corporate investment behavior, increasing output and investment for capacity expansion when corporate profit was at its peak. When investment subsidies reach a certain extent, enterprises are tempted to invest in profit-losing projects, sectors with oversupply and even excessive capacity expansion. That is because the subsidies could offset market losses and still provide considerable gains. Widespread government subsidies resulted in excess input and hence excess capacity, creating market losses across the sector and welfare losses (Cao & Jiang, 2010).

Despite the high market price for land, governments offer cheap land to investors. This practice provides large extra profit to the investors and constitutes an actual subsidy on corporate investment. It also greatly reduces equity investment of projects and externalizes the risks. In actual project implementations, land also plays a crucial role; that is, to be used as guaranty in securing low-interest bank loans equivalent to market value of the land. This loan later becomes an investment fund. In this way, companies would engage in capital-intensive projects with little input by the way of an equity fund and thus build vast production capabilities. It is also noteworthy that accounting treatment on the balance sheet could distort the fact that equity investment is small (by listing the market value of land use rights under equity investment). In addition, local governments would assist major local enterprises and investment projects in "securing" bank loans. This is direct intervention with the credit supply of financial institutions and further reduces the required equity investment, which in turn intensifies the externalization of corporate investment risks. Such risk externalization increases the jeopardy involved in investment behaviors and companies would tend to put too much investment on capacity expansion. Widespread externalization of investment risks would lead to overzealous capacity investment across the entire sector, which would produce overcapacity in times of depression.

## Ⅳ. Mathematical Model for the Formation of Overcapacity

### (Ⅰ) Theoretical Model

We first set up a two-stage game model with $n$ homogenous corporations in $n$ homogenous regions as players. For the local government, its payoff and cost functions of corporate capacity investment are exogenously given and the payoff function of government $i$ is $R(Q_i)$. Since local governments' payoff includes both its fiscal revenue and the effectiveness of officials' work on regional output, its payoff function is also its effectiveness function; so we can use the coefficient of relative risk aversion to describe its payoff function. We first need to make some reasonable assumptions about the payoff function: $R'(Q_i) > 0$, $R''(Q_i) < 0$, $-Q\dfrac{R''(Q)}{R'(Q)} = r$, $0 < r < 1$. The coefficient of relative risk aversion is used here and it means that the payoff curve is relatively smooth and, as capacity increases, the curve shows less change in its shape. Essentially, this implies that the local government is willing to offer subsidies for greater payoff and, as capacity grows, it is less likely to be unwilling. Obviously, these assumptions reflect the reality. The cost on the government for providing one unit of investment subsidy is $\beta$ $(1 \geqslant \beta > 0)$, mainly because the subsidies corporations received could be direct fiscal subsidy or tax reduction and exemption, and huge land profit generated by cheap or free land offered by local governments. Investment subsidies through cheap land sales have leverage effects, that is, the government could provide very high investment subsidies at a relatively low cost. The local government would seek to maximize its return; so during the first stage, corporations would determine their capacity according to the government subsidy function, future market payoff function, their own capacity cost function, and complete their capacity investment. During the second stage, they would set the actual output in accordance with the market situation.

Supposing manufacturers' marginal variable cost equals average variable cost $c$ and there are $n$ manufacturers in the market, then market inverse demand function is $p = a - nq$, where $q$ means actual output and $Q$ capacity. For each unit of capacity investment, the manufacturer receives subsidy $b(Q)$. The investment cost of capacity $Q$ is $kQ$ and $k$ is a constant. Once the manufacturer builds up its capacity, $kQ$ it is deemed as sunk cost.

### (Ⅱ) Equilibrium Analysis

Because government $i$ seeks to maximize its payoff, $R(Q_i) - \beta b_i Q_i$, under the first-stage conditions we can get $b_i = \dfrac{R'(Q_i)}{\beta}$, the subsidy function for manufacturer $i$.

Using backward induction:

At the second stage, market return of manufacturer $i$ is:

$[a-(q_1+\cdots+q_i+\cdots+q_n)]q_i-cq_i$, with $s.t.$: $Q_i \geqslant q_i$ as constraint, which says the manufacturer's output cannot exceed its capacity.

At the first stage, market return of manufacturer $i$ is:

$$\pi_i=[a-(q_1+\cdots+q_i+\cdots+q_n)]q_i-cq_i+b_iQ_i-kQ_i$$

Then: $\pi_i=[a-(q_1+\cdots+q_i+\cdots+q_n)]q_i-cq_i+\dfrac{R'(Q_i)}{\beta}Q_i-kQ_i$

We now set up Lagrangian function

$$L=[a-(q_1+\cdots+q_i+\cdots+q_n)]q_i-cq_i+\frac{R'(Q_i)}{\beta}Q_i-kQ_i+\lambda(Q_i-q_i)$$

K-T condition is:

$$\frac{\partial L}{\partial q_i}=a-(q_1+\cdots+q_i+\cdots+q_n)-q_i-c-\lambda=0$$

$$\frac{\partial L}{\partial Q_i}=\frac{R''(Q_i)}{\beta}Q_i+\frac{R'(Q_i)}{\beta}-k+\lambda=0$$

$$\frac{\partial L}{\partial \lambda}=Q_i-q_i\geqslant 0,\ \lambda\geqslant 0,\ \lambda(Q_i-q_i)=0$$

If $\lambda>0$, then $Q_i=q_i$

Hence $a-(Q_1+\cdots+Q_i+\cdots+Q_n)-Q_i-c+\dfrac{R''(Q_i)}{\beta}Q_i+\dfrac{R'(Q_i)}{\beta}-k=0$

Due to symmetry, we know $Q_1=\cdots=Q_i=\cdots=Q_n$, and so we can get $Q_i$

If $\lambda=0$, $Q_i>q_i$

Due to symmetry, we can get $q_i=\dfrac{a-c}{n+1}$. Hence $\dfrac{R''(Q_i)}{\beta}Q_i+\dfrac{R'(Q_i)}{\beta}=k$.

Because $-Q\dfrac{R''(Q)}{R'(Q)}=r$, $(1-r)R'(Q_i)=\beta k$.

Since $Q_i>q_i=\dfrac{a-c}{n+1}$, when $R'\left(\dfrac{a-c}{n+1}\right)>\dfrac{\beta k}{1-r}$, it will result in excess capacity.

From the above analysis, we know that investment subsidy does not inevitably lead to excess capacity. It has two equilibriums, one of which results in excess capacity and the other not. Only when the subsidy exceeds a certain amount $\left(b\left(\dfrac{a-c}{n+1}\right)=\dfrac{R'\left(\dfrac{a-c}{n+1}\right)}{\beta}>\dfrac{k}{1-r}\right)$, will it generate excess capacity. Obviously, when other conditions remain unchanged, the bigger $n$, the smaller $q_i=\dfrac{a-c}{n+1}$, so $R'\left(\dfrac{a-c}{n+1}\right)>\dfrac{\beta k}{1-r}$ is more likely than not, which means excess capacity; similarly, the smaller $\beta$, the smaller $\dfrac{\beta k}{1-r}$. And it is more likely to make $R'\left(\dfrac{a-c}{n+1}\right)>\dfrac{\beta k}{1-r}$. If bigger $n$ and smaller $\beta$ coexist, the likelihood of excess capacity is even greater. This means that when regional investment subsidies are common, governments have strong preference for capacity investment and their cost of providing per unit of subsidies is relatively low (for instance, local governments currently in general subsidize through cheap land sales), excess capacity is more likely to appear.

### (Ⅲ) Major Inferences

Proposition 1: In an oligopoly market, when investment subsidy exceeds some certain level, it would create social welfare loss. When capacity investment subsidy surpasses some certain level, it would result in excess capacity, creating further loss on social welfare. And as investment subsidy increases, social welfare further diminishes. In a competitive market, investment subsidy would inevitably lead to social welfare loss, whether it creates excess capacity or not.

Validation: when $q = Q$, namely $b\left(\frac{a-c}{n+1}\right) = \frac{R'\left(\frac{a-c}{n+1}\right)}{\beta} \leqslant \frac{k}{1-r}$

If investment subsidy does not exist,

The profit of manufacturer $i$ is $\pi_i = [a-(q_1+\cdots+q_i+\cdots+q_n)]q_i - cq_i - kq_i$

At the first stage, the prerequisite for maximizing the profit of manufacturer $i$ is:

$$a-(q_1+\cdots+q_i+\cdots+q_n)-q_i-c-k=0$$

Due to symmetry, we know that $q_i = \frac{a-c-k}{n+1}$,

Consumer surplus is $\prod = \frac{1}{2}(q_1+\cdots+q_i+\cdots+q_n)^2 = \frac{1}{2}(nq_i)^2 = \frac{1}{2}\left(n\frac{a-c-k}{n+1}\right)^2$,

The surplus of manufacturer $i$ is:

$$\pi_i = (a-nq_i)q_i - cq_i - kq_i = \frac{a-c-k}{n+1}\left(a-n\frac{a-c-k}{n+1}-c-k\right) = \left(\frac{a-c-k}{n+1}\right)^2.$$

If investment subsidy does exist,

For convenience, we assume the subsidy to be a constant, $\bar{b}$

The profit of manufacturer $i$ is:

$$\pi'_i = [a-(q'_1+\cdots+q'_i+\cdots+q'_n)]q'_i - cq'_i + \bar{b}q'_i - kq'_i,$$

At the first stage, the prerequisite for maximizing the profit of manufacturer $i$ is:

$$a-(q'_1+\cdots+q'_i+\cdots+q'_n)-q'_i-c+\bar{b}-k=0$$

Due to symmetry, we can get that $q'_i = \frac{a-c+\bar{b}-k}{n+1}$,

Consumer surplus is $\prod' = \frac{1}{2}(nq'_i)^2 = \frac{1}{2}\left(n\frac{a-c+\bar{b}-k}{n+1}\right)^2$,

Then the profit of manufacturer $i$ is:

$$\pi'_i = (a-nq'_i)q'_i - cq'_i - kq'_i = \frac{a-c+\bar{b}-k}{n+1}\left(a-n\frac{a-c+\bar{b}-k}{n+1}-c-k\right) = \left(\frac{a-c+\bar{b}-k}{n+1}\right)^2$$

Although the cost of government subsidy is $\beta\,\bar{b}nq'_i$, other subsidies come from other sectors in the society and so we can say the total social cost of subsidy is $\bar{b}nq'_i = \bar{b}n\frac{a-c+\bar{b}-k}{n+1}$.

The accrual of consumer surplus is

$$V\Pi = \Pi' - \Pi == \frac{1}{2}\left(n\frac{a-c+\bar{b}-k}{n+1}\right)^2 - \frac{1}{2}\left(n\frac{a-c-k}{n+1}\right)^2$$

$$= \frac{n^2}{(n+1)^2}\left[\bar{b}(a-c-k) + \frac{\bar{b}^2}{2}\right]$$

The accrual of the profit of manufacturer $i$ is

$$V\pi_i = \left(\frac{a-c+\bar{b}-k}{n+1}\right)^2 - \left(\frac{a-c-k}{n+1}\right)^2 = \frac{2\bar{b}\ (a-c-k)\ +\bar{b}^2}{(n+1)^2}$$

So the change of social welfare is:

$$V\amalg = V\Pi + nV\pi_i - n\bar{b}q_i = \frac{n^2}{(n+1)^2}\left[\bar{b}(a-c-k) + \frac{\bar{b}^2}{2}\right]$$

$$+n\frac{2\bar{b}(a-c-k)+\bar{b}^2}{(n+1)^2} - n\bar{b}\frac{a-c-k+\bar{b}}{n+1} = \frac{n\bar{b}(a-c-k) - \frac{n^2\bar{b}^2}{2}}{(n+1)^2}$$

To increase social welfare, it is necessary that $\frac{n\bar{b}(a-c-k) - \frac{n^2\bar{b}^2}{2}}{(n+1)^2} > 0$

Namely, $\bar{b} < \frac{2\ (a-c-k)}{n}$.

So when investment subsidy per unit, $\bar{b}$, exceeds $\frac{2(a-c-k)}{n}$, social welfare would be less than it would otherwise be when investment subsidy does not exist.

Because $\frac{\partial \amalg}{\partial \bar{b}} = \frac{n(a-c-k) - n^2\bar{b}}{(n+1)^2}$,

So when $\frac{\partial \amalg}{\partial \bar{b}} < 0$, we get $\bar{b} > \frac{a-c-k}{n}$,

Namely, when $\bar{b} > \frac{a-c-k}{n}$, as subsidy increases, social welfare begins to diminish. And when $\bar{b} > \frac{2(a-c-k)}{n}$, social welfare is less than it would otherwise be when without investment subsidy. As the subsidy increases, so does the loss on social welfare.

In a competitive market, $n \to \infty$ and $\frac{a-c-k}{n} \to 0$,

So when $\bar{b}$ has a very small positive value, it would cause social welfare loss. Similarly, as $\bar{b}$ increases, social welfare further declines. ① When there is little subsidy, social welfare would increase; this is simply because our model assumes Bertrand competition with only capacity constraints in the market. If we adopt a more competitive model, for instance Bertrand competition model with capacity constraints and random rationing rule, then the equilibrium with a small number of

① This conclusion is not based on the atomistic enterprise hypothesis. In a competitive market with a large number of enterprises, fierce competition, which centers around price and market share, would make total output equivalent or close to the equilibrium output in a perfect competition model. Investment subsidy can only make the total output exceed the equilibrium output (when social welfare is maximized) and therefore cause loss on social welfare. And as subsidy increases, so does the loss on social welfare.

enterprises is closer to the equilibrium in a perfectly competitive market, that is, when $\bar{b}$ has a very small positive value, it would cause social welfare loss.

When $q < Q$, namely $R'\left(\frac{a-c}{n+1}\right) > \frac{\beta k}{1-r}$,

The profit of manufacturer $i$ is $\pi_i = [a-(q_1+\cdots+q_n)]q_i - cq_i + \frac{R'(Q_i)}{\beta}Q_i - kQ_i$. Since $q < Q$, the increase of subsidy would not affect $q$. Now we assume $\frac{R'(Q_i)}{\beta} = b$,

$$\therefore \frac{\partial \pi_i}{\partial b} = Q_i + b\frac{\partial Q_i}{\partial b} - k\frac{\partial Q_i}{\partial b}$$

From the first-stage prerequisite for maximizing profit, we know that $(1-r)\ R'(Q_i) = \beta k$ and $\frac{\partial b}{\partial Q_i} = \frac{R''(Q_i)}{\beta}$

$$\therefore \frac{\partial \pi_i}{\partial b} = Q_i + \frac{R'(Q_i)}{\beta}\frac{\beta}{R''(Q_i)} - \frac{(1-r)R'(Q_i)}{\beta}\frac{\beta_i}{R''(Q_i)} = Q_i + r\frac{R'(Q_i)}{R''(Q_i)}$$

And since $-Q\frac{R''(Q)}{R'(Q)} = r$

$$\therefore \frac{\partial \pi_i}{\partial b} = 0.$$

The accrual of governmenti's subsidy is $Q_i db$, and this increase only expands manufacturer capacity, while output $q$ remains unchanged. Because $q$ is unchanged, neither $p$nor consumer surplus is changed. The manufacturer now has excess capacity; this wastes resources and causes social welfare loss.

Proposition 2: Capacity investment subsidy would exacerbate the fluctuation of capacity utilization rate in economic cycles, further reducing the utilization rate of capacity in times of depression.

Validation: We assume that when the manufacturer is determining its capacity, the probability of market prosperity is $\theta$ and that of depression$1-\theta$; so the demand function in times of depression is $p = a' - nq(a > a')$.

When $q = Q$,

Maximum profit of the manufacturer will be:

$$\pi_i = \theta\{[a-(q_1+\cdots+q_i+\cdots+q_n)]q_i - cq_i\} + (1-\theta)$$
$$\{[a'-(q'_1+\cdots+q'_i+\cdots+q'_n)]q'_i - cq'_i\}$$
$$+\frac{R'(q_i)}{\beta}q_i - kq_i$$

*s. t.* $:q_i \geqslant q'_i$

The constraint means in times of depression, the output is less than the designed capacity, which is the output in times of prosperity.

We now set up Lagrangian function

$$L=\theta\{[a-(q_1+\cdots+q_i+\cdots+q_n)]q_i-cq_i\}+(1-\theta)\{[a'-(q'_1+\cdots+q'_i+\cdots+q'_n)]q'_i-cq'_i\}+\frac{R'(q_i)}{\beta}q_i-kq_i+\lambda(q_i-q'_i)$$

$\because q_i>0,\ q'_i>0$

So K-T condition is:

$$\frac{\partial L}{\partial q_i}=\theta[a-(q_1+\cdots+q_i+\cdots+q_n)-q_i-c]+\frac{R''(q_i)}{\beta}q_i+\frac{R'(q_i)}{\beta}-k+\lambda=0$$

$$\frac{\partial L}{\partial q'_i}=(1-\theta)[a'-(q'_1+\cdots+q'_i+\cdots+q'_n)-q'_i-c]-\lambda=0$$

$$\frac{\partial L}{\partial \lambda}=q_i-q'_i\geqslant 0,\ \lambda\geqslant 0,\ \lambda(q_i-q'_i)=0$$

Suppose $\frac{R'(q_i)}{\beta}=b$ when we try to solve $q_i$ under K-T condition, then $\frac{R''(q'_i)}{\beta}q'_i+\frac{R'(q'_i)}{\beta}=(1-r)b$.

Therefore, we have two situations:

**a. $\lambda=0,\ q_i>q'_i$.**

Due to symmetry, we can get that $q_i=\dfrac{a-c+\dfrac{(1-r)b-k}{\theta}}{n+1}$ and $q'_i=\dfrac{a'-c}{n+1}$

$\because \frac{\partial(q_i-q'_i)}{\partial b}=\frac{1-r}{\theta(n+1)}>0$

So subsidy increase would worsen the fluctuation of capacity utilization rate.

**b. $\lambda>0,\ q_i=q'_i$.**

Due to symmetry, we can get that $q'_i=q_i=\dfrac{\theta a+(1-\theta)a'-c+(1-r)b-k}{n+1}$

$\because \frac{\partial q_i}{\partial b}=\frac{1-r}{n+1}>0$

So when subsidy increases, the output during both prosperity and depression would grow.

But as the output grows, $\lambda=(1-\theta)[a'-(q'_1+\cdots+q'_i+\cdots+q'_n)-q'_i-c]$ would certainly diminish. So when $\lambda=0$, then we get $q_i>q'_i$, which means excess capacity in times of depression.

From the above validation, we know that when $R'\left(\frac{a-c}{n+1}\right)>\frac{\beta k}{1-r}$, it will result in excess capacity. When excess capacity exists, the actual output of the manufacturer during market prosperity will be $q_i=\frac{a-c}{n+1}$ and that during depression will be $q'_i=\frac{a'-c}{n+1}$, $q_i>q'_i$. That is to say, when the payoff margin of local government $R'\left(\frac{a-c}{n+1}\right)>\frac{\beta k}{1-r}$, it would create excess capacity. Only when output is raised to $Q_i$ and $R'(Q_i)=\frac{\beta k}{1-r}$ can there be equilibrium. In this situation, we get that $Q_i>q_i=\frac{a-c}{n+1}$. From the above validation, we know that if the government increases investment subsidy, it would certainly create bigger designed capacity and this certainly amplifies the fluctuation of capacity utilization rate.

Proposition 3: With market uncertainties, risk externalization caused by low equity capital in capacity investment would increase the probability of excess capacity.

In China, local governments offer huge investment subsidies through cheap land sales to attract investment. The land sold can be used as critical guaranty when applying for bank loans. In addition, governments help corporate investors secure those loans. These practices made it possible for corporations to launch capital-intensive projects with extremely low equity capital. This causes serious risk externalization and increases the probability of excess capacity under market uncertainties.

Validation: Suppose variable cost $c = 0$ and there are uncertainties in the market, this means that the probability distribution function of market capacity $a$ defined on an interval $[a_L, a_H]$ is $F(a)$, which is derivable, and its probability density function is $f(a)$. The existence of risk externalization shows that the equity investment of the manufacturer is $ekq_i$, $(0 \leqslant e \leqslant 1)$, where $e$ refers to equity input in capacity investment.

Now we consider two extreme situations, namely when $e = 1$ and when $e = 0$.

**a. When $e = 1$.**

Manufacturer $i$ chooses $q_i$ as its capacity for the first stage, so at the second stage, the output will be $q_i$ or $\frac{a}{n+1}$. When $\frac{a}{n+1} \geqslant q_i$, namely $a \geqslant (n+1) q_i$, the output would be $q_i$; otherwise it would be $\frac{a}{n+1}$.

Then the expected profit of the manufacturer is:

$$E(\pi_i) = \int_{(n+1)q_i}^{a_H} [a - (q_1 + \cdots q_n)] q_i f(a) \mathrm{d}a + \int_{a_L}^{(n+1)q_i} \left(\frac{A}{n+1}\right)^2 f(a) \mathrm{d}a - kq_i$$

Because of the first-stage prerequisite for maximizing expected profit and symmetry, it follows that:

$$\int_{(n+1)q_i}^{a_H} af(a) \mathrm{d}a - (n+1) q_i \int_{(n+1)q_i}^{a_H} f(a) \mathrm{d}a - k = 0 \cdots\cdots 1$$

**b. When $e = 0$.**

Like the situation above, manufacturer $i$ chooses $q_i$ as its capacity for the first stage; and at the second stage, the output will be $q_i$ or $\frac{a}{n+1}$. When $\frac{a}{n+1} \geqslant q_i$, namely $a \geqslant (n+1) q_i$, the output would be $q_i$; otherwise it would be $\frac{a}{n+1}$.

Suppose there is excess capacity, which means the output is $\frac{a}{n+1}$, and the manufacturer suffers loss, the breakeven point would be when $\left(\frac{a}{n+1}\right)^2 = kq'_i$, namely $a = (n+1)\sqrt{kq'_i}$.

Then the expected profit of the manufacturer is:

$$E(\pi_i) = \int_{(n+1)q'_i}^{a_H} [a - (q'_1 + \cdots q'_n)] q'_i f(a) \mathrm{d}a$$

$$+ \int_{(n+1)\sqrt{kq'_i}}^{(n+1)q'_i} \left(\frac{A}{n+1}\right)^2 f(a)\mathrm{d}a - \int_{(n+1)\sqrt{kq'_i}}^{a_H} kq'_i f(a)\mathrm{d}a$$

Because of the first-stage prerequisite for maximizing expected profit and symmetry, it follows that:

$$\int_{(n+1)q'_i}^{a_H} af(a)\mathrm{d}a - (n+1)q'_i \int_{(n+1)q'_i}^{a_H} f(a)\mathrm{d}a - k\int_{(n+1)\sqrt{kq'_i}}^{a_H} f(a)\mathrm{d}a = 0 \cdots\cdots 2$$

Because $\int_{(n+1)\sqrt{kq'_i}}^{a_H} f(a)\mathrm{d}a < 1$, $k\int_{(n+1)\sqrt{kq'_i}}^{a_H} f(a)\mathrm{d}a < k$.

Suppose $y(q_i) = \int_{(n+1)q_i}^{a_H} af(a)\mathrm{d}a - (n+1)q_i \int_{(n+1)q_i}^{a_H} f(a)\mathrm{d}a$

$$\frac{\partial y(q_i)}{\partial q_i} = -(n+1)\int_{(n+1)q_i}^{a_H} f(a)\mathrm{d}a < 0$$

So $y(q_i)$ decreases as $q_i$ rises. And we can know $q_i$ in the first situation is inevitably smaller than $q'_i$ in the second one. That is to say, the capacity is larger when there is complete risk externalization than when there is no risk externalization.

From the above analysis, we know that when the capacity is $q_i$, the probability of having excess capacity would be $F[(n+1)q_i]$. Since $q'_i > q_i$, it follows that $F[(n+1)q_i] < F[(n+1)q'_i]$, which means the probability of having excess capacity is greater when there is complete risk externalization than when there is no risk externalization.

## V. Conclusion and Policy Suggestions

### (I) Major Findings

Due to fiscal decentralization reform and the promotion system of officials that centers on GDP growth, local governments are highly motivated to intervene in corporate investment and use all manner of preferential policies to lure investors. This is especially true in those sectors with high input and output. The stimuli to do so are readily identifiable political accomplishments, greater fiscal revenue, and improved local employment. Meanwhile, government monopoly on land and soft budgetary constraints on the banking sector allow governments to offer cheap land, tax reduction and exemption, other subsidies, and help companies secure financial resources. These are the usual practices adopted by local governments to contend for investments and have become the core of regional competition. Investment subsidies and financial assistance, prevalent in regional competition, distort investment behaviors of corporations and would result in excess capacity: investment subsidies lead to undue investment in capacity expansion, hence excess capacity in the sector and loss of social welfare. Cheap land provided by local governments could be used as guaranty and leverage to help enterprises secure bank loans, reducing the proportion of equity investment and externalizing investment risks. When the expected return is already maximized, companies would still increase their capacity investment and this further decreases capacity utilization rates in times of depression, thus artificially enlarging the amplitude of each economic cycle. Intensifying regional competition would maintain investment subsidies at a very high level, hence serious social welfare loss and more excess capacity.

### (II) Policy Suggestions

Since overcapacity, whose solution requires policy intervention, is not due to market failure but institutional limitations, the key to resolving this problem is to correct current institutions and to improve and expand markets. This means ramping up economic reforms, improving market mechanism, correcting distortions in the behaviors of market players created by existing unreasonable institutions, and greater transparency in disseminating market information. Furthermore, a coordination of supply and demand and phasing out less advanced corporations and capacities is required.

More specifically, the problem of excess capacity should be approached through the following measures: First, modify the fiscal and tax system, in particular clarifying the interest allocation mechanism between the central and local government; the promotion system of officials, which centers on GDP growth, should be reformed to eliminate the strong motivation on the part of local governments to unduly intervene in corporate investments; the local fiscal situation should be made transparent and supervised by the public to prevent the possibility of governments providing fiscal subsidies to local companies. Second, reform the current land management system, clarify land property rights, deepen land market reforms, and establish a market pricing mechanism for land. In this way, local governments could no longer subsidize local corporations with cheap or even free land. Third, further promote financial system reforms, tighten budgetary constraints on banks and straighten out bank-government relations. The proportion of equity investment to total investment should be raised through the market, thus mitigating the problem of risk externalization in corporate investments. Fourth, reform the existing system of environmental protection, ensure the enforcement of environmental protection laws and prevent competition for investment at the expense of the environment. The government also needs to explore formulating and implementing stable, long-term and strict environmental policies, and separate environmental protection targets from industrial policies goals addressing excess capacity. Environmental protection policies should not be loosened even when excess capacity is successfully resolved.

## References

1. Barros, P. P, and L. Cabral. 2000. "Competing for Foreign Direct Investment." *Review of International Economics*, 8 (2): 360 – 371.

2. Bond, E. W., and L. Samuelso. 1986. "Tax Holidays as Signals." *The American Economic Review*, 76 (4).

3. Doyle, C. and S. V. Wijnbergen. 1984. "Taxation of Foreign Multinationals: A Sequential Bargaining Approach to Tax Holidays." *Institute for International Economic Studies*, Seminal Paper No. 284.

4. Facundo, Albornoz, Gregory Corcos, and Toby Kendall. 2009. "Subsidy Competition and the Mode of FDI." *Regional Science and Urban Economics*, 39 (4).

5. Helpman, Elhanan, and Paul R. Krugman. 1989. *Trade Policy and Market Structure*. Cam-

bridge, MA: MIT Press.

6. J. , Peter Neary, and Dermot Leahy. 2000. "Strategic Trade and Industrial Policy towards Dynamic Oligopolies." *The Economic Journal*, 110.

7. Jin, Hehui, Yingyi Qian, and Berry Weingast. 2005. "Regional Decentralization and Fiscal Incentive: Federalism Chinese Style." *Journal of Public Economics*, 89.

8. Osiris, Jorge Parcero. 2007. "Inter-Jurisdiction Subsidy Competition for a New Production Plant: What is the Central Government Optimal Policy?" *Regional Science and Urban Economics*, 37 (6).

9. Qian, Y. , and Roland G. 1998. "Federalism and the Soft Budget constrain." *American Economic Review*, 5.

10. Macroeconomic Study Group, CCER. 2004. "Property Rights, Inefficient Investment and Deflation." *Economic Research Journal*, 09: 26 –35.

11. Cao, Jianhai, and Feitao Jiang. 2010. *China's Industrial Investment: A Research of Redundant Construction and Overcapacity*. Beijing: Economy and Management Publishing House.

12. Guo, Qingwang, and Junxue Jia. 2006. "Local Governments' Behavior, Investment Impulse and Macroeconomic Stability." *Management World*, 05: 19 –25.

13. János, Kornai. 1986. *Economics of Shortage*. Beijing: Economic Science Press.

14. János, Kornai. 2007. *The socialist system: The Political Economy of communism*. Beijing: China Academic Journal Electronic Publishing House.

15. Jiang, Feitao, Weigang Chen, Jianbai Huang, and Guohua Jiao. 2007. "Limitations and Defective Results of Policy of Regulating Investment-Based on Research into Chinese Iron & Steel Industry." *China Industrial Economics*, 06: 53 –61.

16. Jiang, Feitao, and Jianhai Cao. 2009. "Market Failure or Institutional Weaknesses-the Argument, Defect and New Development in Research of Redundant Construction Formation Mechanism." *China Industrial Economics*, 01: 53 –64.

17. Jiang, Feitao, and Xiaoping Li. 2010. "Direct Market Intervention and Restrict Competition: The Orientation of China's Industrial Policy and Its Fundamental Defects." *China Industrial Economics*, 09: 26 –36.

18. Li, Junjie. 2005. "Analysis on Distortion of Local Governments' Economic Behaviors in Economic Transition of China." *China Industrial Economics*, 01: 39 –46.

19. Li, Junjie, and Jun Zhong. 2004. "An Analysis of Chinese Local Governments Economic Action-Under the Viewpoint of Public Choice Theory." *China Industrial Economics*, 04: 27 –34.

20. Li, Yang *et al.* 2005. *The Evaluation of Financial Ecological Environment in Chinese City*. Beijing: People Press.

21. Lin, Justin Yifu. 2007. "Wave Phenomenon and the Reconstruction of Macroeconomic Theories for Developing Countries." *Economic Research Journal*, 01: 126 –131.

22. Lin, Justin Yifu, HoMou Wu, and Yiqing Xing. 2010. " 'Wave Phenomena' and Formation of Excess Capacity." *Economic Research Journal*, 10: 4 –19.

23. Manfred, Neumann. 2003. *Competition Policy-History, Theory and Practice*. Beijing: Pe-

king University Press.

24. Pi, Jiancai. 2008. "Research on the Internal Mechanism of Local Governments' Redundant Construction in China." *Economic Theory and Business Management*, 04: 61 - 64.

25. Tao, Ran, Fei Yuan, and Guangzhong Cao. 2007. "Regional Competition, Land Transfers and Local Financial Effect: Empirical Study Based on the Panel Data of Municipalities in China from 1999 to 2003." *The Journal of World Economy*, 10: 15 - 27.

26. Yang, Peihong. 2006. "The Political Economy of Repetitive Investment: A Model." *Economic Quarterly*, 01: 467 - 478

27. Zhang, Weiying, and Jie Ma. 1999. "The Property Right Foundation of Vicious Competition." *Economic Research Journal*, 06: 11 - 20.

28. Zhou, Li' an. 2004. "The Incentive and Cooperation of Government Officials in the Political Tournaments: An Interpretation of the Prolonged Local Protectionism and Duplicative Investments in China." *Economic Research Journal*, 06: 33 - 40.

29. Zhou, Li' an. 2007. "Governing China's Local Officials: An Analysis of Promotion Tournament Model." *Economic Research Journal*, 07: 36 - 50.

# Pcrt Three
# Government Pouey

# Chapter 10

# China's Sovereign Balance Sheet and Its Risk Assessment*

**Li Yang (李扬), Zhang Xiao Jing (张晓晶), Chang Xin (常欣), Tang Duoduo (汤铎铎), and Li Cheng (李成)**

**Chinese Academy of Social Sciences, Beijing, China**

**Abstract**: Using available data and necessary estimations, this paper provides a tentative picture of the balance sheet of China's sovereign account between 2000 and 2010. The main findings indicate that the net worth of China's sovereign assets had been positive and increasing during the period under review. This implies that the Chinese government has sufficient sovereign assets to cover its sovereign liabilities, therefore the likelihood of a sovereign debt crisis in China is extremely low in the near term. Moreover, although China's leverage ratio (total liabilities/GDP) is far lower compared to advanced economies, it seems higher than that of other major emerging economies such as Brazil, Russia, and India (BRIC). In fact, the leverage ratio has been increasing rapidly over recent years and requires special attention. In particular, according to sector-specific analysis, high corporate liability ratios (percentage to GDP) constitute a major concern of China's national balance sheet. In 2010, this liability ratio exceeded 100%, which exceeds the 90% level observed in OECD countries. Lastly, this paper concludes that a sustainable economic growth and structural transformation of growth model are the fundamental means to taming China's balance sheet risks.

**Keywords**: balance sheet approach, sovereign balance sheet, leverage ratio, transformation of development pattern.

## I. Introduction

Most global economic crises in history went hand in hand with international debt crises. As eco-

---

* Corresponding author: zhang_xj@cass.org.cn

This paper is part of the findings of "Study on China's Development Road" sponsored by National Social Science Funds and led by Professor Li Yang. Project approval number: 10@ZH013. We appreciate the contributions from Sun Tao, Cheng Jinzhui, Zhang Lei, Chen Changbing, Wang Jia, Yin Jianfeng, Zeng Gang, and Cheng Lian.

nomic globalization deepens and the financial sector permeates virtually all areas of modern economic activity, debt crisis constitutes a major component of economic crisis more than ever. In today's world, a country's economic health and its changing dynamics are reflected in its balance sheet. Therefore, in order to reveal the root causes of economic crises and find solutions, investigation on the national assets and liabilities as well as their dynamic equilibriums are sorely needed. Based on such an understanding, a growing body of literature employs the analytical framework of balance sheets to address various macroeconomic issues, especially business cycles. In the view of this research line, most economic crises since the 1980s can be regarded as "balance sheet shocks."

Recently, local financing platforms in China began to see a wave of debt problems, raising concern over China's sovereign debt risks. Faced with these challenges, it is of great importance to formulate China's national balance sheet, especially a government balance sheet, and analyze the sources, status quo, and future prospects of the national and sectoral assets and liabilities.

The national balance sheet identifies the asset-liability of an entire country through a well-designed theoretical framework and a series of data processing methodologies. It reveals the relationships between major economic activities, and is useful in accurately capturing a country's economic health and forecasting the sources and intensity of possible shocks. During financial crises in particular, the national balance sheet can offer references for policy discussions. Furthermore, as a stock indicator instead of flow indicator such as GDP, the national balance sheet enables us to reveal the cumulative effect of a country's economic growth over time. With the help of a deeper analysis on balance sheet structure and the dynamics of different sectors, we may also be able to interpret the structural and institutional characteristics of a country's economy so as to identify challenges facing the evolution of its development pattern.

The concept of a national balance sheet is nothing new. In the late 1930s, American scholars had attempted to apply corporate balance sheet techniques to the national economy (Dickingson and Eakin, 1936). As a sophisticated accounting framework, national balance sheet accounting developed in the 1960s. Goldsmith et al. started the pioneering task of formulating comprehensive and sector-specific balance sheets of the United States for a number of years from the early 20th century to 1980 (see Goldsmith and Lipsey, 1963 and Goldsmith, 1982). Revell (1966) tentatively compiled the UK's national balance sheets between 1957 and 1961. In 1975, these sheets were officially published (see Holder, 1998). In 1990, book and market values of Canada's national balance sheets began being compiled. Now, most OECD member have published financial balance sheets at least, and some have reported the nonfinancial assets as well. Compared to advanced countries, China started late in developing its national balance sheets. Although the National Bureau of Statistics (NBS) published two versions of *Methodology for the Compilation of China's Balance Sheet* in 1997 and 2007 respectively, China's official balance sheets are still in the stage of tentative draft and no data have been officially released to the public. By now, the balance sheets may only be an intermediate reference indicator or intermediate product of national economic accounting. This situation makes it all the more urgent to draft not only a national balance sheet, but especially a sovereign balance sheet for China.

Over a period of time, a balance sheet approach (BSA) entered the research field only as a statistical concept under the overall framework of national economic statistical accounting. Since financial crises in the 1990s in Latin America and Asia, there have been increasingly animated discussions on this approach. There is a natural tendency following these discussions to evolve from pure statistical accounting to a standard approach for macroeconomic analysis[①]. After the global financial tsunami began in 2007, this analytical framework received extensive attention and recognition from academia, governments and international institutions. Some Chinese scholars also conducted preliminary analyses on China's economic issues using this approach (Yi, 2008; Li, 2009). It is fair to say that in current rounds of deliberations about financial disasters, studies using the BSA and national balance sheet have become a major academic school of thought.

Allen et al. (2002) noted that theoretically, four major financial risks can be clearly defined using the BSA: maturity mismatch, currency mismatch, capital structure mismatch and deficient solvency[②]. Analyses on these four risks are critical to unraveling the root cause and transmission mechanism of crises, reactions of micro-level entities to crises, and the development of countermeasure policies. In addition to macro-level analyses, balance sheet studies are further conducted in the following three areas. First, the relationship between the capital structure of a sector (country) and financial stability as well as currency crises, are addressed in Allen et al. (2002), and Hou (2006). Second, the sharing and contagion of inter-sector financial risks are studied in Gray et al. (2007) and Hou (2006). Third, the country case studies on debts, capital structure and financial stability are provided by Haim & Levy (2007; Israel), Mathisen & Pellechio (2006; South Africa), Lima et al. (2006; Columbia) and Rosenberg et al. (2005; emerging market). All of these studies have achieved exciting results.

This paper aims to compile China's balance sheet and address some current debates on China's macroeconomic stability. Given the limitation of data and possible controversies of estimation methodologies, this paper attempts to obtain a reliable framework for the formulation of China's balance sheet, and use this tool to assess China's macroeconomic risks.

This paper is structured in the following manner. Part 1 provides a tentative compilation of China's balance sheet. Part 2 estimates China's overall debt level and leverage ratio. Part 3 examines the mechanism through which China's balance sheet has expanded. Part 4 conducts a risk assessment for China's sovereign balance sheet. Part 5 concludes and proposes some policy recommendations.

Throughout this paper, China's balance sheet is always discussed foremost with an emphasis on sovereign sectors. Then the discussions are extended to the overall national balance sheet, which covers not only government but private business, financial institutions and households as well. It should be stressed that the sovereign and private risks are highly correlated. In fact, the balance

---

① According to Mathisen & Pellechio (2006), between 2003 and 2005, the International Monetary Fund (IMF) published more than ten papers on country-level balance sheet analysis.

② Of which, maturity mismatch, currency mismatch and capital structure mismatch can be referred to as balance sheet mismatch.

sheets of private sectors have expanded largely due to policy factors, indicating government dominance in China's economy. Moreover, the assessment of sovereign debt risks in Part 4 also focuses on the risk contagion from the private to public sectors (such as real estate market). For the same reason, Part 2 examines leverage ratios to explore the range of sovereign debts.

## II. Tentative Compilation of China's Sovereign Balance Sheet (2000 -2010)

The sovereign balance sheet differs from the national balance sheet. The latter includes the assets and liabilities of all economic sectors[①]. In a standard sector-specific balance sheet, there is generally no sovereign balance sheet (only a government balance sheet). Sovereign balance sheets in this paper provide a consolidation of sectors of the government (central and local), as well as state-owned or state-controlled financial institutions (including the central bank) and non-financial state-owned enterprises. In essence it is the government balance sheet in a broader sense. In the sovereign balance sheet, sovereign assets refer to government-possessed or controlled assets including other resources at its disposal, while sovereign liabilities refer to direct liabilities of the government and all contingent liabilities due to implicit guarantees approved by the government.

A sovereign balance sheet is largely opposite to a private sector balance sheet in two fundamental ways. First, the household sector is not included as the government cannot mobilize the assets of the household sector (with the exception of a requisition during wartime or other special periods). Correspondingly, the government normally does not bear any responsibility to repay household liabilities. Second, the private sector is not included as it is not directly controlled by the government and their liabilities are not assumed by the government. Although a crisis in the private sector will spread to the government sector (as what occurred in the US sub-prime mortgage crisis) and worsen the sovereign balance sheet, the private sector itself does not directly enter into the sovereign balance sheet.

Based on the above definition, China's sovereign assets include the following six items: business assets, non-business assets, resources assets, holdings of foreign assets, assets in social security fund, as well as governmental deposits at the central bank. China's sovereign liabilities also include six items: central government debts (internal and external), quasi-government bonds (all government-guaranteed bonds issued by various government departments and policy institutions), local government debts, debts of state-owned enterprises, contingent liabilities due to non-performing loans (NPLs), and implicit pension debts. We next turn to the explanation of data sources and estimation methodology, and then present various items of sovereign assets and liabilities in order to acquire time series data for the period 2000 to 2010.

① The boundary of such relevance (i. e. the government may mobilize the assets of private sectors and has to repay its liabilities) is sometimes subject to the interpretation of government itself.

By consolidating the above-mentioned assets and liabilities items, we show the changes in China's sovereign balance sheet over the years. It can be seen from Figure 1 that during the past 11 years, there had been expansion and the growth of assets outpaced liabilities. As a result, China's government net worth had experienced a continuous increase.

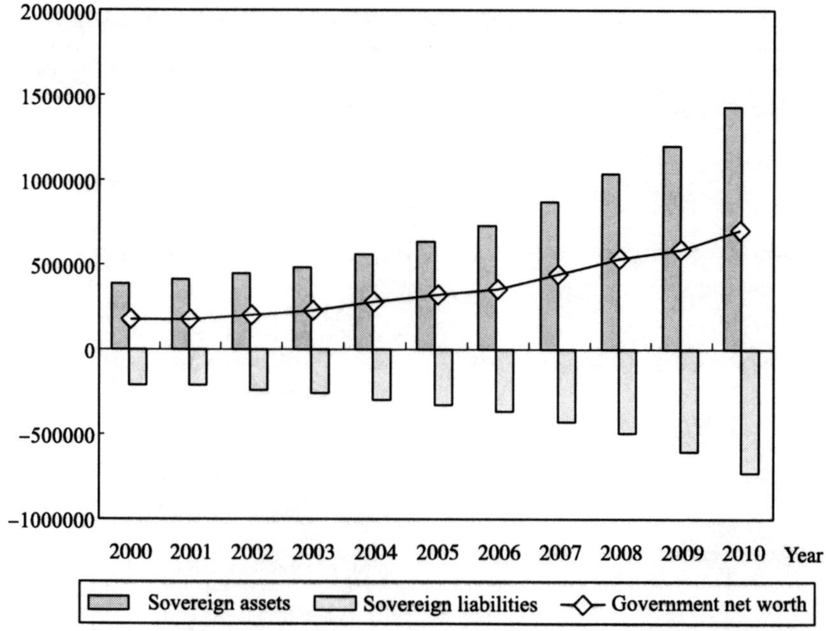


**Figure 1: China's Sovereign Assets/Liabilities and Government Net Worth (2000 -2010)**

Source: estimated by the research group.

With the above analysis on sovereign assets and liabilities, we are able to compile China's sovereign balance sheet between 2000 and 2010. As an example, below a brief analysis on the figures of 2010 is provided.

Table 1 indicates that calculated by broad statistical measure, the net worth of China's sovereign assets in 2010 reached RMB 69.6 trillion. Considering the poor reliability of state-owned assets of administrative nonprofit institutions (due to the performance of government functions) and the limited transferability of state-owned land and resources (land expropriation revenue reached only two or three trillion RMB per year in recent years)①, by narrow statistical measure, i.e. deducting state-owned assets of administrative nonprofit institutions and replacing state-owned land and resources of RMB 44.3 trillion with land expropriation revenue of RMB 2.8 trillion in 2010, China's sovereign assets will fall from RMB 142.3 trillion to RMB 93 trillion. In this way, the net worth of

① If the land expropriation system is to be adjusted in the future and land leasehold system is reformed into an annual land lease system, i.e. replacing one-off collection of land expropriation fund for decades with the collection of land rents on a yearly basis (land use fees), the revenues from land will further decrease.

China's sovereign assets by narrow statistical measure stands at approximately RMB20 trillion. The above analysis indicates that whether observed from a broad or narrow statistical measure, China's sovereign balance sheet has a positive net worth. This indicates that the Chinese government has sufficient resources to remain solvent and is insulated from a sovereign debt crisis in the near term.

**Table 1: China's Sovereign Balance Sheet of 2010 (unit: RMB trillion)**

| Assets | | Liabilities and government net worth | |
|---|---|---|---|
| Government deposits at the central bank | 2.4 | Internal debts of central budget | 6.7 |
| Reserve assets | 19.7 | Sovereign external debts | 2.3 |
| Land | 44.3 | Local government debts except for financing platforms | 5.8 |
| State-owned assets of administrative nonprofit institutions | 7.8 | Local government debts for financing platforms | 9.0 |
| State-owned assets of non-financial sector | 59.1 | Debts of non-financial state-owned enterprises (deducting local government liabilities for financing platforms) | 35.6 |
| State-owned assets of financial sector | 8.2 | Policy banks' debts | 5.2 |
| | | Non-performing loans (NPLs) | 0.4 |
| | | Contingent liabilities due to NPLs | 4.2 |
| State-owned assets of national social security fund | 0.8 | Implicit pension fund debts | 3.5 |
| Total assets | 142.3 | Total liabilities | 72.7 |
| | | Government net worth | 69.6 |

Source: estimated by the research group.

A few points require explanation in regard to the calculation and compilation of the sovereign balance sheet:

On the one hand, there is a risk of undervaluation for assets when using book value. For example, by using the relevant data of listed companies to calculate the market value of state-owned shares, previous studies such as Shen and Fan (2012) concluded that the book values of state-owned assets were undervalued. Additionally, sovereign assets will be overvalued if the state-owned assets of administrative, nonprofit institutions and land are not appropriately deducted. Finally, from an accounting point of view, repetitive calculations may exist, and thus will lead to overvaluation.

On the other hand, it is controversial to simply add up explicit liabilities and contingent liabilities. Obviously, a major problem is how to judge the default risk of contingent liabilities, which definitely affects the valuation of liabilities. Here, we did not select any probabilities for this risk and directly added up these liabilities. Thus, it is a source of overvaluation of liabilities.

Despite the above problems, our overall assessment on China's sovereign balance sheet will not be affected.

## III. China's Overall Liability Level and Leverage Ratio

Although emphasizing the sovereign balance sheet, this paper examines the overall liability level and leverage ratios of various sectors given the risk transfer between sectors. This approach helps understand the overall risks to the economy and provides broader support to the measurement of sovereign balance sheet risks. The reason to include contingent liabilities in sovereign balance sheet calculations is due to the fact that explicit liabilities of other sectors may become contingent sovereign liabilities under certain specific conditions. Therefore, an assessment of the overall liabilities in all sectors should yield a relatively comprehensive appraisal on the scale of contingent liabilities that may occur.

Considering the data availability and characteristics of China's financial system, this paper adopts the definition of liabilities in its narrow sense, i. e. only taking into account currency and deposits, debt securities and loans. Currency is the central bank's liabilities and deposits are mainly the liabilities of commercial banks, which are also a major component of China's money supply. Given that the purpose of examining liabilities is to assess leverage risks while currency and deposits pose little or no risks to financial institutions, we have followed common practices by deducting currency and deposits in calculating the liabilities of the financial sector. According to the definition by the International Monetary Fund (IMF) (2011), standard debt securities comprise nine categories including cashier's checks, commercial instruments, bonds and transferable loans. China's liabilities generally fall into two categories, i. e. bonds and loans. Loans currently comprise the majority while bonds have seen a rapid increase over the past two decades (Figure 2).

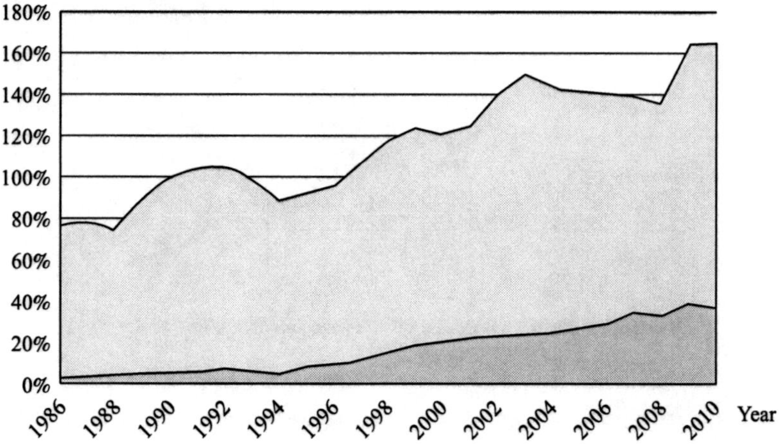


**Figure 2: China's Loans/GDP and Bonds/GDP**

Source: China Economic Information Center (CEIC).

Generally speaking, total liabilities are an aggregate of liabilities of households, enterprises and governments (Cecchetti et al., 2011); in some cases the liabilities of the financial sector are included as well (MGI, 2010; 2012). Here we aggregated liabilities of these four sectors following MGI studies.

Household liabilities are mainly composed of loans. Non-financial corporations' liabilities fall into two categories, i. e., loans and corporate bonds. For financial institutions, liabilities are mainly financial bonds which can be classified as policy financial bonds and other financial bonds after putting aside currencies and deposits. Government liabilities are composed of internal and external debts. To facilitate international comparison, local government liabilities are excluded. Local government liabilities are usually excluded from IMF statistics of government liabilities as well. If local liabilities were taken into account, the percentage of the Chinese government liabilities in GDP would almost double from the current 22.4% to 43.5%.

Figure 3 shows the percentage of China's total liabilities and four sectors' liabilities to GDP. Although the percentage of total liabilities shows an upward trend (there is some decline during 2003 and 2008, caused by deleveraging), the leverage ratio rises rapidly following the Asian Financial Crisis in 1997, the IT bubble burst in 2000, and the global financial crisis in 2008. Evidently, an economic crisis exerts a large impact on the growth of total liabilities.

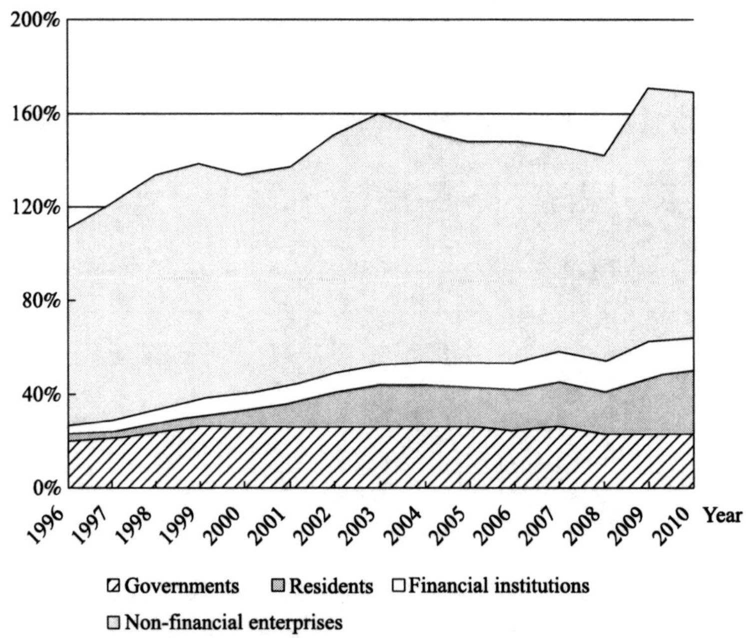


**Figure 3: Percentage of the Four Sector's Liabilities in GDP**

Data source: estimation by the research group and CEIC.

Due to limited space, only China's overall liability level and the leverage ratio from a perspective of international comparison are described in this paper.

Looking at the aggregate, China's overall liability level is lower than most advanced economies but higher than other BRIC countries (excluding South Africa). As shown in Table 2, Japan and Britain's "total liabilities/GDP" exceeds 500%, and the figure for Spain, France, Italy and South Korea exceeds 300% and that for the U. S., German and Canada is smaller but all exceed 270% in 2011. As to BRIC countries, the figure is 148% for Brazil, 122% for India and only 72% for Russia (MGI, 2012) in 2010, all lower than China's 168.9%. Given these figures, China's "total liabilities/GDP" (the leverage ratio) remains moderate and controllable, but vigilance needs to be maintained, especially considering the rapid growth of China's liabilities over recent years and the fact that China's government liabilities will double after taking into account local liabilities.

As Table 2 indicates, the percentage of non-financial enterprises' liabilities is extremely high (the highest among all countries covered), a prominent characteristic of China's liability structure. The percentage is smaller in other sectors, especially households and financial institutions. This is closely related to China's economic development model and characteristics of the financial system. Currently, indirect financing is the most prominent in China's financing system as most monetary resources are allocated through banks. Therefore, Chinese enterprises' liabilities are unavoidably high. During stable economic growth, borrowing from banks is the main source of liabilities. However, in the case of an economic downturn a considerable part of liabilities will go uncollectable and hurt the balance sheet of banks and the enterprise itself. As shown in Figure 2 and 3: although the percentage of non-financial enterprises' liabilities in GDP remains dangerously high, the percentage in total liabilities had dropped from 76% in 1996 to 62.4% in 2010.

**Table 2: A Comparison of the Liability Structure and the Leverage Ratio between China and Advanced Economies (Percentage in GDP, %)**

| | Percentage of households' liabilities | Percentage of non-financial enterprises' liabilities | Percentage of financial institutions' liabilities | Percentage of governments' liabilities | Percentage of total liabilities |
|---|---|---|---|---|---|
| Japan | 67 | 99 | 120 | 226 | 512 |
| Britain | 98 | 109 | 219 | 81 | 507 |
| Spain | 82 | 134 | 76 | 71 | 363 |
| France | 48 | 111 | 97 | 90 | 346 |
| Italy | 45 | 82 | 76 | 111 | 314 |
| South Korea | 81 | 107 | 93 | 33 | 314 |
| U. S. | 87 | 72 | 40 | 80 | 279 |
| German | 60 | 49 | 87 | 83 | 279 |
| Australia | 105 | 59 | 91 | 21 | 276 |
| Canada | 91 | 53 | 63 | 69 | 276 |
| China | 28 | 105.4 | 13 | 22.4 | 168.9 |

Note: data for China are estimated by the research group for 2010; other data come from (MGI) (2012) and are all for the second quarter of 2011 (only the data for Italy are for the first quarter of 2011).

Although there has been no general agreement on the optimal percentage of liabilities in GDP, liability growth is certainly accompanied by greater solvency pressure and risks. There is a threshold in which the disadvantages of growing liabilities will outweigh advantages and may even trigger a financial and economic crisis. Estimating with fund flow statistics of 18 OECD members during 1980 and 2010, Cecchetti et al. (2011) concluded that the threshold (liabilities/GDP) is 85% for governments and residents and 90% for enterprises. From this point of view, it is an alarming sign that the percentage of Chinese enterprises' liabilities in GDP has reached 105.4% in 2010.

More attention might be needed given the fact that all sectors of the national economy interact with each other and liability change in one sector will affect other sectors. A study on Japan by MGI (MGI, 2010) offers a dismal view. In 1995, the percentage of Japanese enterprises' liabilities in GDP was 148%; it dropped to 125% in 2000 and further to 91% in 2005; a decline of 57 percentage points in total within a decade. In the meantime, the percentage of Japanese governments' liabilities in GDP had soared from 84% in 1995 to 131% in 2000, and further to 180% in 2005, namely an increase of 96% within a decade. A direct link, if any, between these movements requires more studies.

## IV. Balance Sheet Expansion with Chinese Characteristics

China's balance sheet has expanded rapidly during 2000 and 2010.

Rapid accumulation of foreign assets, primarily in infrastructure and real estate are major factors in the balance sheet expansion. It records the rapid progress of China's industrialization and urbanization under the export-oriented development strategy. On one hand, with rapid progress of the export-oriented industrialization, China has emerged as the world's processing and manufacturing base, which brings substantial growth of the cargo trade surplus. Under this background, China's foreign assets grew rapidly. By the end of 2011, foreign exchange reserve assets had reached $3.3 trillion. On the other hand, urbanization was accompanied with large-scale investment in infrastructure in China. During 2001 – 2010, China's investment in urban infrastructure had enjoyed 3.57 – fold growth with an average annual rate of 18.4%. The percentage of infrastructure investment in GDP was over 15%, which was far beyond The World Bank's policy suggestion in its report titled, *Providing Infrastructure for Development* in 1994, which stated that the percentage of infrastructure investment in GDP should be no less than 5%. Moreover, along with reform of housing system, urban residents' house assets also amassed rapidly. As estimated, total urban house value witnessed more than a 7 – fold growth from RMB 10.1 trillion in 1998 to RMB 71.9 trillion in 2010.

Liabilities of Chinese governments and state-owned enterprises also saw noticeable expansion that was faster than in the private sector (including private enterprises and households), thus forming sizable sovereign liabilities (namely governments' liabilities in a broad sense). This highlights the fact that economic activities are heavily influenced and led by the government. Furthermore, the speed of economic growth outpaced that of system reform. As a result, this further highlights the typical "intensive infrastructure construction" kind of government. When institutional fund sources became insufficient, the "local government funding vehicle" (LGFV) had burgeoned to support their ambitious investment plans. At the end of 2010, LGFV balances reached RMB4,971billion, accounting for 46.38% of local governments' liabilities. At the end of 2010, the liabilities funds (those issued) of local governments across the country were used for three major purposes: municipal construction, transportation, land purchasing and storage and consolidation, accounting for up to 72% of all purposes. All these are directly linked to urban infrastructure construction. As local governments increased their intervention in economic activities or offered implicit guarantees, non-performing loans of state-owned enterprises and commercial banks and shortfalls in social security funds became their contingent liabilities.

## V. Risk Assessment of China's Sovereign Balance Sheet

Risks of the sovereign balance sheet can be assessed from the macro level.

Factors assessed at the macro level include sovereign countries' liability risks and corresponding solvency risks. As discussed above, the liability level and leverage ratio are main indicators measuring macro risks of the balance sheet.

Structural risks roughly fall into the following three categories.

First, balance sheet mismatch and contingent liabilities. Balance sheet mismatch risks mainly fall into three types. First is the "currency mismatch" risk, mainly "currency mismatch on credit." Specifically, when most of foreign exchange assets are denominated by the U. S. dollar, they will suffer huge losses amidst depreciation of that currency. Second is the "maturity mismatch" risk, which is closely related to a long cycle of urban investment. Commercial banks face the risk of absorbing short-term funds for making long-term loans; for local governments, the risk lies in a serious mismatch between the liability tenure and projects' cash-flow distribution which can lead to "liquidity risks." Third is the "capital structure mismatch" risk, which refers to excessive reliance on debt financing instead of owner's equity. The percentage of China's non-financial enterprises' liabilities in total liabilities was 62.4%, 30 to 40 percentage points higher than that of other countries. The culprit is the characteristics, or weakness of China's financial system. Risks brought about by the above three mismatches can be viewed as liquidity risks.

Contingent liability risks fall into two categories. First, real estate credit risk: by all indicators, direct risk exposure of real estate loans is controllable. However, given several factors like a high percentage of real estate mortgage loans, strong forward and backward linkage of the real estate industry, and the fact that LGFV's heavy reliance on land transfer revenue, banks' indirect risks cannot be ignored as they will turn to real risks upon in-depth adjustment of the house price. An international comparison provided by us (not presented here), the ratio of China's house value to GDP is low, showing China's overall real estate risks are controllable; conversely, the ratio of China's urban house value to residents' disposable income is higher than that of all advanced countries for comparison, showing that risks are being aggravated. The second category is shortfalls in social security funds. With the dual challenge of system transformation and the aging population, the shortfall becomes a prominent issue. So far "empty account" (funds of individual accounts are appropriated for current pension payment) has reached a scale of RMB1. 4 trillion. To bridge the shortfall and ensure pension insurance funds are paid timely and in full amount, the fiscal authority should shoulder the responsibility, which would be even larger if full coverage of pension insurance and "empty accounts" of medical care insurance and unemployment insurance are taken into account. The goal of these contingent liability risks, especially the longevity risk (life expectancy is prolonged thanks to advanced medical care technologies) will translate into more liabilities in the government sector, the ultimate solver of the shortfall.

Second, structural risk is the clearing of liabilities and risk contagion among sectors. Risks of assets and liabilities of all constituents of the national balance sheet are correlated to each other. What's discussed here is about sectoral distribution of liability risks and the property right correlation between assets and liabilities. Based on this, we can sort out the possible liability-clearing path and changes in property rights. Chinese governments own a lot of sovereign assets. Usually, when they are used to cover sovereign liabilities of one sector, they end up being liabilities and risks in the other sector. Liabilities are not truly eliminated. For example, according to the time series data of sovereign liabilities discussed above, banks' non-performing assets declined from 2, 173. 1 billion in 2000 to 433. 6 billion in 2010, but at the same time contingent liabilities formed by disposal of bad assets increased from 1. 4 trillion in 2000 to 4. 2 trillion in 2010.

Third, structural risk is the development path and stability of sovereign liabilities. According to our simulation analysis, the percentage of government liabilities in GDP mainly depends on the difference between the economic growth rate and the interest rate. As long as the difference is maintained at a high level, governments' liability risks won't be big and the percentage of government liabilities in GDP will be stable.

## VI. Conclusions and Policy Recommendations

Based on comprehensive analysis on China's national and sovereign balance sheets, the following conclusions can be reached.

First, China's national balance sheet was rapidly expanded during 2000 – 2010. Rapid accumulation of foreign assets, infrastructures and real estate assets contributed the most to the asset expansion. It could be viewed as a reflection of the rapid process of China's industrialization and urbanization under the export-oriented development strategy. On the liability side, governments and state-owned enterprises experienced faster growth of liabilities than the private sectors, which highlighted a government-led economic system.

Second, overall risks of China's sovereign balance sheet were small and are unlikely to cause a sovereign debt crisis in the near future. However, contingent liability risks deserve attention.

(1) According to the sovereign balance sheet we drafted, the net worth of China's sovereign assets in 2010 calculated by broad and narrow statistical measures reached nearly RMB70 trillion and RMB20 trillion, respectively. In addition, the figure for all years during 2000 – 2010 remained positive and took an upward trend. It indicates that Chinese governments have sufficient sovereign assets to stay solvent, and are very unlikely to suffer from a sovereign debt crisis in the near to medium term.

(2) According to analysis on the overall liability level and the leverage ratio, China's leverage ratio was higher than that of other BRIC countries but far lower than major advanced economies. It was moderate and controllable on the whole. However, it has been rising rapidly over recent years, which deserves attention. Analysis by sector-level data indicated that the enterprises' liability ratios (the percentage in GDP) were very high, which was a prominent characteristic of China's balance sheet. The liability ratio in 2010 was over 100%, higher than the threshold of 90% for OECD countries. At the same time, it is found that China's households' liabilities have great room for growth in the future. According to international experience, the overall liability level will further rise and government net worth will turn from positive to negative along with economic growth. It is a contingency that requires advanced preparation.

(3) Simulation analysis indicates that the percentage of governments' liabilities in GDP mainly depends on the difference between the economic growth rate and the interest rate. Therefore, maintaining sustainable economic growth is a powerful weapon against sovereign debt crisis.

(4) Recent risks of the sovereign balance sheet are mainly centered on the real estate credit and local governments' liabilities. Medium and long-term risks are, however, reflected in foreign assets and liabilities, enterprises' liabilities and shortfalls in social security funds. Most of them are contingent liability risks closely related to the prior development mode.

By assessing risks of the sovereign balance sheet, we believe that transforming the economic development mode should be the fundamental countermeasure against risks in the balance sheet. Specific policy recommendations are proposed as below.

(1) To reduce the currency mismatch risk, China should focus on expanding domestic demands to reduce reliance on foreign demands and slow accumulation of foreign exchange reserves. Meanwhile, holdings of foreign currencies by private sectors, direct investment overseas, and internationalization of RMB are eagerly needed. More importantly, when "currency mismatch on credit" cannot be reversed in the short term, more proactive uses of the *Sovereign Wealth Fund* to reduce currency mismatch risks should be taken.

(2) Chinese governments' should intervene less in economic activities to reduce contingent liability risks. The government-led growth pattern plays a positive role in developing the economy but brings more contingent liabilities to the government than a more mature market economy does. The fundamental way of reducing liability risks is to reduce government intervention in micro-level economic activities by advancing marketization reform and transforming the government's role, thereby crystallizing real debtors of such contingent debt loadings.

(3) China should reshape the fiscal relationship between the central and local governments and

encourage innovations to the financing mechanism for urbanization. First, a top-level design should be deliberated to remove the mismatch between local governments' power in affairs and finance. Second, China should improve the financing mechanism for urbanization, such as fiscal and tax reform to offer new tax sources (such as property tax) for local governments. Some initiatives could also be productive such as expanding pilots of local government bonds to expand funding sources, replacing LGFV with special treasury bonds to be issued by policy banks and the state, and securitizing some public utilities projects or extending the tenure of related loans to remove the maturity mismatch in local governments' balance sheet.

(4) A transition from debt financing to equity financing should be achieved to reduce the leverage ratio and to relieve enterprises' capital structure mismatch. China's financial system is dominated by banks which absorb and allocate most of society's savings. Heavy reliance on banks aggravates enterprises' capital structure mismatch and raises the leverage ratio. Given these, China should transform its financial structure from debt financing to equity financing by developing a capital market that facilitates formation and supply of equity capitals.

(5) China should adjust income distribution patterns and deepen strategic adjustments of the layout of the state-owned economy to bridge the shortfalls in social security funds. The crucial part of the reforms is to increase the business budget incomes of state-owned capitals. For instance, besides central government enterprises, local state-owned enterprises, monopoly enterprises (such as railways beyond control of the State-owned Assets Supervision and Administration Commission), and state-owned financial institutions need to turn over some of their profits to the government. Furthermore, an increase in dividend payment percentages should be undertaken. Operation income of state-owned capitals should also grant more subsidies to social security[①]. Additionally, while maintaining the dominant role of the state-owned economy, some state-owned shares can be sold in domestic securities market to replenish social security funds, such as shares of non-listed state-owned enterprises, holding corporations of listed companies, or listed companies without rights issue.

## References

1. Allen, Mark, Christoph Rosenberg, Christian Keller, Brad Setser, and Nouriel Roubini. 2002. "A Balance Sheet Approach to Financial Crisis." *IMF Working Paper*, WP/02/210.

2. Cecchetti, Stephen G., M. S. Mohanty, and Fabrizio Zampolli. 2011. "The Real Effects of Debt." *BIS Working Paper*, no. 352.

3. Commission of the European Communities, IMF, OECD, UN and World Bank. 2008. *System of National Accounts* 2008, pre-edited version of Volume 1.

4. Dickinson, Frank G., and Franzy Eakin. 1936. "A Balance Sheet of the Nation's Economy." University of Illinois.

5. Goldsmith, R. W., and Robert E. Lipsey. 1963. *Studies in the National Balance Sheet of*

① In 2010, only 0.1% of net profits of central state-owned enterprises, namely RMB1 billion, was appropriated for social security. In 2011, the amount was increased to RMB4 billion, but only represented 0.4% of the net profits of these enterprises.

*the United States*. New Jersey: Princeton University Press

6. Goldsmith, Raymond W. 1982. *The National Balance Sheet of the United States*, 1953 – 1980. Chicago: University of Chicago Press.

7. Gray, Dale F., Robert C. Merton, and Zvi Bodie. 2007. "New Framework for Measuring and Managing Macrofinancial Risk and Financial Stability." *NBER Working Paper*, no.. 13607.

8. Haim, Yair, and Roee Levy. 2007. "Using the Balance Sheet Approach in Financial Stability Surveillance: Analyzing the Israeli Economy's Resilience to Exchange Rate Risk." No. 1/07, Bank of Israel.

9. Holder, Andrew. 1998. "Developing the Public-sector Balance Sheet." *Economic Trends*, no. 540: 31 – 40.

10. Hou, Jie. 2006. *National Capital Structure and Financial Crisis of Emerging Market Economies*. Doctoral dissertation, Renmin University of China.

11. International Monetary Fund. 2011. "Public Sector Debt Statistics: Guide for Compilers and Users." Washington, DC: International Monetary Fund.

12. Li, Yang. 2009. *Asset Bubbles should be Controlled Via the Balance Sheet*, *speech at Summer Davos* 2009. http://money.163.com/09/0910/15/5IS2VHQJ00253NDC.html.

13. Lima, Juan Manuel, Enrique Montes, Carlos Varela, and Johannes Wiegand. 2006. "Sectoral Balance Sheet Mismatches and Macroeconomic Vulnerabilities in Colombia, 1996 – 2003." *IMF Working Paper*, WP/06/5.

14. Mathisen, Johan, and Anthony Pellechio. 2006. "Using the Balance Sheet Approach in Surveillance: Framework, Data Sources, and Data Availability." *IMF Working Paper*, WP/06/100.

15. McKinsey Global Institute (MGI). 2010. "Debt and Deleveraging: The Global Credit Bubble and Its Economic Consequences." www.mckinsey.com.

16. McKinsey Global Institute (MGI). 2012. "Debt and Deleveraging: Uneven Progress on the Path to Growth." www.mckinsey.com.

17. National Bureau of Statistics. 1997 and 2007. *Methodology for the Formulation of China's Balance Sheet*. Beijing: China Statistics Press.

18. Revell, Jack. 1966. "The National Balance Sheet of the United Kingdom." *Review of Income and Wealth*, 12 (4): 281 – 310.

19. Rosenberg, Christoph, Ioannis Halikias, Brett House, Christian Keller, Jens Nystedt, Alexander Pitt, and Brad Setser. 2005. "Debt-related Vulnerabilities and Financial Crises: An Application of the Balance Sheet Approach to Emerging Market Countries." *IMF Occasional Paper*, no. 240.

20. Shen, Peilong, and Huan Fan. 2012. "Research on Chinese Government's Liability Risk Based on "Liquidity Asset" Balance Sheet." *Economic Research*, no. 2.

21. World Bank. 2006. *Where Is the Wealth of Nations? Measuring Capital for the* 21st *Century*, Washington D. C.: World Bank.

22. Wu, You. 2002. "The Comparison and Transforming of National Balance Sheet Account-

ing and Accountancy Balance Sheet Accounting." *Statistical Research*, no. 4.

23. Yi, Gang. 2008. "China Can Withstand the Test of Financial Crisis." *Seeking Truth*, no. 22.

24. Zhang, Guosheng. 2006. "Some Thoughts on Improving Chinese Government's Balance Sheet." *Collected Essays on Finance and Economics*, no. 3.

# Chapter 11

# China's Monetary Policy Instruments (2001 - 2010): Paradox, Analysis and Suggestions*

**Wang Guogang** (王国刚)

**Institute of Finance and Banking, Chinese Academy of Social Sciences, Beijing, China.**

**Abstract**: Through a systematic analysis of China's monetary policy instruments adopted between 2001 and 2010, the author argues that raising *required reserve ratios* (or RRRs) cannot reduce the overall supply of funds, while raising the deposit and loan interest rate expands credit. Compared with the above two approaches, controlling incremental loan scale is more effective. During the 12th Five-Year Plan period (2011 - 2015), China should improve its monetary policy system in five aspects: the balance sheet structure of The People's Bank of China (PBOC), the intermediary objective and operation instruments, market orientation of the deposit and loan interest rate, ultimate objective of monetary policies and establishment of a system framework for prudent macro financial management.

**Keywords**: Monetary policy, instrument, rationale, *required reserve ratios* (or RRRs)

After what may be described as dazzling monetary policy changes from "tight" in 2008 and "moderately loose" during 2009 - 2010 to the current "prudent" policy, PBOC is now focusing more on establishing a system framework for prudent macro financial management. This marks a new era for China's monetary policy control. Against this backdrop, reviewing the entire process, rationale, and the effects of China's monetary policy control in the first decade of the 21st century will carry a significant impact for enhancing China's monetary and financial theory and policy practice.

A monetary policy system includes the ultimate objective, intermediary objective, and operation instruments, and so forth. Operation instruments are the basic means for achieving the intended objective and the mechanism of transmitting monetary policy intentions. Due to limited space and also because Western theories cannot truly explain the operation rationale of China's monetary policy instruments, this paper focuses on exploring reasons for selecting certain policy instruments, the operation process itself and the practical effects. Analysis is made of instruments adopted between 2001

---

* Corresponding author: wgg3806@ sina. com.

and 2010, including RRRs, benchmark deposits, and loan interest rates and control over the incremental loan scale.

## I. The Rationale for Adjusting the RRRs

The RRRs were kept down in the 1990s but have been rising throughout the period 2001 to 2010. As shown in Figure 1, after hitting the trough of 6% in November 21, 1999 the RRRs rose rapidly amidst several monetary policy changes during the first decade of the 21 st century. The RRRs bear "mandatory" attributes. Once implemented, financial institutions should comply without room for any price or quantity "negotiation" with the PBOC. Adjusting the RRRs directly influences financial institutions, their business activities, and loanable funds (creation of derivative money). Theoretically, raising the RRRs directly reduces the supply of money in the financial market, and vice versa. However, there is a major theoretical defect in measuring the effect of RRRs adjustment simply by the money multiplier calculation formula, because it puts aside financial institutions' various reserves, purchases of securities and the examination of solvency of loan customers. It therefore fails to reflect the truth. Moreover, it fails to reflect how these funds acquired by the PBOC (through raising RRRs) are used, and fabricates a deceptive "disappearance" of funds upon accessing the PBOC account.

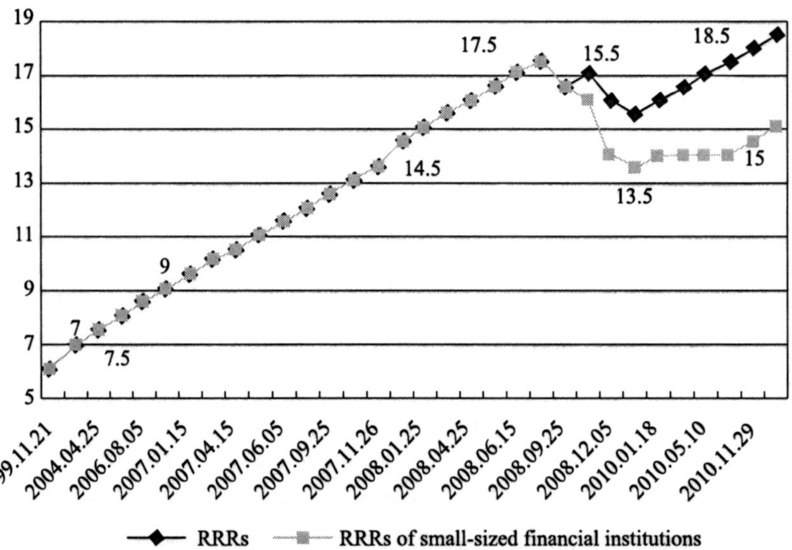


**Figure 1: Trend of the RRRs between 2001 and 2010**

Source: Website of PBOC.

Table 1 lists the amount of legal deposit reserves that financial institutions should pay according to the specified year-end RRRs between 2001 and 2010. It shows that the deposit reserve amount is directly affected by both RRRs and financial institutions' balance of deposits. For instance, at the end of December 2010 the amount of legal deposit reserves were RMB 12. 6 trillion; and where the money multiplier is 5 then over RMB 63 trillion funds would be withdrawn from the market. However, financial institutions' loan balances were only RMB 47. 9 trillion for the same period, which is far short of enough to offset the tightening effect of higher RRRs. If this were to be the real case, China would have been caught up in deflation with a severe economic recession even before other monetary policy instruments, such as control over the incremental loan scale, were adopted after 2003. In fact, China witnessed rapid growth instead of deflation after 2003. Thus, it becomes the focus of this paper to properly explain the funds flow between constant rises of the RRRs.

**Table 1: Reserve Requirement (2001 -2010)**

| Year | RRRs (%) | Balance of deposits (RMB Billion) | Reserve requirement (RMB Billion) |
|---|---|---|---|
| December 2001 | 6 | 13, 840. 39 | 830. 423 |
| December 2002 | 6 | 16, 596. 85 | 995. 81 |
| December 2003 | 7 | 19, 948. 06 | 1, 396. 36 |
| December 2004 | 7. 5 | 22, 933. 43 | 1, 720. 01 |
| December 2005 | 7. 5 | 27, 200. 85 | 2, 040. 06 |
| December 2006 | 9 | 31, 850. 53 | 2, 866. 55 |
| December 2007 | 14. 5 | 37, 306. 70 | 5, 409. 47 |
| December 2008 | 15. 5 | 44, 094. 76 | 6, 834. 69 |
| December 2009 | 15. 5 | 57, 197. 76 | 8, 8656. 52 |
| December 2010 | 18. 5 | 68, 122. 36 | 12, 602. 64 |

Source: Sorted out from data on the website of PBOC.

In Table 2, data in the "deposit of financial corporations" column is larger than that of the "required deposit reserve ratio" for the corresponding year in Table 1 (the gap is "excess reserves"). It indicates that financial institutions have paid the reserve requirement after the RRRs was increased. In this regard, a repeated rise of the RRRs is not a factor in the reduction of funds supply for economic operation. So what's the rationale?

**Table 2: Liability Structure of PBOC (2001 -2010)**

**Denomination: RMB billion**

| Item | 2001 | 2002 | 2003 | 2004 | 2005 | 2006 | 2007 | 2008 | 2009 | 2010 |
|---|---|---|---|---|---|---|---|---|---|---|
| Reserve money | 3, 985. 17 | 4, 513. 82 | 5, 284. 14 | 5, 885. 61 | 6, 434. 31 | 7, 775. 78 | 10, 154. 54 | 12, 922. 23 | 14, 398. 5 | 18, 531. 12 |
| Money issuance | 1, 686. 87 | 1, 858. 91 | 2, 124. 05 | 2, 310. 40 | 2, 585. 40 | 2, 913. 87 | 3, 297. 16 | 3, 711. 58 | 4, 155. 58 | 4, 864. 60 |
| Deposit of financial corporations | 1, 708. 91 | 1, 913. 84 | 2, 255. 80 | 3, 567. 28 | 3, 839. 13 | 4, 845. 93 | 6, 841. 59 | 9, 210. 66 | 10, 242. 92 | 13, 666. 51 |

Continued

| Item | 2001 | 2002 | 2003 | 2004 | 2005 | 2006 | 2007 | 2008 | 2009 | 2010 |
|---|---|---|---|---|---|---|---|---|---|---|
| Margin deposit | 1, 708. 91 | | | | | | | | | |
| Deposit of financial corporations excluded from reserve money | 589. 39 | 741. 07 | 904. 28 | 7. 93 | 9. 79 | 15. 99 | 15. 80 | 59. 12 | 62. 48 | 65. 72 |
| Issuance of bonds | | 148. 75 | 303. 16 | 1, 107. 90 | 2, 029. 60 | 2, 974. 06 | 3, 446. 91 | 4, 577. 98 | 4, 206. 42 | 4, 049. 72 |
| Overseas liability | | 42. 31 | 48. 26 | 56. 23 | 64. 16 | 92. 63 | 94. 73 | 73. 26 | 76. 17 | 72. 01 |
| Government deposit | 285. 05 | 308. 54 | 495. 47 | 583. 22 | 752. 72 | 1, 021. 07 | 1, 712. 11 | 1, 696. 38 | 2, 122. 64 | 2, 427. 73 |
| Proprietary funds | 35. 52 | 21. 98 | 21. 98 | 21. 98 | 21. 98 | 21. 98 | 21. 98 | 21. 98 | 21. 98 | 21. 98 |
| Other liabilities | -51. 68 | 75. 37 | 47. 41 | 210. 60 | 1, 064. 83 | 971. 96 | 1, 483. 71 | 1, 358. 65 | 1, 865. 32 | 759. 22 |
| Total liabilities | 4, 843. 45 | 5, 110. 76 | 6, 200. 41 | 7, 865. 53 | 1, 0367. 60 | 12, 857. 47 | 16, 913. 98 | 20, 709. 60 | 22, 753. 50 | 25, 927. 49 |

Source: Website of PBOC. After 2002, "margin deposit" is no longer listed separately but consolidated into "deposit of financial corporations"; since 2008, "deposit of non-financial corporations" and the sub-item "demand deposit" are deleted, while the item "deposit of financial corporations excluded from reserve money" is added, thus, "deposit of financial corporations excluded from reserve money" is in fact "deposit of non-financial corporations" between 2001 and 2007. Total liabilities of 2011 are calculated from corresponding items.

If the PBOC were to really "freeze" the corresponding amount of funds acquired after increasing the RRRs, they should be booked on the "asset side" of the PBOC's balance sheet. However, we cannot find them in Table 3, nor do they appear as the item "RMB asset. "① Such a huge amount of deposit reserves cannot simply just "disappear" . The only explanation to arise is that the PBOC has used them. But in what way?

As we can see in Table 2 and Table 3, the PBOC's biggest assets on the "asset side" is "foreign exchanges (FX)" registering up to RMB 20. 68 trillion (accounting for 79. 75% of the PBOC's "total assets") by the end of 2010. Such sizable FX assets should be hedged by RMB funds. However, on the "liability side", the figure for "money issuance" is only RMB 4. 87 trillion in 2010, a great gap between RMB 20. 68 trillion "FX" . Given "money issuance" cannot provide enough funding sources to hedge FX assets, it can only resort to other channels. On the "liability side", "deposit of financial corporations" grows fastest between 2001 and 2010, reaching RMB 13. 67 trillion by the end of 2010 and accounting for 52. 71% of total liabilities. "Deposit of financial corporations" is mainly composed of reserve requirement paid by financial institutions. Therefore, the main purpose of raising the RRRs is to hedge FX assets. The basic operation process is: PBOC raises the RRRs → financial institutions pay legal deposit reserves PBOC → PBOC's "deposit of financial corporations" increases → PBOC uses these funds to purchase FX assets from financial

① Please refer to Analysis on PBOC's Regulatory Ability Based on the Balance Sheet by Wang Guogang, Financial Review, Issue 1, 2010.

institutions (so "FX" increases) →the reserve requirement (RMB funds) financial institutions pay to PBOC flows back to financial institutions①. Due to this hedging mechanism, there has been no severe liquidity crunch although the RRRs were repeatedly raised after 2003. Meanwhile, one can deduce that so long as there remains the need to hedge funds that are outstanding for FX, the RRRs have the potential for even further rises.

**Table 3: PBOC's Asset Structure (2001 – 2010) Denomination: RMB billion**

| Item | 2001 | 2002 | 2003 | 2004 | 2005 | 2006 | 2007 | 2008 | 2009 | 2010 |
|---|---|---|---|---|---|---|---|---|---|---|
| Overseas asset | 19860.40 | 23242.85 | 31141.85 | 46960.13 | 63339.16 | 85772.64 | 124825.18 | 162543.52 | 185333.00 | 215419.60 |
| FX | 18850.19 | 22107.39 | 29841.80 | 45939.99 | 62139.96 | 84360.81 | 115168.71 | 149624.26 | 175154.59 | 206766.71 |
| Monetary gold | 256.00 | 337.24 | 337.24 | 337.24 | 337.24 | 337.24 | 337.24 | 337.24 | 669.84 | 669.84 |
| Other overseas asset | 754.21 | 798.22 | 962.81 | 682.90 | 861.96 | 1074.59 | 9319.23 | 12582.02 | 9508.57 | 7983.06 |
| Financial claims on government | 2821.33 | 2863.79 | 2901.02 | 2969.62 | 2892.43 | 2856.41 | 16317.71 | 16195.99 | 15661.97 | 15421.11 |
| Financial claims on central government | – | 2863.79 | 2901.02 | 2969.62 | 2892.43 | 2856.41 | 16317.71 | 16195.99 | 15661.97 | 15421.11 |
| Financial claims on other depository corporations | 11311.60 | 12287.64 | 11982.81 | 10424.2 | 12692.01 | 6516.71 | 7862.80 | 8432.50 | 7161.92 | 9485.70 |
| Financial claims on other financial corporations | 8547.31 | 7240.27 | 7255.95 | 8865.09 | 13226.11 | 21949.75 | 12972.34 | 11852.66 | 11530.15 | 11325.81 |
| Financial claims | – | 206.74 | 206.25 | 136.25 | 66.73 | 66.34 | 63.59 | 44.12 | 43.96 | 24.99 |
| Other assets | – | 5266.29 | 8516.19 | 9300.05 | 11459.57 | 11412.84 | 7098.18 | 8027.20 | 7804.03 | 7597.67 |
| Total assets | – | 51107.58 | 62004.06 | 78655.33 | 103676.01 | 128574.69 | 169139.80 | 207095.99 | 227535.02 | 259274.89 |

Source: Website of PBOC. The 2002 – 2005 data for "financial claim on other depository corporations" is the sum of "financial claim on deposit money banks" and "financial claim on specific depository institutions".

Although raising RRRs to hedge funds outstanding for FX does not reduce money supply on the whole, it effectively prevents inflation however, and an overheated economy and economic and social problems that may arise from the "issuance of huge amounts of currencies" for hedging purposes as well. In this sense, it is effective in maintaining China's financial stability and national economy.

As FX assets are not distributed evenly among financial institutions, those with smaller FX deposits, mainly small and medium-sized financial institutions, will experience the tightening effect because what they pay to the PBOC will not flow back to them. Their loanable funds will be reduced

① Another possible operation process is: PBOC raises the RRRs → Financial institutions pay excess reserves to PBOC → PBOC's "deposit of financial corporations" remains unchanged, but the amount of excess reserves decreases→ PBOC uses these funds to purchase FX assets from financial institutions (so "FX" increases→ financial institutions place these funds at PBOC again, so "deposit of financial corporations" increases. This process has the same result.

by the repeated rise of the RRRs. Although they can relieve funding stress by borrowing from other banks, their interest cost will rise substantially. As a result, they tend to reduce loans to small and micro enterprises or substantially raise the interest rate of disbursements, which are two major causes of small and micro enterprises' difficult access to loans after 2006. In this sense, raising the RRRs is not without any tightening effect or influence on economic operation as a whole. It also explains why "there is a shortage of funds at the micro level despite a relative surplus at the macro level", and forms a long and puzzling paradox.

## II. The Rationale of Adjusting the Benchmark Deposit and Loan Interest Rate

On October 28th, 2004 the PBOC circulated the *Notice on Adjusting RMB Benchmark Interest Rate*, taking a step towards market orientation of the deposit and loan interest rate①. The *Notice* has three key points. Firstly, the "legal interest rate" is reworded as the "benchmark interest rate", thus diluting the administrative color of decisions for the deposit and loan interest rate. Secondly, it stresses that the loan interest rate has a lower limit of 0.9 – fold of the benchmark without cap; for the deposit interest rate, the benchmark is the upper limit and there is no lower limit. Thirdly, all financial institutions are required to "strictly implement the adjusted benchmark interest rate and the fluctuating range, strengthen interest rate risk management and make appropriate decisions on the deposit and loan interest rate based on their own business status, funding cost, and risk status". After April 2006, however, the PBOC adjusted the benchmark interest rate several times through administrative mechanisms, leading to changes in the interest rate market orientation process.

As Figure 2 shows, between 2001 and 2010 the PBOC adjusted the deposit and loan interest rate seventeen times. According to information published by the PBOC, there are two pieces of theoretical basis for these adjustments. Firstly, the interest rate directly controls the supply of funds. According to monetary economics, raising the interest rate reduces supply of funds while reducing the interest rate increases. Secondly such adjustment was made to try to achieve a positive deposit interest rate. Monetary economics believes a negative rate produces several negative effects. However, such theoretical basis is plausible.

Although the theorem "raising the interest rate reduces supply of funds while reducing the interest rate increases" remains common knowledge among all economists, no one has explored the issue of "who raises the interest rate for whom" and "whose supply of funds for whom is reduced or increased". According to the practice of developed countries, the Central Bank raises its interest rate and reduces its supply of funds for financial institutions similar to the way commercial banks do. For example, when the Federal Reserve raises the federal funds rate, it increases commercial banks' cost of borrowing from Federal Funds, thus reducing disbursements to them. Contrarily, when the

① PBOC: Report on Implementation of China's Monetary Policies in the Fourth Quarter of 2004.

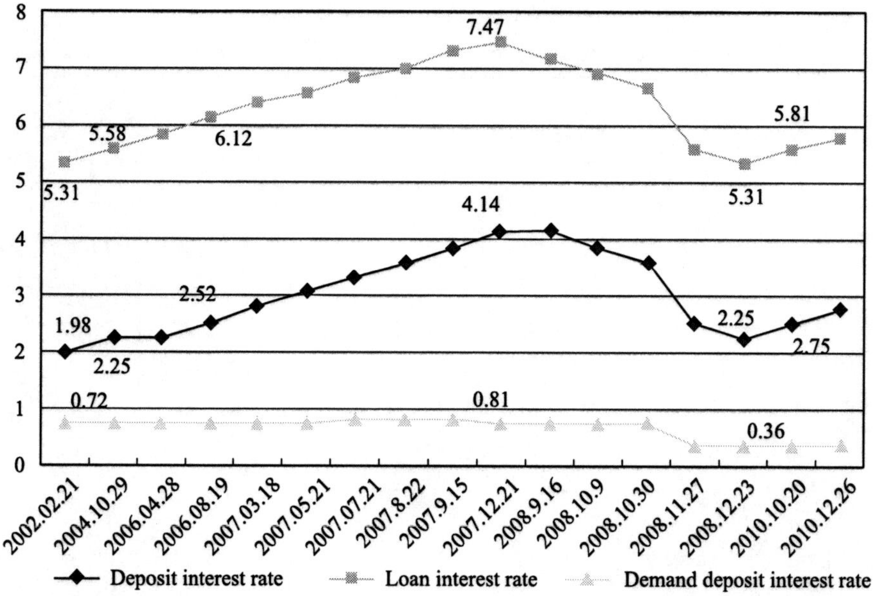


**Figure 2: Trend of Deposit and Loan Interest Rate (2002 –2010)**

Source: Website of PBOC.

Central Bank reduces its interest rate, it increases the supply of funds for commercial banks and other financial institutions. In China however, what the PBOC adjusts is not its interest rate but rather the deposit and loan interest rate of financial institutions (here it bears the characteristics of government pricing), and so the effect of the PBOC's monetary policy adjustment cannot be perfectly explained by the aforementioned theorem.

(1) The PBOC's decision to raise the loan interest rate of financial institutions does not necessarily reduce the supply of funds. It is important to consider two issues here. Firstly, after the *Notice on Adjusting RMB Benchmark Interest Rate* was circulated in October 2004, financial institutions now have the right to decide their loan interest rate based on the benchmark. Given this, is the PBOC's practice (raising the benchmark rate by 0.27 percentage points (0.25 after 2010) through leveraging administrative mechanisms) contrary to the spirit of the "Notice"? Secondly, when financial institutions enjoying an advantage in the loan market, is loan accessibility or the interest rate more important to most Chinese enterprises?

According to Table 4, the percentage of "below the benchmark" and "benchmark" combined tends to rise (from 47.79% in the fourth quarter of 2004 to 63.45% in December 2009), while the percentage of "above benchmark" is declining. Since 2004, the banking industry has witnessed an increasing surplus of funds (excess liquidity), aggravating competition among financial institutions in the loan market and imposing downward pressure on the loan interest rate. Against this backdrop, between 2006 and 2007, PBOC raised the benchmark loan interest rate by eight times, which goes against the market orientation mechanism.

**Table 4: Percentage of Different Fluctuating Ranges for RMB Loan Interest Rate of Financial Institutions**

Denomination: %

| Time | Below the benchmark interest rate | Benchmark interest rate | Above the benchmark interest rate | | | | |
|---|---|---|---|---|---|---|---|
| | (0.9, 1) | 1.0 | Sub-total | (1, 1.3) | (1.3, 1.5) | (1.5, 2) | Above 2 |
| The fourth quarter of 2004 | 23.23 | 24.56 | 52.21 | 28.98 | 9.90 | 10.66 | 2.68 |
| The fourth quarter of 2005 | 24.29 | 26.47 | 49.24 | 26.87 | 8.27 | 11.37 | 2.73 |
| The fourth quarter of 2006 | 25.81 | 26.63 | 47.56 | 27.90 | 7.32 | 10.63 | 1.71 |
| The fourth quarter of 2007 | 28.07 | 27.69 | 44.24 | 27.17 | 7.31 | 8.47 | 1.29 |
| December 2008 | 25.56 | 30.13 | 44.31 | 27.81 | 5.75 | 7.27 | 3.49 |
| December 2009 | 33.19 | 30.26 | 36.55 | 21.38 | 5.13 | 6.64 | 3.40 |
| December 2010 | 27.80 | 29.16 | 43.04 | 25.69 | 5.66 | 8.18 | 3.51 |

Source: PBOC report on implementation of the monetary policy in the fourth quarter of corresponding years.

As a direct outcome of a benchmark rise, businesses pay more funding costs for the same amount of loans. Can such cost rises effectively inhibit their demands on loans? Loan interest is a share of the borrower's business profit. Only when businesses enjoy a big surplus of profit after paying interest will they borrow large amounts; for financial institutions disbursing greater loans to businesses with strong repayment ability. This means the assumption that any rise in the loan interest rate will significantly inhibit demand on loans is not well grounded. A basic fact remains that loan interest is only a small part of the total business cost. When the loan interest rate rises by one percentage point (PP), the impact on the total business cost is far less than one PP. If it can't even afford a 1PP rise in the total business cost, how can it afford a rise in the price of raw materials or spare parts, staff wages, management costs, marketing expenses (such as advertising) and other expenses? (China's PPI rising rate has stayed above 5% for many years) Financial institutions are reluctant to issue loans. Based on such concerns, raising the loan interest rate for financial institutions does not significantly weigh down the demand for loans or slow their growth.

(2) Raising the deposit interest rate forces financial institutions to disburse more loans. As Figure 2 shows, in most cases the PBOC raises the benchmark interest rate for a one-year (1Y) deposit and 1Y loan, simultaneously. According to monetary economics, the direct effect of raising the deposit interest rate is to stimulate deposit growth. What will financial institutions opt for when they have absorbed more deposits with higher cost? Perhaps they would have had some leeway if financial products, like bonds with higher yields than the benchmark deposit interest rate, were available in the financial market. If such products existed they would have purchased them in full capacity before

the benchmark deposit interest rate was raised. On the other hand, the rise of the benchmark deposit interest rate will usually reduce the return on financial products under transaction due to price fluctuations. Besides, products and mechanisms for hedging against the rise of the benchmark deposit interest rate are quite scarce in China's financial market. Due to these factors, the only option for financial institutions is to disburse more loans. Obviously, the result of raising the benchmark interest rate for 1Y deposit and loans is to increase the supply of funds.

(3) As the benchmark rate for 1Y deposits and loans basically shows the same rise, the loan-to-deposit spread sees no big change. However, Figure 2 shows the interest spread between 1Y loans and demand deposit is expanding. In February 2002, the spread shows 3.33 PPs. By December 2007, it has doubled to 6.66 PPs. Normally, the loan interest rate for financial institutions is determined by three factors, according to financial economics. First is the funding cost, namely the deposit interest rate. Second is the business cost, and third is the expected risk, or the default rate that can be mirrored by the net interest spread (NIS). A bigger NIS means greater tolerance of loan risks and therefore a bigger loanable scale, and vice versa. If a commercial bank has 10,000 loan customers when its NIS is 2 PPs, its customers might expand to 20,000 when the NIS increases to 3 PPs, in which case loan disbursements will be bigger, naturally.

On the other hand, if demand deposit has a small percentage in financial institutions' liabilities, a bigger interest spread between 1Y loan and demand deposit exerts little influence on their loan scale. However, as Table 5 shows the percentage of demand deposit in corporate deposit and residents' savings deposit reaches around 50%, so a bigger spread will play an important role in increasing the loan scale. This became more obvious after major commercial banks (both State-owned and joint-stock) were listed after 2006 – as compensation of staff and senior managers is linked to business performance, they were motivated to improve performance through more loan disbursements.

**Table 5: Tenor Structure of Corporate Deposit and Savings Deposit**

Denomination: RMB billion, %

| Year | Corporate demand deposit | Demand savings deposit | Corporate time deposit | Time savings deposit | Total | Percentage of demand deposit |
|---|---|---|---|---|---|---|
| 2004 | 7,450.25 | 4,141.65 | 2,538.22 | 7,813.89 | 21,944.01 | 52.83 |
| 2005 | 8,314.60 | 4,878.75 | 4,522.47 | 9,226.35 | 26,942.17 | 48.97 |
| 2006 | 9,880.26 | 5,857.59 | 5,276.71 | 10,301.14 | 31,315.70 | 50.26 |
| 2007 | 9,171.84 | 6,746.16 | 6,268.55 | 10,828.79 | 33,015.34 | 48.21 |
| 2008 | 9,749.90 | 7,833.68 | 8,070.26 | 14,366.88 | 40,020.73 | 43.94 |
| 2009 | 13,474.73 | 10,054.13 | 10,883.76 | 16,023.04 | 50,435.66 | 46.65 |
| 2010 | 16,453.61 | 12,626.44 | 8,842.42 | 18,090.20 | 56,012.67 | 51.92 |

Source: Website of PBOC.

In April 2006, the PBOC began to raise the benchmark loan interest rate aiming to slow down the ascending loan growth rate. However, the loan growth rate did not drop but rose from 11.29% in March to 15.72% in December; in 2007 from March, the PBOC raised the benchmark deposit and loan interest rate six times in a row, but the loan growth rate rose from 16.99% in February to 17.69% in October. From November to December 2007, the PBOC started to control the scale of incremental loans, an administrative measure that had brought down the loan growth rate. Administrative control indicates that adjusting the benchmark deposit and loan interest rate failed to achieve the intended objective of controlling the loan scale (thereby controlling the quantities of currencies).

Another theoretical basis is to eliminate the negative deposit interest rate. There are three rationales. Firstly, businesses are more likely to apply for loans because they actually enjoy a discount when a price rise leads to a negative interest rate. A loan increase will further push up the price and deteriorates the negative interest rate, which in turn increases their intention to borrow. Such a cycle will overheat the economy and trigger severe inflation. Secondly, when there is a negative interest rate fund owners prefer to purchase other financial products to place funds at financial institutions, but financial institutions' deposits absorbed previously have been disbursed, hence there is a liquidity crunch for financial institutions. Depositors may run on a bank once there are withdrawal difficulties, or a rush to withdraw from other financial institutions once one of them closes down because of insolvency. This will lead to the chain failures of financial institutions, and social and economic chaos. Thirdly, domestic funds may flow overseas in search of higher returns, and this leads to a domestic shortage of funds. To avoid these consequences, there must be a positive deposit interest rate. However, this theoretical basis implies too many assumptions and therefore deviates a lot from the actual situation.

As shown in Figure 3, the negative deposit interest rate occurred three times in parallel with three price rises after 2001, peaking from July to August, 2004 ( − 3.72), February 2008 ( −4.56) and November 2010 ( −2.35). Figure 3 also shows that the main factor in turning the negative deposit interest rate to positive is not due to a rise in the deposit interest rate but rather because of the declining CPI growth rate. The first turning point happened in January 2005 after the CPI growth rate dropped to 1.9%. The second was seen in November 2008 after the CPI growth rate dropped to 2.4%. However, here the positive deposit interest rate is arrived at by comparing the CPI growth rate and 1Y deposit interest rate during the same period; as the CPI growth rate is computed on a "year-on-year" basis, it does not imply accumulative CPI growth based on the constant price, otherwise the 1Y deposit interest rate might still be negative. Table 6 shows the accumulative CPI growth between 2001 and 2010 when we assume the CPI value of 2000 is 100. Obviously, the 1Y deposit interest rate after 2004 all turns out to be negative. Meanwhile, in almost all cases, a rise in the deposit interest rate can hardly offset or outstrip accumulative CPI growth. In this sense, the negative deposit interest rate might be a long-term, irreversible trend.

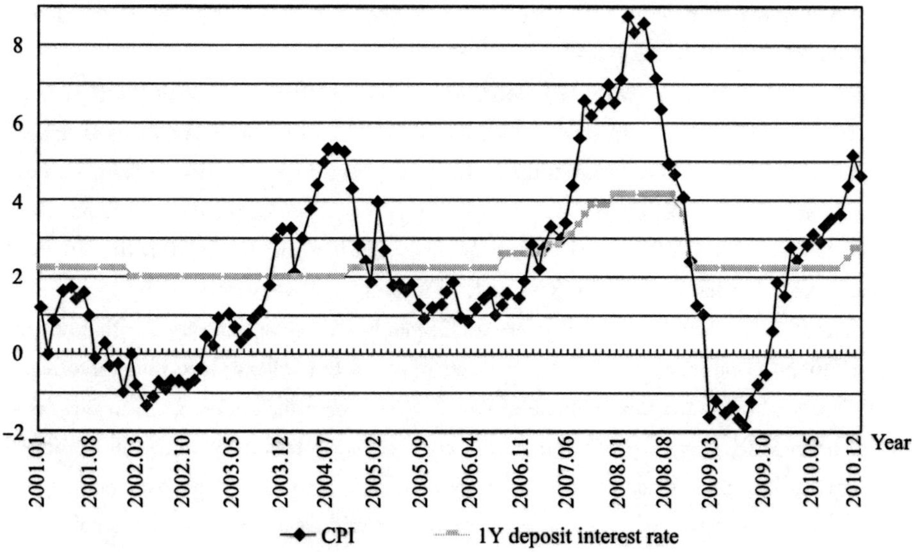


**Figure 3: Trend of CPI Growth Rate and 1Y Deposit Interest Rate**

Source: Website of PBOC and the State Statistics Bureau.

**Table 6: Comparison between Accumulative CPI Growth and 1Y Deposit Interest Rate**

Denomination: %

| Year | CPI growth rate | Accumulative CPI growth | 1Y deposit interest rate |
|---|---|---|---|
| 2001 | 0.7 | 0.69 | 2.25 |
| 2002 | -0.8 | -0.12 | 1.98 |
| 2003 | 1.2 | 1.08 | 1.98 |
| 2004 | 3.9 | 5.02 | 2.25 |
| 2005 | 1.8 | 6.91 | 2.25 |
| 2006 | 1.5 | 8.53 | 2.52 |
| 2007 | 4.8 | 13.73 | 4.14 |
| 2008 | 5.9 | 20.44 | 2.25 |
| 2009 | -0.7 | 19.59 | 2.25 |

Source: computed based on *China Statistical Yearbook* (2010).

Is a negative interest rate bound to increase loans to enterprises? The key point is not enterprises' inner drive to apply for loans (as it also exists when the deposit interest rate is positive) but financial institutions' market initiative and budget constraints. Given major commercial banks have established a complete risk control system and credit accountability system, loan disbursement is not unilaterally decided by enterprises' demands but also by their solvency, capital adequacy ratio, and other regulatory indicators as well as the financial institution's asset structure (like liquidity).

Therefore, loan application under a negative interest rate is not the exclusive factor in financial institutions' decisions to disburse loans.

A negative interest rate will not necessarily lead to financial institutions' shortage of funds. Firstly, we should figure out where funds go if fund owners do not place them in financial institutions due to a negative interest rate. If funds are used to purchase non-deposit financial products, then where do sellers place them? The only possibility is that they deposit them in financial institutions. Track the fund flow and one finds that funds eventually flow into financial institutions as deposits, although the depositor has changed let's say, from residents to enterprises. For financial institutions as a whole, funds inflow does not decrease. Secondly, if many depositors withdraw from one financial institution to purchase on-deposit financial products but sellers place funds into another financial institution; it may cause a shortage of funds at the former institution. Even in this scenario it will not fail because there are mechanisms for alleviating funds stress for financial institutions in the financial system, like inter-bank borrowing, Central Bank's lending and deposit insurance; avoiding the domino effect in case of "depositor's rushing for withdrawal" from one financial institution.

It is well meaning to raise the deposit interest rate, though it actually reshapes the interest pattern in the deposit and loan, and even in the financial market. The monetary policy however, is charged with the mission of regulating macro-level aggregate demands rather than rebuilding the micro-level interest pattern. Therefore, the issue of a negative deposit interest rate can hardly be solved by monetary policy adjustment.

## III. The Rationale of Controlling Incremental Loans Leveraging Administrative Mechanisms

Abolishing management of the credit scale plan in 1998 marked the transition of China's monetary policy from direct to indirect control and an increase in the use of non-administrative mechanisms. From then on, although the intermediary objective of monetary policy has set out the annual loan increment indicator, it is basically non-rigid in nature. Since November 2007, the PBOC began to implement the tight monetary policy and practiced rigid administrative control over loan increments. Between November and December 2007, financial institutions were required not to increase new commercial loans; in 2008, loan increment was controlled within RMB 3.64 trillion and monitored on a quarterly basis. In 2010, the incremental loan scale was still controlled within RMB 7.5 trillion, subject to quarterly monitoring despite the implementation of an eased monetary policy.

According to traditional monetary economics, administrative control over loan increment does not fall within monetary policy instruments. But when instruments such as raising the RRRs, deposit and loan interest rate and issuing bonds fails to achieve the intermediary objective of monetary policy, the administrative control over the loan scale becomes the only viable and most effective alternative, although it has some negative effects given the deposit and loan interest rate has been partly deregulated nowadays.

## IV. Difficulties in China's Monetary Policy Control and Suggestions

Between 2001 and 2010, the PBOC often faced a dilemma in choosing the monetary policy. For instance, promoting economic growth creates more job opportunities but in the meantime requires more loan disbursements, which means more supply of currencies and heavier inflation pressure. This is harmful to a currency's stability. A dilemma also stems from differences between the domestic and overseas economy. If the PBOC does not purchase more FX assets when large sums of foreign exchanges flow in and the central parity rate of RMB increases, it will be adverse to funds operation of financial institutions and the business development of foreign trade enterprises. But issuing more currencies to purchase FX assets will aggravate inflation. Public opinion is another reason. Sometimes the price rise is caused by a shortage of some agricultural products, but the public tends to ask for a tight monetary policy to contain what they deem as "inflation". In this case, a tight monetary policy might produce side effects, but nonaction will incur censuring for "administrative omission".

According to the 12th Five-Year Plan, the goal of improving China's monetary policy system is to "optimize the objective system of monetary policies, the monetary policy decision-making mechanism and the policy transmission mechanism and environment"①. This can be achieved with the following efforts:

(1) Adjust and improve PBOC's balance sheet structure. First is to list "RMB asset" at the "asset side" to show operable RMB funds. Second is to reduce FX reserves; after setting aside sufficient FX reserves, the PBOC should separate remaining FX assets from the BPOC by establishing a Foreign Exchange Stabilization Fund and encouraging the outflow of loan capital and productive capital, so that most of PBOC's assets are used for macro finance control. This will consolidate PBOC's asset control over financial institutions and the financial market. Third is to improve PBOC's liability structure. Currently, the main source of PBOC's liabilities is financial institutions, which is unsustainable. The percentage of "issuance of currencies" should be increased at PBOC's "liability side". By acquiring debt funds through "issuance of currencies", PBOC's asset-controlling ability can be improved.

(2) Enhance the intermediary objective and operation instruments of monetary policy. In light of the experience of the past decade, controlling the credit scale (or the incremental loan scale) is effective in achieving the intended objective of monetary policies, which should be maintained, though administrative control should be fine tuned in the meantime. An option is to make credit policy instruments part of monetary policy instruments. By leveraging credit policy instruments like the capital adequacy ratio, the provision rate, the liquidity ratio and leverage ratio, the PBOC can in-

① Chapter 48 of the *People's Republic of China's 12th Five-Year Plan on National Economic and Social Development.*

directly affect financial institutions' lending activities. On the other hand, the monitoring indicator system should be revised and adjusted, including not only M2 and M1 but also financial aggregation, liquidity aggregation, and aggregate social financing, etc., so that they better reflect China's actual situation and have more measurability, pertinence, and controllability. Apart from improving the balance sheet, an interest rate regulation mechanism ought to be established.

(3) Develop the corporate bond market and advance the process of market orientation of the loan interest rate. Businesses, depositors, financial institutions, and other market participants should be given the right to choose financial products. Corporate bonds carry the same pricing for both fund suppliers and demanders, higher than that of deposits but lower than loans, hence creating a substitute of deposits and loans. An important implication of "developing the corporate bond market" is that the corporate bond issuance scale should match with the loan balance scale. By the end of 2010, China's loan balance had reached up to RMB 48 trillion. To match it, issuance of corporate bonds pursuant to the rules of the *Company Law* and *Securities Law* should be accelerated.

(4) Enhance the ultimate objective of monetary policy. As there are many complicated factors in the changing price and exchange rate (currency issuance is not the only factor), regulating the price and exchange rate is beyond the function of monetary policy. Therefore, it might be more useful to define the ultimate objective of monetary policy as that of "maintaining financial stability".

(5) Establish a system framework for prudent macro financial management. The U. S. financial crisis that broke out in 2008 posed the challenge of strengthening the macro financial management system to the monetary authority, and reflects the intrinsic links among monetary policies, financial stability, and prudent macro management. Establishing the monetary policy system, improving the capital system, strengthening supervision of systematically important financial institutions, shadow banking and derivative transactions are all included in this system framework. Even though China has not yet experienced its baptism of fire through a financial crisis, it still needs to establish such a prudent macro management system. Doing so poses a challenge to China's monetary authority.

## References

1. Bernanke, Ben S., and Mark L. Gertler. 1995. "Inside the Black Box: The Credit Channel of Monetary Policy Transmission." *Journal of Economic Perspectives* (9): 27-48.

2. Blinder, Alan S. 1992. "The Federal Funds Rate and the Channels of Monetary Transmission." *The American Economic Review* (82): 901-921.

3. Blinder, Alan S., Michael Ehrmann, Marcel Fratzscher, Jakob De Haan, and David-Jan Jansen. 2008. "Central Bank Communication and Monetary Policy: A Survey of Theory and Evidence." *Journal of Economic Literature* (46): 910-945.

4. Dai, Genyou, ed. 2000. "Issues Concerning the Current Monetary Policy." *China Finance*, No. 6.

5. Dai, Genyou. 2001. "Practice and Experience of China's Stable Monetary Policy." *Management World*, No. 6.

6. Demiralp, Selva. 2010. "Money, Reserves, and the Transmission of Monetary Policy:

Does the Money Multiplier Exist?" Board of Governors of the Federal Reserve System, Working Paper, May 2010.

7. Fan, Mingtai. 2004. "Financial Structure and Its Impact on the Monetary Transmission Mechanism." *Economic Research Journal*, No. 7.

8. Koop, Gary. 2009. "On the Evolution of the Monetary Policy Transmission Mechanism." *Journal of Economic Dynamics & Control* (33): 997 – 1017.

9. Li, Bin. 2001. "Empirical Study on the Effectiveness of China's Monetary Policy." *Study of Finance*, No. 7.

10. Meltzer, Allan H. 1995. "Monetary, Credit and Other Transmission Processes: A Monetarist Perspective." *Journal of Economic Perspectives* (9): 49 – 72.

11. Mishkin, Frederic. 1998. *The Economics of Money, Banking, and Financial Markets* (Chinese edition). Beijing: China Renmin University Press.

12. Sellon, Gordon, and Stuart Weiner. 1996. "Monetary Policy Without Reserve Requirements: Analytical Issues." *Economic Review*, Quarter IV, 5 – 24.

13. Song, Wang, and Zhengsheng Zhong. 2010. "Impact of China's Financial Disintermediation on the Transmission Mechanism of Monetary Policy: 1978 – 2007". *Economist* (*Jing Ji Xue Jia*), No. 2.

14. Svensson, Lars E. 2003. "What Is Wrong with Taylor Rules? Using Judgment in Monetary Policy through Targeting Rules." *Journal of Economic Literature* (41): 426 – 477.

15. Taylor, John B. 1993. "Discretion versus Policy Rules in Practice." Carnegie-Rochester Conference Series on Public Policy (39): 195 – 214.

16. Walsh, Carl E. 2001. *Monetary Theory and Policy* (Chinese edition). Beijing: China Renmin University Press.

17. Wang, Guogang. 2010. "Analysis on People's Bank of China's Regulatory Ability Based on Balance Sheet." *Financial Review*, No. 1.

18. Wang, Xuebiao, and Zhiqiang Wang. 2001. *Fiscal Policy, Financial Policy and Cointegration Analysis. Dongbei University of Finance and Economics Press.*

19. Xie, Ping, and Xiliang Liu. 2001. *From Inflation to Deflation: China's Monetary Policy in the* 1990*s. Chengdu*: Southwestern University of Finance and Economics Press.

20. Zhang, Chengsi. 2011. "Inflation Persistence, Inflation Expectations, and Monetary Policy in China." *Economic Modeling* (28): 622 – 629.

21. Zhou, Yingzhang, and Zhensheng Jiang. 2002. "Currency Channel, Credit Channel and Effectiveness of Monetary Policy." *Study of Finance*, No. 9.

## Chapter 12

# China's Regional Policy Scenarios for 2011 – 2015 Period*

**Wei Houkai (魏后凯)[1] and Wu Xiaoxia (邬晓霞)[2]**

[1] Institute for Urban and Environmental Studies, Chinese Academy of Social Sciences, Beijing, China

[2] College of Urban Economics and Public Administration, Capital University of Economics and Business, Beijing, China

**Abstract**: In pursuit of more balanced regional development, China should base its regional policy during the period of the 12th Five-Year Plan on the principle of fairness, and tailor it to the specific characteristics of needy areas and development priority zones. The country's master plan of developing the western region, revitalizing the northeast, supporting the rise of central China, and upgrading the east should continue.

**Keywords**: regional policy, balanced regional development, development priority zones, needy areas

## I. Introduction

A well-crafted regional policy can further the Chinese central government's goals of balanced regional growth, optimized spatial development, and efficient resource-allocation. Balanced regional development will be an overarching goal during the period of 12th Five Year plan. Therefore, China should continue to improve its regional policy to coordinate development between well-defined priority development zones; intensify interaction between eastern, central and western regions, strengthen public service, and equalize living standards.

## II. Evaluation of China's Current Regional Policy

To promote balanced regional development, China has implemented a string of policies including the western development program, revitalization of old industrial bases in the northeast, a

* Corresponding author: wei_houkai@263. net.

strategy to accelerate the rise of the central region, and intensified transfer payments to select areas including former revolutionary bases, regions dominated by ethnic minorities, border areas, and impoverished regions. These policies have yielded positive results. Investment in the central, western, and northeast regions has grown increasingly rapidly; regional economic development has been relatively balanced; and poverty alleviation in the rural areas has been progressing well.

Notably, the disparity between per capita gross regional product (GRP) in the east and west of the country has been shrinking since 2003. Per-capita GRP in the western region was 63.0% lower than that of the east in 2003, but by 2009 the difference had fallen to 55.2% (see Figure 1). The gap between average urban and rural household incomes has been shrinking since 2006, as well (Wei Houkai and Xie Xianshu, 2011).

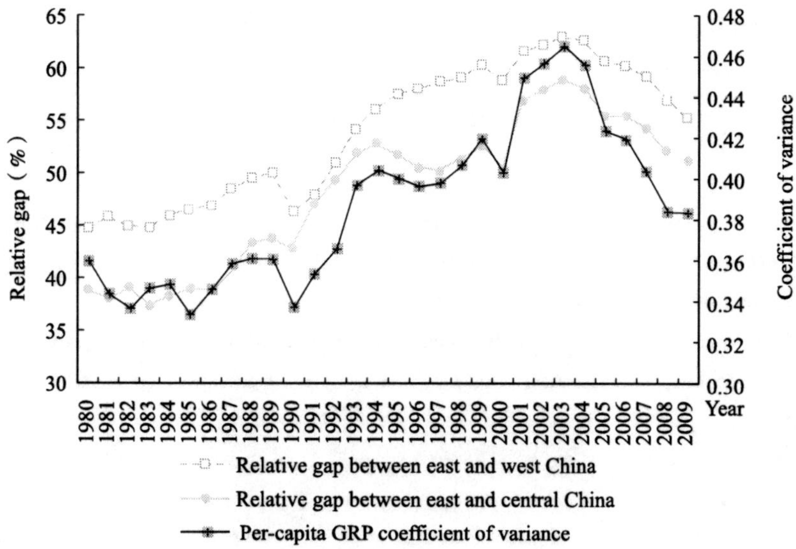


**Figure 1: Relative Disparities in GRP between Three Regions from 1980 to 2009**

Note: East-West Relative Gap Index = (index of the East-index of the Central and West)/ index of the East × 100%

Source: *China Regional Economy in the* 17 *Years after Reform and Opening-up* (China Statistics Press, 1996) and *China Statistical Yearbook* (of each year).

However, China's regional policy has been hampered by weak institutions and a lack of coordination between departments. There has been excessive emphasis on efficiency, with the effect of clustering the majority of the country's special economic zones in the coastal region. Strategies to promote the prosperity of the northeast and other archaic industrial bases were too general to be effective. There were no effective efforts to coordinate relevant agencies including the State Council Leading Group Office of Poverty Alleviation and Development, and the National Development and Reform Commission. Regional development was financed mainly through public expenditure and there was insufficient private investment.

Preferential policies enacted after 2006 have also disrupted China's regional policymaking. In addition to the "Western Development Program," "Northeast Revival Strategy," and the "Rise of Central China Strategy," China launched preferential policies targeting the Yangtze River Delta, the Cross-Strait Economic Zone, and the Tianjin-Binhai New Area. While these favorable policies have increased growth, they have had multiple side effects. Because these policies were not selected by rigorous and uniform criteria but rather due to administrative wishes and pressures from local government, they seriously undermined the impartiality and the rationality of China's regional policymaking system. Local governments may continue to be tempted to lobby or even bribe central government officials to formulate regional policies that favor them. By targeting both poor and wealthy areas, these policies also blurred the focus of regional policymaking, which is supposed to address regional disparities by focusing on less-developed regions. Lastly, these policies cast doubt on the fairness of national policymaking by arbitrarily favoring certain regions over others.

## III. Rationale for China's New Regional Policy

Guided by the Scientific Development Perspective, China has re-focused its regional policy on achieving coordinated regional development as measured along three dimensions. First, development should be comprehensive with a balance between urban and rural growth, coordinated social and economic development, and harmony between human society and nature. Second, development should be sustainable, incorporating resource-saving and environmentally-friendly technologies, strong institutions, and effective policies. Third, development should be guided by mechanisms for regional cooperation, central government-funded support, and eco-compensation, all of which aim at promoting social stability, population well-being, employment, etcetera (Wei, 2009).

China's new regional policy should adhere to three principles. First, the main rationale of regional policy should be more in fairness than in efficiency. The market mechanism usually widens rather than narrows regional disparities (Myrdal, 1957). China's regional policy should therefore prioritize fairness, and focus on supporting those disadvantaged regions that will benefit most from central government intervention (Wei and Wu, 2010).

Second, China's regional policy should be tailored to the areas targeted. For a long time, the country's regional policy has been too general to respond to the diverse needs of its many regions, as witnessed in aspects of the Western Development Program and Northeast Revival Strategy, which suffered from a one-size-fits-all approach.

Third, regional policy should be implemented with greater precision to those areas facing problems. Internationally, regional policies have been used to address areas that are underdeveloped, experiencing depressed growth, or experiencing excessive growth (Zhang, 2005). Given China's transition from a planned to a market-economy and significant urbanization, industrialization, and globalization, the country contains all of these areas and more. The state should help them as long as the problems are truly grave and local government intervention is insufficient to resolve them.

## IV. China's Regional Policy Framework

To promote coordinated regional development, China should adopt a regional policy framework that classifies the country into "Four Regions" and "Two Zones." The Four Regions refers to the division of the country into western, northeastern, central, and eastern regions (Wei, 2006), a categorization with two advantages: it is comprehensive, convenient for macro economic planning and master regional policy formulation, and it maintains the continuity of national strategies and policies (as the 12th Five-Year plan calls for continued implementation of the "Western Development Program," "Northeast Revival Strategy," the "Rise of Central China Strategy," and the "Upgrade of the East"). However, variation within the eastern and western regions are so large that policies for them had better be broken down into five smaller economic regions: the southeast area including Guangdong, Fujian, Hainan, Hong Kong, Macao, and Taiwan; the Yangtze River Delta area covering Shanghai, Zhejiang, and Jiangsu; the Bohai Rim area comprised of Beijing, Tianjin, Hebei and Shandong; the southwest area comprised of Guangxi, Chongqing, Sichuan, Guizhou, Yunnan, and Tibet; and the northwest area consisting of Inner Mongolia, Shanxi, Gansu, Ningxia, Qinghai and Xinjiang. The Two Zones refer to the classification of the country into development priority zones and problems zones. Depending on their resource-bearing capacity, development-density, and development-potential, development priority zones fall into four categories: optimized development zones, key development zones, restricted development zones, and prohibited development zones. Each type of zone should be assigned specific functions and development goals to ensure orderly and reasonable spatial development. Needy areas are classified by the nature and gravity of their problems. Regional aid policy should be administered in needy areas with consideration for these characteristics, rather than as a single blanket policy, thus increasing its effectiveness. In summary, the emphasis in development priority zones is human prosperity, whereas in needy areas the emphasis is regional prosperity. In a country with wide regional disparities, both are discriminatively important.

Within this framework, China's current regional policy formulation and implementation should adhere to the following points. First, the four regions are the basis for overall regional policy planning, but the two zones are the units for regional policy implementation. In fact, the classification of needy areas and development priority zones has increasingly guided China's regional policy. For example, policies to revitalize industries in the northeast have been extended to 26 industrial cities in central China. A pilot program to assist cities previously dependent on resource-extraction has been applied nationwide to 44 cities. Policies implemented to develop the west have also been carried out in 243 localities in the central region. Second, regionalization and zoning are different. The central government's involvement in regionalization and zoning is necessary but the central government should guard itself against bias in its regional policy-making. Third, regional aid policies should be directed to needy areas as a whole, rather than individual provinces or cities (with Tibet and Xinjiang as the only exceptions). In this way, China could build a uniform and differentiated system of state regional aid policy.

## V. Development Priority Zones

A development priority zone is a spatial unit defined by its development priorities according to a universal standard. The intention of demarcating development priority zones is to ensure orderly spatial development, optimum resource allocation, and harmony between human beings and nature (Wei, 2007).

As discussed in the *National Development Priority Zones Demarcation* issued in June 2011, China's territory may be classified according to different standards: by priority, administrative level, or by function. Each type plays an important but varied role in China's socioeconomic development, as listed in Table 1. For example, urbanization zones are the site of human habitation and economic activity, whereas ecological zones contribute to environment protection and restoration.

**Table 1: Scopes, Functions, and Development Goals of National Development Priority Zones**

| Regions | | Scope | Function | Development Goals |
|---|---|---|---|---|
| Urbanization zones | Optimized development zones | Bohai Rim, Yangtze River Delta, Perl River Delta | Important national competitiveness center, national innovation center, national socioeconomic growth center, globally influential economic zones, and economic and population agglomerations | Optimizing spatial structure, urban planning, population layout, industrial restructuring, upgrading development mode and infrastructure |
| | Key development zones | 18 regions including Central and South of Hebei Province, Taiyuan City Cluster and so on | Pillar of economic growth, important entity for regional policy delivery, and population and economic agglomerations | Planning for overall spatial pattern, promoting population agglomeration, forming modern industrial system, and improving infrastructure |
| Agricultural production zones | | 7 major agricultural production zones and 23 bread belts | Safeguard national food security, residential and production areas for farmers, and demo area of socialist new rural area | Restoring the land, building water conservancy projects, optimizing agricultural production structure, and improving processing of agricultural products |

Continued

| Regions | | Scope | Function | Development Goals |
|---|---|---|---|---|
| Ecological zones | Restricted development zones | 25 regions including Daxing'an and Xiaoxing'an Mountains | Safeguard for ecological security and demo area of harmony between human beings and nature | Protecting and restoring ecology, providing ecological products, developing local industries and promoting orderly migration |
| | Prohibited development zones | 1443 places including State-level natural reserves, world cultural and natural heritage sites, key national parks, national forest parks, and national geo-parks | Protection of natural and cultural resources and reserves of rare animals, plants and genetic material | Imposing legally enforceable protection, reducing human impact on natural and cultural heritage, prohibiting illegal development |

The formulation of development priority zones depends on supporting laws, regulations, institutions, a system for evaluation, and policies tailored to the needs of each type of development priority zone.

(1) Fiscal policies. China should accelerate the establishment of a public fiscal institution with the objective of equalizing the public services provided in different development priority zones. This demands: the establishment of national standards for public services and increased transfer payment to major ecological zones for public service provision; a comprehensive review of all environment transfer payment schemes and establishment of the schemes for ecological restoration and eco-migration; establishment of a horizontal payment transfer mechanism and increased transfers to equalize payments for the major ecological zones; and establishment of a long-term mechanism for better compensating the major ecological zones.

(2) Investment policies. Field-oriented investment policies should be integrated with investment policies for development priority zone. Government-funded investment should be directed to public service provision and environmental protection in the major ecological and agricultural production zones, and to infrastructure construction in the key development zones. Government-funded investment should accord with the function and goals of the development priority zones.

(3) Industry policies. The existing industrial restructuring directory should be revised to satisfy the differing needs of the development priority zones. Fixed asset investment tax should be levied at different rates according to the development priority zone, and varying standards for land use, energy consumption, water consumption, waste discharge, and carbon emission should be applied to projects in different priority zones. Optimized development zones should be upgraded in order to move up the value chain and promote indigenous innovation. Key development zones should receive investment in order to enhance their capacity for supporting industry, their industrial carrying capacity, and their competitiveness. Restricted development zones should receive investment for developing ecological and local industries.

(4) Population policies. The intent of population policies is to manage population flows and residence registration. Optimized development zones should encourage inhabitants with stable jobs and permanent residences to obtain residential registration. Key development zones should improve their population carrying capacity and encourage migrant laborers to obtain residential registration. Major ecological zones should encourage voluntary outward migration. At the same time, China should reform its household registration system as well as the household registration-based education, health care, social security systems.

(5) Land policies. Optimized development zones should control new land-use. Key development zones should increase land available for construction. Major ecological zones should tightly control land use and prohibit land-use changes. To maintain fixed acreages of cultivated land, land requisition by urban areas must be offset by increased cultivated land in rural areas.

(6) Environmental policies. First, each type of development zone should satisfy respective natural area indicators. Optimized development zones should be comprised of no less than 30% natural areas; key development zones no less than 40%; restricted development zones no less than 80%; and prohibited development zones no less than 95%. Second, development priority zones are subject to specific requirements for pollution reduction, industrial entry, and waste discharge. Optimized development zones should strictly control pollution and promote environmental protection. Key development zones should increase production while reducing pollution intensity. Restricted development zones should implement as early as possible the deposit regime for post-mining ecological and environmental restoration or even charge higher deposits for the mine environmental protection.

## VI. Regional Aid Policy

During the 12th Five Year plan, China should readjust its regional aid policy to direct funds to each type of needy area based on their characteristics, promoting their self-development and sustaining their growth.

Regional aid policy includes identification of needy areas, establishment of the objectives of regional aid, selection of policy tools, institutional support, and policy evaluation. To deliver assistance that meets the varied needs of different regions, needy areas should first be classified according to the nature and gravity of their problems. Currently, needy areas in China are divided into underdeveloped areas with lagging economic development, aging industrial areas in relative decline, areas dependent on resource-extraction or monolithic industries, grain-producing areas under severe financial burdens, frontier border areas with weak governance, overly-extended metropolitan, and areas vulnerable to natural disaster (see Table 2).

**Table 2: Objectives and Policy Tools of State Regional Aid**

| Problem areas | Aid objectives | Policy tools |
|---|---|---|
| Underdeveloped areas with lagging economic development | Alleviating poverty, promoting comprehensive development | Government-funded investment, infrastructure, training, project, migration and employment |
| Aging industrial areas in relative decline | Stimulating growth, creating jobs, revitalizing old industrial bases | Government-funded investment, tax reduction, training, social security, project, regionalization |
| Areas dependent on resource extraction or with monolithic industries | Identifying new development pathways, ensuring sustainability | Government-funded investment, projects, social security, ecology-protection |
| Grain-producing areas under severe financial burdens | Increasing productivity and farmers' income, improving public services | Government-funded investment, tax reduction, infrastructure, project |
| Frontier border areas with weak governance | Promoting socioeconomic development, harmony, and prosperity | Government-funded investment, infrastructure, project |
| Over-extended metropolitan areas | Mitigating the side effects of over-expansion and ensuring sustainability | Regionalization, infrastructure, public services |
| Areas vulnerable to natural disasters | Preventing, mitigating, and relieving disasters; rebuilding | Government-funded investment, infrastructure, project, migration |

(1) Underdeveloped areas with lagging economic development: China has increased its poverty reduction standards and will intensify its efforts to alleviate poverty. It should continue to pursue a strategy of development-oriented poverty reduction, with additional poverty-reduction funds earmarked for infrastructure construction and skills-training. More projects should be launched to create jobs instead of issuing relief subsidies. Assistance for eco-migrants should also be increased.

(2) Aging industrial areas in relative decline: Old industrial bases are lagging because of their industrial decline and lack of competiveness, a result of unsolved historic problems, social tension, and environment constraints. Various policies tools should be applied to revitalize the old industrial bases. Transfer payment should be increased, and a favorable tax system should be adopted. The laid-off and unemployed should be assisted to find jobs. The social security system should be strengthened. Industries should be restructured and key projects should be supported. Zoning should be adjusted and new zones developed.

(3) Areas dependent on resource extraction or on monolithic industries: Since 2008, the State Council has identified 44 areas that face challenges due to exhausted resources, unemployment, monolithic economies, disproportionately resource-based industries, short industrial chains, or weak substitute industries. The central government should increase its financial support to these areas and establish a fund to aid them in their transition to new industries. Substitute industries should be developed and enhanced. The social security system should be improved. Environmental protection

and restoration should be carried out for sustainable development.

(4) Grain-producing areas under severe financial burdens: The main centers for China's food supply have contributed enormously to the country's food security, yet because of institutions and policies they have experienced slow income growth and high rates of poverty, underdevelopment of their food processing industries, insufficient local revenues, and so on. China's central government should offer more financial support to these areas and reduce their tax burden, construct and upgrade infrastructure, and better support the food-processing industry so as to increase agricultural output, farmers' income, and local fiscal revenues.

(5) Frontier border areas with weak governance: Ethnic minorities and poor population are concentrated in border areas where conflicts frequently occur and social security and infrastructure are inadequate. The central government should launch as soon as possible a development plan for border areas, increase investment in them, improve infrastructure, and carry out more projects in order to facilitate their self-development and socioeconomic development.

(6) Overly-extended metropolitan areas: Characterized by high population density and chaotic urban expansion, China's cities are plagued by traffic jams, insufficient housing stock, and degraded environments. If urban areas continue to expand, their prosperous downtown areas may degenerate into troubled zones. Population and industries should be encouraged to shift away from downtown areas to relieve this pressure; new towns should be developed; public services—particularly public transportation, road infrastructure, and parking facilities—should be provided; and urban planning should be improved.

(7) Areas vulnerable to natural disasters. Early warning systems should be improved in order to provide more accurate observations and forecasts. When disasters occur, increased financial support, human resources, equipment, information, and telecommunication facilities should be delivered in time. During the rebuilding process, the central government should invest more to build infrastructure, develop industries, and assist in outward migration.

## References

1. Myrdal, G., *Economic Theory and Underdeveloped Regions*. London, Duckworth, 1957.

2. Wei, Houkai, and Xiaoxia Wu. 2010. "The Rationale and Direction of China's Regional Policy." *Economic Prospective*, no. 2: 57 – 61.

3. Wei, Houkai, and Xianshu Xie. 2011. "The Drive to Develop China's West: An Inclusive Perspective." *China Economist*, no. 4: 16 – 25.

4. Wei, Houkai. 2009. "60 – Year Evolution of China's Regional Policy and its Prospect." *Henan Social Sciences*, no. 4: 8 – 11.

5. Wei, Houkai. 2007. "Reflections on the Formulation of Development Priority Zones." *China Development Observation*, no. 3: 28 – 30.

6. Wei, Houkai. 2006. "The Modification of China's Regional Policy in the 11th Five-Year." *Study & Exploration*, no. 1: 15 – 23.

7. Zhang, Keyun. 2005. *Regional Policy*, Beijing: Commercial Press, 12 – 13.

# Chapter 13

# Developing Secondary Industry to Drive China's Future Growth*

**Jin Bei** (金碚)

**Institute of Industrial Economics, CASS, Beijing, China**

**Abstract**: Since the second half of the 20th century and especially during the 21st century, world industrialization has experienced a series of historic changes. Although geopolitical changes triggered by political incidents such as the USSR's disintegration have played a significant role, the geographical shift of world industrialization has first and foremost been caused by the tipping of the balance of international economic and industrial development. China's rise has become a massive engine driving this Eastward transition. Due to its impressive rapidity, China's industrialization is often referred to as "compressed industrialization": completion of a long journey in a very short period of time. Chinese industrialization also features many distinctive characteristics that contrast with those of many other countries. Currently, China is in a critical stage of industrial development, moving towards world-class advanced manufacturing. Industrialization is a historic period of economic and social restructuring that is often accompanied by various structural imbalances. It is essentially a process of civilization's progress. China's industrialization is in many ways consistent with Western industrial and technological development, but remains subject to the profound influence of Chinese civilization. China's industrialization features unique differences that are deeply rooted in its institutional systems. After 30 years of brilliant achievements, reform of China's economic and political systems has once again come into the spotlight of public attention.

**Keywords**: Industrialization, globalization, global competition pattern, China's industrial development

As a historical process, industrialization evolved first from a national phenomenon into a global phenomenon. After initially emerging in only a few Western nations, this phenomenon has since swept across the globe and affected every nation on earth. Over the past 100 years, global competition has been a hallmark of world industrialization. Most recently, the rapid industrialization of emerging economies like China's has become the catalyst for shaping a new order in global competition. This process requires change and innovation on the part of emerging economies. As a result, research regarding China's developmental trends in the context of new global competition patterns bears great theoretical and practical relevance.

## I. World Industrialization: History and Modern Tendencies

The overriding theme of world economic development in modern history has been industrialization and the consequent urbanization. Industrialization is the most brilliant chapter of human civilization to date. Despite some resultant conflicts, hardships, miseries and even catastrophes, the tremendous power of industrialization has created unprecedented material wealth, leading to sustained improvement in people's living standards and living conditions, as well as dramatically extending life expectancy in industrialized countries. Countries or regions experiencing this stage of development can expect to rapidly transcend from low-to middle-or even high-income economies. World history indicates that most countries or regions must undergo the process of industrialization before fully achieving economic and social modernization.

As the origins of industrialization in the 17th and 18th century, Western Europe and its immigration countries have become advanced industrial powers and have provided the economic and military justification for modern Western civilization's current domination of the world economy. Modern Western civilization is industrial and capitalist, characterized by massive exploitation of natural resources, relentless expansion into new markets and endless creation and acquisition of wealth. Expansion, occupation and colonization (sometimes involving war and deprivation) constitute the "heroic history" of the industrial era. From this perspective, the two world wars were an extreme but predictable result of Western capitalist industrial civilization.

International industrial competition based on military warfare inevitably wreaks havoc on humanity. Belligerence offers no way out for Western civilization and must be replaced by an alternative, peaceful method for human development. This realization marks the historical backdrop for the development of international rules of competition and of the various institutions governing international relations, all underpinned by the basic principles of open economy, free trade, multinational investment and renouncement of colonial depredation. In the post-war era, some non-Western countries proactively accepted Western civilization but attempted to graft it to their own civilization. These countries intended to Westernize while still retaining many qualities unique to their own civilization. Successful integration of Western industrialization with native culture usually occurs in countries with large economies, such as Russia and India.

Since the era of industrialization, Western civilization has penetrated and affected almost every country in the world. This has naturally transformed the landscape of world civilization. After multiple major conflicts and crises the world has entered a new era of competition among modern civilizations. Instead of a violent "clash of civilizations" with clear boundaries, the competition of modern civilizations is an intricate process of interaction and conflict among major civilizations through mutual convergence, penetration, competition and cooperation in economic, cultural and political arenas.

Since the second half of the 20th century and especially during the 21st century, a series of historic developments have emerged regarding world industrialization. Aside from the drastic collapse of the USSR, the world's geopolitical landscape has been transformed first and foremost by the evolution of world economic patterns. According to a research report by the US National Intelligence Council (NIC), the following tendencies will become apparent in the next 15 years: the eastward shift of wealth and economic power and the rise of "state capitalism" as a hallmark of today's globalization; opportunities and challenges resulting from population growth and aging; increasing scarcity of strategic resources such as water, food and energy due to the rapid growth of the world economy; significant change in the type and source of future international conflicts, the weakening of ideological conflicts, and the preoccupation of most countries with more immediate economic and political challenges; by 2025, the US will still be the most powerful nation in the world but not in a dominant position; China and India will emerge as major powers that compete with the US influence while the EU, Japan and Russia will continue to be key world powers; finally, due to the shift of balance among the great powers, the world of 2025 will become a multi-polar world without multilateralism (Chen Changsheng, 2011).

Today, the term "emerging economies" is slowly replacing "developing countries" to refer to late-starting countries with strong momentum. This is because these countries are much more developed and play a much greater role in the international economic system than the phrases "developing countries" and "developing economies" suggest. For instance, many people in the Western world no longer believe that China still qualifies as a "developing country;" instead, they describe China as an emerging economy. The rise of emerging economies is vastly changing industrial competition and transforming the world's economic landscape. According to IMF vice chairman Zhu Min, "the gravity of world economic growth is shifting from developed economies to emerging and developing economies, which is exerting a major structural impact on all aspects of the global economy" (Zhu Min, 2011).

The gravity of the world economy is shifting eastward. First, according to the UN Database, the economic aggregate of the US and the EU – 15 represented a declining share over the past 50 years of the combined economies of the US, the EU and Asia, while the Asian economy's share continued to increase. Between 1960 and 2010, Asia's share of world GDP increased from 12.3% to 25.8%. In 2009 and 2010, Asia overtook the US and the EU – 15 to become the world's largest economy. Second, world resource consumption has also undergone major structural change. Since the beginning of the 21st century, the oil consumption of advanced economies has not only represented a decreasing share of world consumption but has also decreased in absolute quantity as well. It dropped from 17.1 billion barrels in 2000 to 16.5 billion barrels in 2010 and is projected to further decrease to 16.2 billion barrels by 2015. For emerging economies, this figure jumped from 11 billion barrels in 2000 to 15.3 billion barrels in 2010 and is poised to hit 17.8 billion barrels by 2015, thus overtaking that of advanced economies. That is to say, between 2000 and 2015, world oil consumption will increase by 23.1% but advanced economies will consume 5.3% less oil while the oil consumption of emerging economies will increase by 61.1% (ZhuMin 2011). Third, world demand (import value) is also being dramatically restructured. Despite their continued dominance, developed countries account for a declining share of import demand; emerging economies' share of import demand, on the other hand, is on the rise. This tendency first appeared in the 1970s and has persisted for decades. During the beginning of the 21st century, in particular, emerging economies have experienced a significant increase in their share of world demand for imports. China has played an important role in shifting international demand towards emerging economies and developing countries. Recent years have born witness to the robust growth of Chinese imports and their growing share of total world imports. Between 2001 and 2008, China's imports increased from USD243.6 billion to USD1, 132.6 billion, increasing by 24.6% on an annual basis and accounting for a surging share of total world demand.

As a result of the recent global financial crisis, China's imports suffered in 2009 (dropping to USD1,005.7 billion) but its share in total world imports continued to rise to well above 7%. From the initial inception of industrialization in Western Europe in the 17th century to the second half of the 20th century, about 60 countries and regions completed the process of industrialization. These countries had a total population of 1.2 billion. In other words, it took mankind almost 300 years to bring 20% of world population into industrialized society. This is a brilliant achievement of Western capitalist industrialization. Since the late 20th century, however, the gravity of the world economy has begun to shift eastward, opening a new chapter of rapid industrialization in an Oriental civilization that is home to a significantly larger population. The Chinese mainland alone has a population exceeding 1.3 billion. That is to say, in about 100 years, with China's industrialization, the world population currently living in industrialized societies will be more than doubled. This will transform the world and mark an unprecedented wave of industrialization in human history.

## II. China's Rise: Shifting World Economic Gravity towards the East

Chinese civilization is the only human civilization that evolved uninterruptedly from ancient to modern times. For thousands of years, China functioned as the gravity of the world's economy. According to British economist Angus Maddison, by 1820 China still accounted for 32.9% of world GDP despite 200 years of industrialization in the Western Europe. After the invasion of Western countries and the beginning of direct competition with Western capitalist industrialization, however, China plunged downwards. By 1978, the year of the inception of China's economic reform, the Chinese economy only accounted for 4.9% of world GDP, though it contained 22% of world population.

For more than ten years after 1978, China reflected deeply upon its recent history and transformed its relationship with Western industrial civilization. China became aware that industrialization cannot be skipped, and that the only way to end self-seclusion and backwardness is to accept the world system currently dominated by Western civilization and to accept the rules of international competition and trade developed by Western industrial powers. It is worthy of note that the very ideology of Marxism, embraced by pre – 1978 China to reject Western capitalist civilization, is itself part of Western civilization. In this sense, belief in Marxism cannot lead to the conclusion that Western capitalist civilization ought to be rejected. Nonetheless, China had attempted to adhere to such a rejection and suffered greatly for this choice. It was not until reform and opening-up in 1978 that the Chinese nation began its process of economic rejuvenation. China's entry to the WTO in the early 21 st century marks its audacious integration into the world economic system. Regardless of the capitalist nature or the dominance of developed countries, China has resolved to partake in the harsh environment of international competition as long as it is in the interest of Chinese industrialization efforts, Chinese economic development, and of the delivery of prosperity to the Chinese people.

China's entry into the world economic system and its rapid industrialization surprised both the world and its own citizenry with staggering successes. According to Professor Zheng Binwen's calculations, "starting with per capita GDP of USD155 in 1978, China exceeded the threshold of USD1, 000 in 2001 (USD1, 042) in just 23 years to become a lower middle-income country, which is the first milestone; it took China another nine years to exceed per capita GDP of USD4, 200 to jump from a lower middle-income country to an upper middle-income country, which marks the second milestone. These two historic milestones suggest that if lower middle income and upper middle income stages are seen as two separate thresholds of the middle-income trap, China has already surpassed the initial stage of the middle income trap (lower middle income) and replicated East Asia Speed: this process took Japan seven years (1966 – 1973), Hong Kong seven years (1971 – 1978), Singapore eight years (1971 – 1979) and South Korea eleven years (1977 – 1988)".

Due to its rapid industrialization and economic emergence, China has become a massive engine for the shift of economic gravity towards the East. According to the UN database, Asia's rising share in the world economy before 1995 had been driven by Japan; after 1995, the momentum came from China. Since that time, China has served as a mainstay in resisting further collapse of the Asian economy. After 2000, thanks to China's growing share in the Asian economy, Japan is no longer dominantly the only economic power in Asia. Since 2002, in particular, China has entered a new round of economic growth driven by heavy-chemical industries and has overtaken Japan as the second largest economy in the world. Meanwhile, China's share of the Asian economy has been growing, up 20 percentage points between 2000 and 2010 (up 15.6% in 2000 to 36.1% in 2010), while Japan's share has declined by almost 30 percentage points (down from 60.7% in 2000 to 33.7% in 2010). The balance of power has tipped in China's favor: China has replaced Japan as the primary driver of Asia's economy.

In the course of China's economic rise, the global financial crisis of 2008 came as both a severe test and as a great opportunity for China to prevail in the face of adversity. The repercussions of the financial crisis presented tremendous problems for China's export-dependent manufacturing, which provided most of the momentum for China's 30 years of rapid growth. Fortunately, China's manufacturing has demonstrated powerful capabilities of response and adaptation, emerging from the global financial crisis stronger than ever.

### (I) China Has Overtaken the US as the World's Largest Manufacturer

According to the official database of the International Monetary Fund, world manufacturing value added grew from USD4, 609 billion to USD9, 662 billion between 1990 and 2009. In the same period, the value-added of US manufacturing rose from USD1, 041 billion to USD1, 779 billion, but the US share of world manufacturing declined from 22. 59% to 18. 42%. Japan's manufacturing value-added expanded from USD810 billion to USD1, 050. 6 billion, while Japan's share of world manufacturing decreased from 17. 57% to 10. 87%. Germany's manufacturing value-added increased from USD438 billion to USD567. 9 billion, while Germany's share of world manufacturing decreased from 9. 50% to 5. 88%. France's manufacturing value-added went up from USD200 billion to USD253. 6 billion, while France's share of world total decreased from 4. 34% to 2. 62%. UK manufacturing value-added rose from USD206 billion to USD217. 6 billion, but the UK's share of world manufacturing dropped from 4. 47% to 2. 25%.

China's manufacturing, meanwhile, caught up with and surpassed that of advanced economies in quantitative terms. In 1990, China's manufacturing value-added was a mere USD145 billion, which was far lower than that of the US, Japan and Germany and less even than that of France and the UK, representing 3. 15% of world manufacturing value-added. After China's rapid economic expansion began in 1990, China's manufacturing value-added surpassed USD1 trillion in 2006 and USD2 trillion in 2009. China overtook France and the UK in 1993 and Japan in 2006 to become the second largest manufacturer in the world and surpassed the US in 2008 to become the largest manufacturer in the world. In 2009, China's manufacturing value-added registered USD2, 049. 9 billion, while China's share of the world manufacturing total reached 21. 22%. According to the estimate of US research institute HIS, world manufacturing output totaled USD10 trillion in 2010; China accounted for 19. 8%, while the US share of total manufacturing output was only 19. 4%. In short, China has become the largest manufacturer in the world, thus becoming the first country to outpace US manufacturing since 1895.

### (II) China Has Acquired Sufficient Economic Prowess to Become an Advocate of Free Trade

In the history of the world economy, it has always been competitive trading nations that advocate free trade while less competitive countries call for trade protectionism. Having long supported trade protectionism, China began to cautiously speak in favor of free trade after its entry into the WTO. Due to its changing relative economic status and industrial competitiveness after the global financial crisis, China has turned from passive acceptance to staunch support of free trade. Countries that used to blame China for violating free trade now have to admit that China has worked very hard to observe and maintain the principles of free trade. After the global financial crisis, many countries have readjusted their strategies and rules regarding international competition and trade. Some scholars believe that world policies will reorient from "releasing market power" to "protecting communities." In essence, this shift of focus tends to include more non-conventional factors into conventional rules of free trade, some of which are tailored to meet China's growing trade competitiveness. These changes are also a reflection of China's strengthening trade competitiveness and of the changes in the trade competitiveness of various other countries. In the face of an ever-changing international economic situation, China's responsiveness and maneuverability have significantly improved.

### (III) China Is Making Great Strides in Infrastructure Construction

China has made phenomenal investment in infrastructure construction as part of an attempt to tackle the recent financial crisis. Massive construction projects have been undertaken to build railway, airport, highway, bridge and urban subway systems. China has become the world's leader in high-speed railway lines. Empowered by strong capabilities in industrial production and construction, China has shocked the world with its explosive development of infrastructure. Starting almost from scratch, China has quickly developed some of the most impressive infrastructure systems and conditions for investment and industrial development of any emerging economy. It is foreseeable that in the wake of this drastic improvement in investment and market conditions, world capital, technology and professionals will all move to China on a larger scale and contribute further to the international competitiveness and overall strength of Chinese manufacturing.

### (IV) The Global Financial Crisis Provided an Opportunity for the Breakthrough of China's Resource-intensive Industries

The plummeting international economy eased pressure on scarce environmental resources. Economic recession made it possible to accomplish endeavors that otherwise could not be attempted due to price spikes and severe resource shortages. Meanwhile, the reversal of international asset prices provided the Chinese government, as well as especially powerful Chinese firms, opportunities for strategic international acquisitions. Chinese firms have thus hastened their pace of globalization. China has dramatically increased its investments to meet the challenges of resource constraints and environmental degradation. China's heavy industry grew much faster than light industry during this period, and began to represent an even bigger share of the industrial sector. In 2011 the growth rate of four energy-intensive industries increased dramatically; only petroleum processing, coking and nuclear fuel processing, electric power, and heat production and supply remained relatively constant. Due to advancing technology, energy efficiency in heavy industries has also increased. Despite heavy industries' growing share of the industrial sector, their share of electric power consumption has actually declined, down from 87% at the beginning of 2011 to 83% by the end of the year.

### (V) Chinese Firms Are Becoming Significantly More Competitive

Under the pressure of the global financial crisis, Chinese industries underwent (or began to experience) a reshuffle or a process of "refinement" and invigoration. Responding to the global financial crisis, China took a series of steps that include not only modifications to monetary and financial policies but also the establishment of policies affecting the real economy as well. For instance, it launched a four-trillion yuan stimulus investment plan and key industries rejuvenation plan. These programs are the speediest and most intensive policy reaction to occur since China's reform and opening-up in the late 1970s. Most of these policy measures have already been implemented and are intended to function as "hard" policies that will deliver real benefits to firms.

These programs, intended to stimulate the real economy as a key component of crisis policy, are consistent with China's national conditions and the general patterns of industrialization. Development of industries, especially heavy industries such as those producing manufacturing equipment, electronics and raw materials, provides the basis for increasing national economic power and safeguarding national security. Moreover, the rapid growth of heavy industry is an unavoidable stage of the industrialization process. Unlike the anti-crisis policies of Western countries, China's response to the crisis focused on developing and executing these programs to strengthen the real economy by investing largely in heavy-chemical industries. China took advantage of the economic crisis by launching some projects that were previously considered impractical under normal economic circumstances. Despite the short-term negative impacts of some policies in the industrial rejuvenation plan, these policies will leave a positive overall legacy for long-term economic development. The global financial crisis prompted infrastructure construction activities that may bring energy-intensive industries back to life. Although this may temporarily aggravate preexisting problems with energy conservation and environmental protection, rapid construction of infrastructure will be beneficial for China's long-term economic growth. Despite some wastage of natural resources, these intensive projects have strengthened weak areas of industrial development; short-term sacrifices are likely to translate into future industrial competitive advantage.

### (VI) China Is Earning Greater Influence on the Formulation of International Rules

China's growing economic clout and its potent responses to systemic crises have won widespread recognition of China's influence on the world economy. In fact, many countries often seek help from China to resolve major international issues. As a result, China has gained a much greater say in deciding international affairs and setting international economic rules. As a result, China is now in a better position to implement its strategies and protect its interests in the international economy. China also now faces increasing demands from the international community to shoulder more international obligations and responsibilities as a major international power.

## III. China's Unique Development Path and Tendencies towards Economic Restructuring

China's astonishingly rapid industrialization process is often referred to as "compressed industrialization." Most other countries required far more time to achieve the same degree of industrialization that China has accomplished in little more than 30 years. The Chinese process of industrialization also features many characteristics that are different from or in direct opposition to the industrialization processes of other countries. While most other developing countries suffer from insufficient domestic savings and foreign exchange ("savings gap" and "forex gap"), China has over-abundant savings and foreign exchange. While other developing countries are frustrated by the sluggish development of heavy manufacturing, China's heavy manufacturing seems to be an irrepressible monster. While other countries desire high GDP growth rates, China is worried about GDP overheating and pronounces GDP theory to be heresy. While other developing countries are struggling to reduce trade deficits, the rest of the world condemns China for its consistent trade surplus. These "problem" phenomena that are normally the envy of other countries are indeed consequences of China's phenomenal economic growth, which has led to imbalanced, uncoordinated and unsustainable elements in China's economic development. Some of these structural contradictions are undoubtedly very serious. In order to resolve these issues they must be examined in a scientific manner and cannot be simply ascribed to past mistakes. With the exception of man-made errors, any persistent and intractable contradictions or problems must have fundamental causes.

### (I) Economic Structure Is Influenced by the Equilibrium between Consumption, Savings, Investment and Import/Export Value

In the era of the planned economy, China's high savings rate was considered to be a major symptom of China's irrational economic structure. At the inception of reform and opening-up, there was an extensive discussion in China on the purpose of production and on the importance of consumption to a healthy economy. However, China's savings rate has been on the increase since pro-market reform. Both economic growth and industrialization require a high savings rate. Savings provide a source of investment and growth, which are the main drivers of China's economic achievements. The current concern is whether or not a high savings rate ensures a high investment rate. A high savings rate without equally intensive investment will cause economic recession and macroeconomic policy failure. China's high savings rate is justified by its high investment rate. But there is no denying that excessive savings and investment can cause over-capacity, resulting in imbalanced economic structure and slowing the improvement of people's living standards, which in turn diminishes domestic consumption.

Another defining characteristic of China's macroeconomic situation is China's enormous export of industrial goods. Export of industrial goods is the only way for China to capitalize upon international allocation of production factors within the currently limited bounds of economic globalization. Goods and capital flow freely, while labor tends to be more restricted in its movement. As home to more than 1/5 of the world's labor force, China has long been a destination for the relocation of production capacity and therefore has to achieve supply and demand equilibrium and effective allocation of resources through export of industrial goods. However, excessive trade dependence will subject China to the turbulent international economic situation and trigger trade disputes. An export-oriented growth pattern is also likely to distort price and exchange rate systems, intensifying energy and resource shortages. In fact, judging from the macroeconomic situation, China's massive export economy still has its root cause in high savings. This is because a high savings rate necessitates a low consumption rate and must be offset by a high investment rate in order to ward off economic recession. The danger is that the short-term effect of high investment is increased demand, while the long-term effect is increased supply. Higher supply must be balanced with certain net exports to avoid economic recession.

This situation begs the question: why does China have such high savings and investment? Perhaps the explanation lies in the general patterns of industrialization and in China's industrial development strategies. Or perhaps because within current institutional systems, a greater proportion of national income goes to the state coffer and corporate conglomerates than goes into the pockets of individual consumers; government tends to use its savings on investment and firms rarely distribute dividends to the people ( "people's capitalism" has been practiced in developed countries to create a "wealth effect" that has increased consumption), so that a very limited share of profits has been converted into consumption. Or perhaps it is because the Chinese people have a strong tradition of frugality and wealth accumulation and feel insecure about the future due to an inadequate social safety net. Or perhaps unequal income distribution and a weak middle class have restrained consumption. Whatever the causes, high savings and high investment are a long-term phenomenon in China's industrialization process and cannot be changed overnight.

China's unique macroeconomic situation is an outcome of economic development patterns, development paths and strategies, institutional systems and social psyche. It is simultaneously one of China's unique advantages and one of the most striking representations of an uneven economic structure and an uncoordinated macroeconomic situation. These Chinese macroeconomic characteristics may have been inevitable in the course of the nation's history; the next step is to address these increasing structural contradictions with timely adjustments in order for the country to embark on a brand-new path of industrialization.

### (II) The Importance of a Proper Understanding of the Changing Mix of Primary, Secondary and Tertiary Industries

How to balance the mix of primary, secondary and tertiary industries has been one of China's most discussed economic issues during recent years. On this issue, policy and reality seem to be very contradictory. Although most people believe that China's secondary industry is too large and tertiary industry is underdeveloped, most regions still expect secondary industry to grow at a higher rate than both GDP and tertiary industry. Strangely enough, it does. It is puzzling that although secondary industry grows faster than GDP and tertiary industry, tertiary industry's share of GDP is increasing while that of secondary industry is falling. This paradoxical situation results from the methods of statistical accounting of industries. Agriculture still employs a significant share of China's workforce; far higher than that of other industrialized countries. Measured by current price of finished products, China's secondary industry has reached a fairly advanced level while tertiary industry represents a significantly smaller share of the economy. Measured by purchasing power parity (PPP), however, China's secondary industry is smaller than that achieved by other advanced economies during industrialization, while China's tertiary industry accounts for a significant share of the economy (see Table 1).

**Table 1: Shares of China's Primary, Secondary and Tertiary Industries Measured by Different Price Approaches and Employment**

| Statistical approach | Primary industry | Secondary industry | Tertiary industry |
|---|---|---|---|
| Current price | 10.1 | 46.8 | 43.1 |
| PPP | 4.9 | 40.5 | 54.6 |
| Employment | 36.7 | 28.7 | 34.6 |

Source: estimations by Dr. Li Gang with Institute of Industrial Economics, CASS according to the data of National Bureau of Statistics (NBS) and the World Bank.

Caution must therefore be exercised in the assessment of whether an industrial structure is reasonable or whether it has seriously deviated from the normal track. The same holds true for the assessment of whether China's economy has entered the stage when the secondary industry's share of the economy should decline to make room for tertiary industry. In 2011, China's per capita GDP was 35,000 Yuan or USD 5,555 by year-end exchange rate, which is 11% of the US per capita level. Measured by PPP, China's per capita GDP was 8,210 international dollars①. This is equivalent to the US per capita GDP in the 1940s and Japan's per capita GDP in 1961, calculated in the same manner. By that time, the US and Japan's secondary industries were rising in proportion to total GDP. By the same method of calculation, Japan's secondary industry only accounted for 44.5% and tertiary industry 44.6%.

These statistics and international comparisons can lead to the following conclusion: except for a few regions such as Beijing, most parts of China are experiencing rapid growth of secondary industries, especially manufacturing. Using current-price approach, the share of tertiary industry tends to be smaller, whereas the actual service economy is larger than statistics suggest. This is consistent with how people feel about the service economy in their daily life. Deviation between employment mix and output mix remains an outstanding issue. Whether the secondary industry or the tertiary industry should create jobs for the primary industry's surplus labor is a major strategic issue. With price push picking up speed and current price nearing the level of purchasing power parity, tertiary industry will account for an increasing statistical share and give rise to social consequences that deserve our attention.

Effective industrial restructuring, therefore, requires not just the adjustment of proportion but also the coordination and interaction of primary, secondary and tertiary industries. Primary industry provides an important material basis for secondary and tertiary industries and serves as the premise for the modernization of secondary and tertiary industries. Secondary industry should provide technical support to primary and tertiary industries and is also a source of market demand for primary and tertiary industries. Tertiary industry is a necessity for primary and secondary industries; it should provide highly efficient and comprehensive transport services and information transmission services for both primary and secondary industries. Tertiary industry also provides essential support conditions for increasing the efficiency, branding and extension of primary and secondary industries. Proper understanding of the direction of industrial restructuring is crucial to establishing a modern industrial system compatible with the new path of industrialization that China is currently exploring.

### (III) Drivers of China's Economic Growth and National Competitiveness

The above discussion on the relationship between primary, secondary and tertiary industries suggests that most of China is in the middle stage of industrialization while some regions remain in the initial stage of industrialization. Therefore secondary industry remains the most strategically important sector for China's economic growth. Most of China's powerful corporate conglomerates are in the secondary industry. In 2010, 73.45% of 500 large Chinese corporate conglomerates were in the secondary industry and their operating revenue accounted for 72.6% of the total.

① In 2005 the United States constant price $1 = 1 international dollars.

Through industrial development China has become the world's largest manufacturer and second largest economy with the highest foreign exchange reserve of any country on earth. Secondary industry is the foundation upon which China has become a great power with international influence. Manufacturing is the only area in which China can compete with the other great international powers. A strong secondary industry is crucial to the rejuvenation of the Chinese nation, and further development of secondary industry is essential if China is to improve its people's living standards. As China's production industry targets the development of high-end manufacturing, strong will and great patience will be rewarded with great opportunity. Only a few countries will enter the realm of advanced manufacturing over the next 10 to 15 years, and China must seize every opportunity to join their ranks.

Advanced production industry, especially manufacturing, is essential to meeting almost all economic, social, public welfare and national security challenges confronting China. Admittedly, China's production industry has not yet acquired sufficient capabilities to address all major economic, social and national security issues. China's problem is not the over-expansion of industries but the fact that existing industrial technologies are not well prepared to ensure future economic development. Industrial technology upgrades and innovation are essential to addressing the major problems confronting China. Still more complex and difficult challenges in domestic and international affairs lie ahead, and China's large-country status is accompanied by great economic, political and especially military pressures. Triumph over these problems and pressures will require rapid industrial development, especially the development of advanced industries that focus on cutting edge technology and refined manufacturing.

As early as in the 1980s, European scholars claimed that mankind had entered an era of "risk-based society" where security issues are becoming increasingly significant. China's development will redefine national security interests. China's national interest is tied not only to its 9.6 million square kilometers of land but also to its vast seas and economic zones, offshore islands, airspace, global navigation channels and even to the overseas investment locations of Chinese firms. Without powerful military equipment and emergency response capabilities, these security interests will be in jeopardy. Only China's indigenous industries can satisfy these emergency response and military equipment needs. This is becoming a national issue of growing urgency, requiring that China speed up the development of technologically advanced manufacturing capabilities. Without these capabilities it will be difficult for China to become a truly powerful country and to assume its greater international responsibilities. Under the new patterns of global competition, China's international strength and competitiveness are fundamentally tied to the strength of its industries.

In the 19th century, the problem of uneven and uncoordinated industrial development had already emerged among major capitalist countries and aroused intense public criticism. By the middle of the 20th century, apparent resource and environmental constraints on industrialization gave rise to an intellectual ferment about "growth limits" (Rome Club Report) and the possibility of a non-industrialization or "middle" path (*Small is Beautiful*, E. F. Schumacher). Despite some reasonable elements in these theories that merit our attention, the worldwide process of industrialization never stopped advancing and accelerating. For an emerging power like China, all stages of industrialization are inevitable. For instance, resource-intensive industries are inevitable and cannot be renounced for the sake of industrial restructuring before China catches up with developed countries in these industries. Although steel manufacturing seems to be at serious "overcapacity," this is probably because China's cumulative steel reserves are far lower than that of developed countries. Developed industrialized countries such as the United States and Japan all have a very high level of per capita steel inventory: 11 to 12 tons. China's per capita steel inventory was only 1.5 tons in 2004. After great increases in steel capacity over recent years, China's per capita steel inventory in 2011 may have reached 4 tons, which is still much lower than that of developed countries. China's economic development cannot stray from the path of human industrial civilization. The key is to enhance technological and managerial innovation for resource-intensive industries in order to make production both cleaner and more efficient. More rigorous standards governing the development of resource-intensive industries will also incentivize the technological innovation necessary for energy conservation and environmental protection.

Building an industrial power is not only a matter of producing manufactured goods. The essence of industrialization is not confined to the growth of material wealth; it also entails the transformation of economic and social structures, as well as the social attitudes of the entire country. Given the universal importance and relevance of industrialization, households should think about sending their sons and daughters to engineering schools and universities. Why do the brightest students choose to study finance and other non-engineering majors? The education industry should think about whether educational resources should be devoted to the training of industrial professionals or to people who are far from the production line. Our society needs to reflect upon whether we are paying sufficient respect to manufacturing, the core of the Chinese economy. Should manufacturing be a fountain of wealth for the middle class or a mere gathering place for low-income citizens? The development of industry will determine not only the quality of China's material goods but also the quality of the Chinese people.

## IV. The Arduous Journey of China's Rise as an Industrial Power

The history of world industrialization tells us that most countries and regions in the world will undergo the process of industrialization to achieve economic development and become an industrial society. However, it is after this process that these countries will reach a fork in the road: some will emerge as industrial powers while others will not. Having reached a certain income level, some countries will lose their competitive edge in manufacturing and rely on the service sector to support their national economy. Most of these countries are unlikely to retain their roles as leaders of economic development, science and technology. Several countries in southern Europe, such as Greece, fall into this category. After completion of the industrialization process, some other countries still manage to maintain competitive advantage in certain areas of manufacturing. Although losing cost advantage, these countries are still able to occupy certain international status in conventional and advanced manufacturing sectors by virtue of the specialized technology, processes and brands that they have developed in these sectors. This is the case with several countries in Western Europe. The third category of countries are those that have firmly occupied superior technological positions and advanced manufacturing technology platforms for various reasons, often including effective institutional systems, conducive cultural norms, successful national strategies, solid industrial foundations and enterprising, well-educated workforces. After three hundred years of industrialization, only a few countries such as the US, Germany, Japan, Switzerland and Sweden have entered this third category of industrial power and firmly secured their continuing superiority in manufacturing. When China becomes the world's largest manufacturer, most of its industries will still lag far behind in terms of technology, manufacturing capabilities and especially core competencies. For China to become a real industrial power, the journey ahead will be long indeed.

So far, China's industrialization has roughly followed the technological path of industrialization in Western countries. From a global perspective, China's industrialization has depended upon a dispersion of technology from the Western world as industry has shifted from West to East. As a developing country and an emerging economy, most of China has experienced the four phases below:

The first phase is international reallocation of production capabilities, i. e. relocation of processing, assembly and manufacturing capabilities from developed countries to China where the cost of production is low. This process is driven by inexpensive land, natural resources and labor, as well as by low environmental standards. Developed countries take advantage of these low production costs by shifting low- and mid-level production processes to the developing country. As multinational firms in the developed world shift production to low-cost countries, the branding of the developing country's manufactured goods changes. A sign of this phase is that "Made in China" goods are no longer considered cheap and shoddy; instead, they have gained a reputation as inexpensive goods that average people around the world cannot live without.

The second phase is the international reallocation of production equipment and skills from developed countries to China. This process of international migration is accompanied by two significant economic factors: first, corporate capabilities for capital accumulation and equipment investment (especially procurement of advanced equipment) rise; second, education and training of engineers and skilled workers improves and a "craftsman" culture is developed. For developed countries and multinational firms in particular, this process means intensive localization and outsourcing of production; for China, it means technological progress and improvement in industrial production. During this phase, Chinese goods develop an even better reputation for their superior quality and an increasing number of "Made in China" products are sold by mid-range stores around the world.

The third phase is the international reallocation of R&D capabilities from developed countries to China, making China as their research base with innovative competence in core technologies. This process of international migration is accompanied by an overall improvement in China's social economic environment and the formation of innovation mechanism and culture. For developed countries and multinational firms in particular, this process means 'root transplantation' of manufacturing industry; for China, it means climbing up the industrial commanding height. During this phase, Chinese goods develop a reputation of high-tech boutiques and an increasing number of "Made in China" products are fashionable goods.

The fourth phase is the international reallocation of branding advantage, i. e. the most competitive brands featuring technological superiority and cultural appeal shift from developed countries to China. This process of relocation is driven by comprehensive economic, technological and cultural strengths and by the "psychological conquest" over consumers. For developed countries and especially for multinational firms, this phase marks a complete transformation. For China, it marks the beginning of far greater industrial prowess. After the fourth phase, Chinese products will be unrivalled on the world market.

Obviously, most Chinese industries are in the first and second stages of development. Even China's most competitive industries like textiles have not yet reached and completed the third phase. Therefore China has a long way to go before becoming a strong industrial power. We must remain cognizant that for China at its current stage of development, production industries, especially manufacturing, are its most important industries. Without long-term efforts to further develop manufacturing, it will be impossible for China to become an industrial power or even to maintain its current competitive edge. More importantly, production industries are a vehicle of innovation. Without advanced industries, it is unlikely for scientific discoveries and technological inventions to be applied in mass production. In short, an advanced manufacturing sector is the foundation for building an innovation-oriented country. Without strong industries, a country cannot expect to be innovation-oriented. This is the primary reason the US has called for the rejuvenation of its manufacturing industry.

Given the enormous scale of Chinese manufacturing there will undoubtedly be difficulties with its further development. Some of the most striking complications are related to resource and environmental constraints. Growing resource and environmental constraints cannot be addressed by abandoning industrial enterprises. On the contrary, developing stronger industry is the only sensible response to resource and environmental limitations. The most fundamental way to address resource and environmental constraints is to move up the industrial ladder and increase the efficiency, conservation, cleanliness and refinement of the entire industrial chain.

Today, most of China's industrial sectors are beneath the levels of developed countries by large margins. It is imperative for China to strive for high-end development in all industries, achieve refined and lean production throughout the industrial chain, and develop more competitive modern industrial systems with higher resource efficiency and environmental standards. To this end, China should develop a culture of modern industrial civilization, which is the irreducible DNA of any strong industry.

Since the beginning of the 21st century, industrial restructuring and upgrading have received ever-increasing attention, dominating the agenda for the transformation of economic development in China. When creating strategies for industrial development, China's industries and regional planners have been trying to interpret the essence of industrial restructuring and to align industrial development priorities with viable paths of industrial restructuring and upgrading. According to the above analysis of international industrial competition, almost all Chinese industries, including even the most competitive industries like textiles and apparels, have more or less completed the international relocation of production capabilities, equipment and skills but are far from absorbing the core technologies, innovation capabilities and branding advantages of foreign countries. This is an indication that China suffers from more than the simple absence of technology. China is still at a great distance from the peak of world industry!

Indeed, China needs to fashion a modern industry through industrial restructuring and upgrading, as well as through the strategic development of emerging industries. Nevertheless, this does not mean a reckless renouncement of conventional industries for the single-minded pursuit of high-tech industries. In fact, embedding high-tech elements into conventional industries is an effective way to upgrade an industry. For China as a whole, there is no sunset industry and great potential exists in conventional industrial sectors as well as in various sectors of advanced manufacturing. Far from "giving up," the intention of industrial upgrading is to "hold tight," making China's industries more competitive internationally in all respects. Bringing industrial sectors (including conventional industries and high-tech industries) up to speed with advanced world levels should be an urgent priority for China's industrial transformation. Given these considerations, the following important issues must be properly understood and handled:

First, with respect to the upgrading of conventional industries: given varied competencies in the workforce, China's industry needs to accommodate various types and levels of skill and it should target employees who will cater to a diverse industrial structure. Industries are fundamentally continuous and are not divided by absolute boundaries or distinction between superiority and inferiority. Powerful firms can emerge from virtually any industry. For example, it is not only aviation/aerospace and high-end manufacturing industries that make the US strong, but also conventional enterprises such as Coca-cola, Wal-Mart, jeans and MacDonald's.

The improvement of technology and international competitiveness in conventional industries is a common goal for industrial powers. Most high technologies are developed to be applied in conventional industries. There is no absolute high & low-value attribute attached to high-tech industries and conventional industries. Conventional industries may also have high-tech attributes and generate high value addition. By the same token, high-tech industries may also have low-value activities as well. Therefore industrial restructuring should not be industry-discriminative. Technological remodeling is one of the most effective ways to achieve industrial upgrading.

A specific example is IT application for the achievement of industrialization. As a matter of fact, many Chinese manufacturing enterprises have made considerable headway in the integration of IT application and industrialization. Fairly advanced information technologies have been applied not only in R&D, design, production and sales networks, but also in the monitoring of product performance after sales. Innovative IT application should be greatly encouraged.

Second, with respect to the development of strategic emerging industries: emerging industries are industries for the future, characterized by the uncertainty of technological options and by the immaturity of the application of technology. For most emerging industries, core technologies are not yet fully ready even in developed countries and must therefore rely on government subsidy. Besides, relatively mature and applicable technology options that have proven successful in developed countries may not be entirely suitable given China's national conditions.

Considering the reality of China's industrial development, strategic emerging industries include high-end industries and industrial chains that have appeared in developed countries but are not yet ready in China, together with new industrial sectors that are being explored in other developing countries as well. Although it is easier to copy preexisting industries from foreign countries, indigenous innovation is a better investment due to the barriers in the international relocation of technologies. However, the development of entirely new industries can only rely on indigenous innovation and thus involves considerable R&D cost, risk and uncertainty.

It is unwise to roll out production capabilities in low-end industrial chains when the technology is not ready. "Strategic emerging industries" generally involve long industrial chains, in which some processes are resource-efficient and environmentally friendly while others are not, even involving energy-intensive and dirty processes. Hence, development of strategic emerging industries should strive for technological innovation in some industrial activities but aim to ultimately achieve technological maturity and efficiency throughout the entire industrial chain and even the entire lifecycle of the industry.

Third, modern services: Many people are concerned that China's service sector is backward while secondary industries represent an excessive share of the economy. Most regions are worried about how to speed up the development of services and increase the share of the tertiary industry. The reality is that it takes time for modern services to flourish. Once economic development reaches a certain level, the service sector will naturally achieve a significant share of the economy. With industrial development comes the improvement of industrial technologies, further division of labor, decomposition of industrial chains and integration between industries, all of which will broaden the scope of the service sector. Highly dependent on industrial technologies, modern services (such as communications, logistics, Internet-based economies and the information industry) cannot develop without the application of industrial technologies, institutional reform and broader scope of access. As industrial goods become cheaper and services more expensive, the economic share of tertiary industry measured by current price will increase faster than expected.

Fourth, regional development strategies of industrialization: as China's industries continue to grow and develop, the geographic distribution of industry will change. Over the past 30 years of reform and opening-up, China's industrialization first occurred in urban regions near China's coastline in the east. These regions include the Yangtze River Delta, the Pearl River Delta and the Bohai Rim Economic Circle, etc. There are also certain central cities and economic zones that have experienced rapid development in the interior region, but these interior provinces have generally lagged behind the coastal region. In particular, many county economies are significantly less developed than China's central urban economies. Where agriculture remains the dominant industry, the countryside rarely boasts advanced industries and services. In fact, agriculture itself is not yet backed by sufficient utilization of modern techniques of production. The overall situation in China is defined by the co-existence of well-developed central urban hubs and an underdeveloped rural economy.

China's regional disparities are striking and are a major source of the imbalanced, uncoordinated and unsustainable development of China's economy. Thus, China's future industrialization must march forward into the underdeveloped parts of the coastal, central and western regions, as well as into all of China's agricultural countryside.

After 30 years of rapid industrialization, China has acquired both the necessary and prerequisite conditions to develop on these various fronts. It has accomplished considerable economic development and acquired substantial technological competency, capital, and human resources. Thanks to drastic improvements in national infrastructure, the inferior location of these regions is no longer an issue. Furthermore, there has emerged a squadron of intrepid entrepreneurs who are seasoned in business operation and risk prevention. Central cities have become more mature and are beginning to exert greater regional influence. Instead of absorbing resources from the region, Shanghai now exerts a beneficial influence on the surrounding region and the economic prosperity of the Yangtze River Delta is now expanding far upriver. This permeation effect will stimulate rapid growth of the hinterland economy.

Industrial development on these three fronts reflects great diversity, equilibrium, integration and tendency towards domestic consumption. First, during the initial three decades since reform and opening up, China's economic growth was fueled by first-tier and coastal cities. Except for these first-tier urban centers, most of China, including most cities, was relatively backward in its economic development. Now these first-tier cities are being overcrowded and their pace of development has slowed. The only way to ensure sustained economic growth is to develop new sources of growth in the coming 15 to 20 years. Second, China's economic development is characterized by gradual reform and differentiated levels of development, resulting in uneven development across regions. Only through industrial development in the interior regions will China be able to achieve balanced economic growth. Third, economic integration will occur between provincial capitals and their surrounding regions, across separate provinces and previously separate markets, as well as between cities and the countryside. Economic integration is an effective recipe for local protectionism. Only with a united domestic economy will China be able to productively partake in the global economy for its sustainable development, thus avoiding the "middle-income trap". Lastly, only through economic permeation to and interconnection with relatively secluded interior regions will China's economy be able to effectively increase domestic consumption. Currently, a major reason for China's sluggish domestic consumption is that its economic hinterland is relatively secluded while first-tier cities are highly open, so that central coastal cities are much more integrated with the world economy than with the economy of the Chinese hinterland. Massive production capabilities are disconnected from the narrow hinterland market. All-around opening-up of the hinterland economy to the rest of China and the rest of the world is the only way to achieve the sustained growth of domestic consumption.

Fifth, the strategy of "going global" in the context of the world economy, China's industries should not only abide by the WTO rules on free trade but also prepare themselves to come to terms with strict rules regarding international competition. The problem is that most Chinese enterprises are unfamiliar with international rules and lack practical experience with international operation. In particular, the organizational structure of Chinese enterprises does not prepare them for international operation and must be improved in order to "go global" on a larger scale. In particular, greater reform of state-owned enterprises will be necessary to enable them to compete in a global context.

"Going global" is a difficult project with far-reaching significance. What kind of enterprises should invest abroad? Why should they go global? The payoff can be found in the alternative outlets for excess production capability, in the acquisition of the most cutting edge technology and in the development of powerful international industrial chains and networks. Strategically, going global will induce more powerful corporate organizational structure and international competitiveness in the global supply chain.

## V. Concluding Remarks

Industrialization creates an era of economic and social transformation and structural imbalances. It is essentially a process of the progress of civilization. China's industrialization builds upon Western industrial technologies but remains subject to the deep influence of Chinese civilization. Although Chinese and Western industrialization have followed similar paths, China's industrial development is characterized by unique institutional systems flawed by incomplete reform and opening-up, institutional imperfections and by many unique national conditions. One of these conditions is government intervention in deciding economic structure and economic affairs. In a contest for "leapfrog development", local governments tend to exert influence on the market to increase the pressure for "brilliant achievements," often at the cost of market distortions. Then, reverse-market policies have to be adopted to address the structural deviations developed under the effect of pro-market deviations. In a word, most of China's structural economic issues are related to excessive government intervention. That is why China is troubled by a high savings rate, high investment rate, massive industrial output, strong export competitiveness and enormous foreign exchange reserves that, though envied by other developing countries, frequently create problems in the Chinese economy.

Government administration is important and can direct resources to urgent endeavors to achieve swift results. But it is crucial to develop a market-based mechanism of resource allocation. Imbalanced, uncoordinated and unsustainable elements in China's economy almost all result from institutional glitches. Under intensive government intervention, China's industrial development over the past thirty years has been highly dependent upon various favorable policies and special treatment. These short-term policy maneuvers cannot persist; otherwise corporate competition will become little more than the competition for policy preferences and special treatment. Under a perfect market economy, the most effective development policy is fair competition without discrimination. Therefore as China stands at the threshold of becoming a true industrial power, economic and political reform has once again come into the spotlight of public attention.

## References

1. Chen, Changsheng. 2011. "The U. S. Forecast on the World in the Following Fifteen Years and Its National Strategy-Comment on the 'Global Trends 2025' by National Intelligence Council (NIC)." *Review of Economic Research* (46).

2. Institute of Industrial & Technical Economics of NDRC etc. 2012. Development Report on Top 500 Big Enterprises Group in China (2010 – 2011). *Review of Economic Research* (15C – 1).

3. Institute of Industrial Economics of CASS. 2011. *China Industrial Development Report-Transformation and Upgrading of China's Industry.* Beijing: Economic Management Press.

4. Jin, Bei, and Gang Li. 2011. *China's Development Pattern – Exploration of Chinese Economists.* Beijing: Economic Science Press, 2011.

5. Jin, Bei. 2010. *Competitiveness Report of China's Enterprises* 2010. Beijing: Social Sciences Academic Press.

6. Jin Bei. 2011. "Resources Constraint and China's Industrialization Path." *Seeking Truth Magazine* (8).

7. Jin Bei. 2011. "Transformation and Upgrading of China's Industry." *China Industrial Economics* (7).

8. Jin Bei. 2011. *Jin Bei Collections.* Beijing: China Modern Economics Publishing House.

9. Jing, Christopher. 2011. *Reflections on China-What We Have Done Wrong.* Jiangsu: Phoenix press.

10. Li, Yining. 2009. *Chinese Economy in Disequilibrium.* Beijing: Encyclopedia of China Publishing House.

11. Li, Zongnan, and Feng wen. 2011. *China's Trends II: Innovation Changes China.* Beijing: China Industry & Commerce Associated *Press.*

12. National Institute for Research Advancement (NIRA). 1989. *Japan in the* 1990*s*. Beijing: Economic Management Press.

13. Omae, Kenichi. 2010. *Economics Psychological Aspects.* Beijing: China CITIC Press.

14. Senor, Dan, and Saul Singer . 2010. *Start-up Nation-The Story of Israel's Economic Miracles.* Beijing: China CITIC Press.

15. Zhang, Weiwei. 2011. *The Rise of a 'Civilization State'* . Shanghai: Shanghai People's Publishing House.

16. Zheng, Bingwen. 2011. "Middle Income Trap and China's Path to Development: In Perspective of International Experiences and Lessons." *Strategy and Management* 5/6.

17. Zhu, Min. 2011. "Profound Changes of World Economic Structure and Challenges for Emerging Economies." *International Finance Research* (10).

# Chapter 14

# Domestic Demand-based Economic Globalization: Strategic Choice for China to Profit from the Second Wave of Globalization*

**Liu Zhibiao (刘志彪)**

**Center for the Yangtze River Delta Socioeconomic Development of Nanjing University, Nanjing, China**

**Jiangsu Provincial Academy of Social Sciences, Nanjing, China**

**Abstract**: China's first wave of economic globalization is characterized by its full utilization of foreign advanced, especially innovative, production factors in the domestic market to develop its innovation economy. China's participation in global economy can be described as fully utilizing domestic low-end production factors through foreign markets. This type of participation has been overdone. As China aims to engage in a second wave of economic globalization, the focus is to implement an in-depth globalization strategy under the condition of expanding domestic demands, namely and to develop the global economy based on domestic demands. The purpose is to achieve an economic rebalance with the world and help China out of its overcapacity predicament in weaker global economic climates. Moreover, it will bring China a chance to introduce foreign advanced factors to accelerate growth and develop innovation economy by taking advantage of economic crisis in the West.

**Keywords**: domestic demands, export orientation, economic globalization and China's economic development

After three decades of reform and opening, China has become one of the world's biggest winners of economic globalization after World War II. Globalization has enabled China's economy to take off and develop rapidly into the world's factory with its cheap labor. However, it has been increasingly recognized since 2008 that China, as a big economy, should have a rebalance its position within the world economy, because the sort of export-based dividend China used to enjoy from the

---

* Corresponding author: zbliu@ nju. edu. cn.

This paper is a phase result of a major project funded by Major Research Base of Humanities & Social Sciences, Ministry of Education-*Research on Improving the Opening-up Level of the Yangtze River Delta under the Condition of Expanding Domestic Demands*. Project number: 11JJD790036.

first wave of globalization by embedding low-end factors into the global value chain (GVC) has been reached its limit. Therefore, China's globalization strategy should be transformed and upgraded.

The transformation does not mean that China should draw back to an internally oriented economy. Instead, it means China should further take advantage of the world economic crisis to launch a new development strategy to respond to the second round of economic globalization-implementing an in-depth globalization strategy under the condition of expanding domestic demands, namely, developing the global economy based on domestic demands.

According to China's 12th Five-year Plan (2011 – 2015), China will develop a world leading domestic market. This requires an expansion of domestic demands in conjunction with a new strategy that leverages the linkage between the domestic and global market. With these efforts, China can maximize the use of global advanced innovative factors, facilitate economic transformation and upgrading, and accelerate fulfillment of the goal of building an all-around well-off society and achieving modernization.

Developing a domestic demand-based global economy is neither a new economic phenomenon nor a new concept. It is a shared economic pattern across the world's advanced, populous countries. The United States is a typical example. Owing to its large population who earns large income and to its strong purchasing power, the U. S. has the world's largest final demand. This is the main condition for the U. S. has relied upon to become the global market governor. Another reason is that such strong domestic demand plus other non-economic factors have shaped and maintained a dominant position of the U. S. dollar over a fairly long period. This attracts global production factors and exporters, so that the U. S. can always gain low-cost factors and products easily. Finally, thanks to its sizable domestic market and a good many job opportunities, the U. S. becomes the biggest absorber of various factors, especially advanced innovative factors. Among developed countries, the U. S. absorbs the most foreign direct investment (FDI) and top-level talent from all over the world.

Admittedly, the domestic demand-based global economic system of the U. S. is supported by its own conditions and complex backgrounds such as its consumption culture, political and military strength. For China, which is also a big economy, its major development strategy is undoubtedly to establish a similar global economic system with Chinese characteristics. In this paper, the author will comprehensively discuss the basic background, connotation and policy orientation of this strategy.

## I. Background of the Need for China to Launch the Second Round of Globalization Strategy Soon

Below are some major characteristics of China's participation in the first wave of globalization since the 1980s and especially since 1992. They represent some changes in China's rebalance with the world economy and also main reasons for the need to change the globalization strategy.

Being a resource-poor country, China is a big resource consumer because it sits at the low end of the GVC. In a complete goods and service chain, resource consumption and occupation mainly happens during processing, manufacturing, assembling and production. Due to China's comparative advantages at the bottom of the value chain, it is bound to undertake resource consumption transferred from western countries which then focus on research & development (R&D), designing, brand, marketing and other high-end elements of the value chain. Even though China's total resource consumption will the same, it will consume and occupy more resources after western countries transferring over production through intra-product specialization. Relying on resource-consuming production and processing, China's trade and economic growth inevitably follows an extensive growth mode.

Another reason for China's need to change its globalization strategy is that it the biggest FDI absorber among developing countries. As such a poor country, it has been providing much direct and indirect financing for rich countries. As of the end of June 2011, China's foreign exchange reserve balance has reached USD3. 1975 trillion, accounting for 69% of its external financial asset; foreign investment in China values at USD1. 58. 8 trillion, accounting for 60% of its external financial liabilities. It fully shows that both China's external financial assets and liabilities have a compact structure. External financial assets are concentrated in government agencies in the form of foreign exchange reserves, while external financial liabilities are concentrated in the private sector in the form of direct investment①. Such a pattern has five financing effects. First, absorbing FDI for original equipment manufacturer (OEM) at the bottom of GVC leads to competitive export of low-end factors, which constantly brings down the input cost of enterprises in the importing country, especially in high-end manufacturing industry. Second, by undertaking manufacturing outsourced goods, China reduces the outsourcer country's investment in fixed assets like factories and equipment, thus reducing their capital formation rate. Third, exporting cheap consumption goods to rich countries is equal to improving their residents' income, enabling them to invest more of their income in financial assets while maintaining a high living standard. Fourth, rich countries' manufacturing can obtain higher profits and invest them in virtual economic activities like merger & acquisition (M&A) and dividend payment. Fifth, China's foreign exchange income gained from export is not used to purchase raw materials or equipment but is refluxed to rich countries through constant purchasing of their treasury bonds or other riskier financial products. Consequently, excessive foreign exchange earnings result in more issuance of Renminbi and severe domestic inflation; on the other hand, it fuels rich countries' financial bubble and puts its foreign exchange wealth in the danger of being constantly depreciated.

Globalization is in essence a contest for jobs by all countries. As an "operator at the bottom of the world," China fights for low-end jobs emptied out by developed countries during industrial restructuring but at the cost of losing high-end jobs to rich countries. However, western rich countries argue that China's export has ruined their industrial and employment base. For instance, Autor, *et*

① China had become the biggest net capital exporter last year. Please refer to http: //dycj. ynet. com/3. 1/1112/06/6569942. html.

*al.* (2011) holds that imports from China cause negative effects on the U. S. economy: imports from China are negatively correlated to employment in corresponding manufacturing industries and labor markets in the U. S. ; they reduce the wage of workers and raise government spending on unemployment and medical security①. They call this "the China syndrome." In fact, exports from China offer a chance for the U. S. to restructure its industry at a low cost; but in the meantime, China loses the chance to absorb advanced factors essential for industrial upgrading.

Finally, western technologies are sorely needed by China's manufacturing, but they crowd out China's independent innovation, bereaving China's manufacturing of a "heart" and "head." Long-term export-oriented OEM using low-end production factors enables China's manufacturing enterprises to profit decently without having to input in R&D, designing and brand network. This leads to two negative results. First, China's own R&D and heavy equipment industry cannot survive due to a lack of demands. Second, China's manufacturing suffers from two diseases. First is the "heart disease" caused by a lack of core technologies that are mostly grasped by multinational enterprises of developed countries. Chinese manufacturers can only utilize other countries' technologies at a high cost. The other disease is "neuropathy," symptoms of which include a low intelligence level of "China-manufactured" products, backward software development and application.

From the perspective of a balance between aggregate demands and supplies, "deleveraging" of consumption in the U. S. and European countries will go parallel and interact with China's "de-capacity." "Deleveraging" of consumption requires the U. S. and European countries to increase savings and reduce excessive consumption, while "de-capacity" requires China to reduce overcapacity, especially that of traditional low value-added industries. Implementing the strategy of expanding domestic demands is the best means to "de-capacity," which is a controllable policy instrument of the Chinese Government and also the core to China rebalancing with the world economy. It requires China to embrace a domestic demand-based economic development mode. There are, however, many challenges associated with this strategy.

First, China's economy has three low ratios: a low ratio of investment for people's well-being, a low ratio of the service industry and a low ratio of middle-income earners. This is the reason why it is hard to expand China's domestic demands. Consequently, the investment-driven growth mode is self-reinforced and it constantly builds up excess capacity, hence heavier reliance on export. In case of an external crisis, the economy will unavoidably go down. This vicious circle will not be solved unless we increase the three ratios, which requires long-term efforts. In the short term, stabilizing external demands remains the most important way of ensuring economic growth.

Second, the real challenge for China now lies in how to expand domestic demand and how to improve industrial competitiveness throughout the process. Determinants of expanding domestic demand lie with the demand side seemingly, and it seems that if China multiplies people's income, balance income distribution and enhance consumption infrastructures, China will automatically ex-

① Autor, David H., David Dorn, and Gordon H. Hanson. 2012. "The China Syndrome: Local Labor Market Effects of Import Competition in the United States." NBER Working Paper No. 18054, Issued in May 2012.

pand domestic demands. However, the crux actually lies with the supply side. Given the huge technological gap between China and western countries, expanding domestic demands will end up with stronger demands on western surplus products and even luxuries① instead of Chinese products! In the long term, if expanding domestic demands is not combined with industrial upgrading to improve competitiveness of Chinese products, China's overcapacity will not be digested by either domestic or foreign markets.

Third, at the micro level, there is only weak technology and product but there exists no weak market. Independent technical innovation is the ultimate solution of expanding domestic demands in the long run. In the past, China upgraded industries by absorbing western technologies and capital that produced the "technology spillover" effect. However, by swapping the market with technologies, China cannot acquire real advanced technologies. Learning and imitating do not promise smooth technological development. Therefore, many people advocate that the government should increase R&D and marketing input in China's domestic enterprises and brands. During economic globalization, closed, independent R&D can hardly produce practical effects. China should seek to be market-oriented to utilize advanced usable factors, including western technologies, knowledge and talents so as to build its own international competitiveness.

## II. Domestic Demand-based Economic Globalization: Basic Contents of the Second Round of Globalization Strategy

The strategy of expanding domestic demands does not run counter to globalization, nor does it conflict with participation in economic globalization. Expanding domestic demands is about utilizing the domestic market; hence there is no direct linkage to participation in the global economy. It can be operated in an open manner, like importing foreign factors, processing them in China and selling them in both the domestic and overseas market. It can also be done in a closed manner, such as completing the whole value-adding process of the industrial chain without any linkage to the international economy. "Economic globalization" refers to a trend of the market economy and cross-regional flow of factors on the global scale. It is only the opposite of closed flow of factors within a closed economy. The domestic demand-based economic globalization, in essence, is about developing one's own economy by leveraging global quality factors. In an open environment, big economies are generally "domestic demand-based" in nature due to huge domestic demand potentials. For small economies like Singapore, Taiwan, South Korea, *et al.*, as their limited size of population and the domestic market cannot digest supplies of economies of scale, they are generally "export-oriented."

For such a big economy with huge market potential as China, the export-oriented economic globalization strategy is unsustainable. No country in the world can accommodate long-term export from

① For instance, the sales volume of Bentley motors hit a new record in 2011. Its sales volume almost doubled in China with a record of 1839. For the first time, China overtakes the UK to become the second largest market of Bentley motors.

such a huge producer, or would allow its industries to be entrapped for long in fierce competition ignited by China's cheap products. Generally speaking, aside from market demands, the second wave of economic globalization has the following fundamental differences from the first wave in terms of basic strategic content:

First is the strategic precondition. The first wave of economic globalization is characterized by an export orientation. Its precondition is a comparable advantage in the price of low-end factors; when domestic income is low and domestic demand is too weak to support rapid economic growth, China's cheap production factors have great competitiveness in the global market. The domestic market has strong demands on low-end factors but weak demands on high-end factors, which is the main reason why China becomes the world's manufacturing factory but its independent innovation and producer service are underdeveloped. The preconditions for the second wave of economic globalization is fundamentally different. It lies more in improvement in the quality and production efficiency of factors. Specifically, the factor price is rising gradually and comparable advantages of low-end industries are vanishing. We can no longer subsidize foreigners by sacrificing laborer's interests, consuming and occupying huge amounts of capitals and destroying domestic ecological environment. To occupy the domestic market, domestic enterprises will have strong demands on advanced factors. Meanwhile, the rising price of factors will edge out low-end industries, hence innovation-driven economic growth, improvement in the production efficiency and great development of the service industry.

Second is the strategic purpose. The first round of globalization strategy aims more at finding an outlet for domestic overcapacity. Its strategic purpose can be summarized as fully utilizing domestic low-end production factors through foreign markets." The purpose of new strategy can be summarized as fully utilizing foreign advanced production factors, especially innovative factors in the domestic market to accelerate development of China's innovation economy[①]. Insufficient domestic technologies can be supplemented by attracting over foreign factors. The purpose of taking advantage of the second wave of globalization is to help China out of the overcapacity predicament when the world's economy weakens and to bring China a chance to introduce foreign advanced factors.

Third is the strategic core. For the first wave of economic globalization, the core is to implement the "import substitution" strategy from the beginning. Since 1992, the strategy has evolved into "increasing export by absorbing FDI" and "swapping market with technologies." For the second wave, the core is to implement an in-depth globalization strategy under the condition of expanding domestic demands. Generally, the depth is mainly manifested in striving for more advanced innovative factors from all over the world and improving the ability of allocating innovation factors on the global

① The "Home Market Effect" theory proposed by Krugman (1980) can explain the fact that where increasing returns and trade cost exist, countries with bigger domestic demands will motivate enterprises to choose to engage in production in their home country; a bigger market will attract over more enterprises producing differentiated products; besides, due to increasing returns to scale, a country tends to export products catering to demands of the home market. Please refer to Krugman Paul R. Scale Economies, Product Differentiation, and the Pattern of Trade. American Economic Review, 1980 (70); and Amiti M. Inter-industry Trade in Manufactures: Does Country Size Matter? *Journal of International Economics*, 1998 (44).

scale. Specifically, it includes at least three points. First, utilizing the siphon effect of China's sizable domestic market to absorb global innovative factors to serve China's industrial upgrading; second, utilizing the scale effect of the domestic market to create export differentiation and low-cost competitiveness and upgrade export; third, utilizing the scale effect of the domestic market to develop China's multinational corporations, foster industrial chain owners and shape a global monopolistic competition pattern.

Fourth is the strategic roadmap. The basic roadmap of the first round of globalization strategy is to embed low-end factors into the GVC. With advantages in R&D, marketing, network and brands, governors sitting at the top end of the GVC transfer over production to Chinese enterprises that are at the low end of the value chain. In order to cater to demands of foreign consumers, Chinese enterprises often import foreign equipment and technologies to increase exportable capacities. Without domestic demands, China's equipment manufacturing is declining despite soaring export of consumer goods. For the second round, the strategic roadmap is to encourage enterprises to join or develop the domestic value chain (DVC)[①], and then develop a GVC where domestic large or multinational corporations will be the governor, who will outsource production to other domestic and foreign enterprises, make global production factor suppliers their own suppliers, or develop a GVC and then sell products across the world based on domestic and overseas demands, independent R&D and designing.

Fifth is strategy implementation. During the first wave of globalization, China has mainly utilized foreign economic factors by absorbing foreign funds. After sacrificing resources and the environment, China is only positioned at the bottom of the value chain to engage in the least-profitable production and processing. During the second wave, foreign economic factors will be utilized through three approaches. First is to establish factories overseas or merge and acquire overseas companies. Through capital control, China can strengthen integration and control of overseas economic factors, thus controlling more profitable and higher-end elements of the value chain like technology, brand and channel and transforming the development model[②]; second is to utilize the huge domestic market and the scale effect to develop reverse outsourcing and absorb foreign advanced factors[③]; third is to build various infrastructures to attract overseas high-tech talents to engage in R&D to facil-

① About the domestic value chain, please refer to Liu Zhibiao and Zhang Jie. Formation, Breakthrough and Countermeasures of Developing Countries' Capturing Network under Global OEM System. *China Industrial Economics*, issue 5, 2007.

② High-end technologies and factors can be acquired based on domestic demands. For instance, Jiangsu JinSheng machinery co., Ltd, a private company, purchased 50% of stock equity of German's EMAG with 100 million Euros in early 2011. With a history of 140 years, EMAG's is the third largest high-end numerical-control machine tool manufacturer in Europe. It owns over 200 international patents, and 60% of its products serve Mercedes-Benz, BMW and Porsche. As planned, two parties will establish EMAG (China) Company in Jintan, Jiangsu Province with a registration amount of 60 million Euros after the merger and acquisition. By investing RMB 4.9 billion in total, the company directly introduces a whole set of EMAG's technologies and production equipment that are three decades ahead of domestic peers and builds an Asia-pacific manufacturing center with an output of 30 million high-end machine tools.

③ For this proposition, please refer to Liu Danlu and Yue Zhonggang, Reverse R&D Outsourcing and Growth of Chinese Enterprises-Case Study Based on China's Own Automobile Brands in the Yangtze River Delta, *Industrial Economics Research*, issue 4, 2011.

itate China's industrial upgrading.

Sixth is about the industry to rely on. During the first wave of globalization, China holds a comparative advantage in low-end production factors, so burgeoning industries are mainly exportable, including labor-intensive processing industries. During that period, China relies on the heavy chemical and real estate industry, which aggravates reliance on investment. During the second wave, however, China will rely on manufacturing and the modern service industry, especially the advanced producer service which features intensive knowledge, technologies and human capitals. These two industries will dominate the modern industrial system. Taking manufacturing for example, to become the world's manufacturing power, China should develop the automobile, high-speed rail, airplane and heavy machinery sector. At present, China-made automobile manufacturing is at the climbing stage, airplane manufacturing is just taking off, heavy machinery is the world leader in some areas, and high-speed rail has gradually outstepped advanced countries. If advanced technologies and talents support these sectors during the climbing stage, it will take less time for China to surpass developed countries. In order to make developed countries the factor supplier of "China-made" and "China-created" products, developing a world's leading market in China is a basic prerequisite.

Based on the above, the strategic focus of China's participation in the second wave of globalization is to achieve a transition from enterprises' accession into the GVC to an accession into the global innovation value chain (GIVC) and to develop the innovation economy in an open environment leveraging domestic demands while transforming the demand structure. The concept of the GIVC is an innovative point of this paper. Detailed expounding will be our future research tasks. Here, we make a brief introduction below:

First, the transition from accession into GVC to GIVC falls into two stages. The first stage witnesses a transition from GVC to the national value chain (NVC) and two shifts happening to domestic enterprises: from being suppliers and "the captured" in the GVC to being outsourcers and governor of the NVC. At the second stage, GIVC is formed through an open globalization strategy based on NVC. The controller of NVC attracts global advanced production factors with appeal of the domestic market. For instance, foreign talents can be attracted over to work in China by taking advantage of the world economic crisis. Alternatively, Chinese enterprises can directly purchase overseas R&D companies①.

Second, although we have repeatedly discussed that only based on domestic demands can China develop brands with proprietary intellectual property rights, it is a very challenging task in practice. To transform themselves from being OEM producers to being a proprietary brand, especially international brand owners, Chinese enterprises need to spend tremendous advertisement and channel

① According to the report by the U. S. National Science Board, as the U. S. enterprises expand their R&D laboratories in China and other Asian areas, the U. S. is rapidly losing high-tech jobs. Within six years as of the end of 2009, about 85 percent of incremental R&D employees of the U. S. multinational companies work overseas. Although the U. S. enterprises usually do not close their domestic laboratories, they prioritize overseas laboratory expansion. The percentage of overseas R&D employees in U. S enterprises has risen from 16 percent in 2004 to about 27 percent in 2009. Please refer to http: //cn. wsj. com/gb/20120119/atc072217. asp.

construction fees; besides, efforts may be stranded due to a lack of familiarity with the global market, branding and marketing talents. Moreover, if the previous "outsourcer-supplier" partnership turns into life-or-death competition, powerful international outsourcers (international brand owners at the top end of the GVC) may issue competitive threats like forceful blockade and containment lest they should be replaced by late-comers. All these reasons are micro-level difficulties in developing countries' industrial transformation and upgrading. Do we really need to divide the transition into two clear-cut stages as stated above? Or formation of the NVC and the GIVC is essentially two aspects of one question? We still lack empirical studies in this respect.

## III. Policy Orientation of China's Participation in the Second Wave of Economic Globalization

At present, China still clings to the first wave of globalization, painfully struggling for a balance between expanding domestic demands and stabilizing foreign demands. It is not well-prepared or well-adapted for the second wave of domestic demand-based economic globalization. We discuss this controversial argument from the following aspects.

Putting aside several deciding factors in a country's comprehensive competitiveness like politics, military force and culture, there are three criteria measuring China's competitiveness from an economic perspective: it must at least own a new globalization concept and supportive strategies and policies which adapt to the second wave of economic globalization; it must own powerful multinational companies which are at the top end of innovation value chain; it must own a great many high-end human capitals with international visions. Judging from these criteria, we conclude that China is not well-adapted.

First, China has not developed a new globalization concept or supportive strategies and policies which adapt to the second wave of economic globalization. China always holds a concept that "export is the engine of economic growth." It views the world as a battlefield where China, as a populous developing country, competes fiercely with other countries in order to develop into an economic power. It aims at maximizing China's export scale and perceives the low price as the main source of China's competitiveness. Guided by this concept, the globalization strategy bypasses the technological gap between domestic and multinational enterprises and makes effective use of surplus production factors at the domestic and overseas market. To some extent, it has utilized the "technology and management skills spillover effect" provided by western countries. However, this strategy can no longer ensure a balance between China and the world during the next round of global competition. As western countries' market potentials are declining, the international market has been unable to accommodate overcapacity from such a big producer as China. Furthermore, western countries will sink into a long period of economic recession in the future, and their ability of utilizing advanced production factors are weakening. Given these realities, if China does not expand domestic demands, the new round of globalization will not be sustainable, which will deprive China of the chance to accelerate growth and profit tremendously from therein. Therefore, what is needed most for China to implement the new globalization strategy is to draw up independent globalization policies and action plans with opener mind and international visions.

Second, according to international experience, to enjoy competiveness in the world economy, a country must own powerful multinational companies which are at the top end of the innovation value chain, especially private-owned ones because they are the leading actors, pioneers and international rule makers of economic globalization. In fact, China lacks large private-owned multinational companies. Although many state-owned Chinese enterprises have been listed among world top 500 after restructuring, they cannot change China's disadvantageous position. Due to their "soft budget constraint," they lack efficiency during transnational operation and overseas M&A. Moreover, they are more apt to be sanctioned by western countries' anti-dumping law and may even arouse western people's hostility against China. During the first wave of globalization, China has acted as the "world operator" dealing with low-end manufacturing outsourcing and labor-intensive processing, while multinational companies of the U. S. and European countries undertake R&D, designing, marketing and brand network, so China enjoys complementary and reconciliatory interests with western countries then. During the second wave, however, China will vie with western countries for advanced production factors and the status as the innovation center. At some higher ends of the value chain, China will try to replace the current controllers which may resist desperately. Then again, game rules of the world economy are made by the powerful ones. If China lacks privately owned multinational companies, which can take part in the game, it would not truly grasp the precious opportunity brought by the second wave of globalization.

Finally, a governor of economic globalization must own a great many high-end talents with international visions. China is not short of general talents but really lacks leading talents who can contribute to developing China's own multinational companies. As required by the new strategy, China should develop a world-class technological innovation center, a high-end talent accumulation areas, a world's leading R&D and leading-edge standards-setting area and a globally influential high-tech industry radiation area in eastern regions, especially big cities in next several years. To achieve these goals, China must immediately draw up policies on attracting and cultivating high-end leading talents, gather R&D and entrepreneurial teams led by strategic scientists and high-end talent, build world-class scientific research institute, R&D centers and entrepreneurial service teams. Language is a barrier in cultivating high-end talents of international visions in China. Besides, China's technological and education environment is not good enough to cultivate competent talents in all arenas. As a remedy, attracting Chinese students studying abroad back is an important means of marketization and internationalization of high-end talents. Most of these returned talents have obtained the doctor's and master's degrees at prestigious overseas universities. They own both practical experience of leading-edge technologies and profound understanding of the market economy and modern management; some not only own proprietary intellectual property rights and patents but also keep close touch with overseas experts and companies. Therefore, they will be an important force in the rise of China's economy.

Accordingly, we can propose the following policy orientations for improving China's competitiveness during the second wave of economic globalization:

First, China should form a new globalization concept and supportive strategies and policies which adapt to the second wave of economic globalization. The most critical objective is to build some economic vehicles for expanding domestic demand and attracting global advanced factors. The first vehicle is manufacturing. A strong manufacturing is the vehicle of modern technologies. Over a long period of time, China will need to develop modern manufacturing to boost economic growth. This vehicle will become the pioneer and leading force of expanding domestic demands. Second is urbanization. According to international experience, urbanization is mainly driven by investment initially. Once infrastructure investment is completed, it will be driven by consumption. About half of China's population still needs to be urbanized now. Accelerating the urbanization process will help expand the domestic demand market. The third vehicle is composed of foreign trade, foreign capital, foreign economy, foreign intellects and outsourcing which absorb global advanced factors. Fourth is producer service. By incorporating advanced technologies, human capital and intellectual capitals into the goods production process, producer service is a major input factor deciding international competitiveness of modern industries. Developing producer services including finance, commerce, logistics, designing and technical service will directly absorb domestic and overseas advanced factor. Fifth is residential consumption.

Next, China should develop powerful multinational companies sitting at the top of the innovation value chain, especially private-owned multinational companies. First, the government should break up monopoly of state-owned enterprises in some industries by offering consistent national treatment to foreign, state-owned and private enterprises. The private sector should enjoy more freedom to enter competitive industries. Second, private enterprises should be encouraged to merge and acquire other domestic companies so as to develop into a giant corporation owning certain market control. Third, given the current economic crisis in western countries, private enterprises should be encouraged to join up to acquire western enterprises which have technologies, talents, brands and channels, and throughout this process achieve property right integration and asset restructuring. The key here is to encourage private enterprises to merge and acquire domestic and overseas rivalries to expand themselves.

Finally, China should own plentiful high-end human capital of international visions. The key is to introducing foreign talents in parallel with cultivating local talents. By taking advantage of economic slump in some western countries, we can purchase their powerful listed companies, the main purpose of which is to utilize their talents, especially high-level and urgently-needed talents aside from liquidizing their assets. These talents will provide R&D and designing service required for Chinese enterprises to expand domestic and overseas markets.

# Part Four
# Industrial Development

# Chapter 15

# China's Industries in the Beginning of Its 12th Five-Year Plan Period*

**Jin Bei (金碚)**

**Institute of Industrial Economics, Chinese Academy of Social Sciences (CASS), Beijing, China**

**Abstract:** Complex international and domestic economic scenarios and the short cyclical nature of macroeconomic policies characterizes the beginning year of the 12th Five-year Plan period. It reflects the difficult policy choices that arise among three major regulatory targets for growth, structure, and prices. In the transitional period of intertwined challenges, a spirit of commitment and dedication to real industries will allow China to occupy vantage points in world manufacturing and become an industrial power in the real sense. To a certain extent the beginning year of the 12th Five-year Plan period (2011 – 2015), while fraught with challenges and pain, marks a departure from cutthroat competition to quality growth for Chinese enterprises and entrepreneurs. From 2012, China's industrial and market economic systems will both head towards more sophisticated stages of development. China's industries will develop along environmentally sustainable, delicate, high-end, IT-based and service-oriented paths, while expediting the country's economic restructuring, industrial upgrade capabilities and its pursuit of innovative industrialization, and it will do so with strides more remarkable than ever before in its history.

**Keywords:** 12th Five-year Plan, new approach of industrialization, industrial transformation and upgrade

The 12th Five-year Plan of China's Economic and Social Development (hereinafter referred to as the "12th Five-year Plan") took effect in 2011. A year later, China's economy has experienced dramatic changes. Its economy is almost repeating the turbulence of 2007 to 2009, with the regulation of macroeconomic policy having swerved in the past year. The economic slowdown just a few months into the first year of the 12th Five-year Plan period forced central economic policymakers to relax macroeconomic regulation. Unfolding potential contradictions that are deeply entrenched and in-

---

* Corresponding author: jinbei8859@163.com.

This paper is the overview chapter of *China Industrial Development Report* (2012) – *China's Industries in the Beginning Year of the 12th Five-year Plan Period.*

tertwined suggest that China's industrial growth is not yet free of its dependence on the old path, and that China's industrial development has entered a decisive moment of change. At this juncture, it is of great theoretical and realistic relevance to study the fundamental perceptions and patterns of China's industrialization. It is fair to say that even technical and descriptive analysis of China's economic situation, and particularly industrial development and prospects, cannot dwell on superficial phenomena. Key questions and issues concerning China's industrial transformation from quantitative growth to qualitative growth must be addressed at a more fundamental level.

## I. From Good Start to Complex Economic Restructuring

In 2011, China's economy restored its high growth path after having successfully withstood the global financial crisis that erupted in 2008. Instead of taking another round of an upsurge, the economy grew steadily and entered a period of adjustment fraught with challenges. Despite the repeated attempts of macroeconomic policymakers to boost the economy, setbacks were inevitable.

The last three years of the 11th Five-year Plan period (2006 – 2010) saw the eruption of a global financial crisis, and yet China still achieved most of the targets set for the five-year period. Today, although three to four years have elapsed since then, the international and domestic economic situation remains very complex and uncertain. Moreover, great successes in tackling the crisis notwithstanding, China's massive stimulus policy has left significant repercussions on its economy. An economic stimulus policy released massive liquidity that presented the 12th Five-year Period with growing inflationary pressures and excessive price rises. It is against this backdrop that the State Council decided in the first half of 2011 to "fight inflation as the primary economic problem". Based on this assessment, a series of austere macroeconomic policy measures were taken and the housing market was subjected to tight restrictions.

Meanwhile, macroeconomic policy deliberately played down attention on the GDP growth rate. It was publicly announced that a high growth rate could be sacrificed in the interests of a structural adjustment. Thus, multiple regulatory measures were taken to dampen the growth rate in order to favor steady progress. In 2012, the Chinese government officially announced its economic growth target of 7.5%, lower than the (actual) target to secure 8% growth after the eruption of the global financial crisis (whether this target is achieved or not was taken as a vital indicator for the success of fighting the global financial crisis). This policy sent a clear signal to the market: GDP growth rate is no longer the primary or No. 1 macroeconomic policy target. Nevertheless, it was widely believed that a low-growth policy would be resisted at the local level and would fail to achieve expected results. In any case GDP growth rate seems less important than before. Some economists and research institutes have claimed that China's economy will soon enter a period of medium growth and will avoid setting a high GDP growth rate as a mandatory target, so naturally some decline in the growth rate will appear. Others have become superstitious, believing in a theory of the "GDP curse"; setting a GDP growth rate as a policy target and government performance metric is the root cause for the intractable problems China has to face today, according to them.

It was beyond people's expectation that under the joint effect of insufficient demand at home and abroad, and the policy tightening in the face of rampant inflation, China's economic growth in 2011 suffered a slowdown month after month. By the first quarter of 2012, China's economic growth rate slowed to 8.1%, the lowest in three years. Based on this performance, the World Bank revealed in its press conference for the East Asia Economic Half-year Report that the expectation for China's GDP growth rate in 2012 was lowered from 8.4% half a year ago to 8.2%. The growth rate for April further decreased. In a word, although China's economic growth rate is not beyond the regulatory range, some major economic indicators are falling at an unexpected pace and excessive economic slowdown under the joint effect of the economic cycle and policy changes has reappeared (See Table 1).

**Table 1: GDP Growth Rates in 2011 and the First Quarter of 2012 (Unit: %)**

| Q1, 2011 | Q2, 2011 | Q3, 2011 | Q4, 2011 | Q1, 2012 |
|---|---|---|---|---|
| 9.7 | 9.5 | 9.1 | 8.9 | 8.1 |

Source: NBS (National Bureau of Statistics, the same below).

The industrial growth rate moved in the same direction. In the first four months of 2012, the value added of large industrial enterprises in China registered a year-on-year growth of 11%, which is down by 3.2 percentage points over the same period of the previous year. Specifically, China's industrial growth registered 11.6% in the first three months of 2012 and declined by 2.6 percentage points in April from March's 11.9% to reach 9.3%. The slowdown of heavy industries is particularly striking. During the first four months of 2012, the value added of China's light industries reported a year-on-year growth rate of 12.3%, down by 0.6 percentage points, and the value added of heavy industries grew by 10.5%, down by 4.2 percentage points. By May 2012, the situation changed somewhat yet the tendency towards a slowdown prevailed. In May, actual growth of value added of large industrial enterprises registered 9.6%, up 0.3 percentage points over April. Between January and May, value added of large industrial enterprises had an actual year-on-year growth of 10.7%, which is lower by 0.9 percentage points compared with the first quarter; the value added of heavy industries increased by 9.8% year-on-year and the value added of light industries grew by 9.1%. All are below the growth rates of the first four months (see Table 2).

**Table 2: Growth Rate of Industrial Value Added between 2011 and May 2012 (Unit: %)**

| Q1, 2011 | Q2, 2011 | Q3, 2011 | 2011 (whole year) | Q1, 2012 | January to May, 2012 |
|---|---|---|---|---|---|
| 14.4 | 14.3 | 14.2 | 13.9 | 11.6 | 10.7 |

Source: NBS (National Bureau of Statistics, the same below).

An economic slowdown is also reflected in price indices. In April 2012, China's industrial producer ex-factory price index and purchase price index fell from the height of 107. 5 and 110. 5 in July 2011 to 99. 3 and 99. 2, down 8. 2 percentage points and 11. 3 percentage points respectively. Meanwhile, prices of bulk commodities dropped to a noticeable extent. In May, China's industrial producer ex-factory price fell by 1. 4% on a year-on-year basis and 0. 4% on a quarterly basis. The purchase price of industrial producers dropped by 1. 6% on a year-on-year basis and 0. 3% on a quarterly basis. Between January and May, industrial producer ex-factory prices dropped by an average 0. 3% and the industrial producer purchase price grew by an average 0. 1% (as indicated in Figure 1 and Figure 2). In a nutshell, judging from the industrial price indices, industrial prospects and corporate profitability have worsened, in fact.

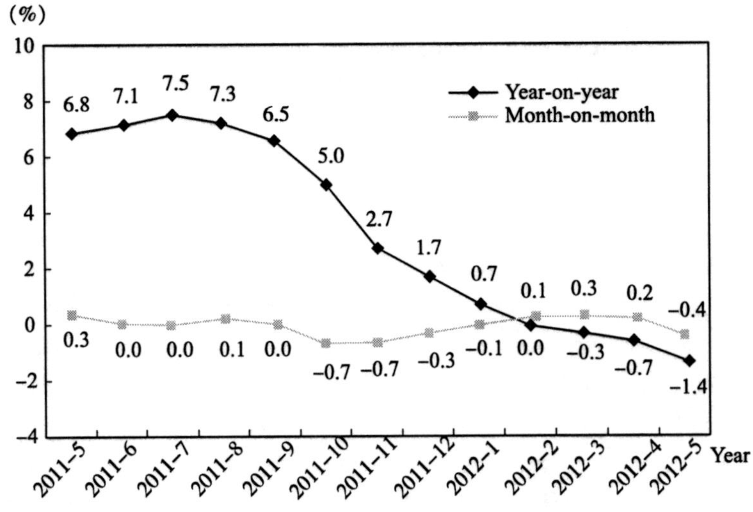


**Figure 1: Ex-factory Price Fluctuations of Industrial Manufacturers**

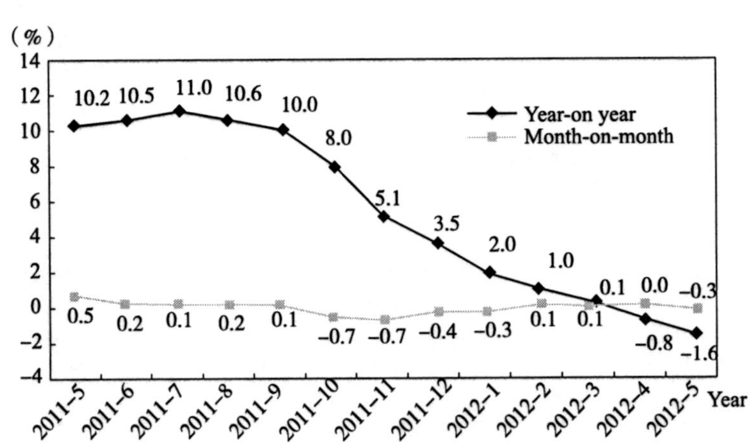


**Figure 2: Industrial Manufacturer Purchase Price Fluctuations**

The economic growth rate has a strong correlation with corporate profitability. With the slowdown in 2011, the overall profits of China's industrial enterprises declined. This downward trend continued into 2012. Between January and March 2012, large industrial enterprises reported a reduction in their total profits by 1.3% and as much as 19% of these industrial enterprises reported losses, with the amount of losses increasing by 76.3% over the same period of the previous year. Of these, the metallurgy industry has seen a reduction in profits by 59.2% with profitability of only 1.3%; major medium-sized and large steel enterprises made a net loss of RMB 1.03 billion-in contrast to the net profit of RMB 15.8 billion in 2011. Between January and April, large industrial enterprises achieved a net profit of RMB 1,452.5 billion, down 1.6% year-on-year. April's profit of RMB 407.6 billion is down 2.2% year-on-year. Between January and April, large industrial enterprises achieved a main business revenue of RMB 27,041.6 billion, up 12.7% year-on-year, which is the lowest growth rate since 2011 (see Figure 3).

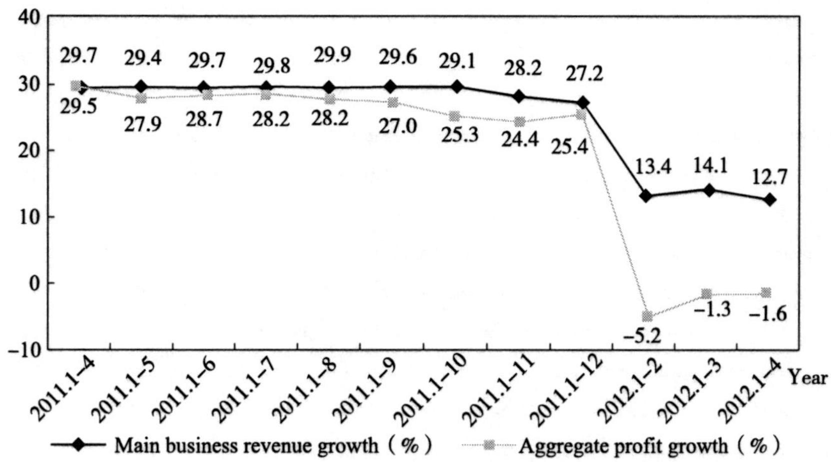


**Figure 3: Aggregate Profit and Main Business Revenue Growth of China's Large Industrial Enterprises**

A bleak industrial situation slashed China's treasury revenue. On a cumulative basis from January to April 2012, China's national fiscal revenue increased by 12.5% over the same period for the previous year, down by 18.9 percentage points, of which tax revenue increased by 8.1%, down by 22.4 percentage points. In April, China's national fiscal revenue grew by 6.9% over the previous month, down 20.3 percentage points year-on-year. The fall in fiscal revenue growth by such a large margin has never happened over a period of many years.

Growing investment demand, consumption, and export was lower than expectation, and enterprises universally reported operational difficulties worse than that of the financial crisis of 2008 and 2009. Given the situation, the State Council returned its attention to the economic growth rate and vowed to "give more prominence to growth stability". Given the international market drives external demand, and consumer demands are unlikely to experience a substantial increase, investment became an important policy factor in order to stabilize growth. On May 23, 2012, a State Council executive meeting proposed the following measures: "to accelerate the implementation and expand the scope of public welfare projects, expedite the installation of new energy products such as self-supplying solar energy, increase the penetration of optical fibers, and step up support to the construction of affordable housing and the renewal of rural shanty houses. Expedite the implementation of major projects of the 12th Five-year Plan, initiate a series of major projects with extensive influence and driving effect, and speed up preparations for approved projects in such areas as railway, municipal construction, energy, telecom, education, and healthcare. Great support should be given to the entrepreneurship of small businesses. Take stock of ongoing projects, identify and resolve problems, and prevent the occurrence of unfinished projects. Encourage private investment in such areas as railway, municipal construction, energy, telecom, education, and healthcare. Vigorously support the entrepreneurship of small businesses"① . The purpose of all these measures-despite improving public welfare, infrastructure, construction and the promotion of an IT society-boils down to the expansion of the current phase of investment. The short-term macroeconomic effect of increased project approvals fuels demand.

The multifarious complex of international and domestic economics and the short cyclical nature of government macroeconomic policies (government macroeconomic policies swerving in short periods of time) remain striking features of China's economy in the beginning year of the 12th Five-year Plan period. The difficult task of policy balance among major regulatory targets for growth, restructuring, and commodity prices reflects this. At a deeper level, China's industrialization has passed the stage of rapid expansion and must reduce its dependence on a conventional growth path while pursuing a brand new approach to industrialization. This critical juncture reveals complex problems never before seen in such a short time frame. It is fair to say that long-term economic transitional issues have found expression through a short-term phenomenon of cyclical fluctuations, i. e. short-term changes in macroeconomic supply and demand are contradictory and corresponding shifts in government macroeconomic policies actually reflect key changes in China's economic development stages and patterns.

## II. Weaning from a Conventional Growth Pattern

From a global perspective, humans are currently in the stage of industrialization, with only about 20% of world population having fully entered industrial society. This process has a history of 200 to 300 years. There are achievements through industrialization that historically haven't been seen before, yet all know its cost and challenges. During the early stages of industrialization capitalism came under fierce criticism. By the middle of the 20th century, industrial manufacturing based on

① Chinese Government Network, May 23, 2012 (17): 45.

fossil fuel proved to be increasingly unsustainable. As a result, some concluded that the economic growth of human society required boundaries and "zero-growth" was the only way to save the planet. The Club of Rome, by the famous report *The Limits to Growth*, represents this faction. Alternately, others have argued the only way for humanity to address resources and environmental constraints while maintaining growth is by renouncing modern industrialization and pursuing "middle technologies" that do not depend on fossil fuel energy. This opinion is represented by the masterpiece *Small Is Beautiful* by E. F. Schumacher.

China, as a matter of fact, had recognized the problems of industrialization based on fossil fuel and mass mechanical manufacturing over the past two centuries, and was ambivalent when it came to pursuing a traditional industrialization route. The notion that "China cannot let its households possess cars" for example, had a long-term impact on national strategies and policies for the automotive industry. Even today, the view continues to achieve a reasonable amount of circulation. Many people argued that China should not develop industrial technologies of mass mechanical manufacturing adopted by the Western world, but should rather focus on the development of "fit-for-use" technologies. Such a proposition was even written into official government documents. However, that China's industrialization has followed the path of Western countries is undeniable. China's industrialization is essentially a dispersion and transfer of technologies from the Western world. In reality, China did not invent "fit-for-purpose" technologies essentially different from the technology path of the Western world; it took proactive measures to introduce capital and technologies from developed nations.

This traditional approach to industrialization is the root of many problems today. "Imbalanced, uncoordinated and unsustainable" issues are particularly striking. However, the reality is that we ignore rational elements and the historic contributions of industrialization while enjoying the benefits of industrial development and civilization. There is no free lunch in the world, and all progress comes at a price. Nevertheless, we cannot turn a blind eye to traditional industrialization's defects. In particular, economic development through traditional industrialization is subjected strongly to a path of dependence. Technology, interest, concepts and institutional drawbacks won't disappear by themselves. It takes great effort to push the rapid train of China's industrialization out of the old rut and onto a brand new track of industrialization, and wean from a path of dependence. The 12th Five-year Plan period is such a difficult transition indeed.

Firstly, dependence on low-cost resources must be reconsidered. Since the 1980s, China's industrialization has followed a path of "cutthroat" competition. The positive significance is the complete rejection of a planned economy and developmental approach, at a time when China's industries were not internationally competitive. An extensive growth pattern is therefore an inevitable choice. To a large extent, efforts were made to achieve growth at all costs. Economic competition took place not only in the business community, but also largely through government intervention in local competition. Local competition is characterized by the following pattern: "maximum use of immovable factors (cutting prices) to attract movable factors" . Immovable factors here refer to taxation, infrastructure, land, natural resources, and the environment. Internationally, labor is not a highly movable factor. Movable factors mainly include capital, entrepreneurs, and technologies. Between regions, labor is highly mobile.

It is worth noting that the government determines the prices of immovable factors. When local governments become major players of regional competition, they naturally slash prices of immovable factors resulting in: tax credits, land grants, cheap resources, meager labor protection and sloppy environmental standards. This has inevitably caused an extensive pattern of economic growth characterized by mass input of low-price factors.

During industrialization's early stages, the extensive growth pattern acquired cost advantages by virtue of low-cost resources. Low-cost resources can increase the competitiveness of users, and still create a demand for resource suppliers. At low levels of economic development, the opportunity cost of resource materials was very low and the use of resources on a mass scale was economically viable in the short-term. That is to say, without industrial technologies and prior to reaching a certain level of industrial development, most of the earth's materials are not considered valuable resources. This scenario presents scarce technology because it is costly and time-consuming to develop; hence the importance of acquiring a competitive advantage by substituting expensive and scarce technologies with low-cost resources. From another perspective, technology's progress relies on industrial development and capital accumulation, while industrial development and capital accumulation cannot be achieved without resource consumption. In this sense, extensive resource consumption in a short period of time is unavoidable for the foundation for the highly efficient use of resources in the future. If alternatives are discovered or invented before specific resources are exhausted, a rational choice to use them as a means to acquire competitiveness is taken.

Extensive growth, although justified under a certain historical period, comes at a high cost and is unsustainable. When the drawback of extensive growth patterns becomes increasingly pronounced, the immediate effect on the market is the end of low-cost resources. At the threshold of the 11th to the 12th Five-year Plan period, we saw an upsurge in prices for all kinds of resources. It was interrupted by outbursts of economic crises that led to sluggish demand but nonetheless denoted an irreversible upward tendency. In particular, China's labor resources, which seem to be the most abundant of all, abruptly experienced a major turnaround. In 2011, wage increases swept across China and labor shortages caused serious dilemmas for manufacturers. This situation not only affected the coastal region of eastern China, but became evident in populous interior places such as Sichuan and Henan provinces.

These signs mark the end of low-cost resources for China and the "cutthroat" competition must be halted. However, China's industries have over the years developed a strong dependence on low-cost resources, i. e. dependence on a crude extensive path of growth. It is no easy job to wean from such a path of dependence. The industrial economic situation since 2011 has highlighted the difficulties of an extensive growth pattern built upon low-cost resources. For instance, once the growth rate slides, enterprises are less profitable and even lose profits. Enterprises are not resistant to rising resource prices, and such growing prices will rapidly offset corporate profits. While local governments still promise land grants and tax credits to attract businesses, we can still see, at the inception of the 12th Five-year Plan period, many signs that China's industrial development is beginning to wean from resource dependence.

Secondly, dependence on investment expansion must be reconsidered. From the perspective of macroeconomic equilibrium, the high savings rate of China's economy will inevitably lead to a high investment rate, otherwise the economy will decline under the effect of oversupply. The problems afflicting China's economy, however, are not that simple. Due to the inefficiency of fixed asset investment, it takes more investment to reach the same level of economic growth, and for capital-output ratio to maintain an upward tendency. That is to say, both China's economic development and industrial growth are highly dependent on the expansion of investment.

In particular, as a means of macroeconomic regulation, the encouragement or restriction of investment almost becomes the most frequently used and most potent policy instrument. In 2008, one of the most effective policies to fight the impact of the global financial crisis was the "RMB four trillion fixed asset investment" . The plunge in economic growth in 2012 is largely a result of a vacuum of follow-up investment, after expired projects initiated during 2008 and 2009. Once again, fixed asset investment became the solution. To some extent, China practices an investment-dependent economic model. In stark contrast to other developing countries, China has massive savings to support investment.

Although the path of dependence on investment remains irreversible in the short-term, some attempts have been made since the inception of the 12th Five-year Plan period to it. The most significant measure is the transition from extensive investment expansion to innovative investment pulling. The nature of the former is that investment tends to pull growth from demand side, and policies are targeted at short-term macroeconomic supply and demand equilibrium. The nature of the latter is that investment tends to promote innovation and structural improvement from the supply side, with policy target towards long-term efficiency gains and industrial upgrade. of course, China's economic dependence on investment is stubborn and difficult to change. For instance, investments on strategic emerging industries are intended to promote industrial restructuring and upgrade, but have turned out to support low-end processes of emerging industries. Another example, the "innovative industries park", "software park" and "animation industry park", originally aimed to promote innovation but have turned out to be investment expansion and housing projects under government subsidies. Despite these setbacks, positive performance has already been made in moving away from investment dependence in the 12th Five-year Plan period. In addition, there are internal motives for such a tendency to continue. Indeed, new problems and contradictions are bound to occur in the process of getting rid of an investment path of dependence and deserve our careful observation and research.

Thirdly, excessive dependence on external demand must be reconsidered. China's economic circle and academics generally accept the view that China's economic growth is driven by external demand. In fact, this assessment is inaccurate. Given the magnitude of China's consumer demand and investment demand, net export contributes a smaller share to macroeconomic growth than does domestic demand (consumption + investment). Since 2000, the contribution of next export was the highest in 2005, with net export contributing 23% or so to economic growth. Over the past few years, under the effect of the global financial crisis, the contribution of net export to China's growth rate has plunged, particularly in 2009 when net export contribution fell to –40%. In 2010 and 2011, net export made even no contribution to China's economic growth. However, judging from the size of import and export, the external dependence of China's economy is high. This suggests that China's industries are very open and closely connected with the international economy. Some of China's industries and businesses are highly vulnerable to external fluctuations. Once external demand falters, the growth rate of some of China's industries and businesses will suffer, and may even decline.

As described above, China's economic growth no longer depends on the pulling of external demand. Although dependence on foreign trade remains high, China's position and role in the international division of labor are changing and domestic demand will have a dominant contribution. Some industries and enterprises that used to rely on overseas markets are shifting towards the domestic market. Despite the macroeconomic situation or the observation of the industrial and corporate levels, China's economy must be weaned from excessive external dependence and shift towards a growth model characterized by the balanced pulling of domestic and external demand.

It must be clarified that shifting from excessive external dependence does not mean that industrial imports and exports hold any lesser position of importance. Due to an uneven distribution of resources across the world, and the significance of the international division of labor to achieve effective resources allocation, particularly in light of China's needs to import industrial goods and resources that are not readily available at home yet essential to securing economic growth, the expansion of international trade and investment will be an important task for China in the long-term period. Furthermore, China's hundreds of millions strong labor force remains unable to cross borders and can only be employed at local manufacturing workshops that are part of a global supply chain. Increasing growth in the export of industrial goods has to be a long-term strategy for China. Based on these considerations, the essential implication of reducing the dependence on external demand is to promote domestic demand, particularly the growth of domestic consumption, and make manufacturing and consumption equally important drivers of growth.

A fourth reconsideration is dependence on virtual finance. In various economic sectors, manufacturing has gone through the most complete reform and highest level of openness, competition in the manufacturing sector is therefore the fiercest. Compared with the manufacturing sector, reform in other sectors lags behind and this is especially the case for financial industry. In spite of such slow progress, China's economy has become increasingly dependent on the financial industry, under the effect of a high dependence of developed economies on the financial industry and a host of other domestic factors. At the macroeconomic level, the effect is that economic growth becomes increasingly subjected to the decisive influence of monetary and financial policies of financial liquidity, and national monetary and financial policies and financial liquidity (money supply) is essential to support and stimulate economic growth. At the industrial level, the representation is the rapid expansion of a virtual economy and growing intervention of the financial industry and virtual economy in real assets (such as real estate), and asset bubbles are a striking phenomenon. At a corporate level, real industries including manufacturing enterprises increasingly tend to engage in financial and asset investment. For some manufacturing enterprises, their sideline businesses of an investment nature have exceeded their core businesses. Considering that a virtual economy such as a financial intermediation is much more profitable than real industries, together with a deteriorating business climate and the increasing burdens on enterprises, more companies are losing confidence in real industries. Given that real industries, particularly that of manufacturing, are not yet sophisticated or competitive, their reliance on the financial industry means a serious negative effect on China's industrialization prospects.

How then can we define real economy? At the 33rd collective workshop of the Politburo held on May 28, 2012 on the theme of "adhering to a brand-new path of industrialization with Chinese characteristics and advancing strategic adjustment of economic structure", General Secretary Hu Jintao highlighted that "industries are the mainstay of real economy and forefront of transforming economic growth pattern and optimizing industrial structure". This reaffirms the notion that China's economy cannot become over-dependent on the financial industry and must reverse the tendency towards excessive expansion in the virtual economy, and that industries will be developed as the most important sector of a real economy. This statement is a key indication for China's economic development in the beginning year of the 12th Five-year Plan period.

In summary, various international and domestic factors have jointly formed tremendous pressures and momentum that vigorously drives China's economic and more particularly its industrial transformation. In 2011, we have seen both the positive effects of this trend and the setbacks as a result of attempts to shake off a reliance on a conventional path of development. Nevertheless, both the positive signs and frustrating setbacks form an important precursor to the major and fundamental transition along China's industrialization path during the 12th Five-year Plan period.

## III. Period of Intertwined Challenges

Economic restructuring, especially that of industrial upgrade achieved through innovation, is the fundamental way to extricate China's economy from the reliance on a traditional path of development. For this transition to be achieved at an early date, China must develop the incentives and capabilities for innovation. However, both conditions can hardly be available at the same time. When economic growth is on a fast track, corporate profitability will be strong, yet the need for restructuring and upgrade seems unjustified. When the economy dips, although businesses feel under great pressure to restructure and upgrade, poor profitability means a shortage of funds and the issue of survival overrides innovation.

In the beginning year of the 12th Five-year Plan period, China's economy has once again encountered a period of intertwined contradictions of restructuring and industrial upgrade. Some scholars pointed out that in the 12th Five-year Plan period, international economic prospects appear very bleak. "World economic growth engines are uncertain; excessive easing of money led to inflation; manufacturing and innovation received little attention during the period of bubble economy (since

2000, the United States had a decline of more than 20% in the application for invention patents in all technological areas); continuing global sovereign debt crisis; re-industrialization of Europe and the US and the prospects of a stagflation of world economy" (Zhang, 2012).

In fact, China's economy faces complex situations; its economic growth rate has slowed, business costs have increased. According to National Bureau of Statistics data, in 2011 the annual average salary of employees of non-private enterprises in cities reached RMB42,452, which is a nominal increase by 14.3% year-on-year, with a growth rate higher by 0.8 percentage points over 2010. After adjustment for inflation, the actual growth is 8.5%; the annual average salary of employees of private enterprises in cities reached RMB24,556, which is a nominal growth of 18.3% over the same period of the previous year, up 4.2 percentage points or 12.3% after adjusted for inflation. In 2011, the monthly average income of migrant workers exceeded RMB2,000, reaching RMB2,049, which is higher by RMB359 over 2010, or up 21.2%. Between various quarters of 2011 to the first and second quarters of 2012, corporate profit growth slowed and inflationary potentials remained. If liquidity is once again pumped to stimulate the economy, commodity prices will be difficult to control and inflation may reoccur. The Chinese government has developed great competence for macroeconomic regulation and has more regulatory measures at hand than does other market economies. It cannot only take economic measures, but also administrative ones to achieve immediate effects. However, in the 12th Five-year Plan period, the room for macroeconomic maneuver is diminishing. Regulatory policies, especially those that are excessively vigorous, will cause significant side effects. Therefore, macroeconomic regulation must be practiced in a more cautious manner and intense administrative regulatory measures must be avoided.

Desirably, the 12th Five-year Plan period should not pursue high GDP growth and may make greater effort in economic restructuring when the growth rate dips below the range of 7.5% to 8.0%, aiming to achieve the transition from investment-driven growth to innovation-driven growth. The problem arises when the GDP growth rate is really below or near 8%, if relaxed macroeconomic policies and growth-oriented industrial policies are not taken, the growth rate is likely to further drop to reach the lower limit of the regulatory target range and may even dip beyond this range to cause recession. In addition, the decrease of the economic growth rate will inevitably cause fiscal revenue growth to decline. Under tight fiscal conditions and even fiscal difficulties in some regions, tax authorities will increase tax collection intensity and force a greater burden on businesses at a time of declining profitability. Hence, although policies call for reducing business burdens and "structural tax cut", the outcome is easier said than done.

At this juncture, the government will also issue a string of policies to encourage private business investment, and open more sectors for business investment such as railway and highway infrastructure, in order to alleviate financial shortages. However, cash-strapped private businesses face an apparently insincere promise of opening infrastructure construction sectors (currently under state monopoly), and only a short-term solution to make up for tight fiscal deficits, instead of equal rights to private capital from a higher legislative level. In fact, at a time of intertwined challenges, private businesses are not in good financial shape and their market credibility suffers. As a result, businesses cannot be expected to invest as heavily as they could during better times.

More importantly, during the period of intertwined financial problems, the business philosophies of entrepreneurs are under a tremendous challenge: that is, whether should they pursue maximal profits, financial conservatism and opportunism, or remain committed to the development of real industries despite the difficult situation? The 12th Five-year Plan period will weed out the less competitive enterprises and may even instigate a period of reshuffle. One of the greatest achievements made during the 30 years of China's transition to a market economy is the emergence of entrepreneurs who can maneuver their businesses to achieve exciting performance outcomes in an ever-changing market. During the 12th Five-year Plan period, the further advancement of China's industrialization calls for a large number of entrepreneurs and managers who have in-depth understanding of the essence of industrialization, and who can lead their businesses to track innovation and of a new approach to developing industrialization. Overcoming the current stage of intertwined challenges and bringing China's industrial development to a higher level requires a commitment to real industries, and the tenacity of modern industrial civilization. Only by accomplishing this transition can China become a future industrial power in a real sense. To some extent, although fraught with pain and challenge, the beginning year of the 12th Five-year Plan period will mark the end of cutthroat competition and the beginning of sophisticated and qualitative development.

## IV. China's Industries towards Quality Growth

All economic and social phenomena emerging in the beginning year of the 12th Five-year Plan period suggest that China's industrialization is at a crucial period. The option is either to repeat the cyclical fluctuation from expansion to inflation, contraction, slowdown, stimulation, and back to expansion, deepening the problems accumulated in the economic system and further entrenching imbalanced, uncoordinated, and unsustainable growth; or resolutely wean from a traditional path of development and pursue quality growth. Obviously, through great achievements of industrialization, China has already accumulated great economic and technological prowess and is fully capable of becoming an innovation trailblazer, accomplishing the industrial transition and achieving industrial power in the real sense. To this end, China should take steps to achieve a new model of development that is green, delicate, high-end, IT-based, and service-oriented.

(1) Green: the process of industrialization not only means the application of more advanced technologies for material production. At a deeper level, it is a process of civilization. It is through industrialization that humanity evolved from barbarism to modern civilization. In the early stages of industrialization, there were indeed barbaric activities and plunder; the human race emerged from this barbarism, so to speak. The essence of barbarism is undisciplined willfulness and unscrupulousness, while the moral nature of civilization is self-discipline. The spirit of self-discipline is a symbol of human progress. For industries, a key element of civilization is green development. The nature of technology is to turn waste into resources and manufacture products that can meet people's needs and

increase their welfare. Industrial manufacturing must be carried out in a resource-efficient, clean and safe manner, which this paper refers to as "green" and considers an intrinsic element of industrial civilization. The problem is that industrial competition could lead to unscrupulous and barbaric actions under the principle of "efficiency supremacy", which is misinterpreted as "profit supremacy" without proper restraint on those actions to seek maximum profits. Green industrial development calls for the return of industrial civilization: industrialization is an age of efficiency, cleanness and safety. The longest life expectancy, the best health conditions, and the highest populations with access to material and moral welfare characterizes this era. Despite a vastly increased world population and tremendous resources and environmental pressures, the establishment of advanced industries ultimately provides the technical and material circumstances to achieve resources efficiency and environmental improvement.

Green manufacturing means an overall improvement of industrial performance, instead of the closure or relocation of a few factories or the manufacture of a few new products, and less excessive expansion of investment and output capacities in favor of pursuing new energy equipment and industries. Government-led investment and subsidies for new energy have often led to unsophisticated and cost-inefficiency "high-tech" products at the expense of massive waste of fiscal subsidies. In many cases, "clean energy" is generated at the expense of consuming massive fossil fuel energy (electricity). Dirty and unsophisticated technologies were employed to manufacture clean energy equipment. "The devil driven out of the door has come in through the window". Green industries must become a systematic project covering all industrial sectors, and even society at large. Just as clean living is for modern human civilization, green industries are a symbol of modern industrial civilization. Actually, humanity mainly relies on the development of modern industries to achieve a clean lifestyle. Green industries must be achieved through the comprehensive progress of industrial technologies, and the system of a circular economy based on such progress. In a word, the essence of green industries is to create a more advanced system of modern industries. The 12th Five-year Plan period is just such a new stage for China's industries to evolve into a more advanced system of modern industries.

(2) Delicate: delicate manufacturing is an essential symbol of manufacturing civilization. Industrialization universally and unremittingly applies scientific discoveries and technology inventions and supports more discoveries and inventions to be made. The economic essence of manufacturing is to apply scarce resources in the most economical and productive ways and create finished goods that are fit for the purpose of use with the highest quality and constantly improve quality standards to meet growing needs of users. High technologies and refined processes and products are the character of industries and essential to achieving sustained competitiveness. The market is bound to reject shoddy goods.

Delicate manufacturing is not only a technical norm, but a culture and behavioral pattern distinctively different from that of an agrarian, nomadic, or mining civilization. Whether a country's industries can achieve delicate manufacturing or not is actually an important indication of whether industrialization has indeed arrived and is deeply rooted. If cheap resources and the comparative cost advantage are the only means for a country to expand industrial manufacturing without a commitment to delicate manufacturing, the country will fail to become a future industrial power.

Delicacy needs artistic creativity to be an ally of industries. Delicate industrial goods must be aesthetic in the first place. American, German, French, Japanese, and Italian goods are all very delicate but differ in terms of their respective qualities and detail, and each occupies different industrial vantage points that are insurmountable for other countries. Whether China can be an industrial power will depend on the creation of such a delicate manufacturing culture.

(3) High-end: high-end manufacturing represents the enterprising spirit and the nature of science. Industries are an important carrier of technological innovation. Industrial progress derives from and depends upon science and technology. As science and technology become more advanced, industries will become increasingly sophisticated. As a late-starting country, China has achieved its industrial development over the past 60 years, basically by following the path of Western industrial development and is thereby characterized by imitation. Given the current level of technology across various industries, this process is yet to unfold. After 60 years of following the old path, China now must explore its own way in climbing to the peak, occupying industrial and strategic vantage points with great courage and unyielding spirit.

High-end does not mean capturing profit opportunities. In an economic sense, "high-end" and "high technologies" are not synonymous with greater profitability and even "low-end" and "traditional technologies" may not necessarily be unable to bring about high profitability; the economic justification for high profitability is the possession of unique capabilities regardless of high-end or low-end capabilities. Even if some Chinese companies entered into the so-called high-end emerging industries, they are likely to encounter serious losses, over-capacity, anti-dumping and anti-subsidy countermeasures by countries such as the US. The reason for their frustration is that these companies actually invested in high-end or emerging industries in an expansive manner and only entered into "statistically emerging industries", i. e. low-end processes of these sectors. For industrial development to upgrade into high-end processes, a company must explore where it has developed a unique advantage through technological innovation and business model innovation.

(4) IT-based: integration between industrialization and IT application is a basic direction in modern industrial development. IT application not only promotes industrial productivity and enables green and delicate manufacturing, but transforms the way industrial manufacturing and competition are carried out as well. For instance, it enables the numeric control of industrial equipment and transforms from standardized manufacturing products to flexible manufacturing and individualized products, and may induce substantial change in the economic nature of industrial goods. Due to asymmetric information between manufacturers and consumers (users), industrial goods fall into three basic types: search goods, experience goods, and credence goods. The common nature of these products is that for consumers, they cannot acquire information about the manufacturing process and the only way to assess quality is through observation (search), use (experience) or subjective recognition (trust). Other means include selective information dissemination through advertisement placements or disclosure of quality information under government requirements. Secrecy,

or the prevention of information leakage, is a basic means for businesses to keep their competitiveness. As information application becomes integrated into the process of industrialization, advanced information systems are likely to change the economic nature of products and bring their information under public scrutiny. The Internet enables buyers to know more about these products, and even to learn about the entire processes under which they are manufactured. This has changed the rules of the game: businesses disclose their manufacturing information to a maximal extent, rather than trying to keep their secrecy, in order to gain the trust of customers and especially consumers and stay more competitive in the market. Noticeably, some leading businesses are developing further in this direction. Some foreign companies, for instance, now provide via electronic information to consumers almost every process of their manufacturing. It is possible that if a dairy company develops an information system that provides all information about their manufacturing processes to consumers that consumers may even observe on a real-time basis the dairy production process (technically, through the transmission of production coordination and monitoring of the center's computer screen information to the Internet). Transparency powerfully boosts the competitiveness of these businesses, putting those that only rely on advertisements at a complete disadvantage. When one company reveals information in such a manner, others must follow suit. The Internet transmits both manufacturing information and information about corporate social responsibilities. In this way, businesses move from the "black box" assumed under conventional economics to the "white box" with considerable information transparency. Information will be much less asymmetric and information transparency becomes a major factor of competitiveness. Integration between IT application and industrialization will vastly change the way industries compete, improving their overall performance. Some overseas businesses have already declared that "we have nothing to hide from the media and consumers", indicating that information openness is a more powerful way of competition than secrecy, for example. We must approach the impact and challenge of information and its application on China's industries.

(5) Service-oriented: modern services are shaped by industrial spirit. An increasing share of services in the economy does not mean a trade-off between industries and services, but rather an extension of the manufacturing industrial chain into services. It is essentially the deepening and extension of a manufacturing civilization. The nature of modern services is "industries", thus the reference here is to industrial services or high-tech services including: product design, division of functions, creation of production lines, reengineering of processes, organizational control, technology application, and cost accounting. A country or region without the foundation of a manufacturing civilization will struggle to develop competitive services.

The boundary between industries or manufacturing and services is largely artificial. The process of industrial manufacturing contains extensive service-oriented labor, and whether an activity is essentially manufacturing or service in nature will be difficult to define and subject to our arbitrary definition. Steelmaking is manufacturing, for instance, and operations of steelmaking furnaces are manufacturing activities. But should the commissioning of steelmaking computer programs still be defined as a manufacturing activity? Should the maintenance and upgrade of this software system become a manufacturing activity? Will an activity be defined as manufacturing or service if one manufacturer's activity is performed by another (such as a software developer, or commissioning and maintenance of moulds)? In fact, apart from the financial industry that provides trading instruments to the real economy, services include direct and industrial services, and whose boundary is not absolute. According to the definition, direct services require physical and mental labor without the carrier of physical products (labor does not need to be materialized into physical products and does not rely on the tools and equipment of service activities). Direct services provided without using industrial goods as instruments are very few. Industrial services are service activities supported by industrial goods (equipment) and based on industrial culture; they are essentially the decomposition and specialization of industrial processes. The difference between industrial services and manufacturing lies in the fact that the former provides "product utility" normally without physical carriers (needless to be materialized into products) and employs physical finished goods as instruments or objects of labor, while the latter manufactures products that are in physical form (materialized into finished goods). With industrial development, more and more manufacturing processes will be decomposed. In particular, the extensive application of industrial goods will give rise to an increasing number of industrial services. For instance, the use of telephone services becomes increasingly sophisticated and generates the telecom industry on a huge scale; the development of transport equipment gives rise to a massive logistics sector. Hence, service-oriented industries are an inevitable trend and boil down to a high degree of division of labor, specialization, and the extensive application of industrial goods and technologies. On the eve of the Chinese Lunar New Year, hundreds of millions of people sit in front of the TV to watch the National Spring Festival Gala. It is an artistic performance delivered through the application of industrial goods, technologies, and organizational methodologies. China's transportation peak before and after the Spring Festival is the largest service activity in the world. It is apparently a massive application of industrial products, technologies, and organizational methodologies. In fact, as long as industries or corporate organizational patterns separate product utility from product physical entity, then services can be created from manufacturing. The automotive industry is one of manufacturing, yet services can be created by separating design, sales, repair, refitting, and decoration processes to be performed by specialized businesses. This process is actually a decomposition of the industrial chain, and the replacement of the internal division of work with an external division of work. We may even imagine that all manufacturing processes of the automotive industry can be outsourced to businesses specializing in industrial services, and automobile manufacturing can become a process composed of a series of services where participant businesses are referred to as "automobile manufacturing service providers", while manufacturers become product owners.

Numerous service sectors are derivatives of manufacturing, and take industrial goods as service instruments and objects. Arguably, modern services are essentially the deepening and extension of the greater manufacturing civilization. Without an advanced manufacturing civilization, there will not be advanced modern services, yet a sophisticated manufacturing sector will inevitably give rise to a developed modern services sector. Hence, the service-oriented development of manufacturing is an inevitable trend of industrialization, and the statistically increasing share of services (tertiary industries) will be a natural phenomenon.

In the beginning year of the 12th Five-year Plan, the tendency of Chinese industries shifting towards green, delicate, high-end, IT-based and service-oriented developments is expediting economic restructuring and industrial transition towards quality growth, and doing so in a far-reaching and more remarkable way than we have ever before witnessed. This marks a milestone in China's industrialization process.

## References

1. Jin, Bei. 2012. "China Must Be Firmly Committed to Developing the Real Economy." *Seeking Truth*, 4 (7).

2. Jin, Bei. 2012. "Global Competition Pattern and China's Industrial Development Tendencies." *China Industrial Economy*, (5).

3. Li, Zongnan, and Feng Wen. 2011. *China's Overall Trend 2: Innovation Changes China*. Beijing: China Business Association Press.

4. Lu, Junqing, Fangying Chou, and Xueshun Liu. 2011. *The Fourth Wave: Green Civilization*. Beijing: CITIC Press.

5. Zhang, Yansheng. 2012. "International Economic Environment Facing China in the 12th Five-year Plan Period." *Scientific Development*, (4).

6. Sustainable Strategies Research Group, China 21st Century Agenda Management Center. 2011. *Development Patterns-China's Resource, Environmental and Social Evolutions*. Beijing: Social Sciences Literature Press.

# Chapter 16

# Relying on Secondary Industry to Drive National Policy and Reinvigorate China's Economy*

**Huang Qunhui** (黄群慧)

**Institute of Industrial Economics, Chinese Academy of Social Sciences, Beijing, China**

**Abstract**: China is a large, developing economy now entering the second half of the intermediate stage of industrialization. It is inadequate for China at this time to perceive industrial development as a part of its industrial strategy. Rather, industrial development should be discussed and developed using a wider lens, as part of state strategy and responding to national conditions. This paper argues that, for China to progress further, it must transition from being simply a large industrial country to being a true industrial power. The paper presents characteristics and indicators that describe the world's industrial powers. China should focus strategically on development via invigorating industry-this idea and its related objectives, key tasks, and policy directions make up the Industry-Invigorating-China Strategy. The author predicts that China will develop the basic qualities of an industrial power by 2020, and it will achieve full industrial power status by 2040.

**Keywords**: large industrial country; the Industry-Invigorating-China Strategy; industrial power

All over the world, the financial crisis has laid bare the importance of the real economy. Bearing this in mind, China's Central Economic Working Conference at the end of 2011 declared that China should make the real economy a high priority. The virtual side of China's economy has seen windfall profits in recent years in the wake of financial engineering and innovation, and the real economy has been losing talent and funding to the virtual economy. Manufacturing in China is now seen as less significant than it ought to be. China launched the *Plan to Adjust and Revitalize the Top Ten Industries* after the financial crisis. This plan outlined a proposal to establish a modern industrial system with optimized organizational methods, advanced technologies, clean and safe means of

---

* Corresponding author: huang. q. h@263. net.

This paper is funded by the "Study on the Relationship among China's Industrialization, Informationization and Industrial Modernization" at the Chinese Academy of Social Science.

production, high added value and more employment. This proposal was part of the 12th Five-year Plan, formally released in the *Industrial Transformation and Upgrading Plan* (2011 – 2015) on December 30, 2011. These initiatives all regard industrial development merely as one part of industrial strategy. But this secondary emphasis on industrial development is not sufficient for China, a large developing country in the second half of the intermediate stage of industrialization. This oversight does not sufficiently incorporate national conditions and broader, nation-wide strategies.

## I. China: A Large Industrial Country

China was once accurately described as a large agricultural country, but market-oriented reforms and industrialization set against a backdrop of informationization and globalization have brought China rapid growth over the past three decades. China is no longer merely an agricultural economy but the world's second largest economy; per-capita GDP has risen from less than USD100 in 1978 to more than USD 4, 000 in 2011.

In 2005, the author of this paper co-proposed a framework to classify China's basic national economic conditions using a sector-based structure (Chen and Huang, 2005). The development framework for a large economy is as follows: a large agricultural country→a large industrial country→an industrial power→a large service country. This trajectory describes an economy moving from early industrial economy to intermediate industrial economy, late industrial economy, and eventually post-industrial economy. This framework is useful in that it translates vernacular terms-large agricultural country, large industrial country, industrial power, etc. -into economic terms that can be used to develop a research paradigm for development economics.

Since the turn of the century, China has transitioned from being a large agricultural country to being a large industrial country, and now it is moving towards becoming an industrial power. China's current economic status corresponds to the intermediate and late stages of industrialization. China's status as a large industrial economy means the following:

First, let us look at China's aggregate economy. The term "large country" refers to economic size and not political power as defined by international politics, wherein a country is judged by its capacity to wage and win a war with military supremacy (Guo Shuyong, 2006). China is the largest country in the world by population, and its aggregate economy ranked 6th in 2000, 5th in 2005, 3rd in 2007, and 2nd since 2010.

The second feature associated with China's status as a large industrial economy relates to the dominant role of industry in the national economy. Industry's contribution to national GDP far exceeds that of agriculture both in terms of aggregate economic size and also economic growth. Agriculture was dominant before the 1970s, but in recent years the proportion of China's industry, services and agriculture have accounted for around 50%, 40%, and 10% of GDP, respectively. The export of industrial goods accounts for over 90% of total exports leaving China. These figures demonstrate how dominant industry is within the national economy.

The third feature is China's proportion of gross industrial income in total world industry. China's gross industrial production, a figure which includes the value, output, and variety of industry, accounts for a great proportion of the world's industrial production. By 2000, China had become an industrial powerhouse on the world stage, ranking high in the output of many major industrial products. It was ranked first in crude steel, coal, cement, fertilizer and televisions, second in power, chemical fiber and cotton, fourth in sugar, and fifth in crude oil. China's industrial added value reached USD2,364 billion in 2010, 1.04 times that of the U.S. Its manufacturing output value reached USD1.96 trillion or 19.8% of the world total. Out of the world's 500 major industrial goods, China ranked first in the production of 220. Certain sectors in China such as steel, ship-building, automobile production, power, chemicals and home appliances have developed to massive scale. The output of certain products like crude steel, electrolytic aluminum, cement, refined copper, ships, computers, air conditioners and refrigerators account for over half of the world total.

The next key factor is that China has not actually achieved full industrialization yet-China is a large industrial country, but not yet an "industrialized nation." The industrialization process has four stages: agricultural, agricultural-industrial, industrial-agricultural, and industrialized. China is essentially on the third of these steps now, the industrial-agricultural. There is a key distinction to make here between a large industrial country and a large industrialized country. China reached this third stage by 2008 (Huang and Zhong, 2010), so today it remains a middle-income country that must still avoid a middle-income trap.

Fifth and last, China is still not an industrial power. By calling China a large industrial country, this necessarily precludes China from being an industrial power. Although size and power are related, there is by no means a one-to-one ratio. Size is about scale and quantity, whereas power requires efficiency and quality. Given its lacking in industrial modernization, weak international competitiveness, and moderate-at-best industrial quality, China cannot yet be called an industrial power. Our estimates show that the composite index of industrial modernization by the mid to late period of the 10th Five-Year plan was 36.44 out of a possible 100 (Chen and Huang, 2009).

In discussing whether or not China is currently a large industrial country, there are both pessimistic and an optimistic schools of thought. The pessimistic view holds that China remains a large agricultural country since China's agricultural sector is its largest in terms of number of workers. Agricultural employment has been declining steadily since 1991, and, as of 2009, primary industry (agriculture) had 297.08 million workers, secondary industry (industry/manufacturing) 216.84 million, and tertiary industry (service) 266.03 million. This means that agriculture still has the largest workforce in China by a slim margin. However, it is important to consider that a) there are 100 – 200 million migrant workers in China who are generally engaged in non-agricultural work, and b) most farmers simply engage in household agriculture (many using just their spare time to engage in agricultural work). This means that real employment in the agricultural sector may not be as large as statistics would make one think. Furthermore, China's employment structure is somewhat distorted because of the country's population and constrains in economic structure. The transformation of employment structure lags behind that of economic structure. Therefore, China's actual status cannot be judged by just looking at the base employment in each of the three main industries, and the dominance of industry should not be obscured by China's flawed employment structure. It would be more effective to look at national economic output values in order to determine the country's economic structure. Due to factors like the household registration system and industrialization outpacing urbanization, the majority of China's population remains officially rural. So even though China has a large agricultural population, it is not in fact a large agricultural country. ①

The optimistic view holds that China transformed from a large agricultural country to a large industrial country in 1978 and became an industrial power in 2010 (Hu, et. al, 2011). The first point is based on two facts: the establishment of a relatively complete industrial system, and industrial output becoming greater than that of the primary or tertiary industry. However, at that time China had a very low per-capita GDP, and few industrial goods were exported. China's economy at the time could hardly meet residents' basic demands. This disproves the first of the two facts. As for the second point, it is undeniable that China has taken great strides towards becoming an industrial power since the turn of the century, but this fact does not fundamentally change China's economic status. Specifically, China's industrial structure still needs to be upgraded; China's industry still stands at the low end of the global value chain, and there are very few Chinese multinational companies that have the industrial and R&D capabilities to compete on the world stage. Industrial productivity remains very low, and the proportion of technology-intensive exports with high added value is low. These weaknesses mean that China remains a large industrial country that has yet to become a true industrial power.

## II. Characteristics of an Industrial Power

A large industrial country is one with a massive industrial system and large amounts of industrial products. An industrial power, by contrast, has a modern, highly-efficient industrial system and advanced, quality industrial goods. An industrial power is a country with a commanding economic position that plays a leading, influential role across global industry or at least some industrial sectors. According to this definition, industrial powers fall into two categories. The first category includes countries like the U. S., Germany and Japan-strong and influential in almost any industry; the second category includes countries like Britain, France and Switzerland-strong in some industrial sectors and less so in others.

Industrial powers have some common characteristics. Firstly, they own the world's leading industrial technologies and innovative capabilities and play a leading role in industrial innovation. Advanced technologies serve to guarantee their commanding position in the world. Secondly,

① Urbanization in China exceeded 50% for the first time in 2011. The latest statistics show that the urban and agricultural population are 690. 79 million and 656. 56 million, respectively, as of 2011; the urban population accounts for 51. 27% of the total. As these urban population statistics include 100 – 200 million migrant farmers who have worked at a fixed place for more than six months, China's urbanization rate is not actually as high as statistics indicate, and the agricultural population remains in the majority under the current household registration system.

industrial powers have a high-grade industrial structure. Within a given industry, these economies leverage high-quality, new technologies (including information technologies). Their products have high added values, their industries are at the upper end of the global value chain, and their industrial organization is at least solid. High-tech industries, high-processing level industries, and technology-intensive industries are key for these industrial powers. Industrial powers also focus on sustainable development. By establishing an environmentally friendly, modern production system, these powers have moved a great distance towards solving resource and environmental problems, laying a foundation for sustainable economic development. Industrial powers also have world-leading production efficiency, a comprehensive reflection of their economic strength. Lastly, industrial powers possess many large-scale multi-national companies with strong international competitiveness and world famous brands. This is a macro-level manifestation of the desirable economic might industrial powers enjoy.

The characteristics listed above are elaborated in Table 1. of special note here is that some of these indicators are statistical in nature, some can be compared across national borders whereas some are specific to China, and some are more readily available than others. The purpose of listing them is not to evaluate the strength of industrial powers① but to simply provide a more detailed description of their characteristics. Industrial powers should have high ranks in many of the traits listed in Table 1.

**Table 1: Characteristics of Industrial Powers**

| Item | Explanation of indicator |
|---|---|
| Advanced technologies | This trait can be described by input and output of technical innovation. Input-related indicators include the percentage of R&D expenses in industrial added value, the ratio of R&D employees out of every ten thousand industrial workers, the per-capita net value of fixed assets, the value of machines per worker, and the fixed assets coefficient (net fixed assets/original value). Output-related indicators include the number of patents for an invention owned, the rate of new products, and the sales income percentage of new products. There are also sector-specific indicators reflecting technical sophistication. |
| A high-grade industrial structure | A high-grade industrial structure can be demonstrated by indicators of industrial organization in a nation-industrial concentration, average corporate production scale, number of industrial clusters; indicators of industrial informationization-the penetration rate of digital design tools in large and medium-sized enterprises, the numerical control rate of key technical process in main industrial sectors; indicators of high-end industry-industrial added value rate, number of proprietary brands, and number of proprietary research centers; indicators of high-processing rate for the industrial structure-percentage of exported industrial goods in industrial added value, total exports, the ratio of industrial added value to the raw material industry's added value; indicators of technological intensity-percentage of output of high-tech industries in industrial added value, percentage of exported goods manufactured with advanced technologies, percentage of value-added to strategic emerging industries (proposed by China). To serve as an example, the industrial added value rates of the U. S. and Germany usually exceed 40%, while the same stat for China was only 26.5% in 2010. |

① A ranking list of global industrial powers can be worked out through some indicators with great comparability and easy access to data after non-dimensional-normalization processing. However, this is not the focus of study in this paper.

Continued

| Item | Explanation of indicator |
|---|---|
| Sustainable development | Sustainable development focuses on energy saving and emission reduction. Specific indicators include industrial added value produced by unit of energy or water used, industrial carbon dioxide ($CO_2$) emission intensity, chemical oxygen demand and sulfur dioxide ($SO_2$) emission intensity, comprehensive utilization rate of industrial solid wastes, and the emission intensity of ammonia nitrogen and nitrogen oxide. |
| Overall economic efficiency | The overall economic efficiency of a country can be measured by indicators such as gross labor productivity (the industrial added value created by each worker in a year), the contribution rate of total assets, the productivity of industrial land, the composite index of industrial economic benefits, and the industrial added value created by a unit of labor cost. Gross labor productivity is a particularly significant indicator of an industrial power, and the U. S. has the highest gross labor productivity in the world. |
| International competitiveness of enterprises | There is no direct statistical indicator for the international competitiveness of enterprises. This figure can be roughly measured by looking at the number of industrial enterprises from a country that are ranked in the world's top 500 enterprises and brands, the ranking of enterprises in all industrial sectors, and the trade competitiveness of a country's industrial goods. As enterprise rankings are mainly based on operating revenues, this figure reflects corporate scale, one dimension of strong competitiveness. |

Source: Compiled by the author from related materials.

## III. The Industry-Invigorating-China Strategy: Proposal

Given China's current national economic condition, developing China into an industrial power has become necessary both strategically and economically. Efforts to transform China into an industrial power have been ongoing since the mid – 1990s; before that time, China's economic development was more focused on quantitative expansion and extensive growth with heavy resource consumption and severe environmental pollution. Though this strategy benefited China, this extensive growth has also brought extensive problems.

It was explicitly laid out in the 9th Five-Year Plan, released in 1996, that China should turn from extensive to intensive growth. Starting in 1997, China has looked to transition from a large industrial country to an industrial power. This new goal for growth is partially laid out in Table 2, which focuses on the 1996 – 2011 *Report on China's Industrial Development*, the most authoritative research report on this aspect of China's ongoing move from large industrial country to industrial power.

**Table 2: 1996 – 2011 Landmark Recommendations and Implementations from the *Report on China's Industrial Development***

| Year | Subject | Implication |
|---|---|---|
| 1996 | Transitioning from the 8th Five-Year Plan to the more challenging 21st century | This report summarized China's industrial achievements from the 8th Five-Year Plan and set out a vision for the 9th Five-Year Plan, noting problems to be faced and the role of industrial development. |

Continued

| Year | Subject | Implication |
|---|---|---|
| 1997 | Transformation from quantitative expansion to quality improvement | This report proposed upgrading and refining China's industry, emphasizing quality over quantity for the first time. |
| 1998 | Systematic innovation, organizational change, and policy adjustment | This report reviewed China's industrial development according to three major influencers: economic system reform, industrial organization changes, and policy choices. It proposed suggestions for further systematic reforms that would rationalize industrial organization and develop scientific industrial development policies. |
| 1999 | China bids farewell to the age of the shortage economy | After two decades of rapid industrial development and industrialization, China has bid farewell to the age of shortage economy. China's industry is flourishing after passing through a certain industrial pubescence. Industrial development and quality improvement are key points. |
| 2000 | China's strategy in the new century-moving from a large industrial country to an industrial power | Several indicators show that China has become a large industrial country-the number of industrial goods produced, the aggregate added value, the proportion of each of the three industries, and the number of imported and exported industrial goods. However, the international competitiveness of China's industry remains relatively weak; quality as the focus of industrial development in the 21st century is stressed for the third time. |
| 2001 | China's industry against a backdrop of economic globalization | This report placed China's industrial development in the context of globalization, paying attention now to the international arena and looking to improve China's industrial quality. |
| 2002 | Corporate and governmental behaviors governed by WTO rules | Again this report focused on China's industry against a backdrop of economic globalization, especially relevant after China's entry to the WTO. |
| 2003 | China's manufacturing under the global labor division system | How can China transform its low-cost "Made in China" branding in order to create higher added value products? How can China do this against the global pattern of labor division given the low-cost international competitiveness of China's industrial goods? These questions about China's manufacturing development were central to this year's report. |
| 2004 | China's industrial technical innovation | The key to improving China's industrial quality and international competiveness is to build up China's technical innovation capabilities for industry. Technical innovation is the core to China's industrial development and modernization. |
| 2005 | China's industrial development under resource and environmental constraints | China's rapid industrial development needs resources to support it, and resources tax the environment. It is necessary to strike a balance between industrial development and resource and environmental constraints. This requires a shift away from extensive growth towards intensive growth. |

Continued

| Year | Subject | Implication |
|---|---|---|
| 2006 | The Scientific Concept of Development and the transformation of China's economic growth model | This report summarized China's industrial development during the 10th Five-Year Plan, analyzing issues faced in industrial development like resource and environmental constraints and weak independent innovation capabilities. It proposed transforming the economic development model under the guidance of the Scientific Development Concept. |
| 2007 | An analysis of industrial development benefits | This report analyzed the overall, regional, sectoral and corporate industrial development benefits and the balance between industrial growth and economic benefits, and proposed policy recommendations on improving China's industrial development benefits. |
| 2008 | China's industry over the past three decades since reform and opening | This report reviewed and summarized China's industrial achievements and learning experiences over the decades since reform and opening. It also proposed suggestions for further deepening reforms. |
| 2009 | China's industry over the past six decades | This year's report reviewed China's industrial development over the past six decades since the founding of the PRC, analyzing characteristics of different development stages and pointing out industrial development bottlenecks to be avoided in the future. |
| 2010 | China's industry in the global financial crisis | The report in 2010 described the performance of China's industry and the significant contribution of industry to China's recovery following the crisis. It recommended that China's industry be transformed and upgraded after the crisis. |
| 2011 | Transforming and upgrading China's industry | In 2011 the report summarized the progress of China's industry towards transformation during the 11th Five-Year Plan, discussing key developmental issues to note during the 12th Five-year Plan period. |

Source: *Report on China's Industrial Development* (1996 – 2001). This annual report has been published 16 times as of 2011.

Specific subjects in the report include the transformation itself (1997: transformation from quantitative expansion to quality improvement; 1999: bidding farewell to the age of the shortage economy; 2000: moving towards becoming an industrial power; 2006: transforming the economic growth model under the guidance of the Scientific Development Concept; 2011: industrial transformation and upgrading), the international background of the transformation (2001: economic globalization, 2002: China's entry into WTO; 2003: the international labor division system; 2010: the global financial crisis), and the key to transformation (1998: systematic innovation; 2003: developing competitive advantage within China's manufacturing sector; 2004: technical innovation; 2005: resource and environmental constraints; 2007: the benefits of industrial development). Particularly relevant is the subject of the 2000 edition of the report-China's Strategy in the New Century: Moving from a Large Industrial Country to an Industrial Power. The 2000 edition of this report is the first time when the Industry-Invigorating-China Strategy was proposed. The Communist Party of China (CPC) Central Committee proposed a new industrialization path with the Scientific Concept of Development. This was also raised in the 11th Five-year Plan, the *Plan on Adjusting and Revitalizing Top Ten Industries* proposed after the financial crisis, and the 12th Five-year Plan. Despite the rhetoric surrounding this new development paradigm, however, this strategy has not yet been formally raised as a state strategic plan or policy.

The Industry-Invigorating-China Strategy is an economic development strategy designed to develop China into an industrial power. To implement this strategy, the government has much important work to do: working out the specific mission of the plan, determining relevant environmental and economic conditions, breaking down the necessary timetable, objectives, and milestones, and determining the specific tasks, conditions, and implementation measures required. A final plan should meet four requirements. First, it should be national in scope and not focus merely on industrial development. Second, it should be systematic, thinking through all of the necessary steps for building an industrial power: scientific research, education, administration, society, culture, etc. Third, scope-a finalized plan should be ten or twenty years in scope if not longer, keeping in mind the goal of China becoming an industrial power within the next two decades. Fourth, the plan should consider the development of global rivalries, with specific steps to cope with international competition in the meantime.

Such a national strategic plan is absolutely essential if China is to completely transform its development model. Given that China is a large industrial country, the key to changing its economic growth model is to change its industrial development model according to exact scientific criteria. Although the CPC Central Committee already proposed the transformation of China's economic growth model based on the Scientific Concept of Development in 1996, 2003 and 2006, not much progress has been made. This is essentially because the government lacks a leverage point, a means to push transformation throughout China's industrial sector. An organized high-level strategy would therefore be quite useful.

Development also must be conducted with the main focus on the real economy. The real economy refers to economic activities which provide material goods and services-agriculture, industry, transportation, trade, logistics, constriction, and, especially, manufacturing. Contrast this to the virtual economy, which essentially is made up of equity transactions of nontangible capital. The purpose of the virtual economy is to allocate financial resources efficiently to increase the value of a given amount of capital. Ideally, the virtual economy optimizes fund allocation and promotes technical advances as well as the development of the real economy. Under an imperfect financial system, however, the virtual economy becomes divorced from the real economy, leading to the creation of bubbles and financial crises. It is precisely this separation of virtual from real economy that had led Western advanced economies to flounder in the global financial crisis. As a large manufacturer, Germany has been particularly susceptible to the European Debt Crisis. The examples of advanced economies in recent years prove the importance of an advanced real economy to prevent economic crises.

In recent years, China has been witnessing extensive asset speculation and a thriving virtual economy that has become somewhat divorced from its real counterpart. Much capital flows to informal lending and real estate, injuring the real economy and especially manufacturing by making financing more difficult to come by and more expensive. This not only affects economic development and helps expand the income equality gap in China but also adds to financial and social risks. Because of this, the Central Economic Working Conference of 2011 proposed that the real economy should be far and away the number one priority in national economic development. At the National Conference on Financial Work in early 2012, one major priority was ensuring the flow of funds to the real economy in order to prevent over-inflation in the virtual economy and the hollowing-out of industries. A national strategy for invigorating China through industry is necessary.

Guiding local governments' planning of development scientifically requires this kind of strategic national plan. Although a national Industry-Invigorating-China Strategy is not available just yet, several local governments-Guizhou, Anhui, Yunnan, Gansu, Sichuan and Hubei-have set a goal to invigorate provinces and cities through industrial development. Nearly one hundred county-level cities have put forth similar goals[①]. However, what they propose is slightly different from what we are proposing in this paper. Some local governments (especially in central and western regions) focused on expanding local industrial scale in order to strengthen one province or city. This is similar to the quantitative expansion China experienced before the intermediate stage of industrialization. The national strategy, however, stresses quality and aims at developing the whole country into an industrial power. The impulse of local governments to expand scale will aggravate resource and environmental constraints already encountered during China's heavy-industrialization stage. By contrast, a national strategic plan proposed by the central government will promote scientific development of local economies.

Using a national strategy to promote industrial development, especially manufacturing development, is common practice among developed economies. Some developing countries have established a national manufacturing development strategy as well. For instance, South Africa proposed *South Africa's Advanced Manufacturing Technology Strategy* in the form of a government report in 2009, and India's National Manufacturing Competitiveness Committee authored the *National Manufacturing Whitebook* in 2006 (Sun Linyan, 2009). After the financial crisis, developed countries have become aware of the deindustrialization issue and therefore have attached more importance to the real economy by launching a state plan to revitalize and develop their manufacturing sectors.

On June 24, 2011, the U. S. President's Council of Advisors on Science and Technology (PCAST) submitted the report *Ensuring American Leadership in Advanced Manufacturing* to President Barack Obama. According to this report, although U. S. manufacturing has maintained leading position in the world for more than a century, it has declined rapidly over recent decades. The report proposes that close cooperation among the government, enterprises, and academia is urgently needed in order to revitalize American manufacturing. Based on this report, President Obama launched

① Searching Baidu with keyword "Industry-Invigorating-Province Strategy" yields 724,000 results; searching with keyword "Industry-Invigorating-City Strategy" yields 2,210,000 results.

the Advanced Manufacturing Partnership (AMP), jointly led and implemented by Dow Chemical Company and the Massachusetts Institute of Technology. The plan contains four commitments: building domestic manufacturing capabilities in critical national security industries, reducing the time needed to make advanced materials used in manufacturing products, establishing U. S. leadership in next-generation robotics, and increasing the energy efficiency of manufacturing processes.

France put forward a similar series of objectives and measures for domestic industrial development on March 4, 2010. This represents a fresh start for France's ambitious plan to rejuvenate its industries. It calls for 25% industrial output growth, eliminating France's industrial trade deficit except in energy, bringing up the percentage of France's industrial added value to Europe's total industrial added value by 2%, and maintaining current employment numbers in the industrial sector over the next five years.

China should take note of and learn from such strategies. The industry-rejuvenating policies of these and other developed economies following the financial crisis will make international competition even fiercer. This further demonstrates how vital it is that China develops its Industry-Invigorating-China Strategy.

On December 30, 2011, the State Council circulated the *Industrial Transformation and Upgrading Plan* (2011 - 2015), which proposed the necessary thinking, major objectives, and key tasks necessary for industrial transformation and upgrading based on the achievements made and challenges left to overcome from the 11th and 12th Five-Year Plans. Specifically, this plan aims to transform Chin's industrial development model following a new path of industrialization and upgrading industrial infrastructure by optimizing industrial technologies and organization in various sectors. This is the first industrial plan to be proposed and circulated by the State Council since China's reform and opening. It explicitly pointed out that industrial transformation and upgrading is the only road for China to move from being a large industrial country to being an industrial power. However, this plan is but an extension of the *Plan on Adjusting and Revitalizing Top Ten Industries* and the 12th Five-year Plan, and is not a real Industry-Invigorating-China Strategy. Any plan that does not set out a timetable listing all of the required steps and milestones necessary for China to become an industrial power is not a sufficient and long-term plan[①]. This latest plan is perhaps better viewed as a four-year sub-plan leading up to the true Industry-Invigorating-China Strategy.

## IV. Objectives and Tasks for the Industry-Invigorating-China Strategy

The process of improving a country's industrial quality and efficiency to meet advanced global standards is essentially economic modernization. According to modernization theory, this process is

① Although it is a Five-Year Plan (2011 -2015), it was not circulated until December 30, 2011, so the actual implementation period covers only four years.

known as industrial modernization. Industry is a leading force of many national economies, and industrial modernization is the engine of economic modernization. Only by driving industrial modernization can China develop into an industrial power and truly achieve economic modernization. According to our estimates, China's industrial modernization reached 40% by the end of the 10th Five-Year Plan (2001 - 2005). If we simply look at the average annual growth rate recorded during the 10th Five-Year Plan without considering other factors, China will be 60% industrially modernized by around 2020 and 100% modernized by around 2040 (Chen Jiagui and Huang Qunhui, 2009). This is basically in line with Deng Xiaoping's three-step strategy for China's modernization. That is to say that China will become an industrial power in some respects by around 2020 and a complete industrial power by around 2040. According to a research report by the Sadie Research Institute under the Ministry of Industry and Information Technology, China will have established a modern industrial system with certain strengths by 2015, have basically developed into an industrial power by 2020, and have truly developed into a world-class industrial power by 2050 (Qiao Biao, *et. al*, 2011). We have come to similar conclusions in our research. Furthermore, China aims to develop into a leading economic power in terms of human resources, talent, and technical innovation by 2020 as proposed in the *Country's Medium and Long-term Talent Development Plan* (2010 - 2020) (June, 2010), *National Medium and Long-Term Program for Education Reform and Development* (2010 - 2020) (July, 2010) and *National Medium and Long-Term Program for Science and Technology Development* (2006 - 2020) (February 2006), respectively. These objectives are aligned with the goals of the Industry-Invigorating-China Strategy.

The Industry-Invigorating-China Strategy should focus on establishing three major things: an advanced technological system, a modern industrial system, and a highly efficient management system.

(1) China should vigorously carry out technical innovation and establish an advanced technological system-an industrial power needs to own advanced technologies. Although in recent years China has built a relatively complete technological system with increasing levels of R&D and technological innovation intensity as well as steadily rising industrial innovation capabilities, it still falls behind countries like the U. S., Germany and Japan, especially in core technologies and national technological systems. In 2008, the average R&D intensity of OECD countries was 2. 33; the R&D intensities of the U. S., Germany and Japan were 2. 89, 2. 64 and 3. 42, respectively; China, by comparison, was only 1. 54 (growing to merely 1. 71 by 2010). As for the self-sufficiency rate of key technologies, the percentages of China's imports of textile machinery, high-end machine tools, high-speed offset printers, integrated chip manufacturing equipment, and optical fiber manufacturing equipment are 70%, 75%, 75%, 85% and 100%, respectively. These figures demonstrate that China is highly dependent on other countries for its advanced manufacturing machinery. As for patents, in 2010 China applied for 12, 337 international PCT patents, only one fourth of the U. S.'s figure and one third of Japan's. From 2004 to 2006, the U. S., Japan and Germany owned 43%, 17% and 10% of patents on nanotechnologies, respectively (and 70% in total), while China held very few (Department of Industrial Policy under Ministry of Industry and Information Technology

and Institute of Industrial Economics, CASS, 2011).

Possessing world-leading technologies and innovative capabilities are basic requirements for an industrial power hoping to compete from an advantageous position. The reason for China's inferior position in global competition is a lack of either advanced technologies or an advanced technological development system. Therefore, building an advanced technological development system through technical innovation is the first thing that must be done. Originality and intellectual property rights are growing ever more important, so China must increase inputs in basic science. Generally, given huge leap-frog benefits from the introduction of advanced technologies, emerging countries tend to make technical progress by imitating or importing technology from developed countries over a fairly long time period. China has followed this pattern since reform and opening. However, now that China has become a large industrial economy in its own right, it must also build up independent innovative capabilities and its own system of intellectual property rights. This is especially important for strategic, fundamental technological areas. Therefore, aside from applying and modifying imported technologies, China must also stress original research and domestic innovation.

(2) China should also upgrade its industrial structure and establish a modern industrial system. Transforming and upgrading its industrial structure is an arduous task with four distinct steps or aspects. First, Chinese enterprises have been at the low end of the global value chain for a long time. Embedded in the global value chain via OEMs, Chinese enterprises mainly deal with labor-intensive production-low levels of technological content and high labor input. This leaves little room for Chinese enterprises to add value through product design innovation, high-end manufacturing, and advanced brand management and marketing. Among the world's top 500 brands in 2009, China had only 18 compared to 241 for the U. S., 46 for France and 40 for Japan (Qiao, *et. al*, 2011).

Second, concentration for most industries in China remains unfinished. Although the period from 2002 to 2011 saw many enterprises scaling up in terms of size, concentration has actually declined recently in most industries (Li, *et al.*, 2011). China's top 500 firms are far weaker than many multinational companies and are simply not yet able to compete.

During the 11th Five-Year Plan, heavy industry accounted for over 70% of China's secondary industry. This demonstrates that China's industrial structure has not yet transformed from capital-intensive to technology-intensive. Equipment manufacturing has grown the fastest, but the percentage of high-technology industry and high-tech-intensive industry within total industrial output value were only 27.6% and 11% in 2009, respectively (Department of Industrial Policy under Ministry of Industry and Information Technology and Institute of Industrial Economics, CASS, 2011).

Fourth, overall efficiency indicators such as labor productivity, industrial added value, and industrial energy consumption efficiency are far lower than in developed economies. China's labor productivity in equipment manufacturing was USD19,000 per person per year in 2007. Compare this to figures from 1996 for the U. S. at USD98,000 and Japan at USD110,000. In 2009, China's industrial added value rate was 26.5%, while the rates for the U. S., Japan, and Germany were 68.0%, 43.6%, and 43.4%, respectively. In 2008, China needed 1.1 tons of standard coal to produce 10,000 Renminbi of GDP output, three to four times the consumption in developed economies (Qiao, *et al.*, 2011).

These weaknesses help demonstrate just how vital it is that China upgrades its industrial structure to establish a modern industrial system. *The Industrial Transformation and Upgrading Plan* (2011 – 2015) is significant in that it proposes that China must improve its independent innovation capabilities, accelerate interaction between informationization and industrialization, boost strategic emerging industries, upgrade traditional industries, speed up development of its producer service industry, optimize overall structures, and build core industrial competitiveness and sustainable development capabilities. If this plan is implemented effectively, China will soon establish a modern industrial system on top of a solid agricultural foundation, an optimized industrial structure, and rapid service industry development. Technological advances will be key to developing such a future.

The strategic development of the primary and tertiary industries will be altered under the Industry-Invigorating-China Strategy. The strategic mission of the first industry should be for the agricultural market to benefit industrial development. This requires funding agriculture and increasing farmer incomes in order to create more demand for industrial technologies and products, thereby promoting industrial development through agricultural development (Huang and Wang, 2000). The strategic mission and development orientation of the tertiary industry have two key points. First, the tertiary industry should serve as a main channel for surplus labor created by higher industrial productivity. Second, the tertiary industry will assist in upgrading China's industrial structure by developing producer and manufacturer services. This will help give China momentum to become a large service economy.

(3) China should deepen reforms and establish a highly efficient administrative system. China's practices since reform and opening show that economic modernization should be supported by industrialization and market-oriented reforms. Some fundamental institutional barriers are impeding modernization in China, and China should advance reforms and perfect its market-economy system in order to do away with these hindrances. Turning thinking into action will involve a long-term and all-encompassing innovative process wherein a scientific and efficient administration leads China to implement deeper and more effective reforms.

China's existing administrative system is insufficient for China's long-term needs in several ways. For one, industrial development is concurrently administrated by multiple authorities-the State Development and Reform Commission (SDRC), the Ministry of Industry and Information Technology, the State-owned assets administration departments, the department of science and technology, the department of economy and trade, the land department, and the urban construction department. These bodies need to be streamlined into a system which facilitates communication and coordination among the different authorities so as not to impede industrial modernization.

Furthermore, a more effective administration system could help boost key scientific research. China's scientific research input has indeed increased substantially in recent years. R&D input in 2010 was 706.26 billion RMB, an increase of 126.05 billion RMB, or 21.7%, from 2009. This increase far outstrips basic GDP growth. However, technological innovation efficiency is low because of the current scientific research management system. An empirical study has shown that when China's R&D input increases by one unit, the number of SCI papers increases by 0.852. This figure is 1.263 for Japan and 1.755 for Korea. For each additional unit of input to China's R&D, the number of approved patents increases by 1.386. This figure is 2.652 in Japan and 1.676 for Korea (Li and Li, 2008). Based on this, it is clear that China must reform its management systems for industry, education, human capital, and science and technology, among others.

China should specifically look to establish a coordination mechanism to facilitate communication among China's many different administrative authorities. It should also deepen reforms in monopolized industries, perfect its investment mechanism, and create equal market access and a fair, competitive environment. China should also further reforms in educational and talent management to assure that China's talents are being cultivated and not lost. Reforming science and technology administration is another priority which can help China ensure that enterprises play a major role in technical innovation and help improve technical innovation efficiency. One more point to make is that the industrial department is not the only authority involved in the Industry-Invigorating-China Strategy. This strategy is a top-level, systematic plan for developing the whole country, and it should be aligned with other national development objectives stated in the *Country's Medium and Long-term Talent Development Plan* (2010–2020), *National Medium and Long-Term Program for Education Reform and Development* (2010–2020) and *National Medium and Long-Term Program for Science and Technology Development* (2006–2020).

## V. Policy Suggestions

The Industry-Invigorating-China Strategy is, in its current stage, important thought work. More important than theorizing, though, is turning these thoughts into actions. China should now follow the plan-do-check-adjust (PDCA) cycle and firmly set down policies to guarantee physical implementation of these ideas. China's extensive industrial growth model has brought about environmental pollution and inefficient energy consumption in recent years. This, combined with the great risks involved in industrial transformation, upgrading, and innovation, means that China's industry sector is currently in a disadvantageous position. Its current position is disadvantageous when compared with the virtual economy in terms of available financing, talent, and even land. Therefore, policies should encourage resources to flow to the real economy. There should also be policies regulating financial activities and cracking down on speculation so that the virtual economy can fulfill its original function of serving the real economy and not vice versa.

There should be preferential financial policies for real economy enterprises such as structural tax breaks and special funds available for technological innovation and industrial upgrading. These policies should benefit the real economy and be especially geared towards manufacturing and small-and micro-sized enterprises. China's financial revenues have grown rapidly for many years, so the financial system should be ready to play its necessary role for the good of the economy at large.

China should continue to reform its financial system and financial regulatory bodies with the goal of creating a financial system that can support the development of an innovative economy. China must experiment and try new things in its efforts to establish a policy-based financial system, appropriate mechanisms for venture capital investment, and a viable system of capital markets. Disciplining the financial system is a top priority if the virtual economy is going to fill its original role of optimizing the allocation of resources and serving the real economy. It is unacceptable for there to be adequate liquidity in China's capital markets when no such financing is available for its industrial economy.

Industrial policy should prioritize the development of modern manufacturing, especially strategic emerging manufacturing, and eliminate old-fashioned, backwards production methods. Although manufacturing will shrink in percentage of GDP as China approaches the late stages of industrialization (perhaps by around 2020) (Chen Jiagui and Huang Qunhui, 2007), manufacturing should and will remain significant. For the service industry, the focus should be on producer services incorporating R&D, finance, logistics, information services, and after-sales services. The purpose here is to improve industrial efficiency and promote industrial transformation and upgrading.

As for price inflation and income inequality, China's leadership should put forth policies to improve profits for the real economy. The virtual economy and monopolized industries are each currently taking too large a slice of profits. The average profit of the banking sector, for example, exceeds that of the manufacturing sector to a dangerous degree. The goal should be to increase the proportion of labor income in national income so as to create an atmosphere that is respectful towards labor and the real economy.

As for market competition, China should dismantle administrative monopoly which, though beneficial in some ways, tend to block technical innovation and industrial upgrading. China's leadership should also encourage private enterprises to participate in competition and protect traditional industries when they take the initiative and try to upgrade or modernize. Market competition should be regulated, and speculators pocketing windfall profits should be punished harshly. As for talent and innovation, Chinese policies should encourage more innovative talents to flow to the industrial sectors where innovation is needed. China should push forward with reforms in education, human capital, and scientific and technological management in order to implement the recommended strategy.

By perfecting the above policies and systems, the Industry-Invigorating-China Strategy can be implemented successfully, and China will become a more competitive, wealthier, and happier country.

## References

1. Chen, Jiagui, and Qunhui Huang. 2005. "Industrial Development, Changing National Situations and the Strategy of Economic Modernization: An Analysis of National Situations for China's Growing into a Large Industrial State." *Social Sciences in China*, (4).

2. Chen, Jiagui, and Qunhui Huang, etc. 2007. "Report on the Progress of Industrialization in China-Evaluating and Researching the Industrial Level in 31 Provinces and Regions during 1995 – 2005." Beijing: Social Science Academy Press.

3. Chen, Jiagui, and Qunhui Huang. 2009. "Achieve Industrial Modernization—Analyzing

and Evaluating Modernization in 15 Key Industries." *China Industrial Economy*, (4).

4. Department of Industrial Policy under Ministry of Industry and Information Technology and Institute of Industrial Economics, Chinese Academy of Social Science. "Report on China's Industrial Development and Industrial Policies (2011) -Adjustment and Upgrading." China Citic Press, 2011.

5. Guo, Shuyong. 2006. "The Logic of the Great Power Growth: A Study of the Rises of Western Powers from the Perspective of International Political Sociology." Beijing: Beijing University Press.

6. Huang, Qunhui, and Hongwu Zhong. 2010. "China's Industrialization and Problems during the Intermediate Stage of the 'Eleventh Five-year,'" [A]. China Economic Research Report (2009 - 2010) [C]. Beijing: Economy and Management Publishing House.

7. Huang, Taiyan, and Jiangui Wang. 2000. "Transformation of the Fundamental Role of Agriculture in the New Industrial Stage." *Social Sciences in China*, (3).

8. Hu, Angang, Yilong Yan and Xing Wei. 2011. "China Will Achieve Common Prosperity by 2030." Beijing: China Renmin University Press.

9. Li, Junjiang, and Zheng Li. 2008. "China's Scientific and Technological Innovation System: Reform, Development and Achievement." Jilin University Journal Social Sciences Edition, (6).

10. Li, Jianming, Rong Miao, and Yufeng Hao. 2011. "The Growing Trend of China's Top 500 Companies over the Past Decade." *China Industrial Economy*, (10).

11. Qiao, Biao, Yaguang Li, and Hu Sun, etc. 2011. "Thinking and Strategies of Advancing the Building of an Industrial Power in the New Era." [R]. *Research on Industry and Informationization*, (4). http://image.ccidnet.com/ccidgroup/gyhxxhyj/gyhxxhyj12.pdf

12. Shanghai Economic Commission and Shanghai Institute of Scientific and Technical Information. "The Developments of Key Manufacturing Industries in the World." Shanghai: Shanghai Scientific and Technological Literature Publishing House, 2008.

13. Institute of Industrial Economics, Chinese Academy of Social Sciences. "Report on China's Industrial Development." Beijing: Economy and Management Publishing House, 1996 - 2011.

# Chapter 17

# Recalculating the Significance of Secondary and Tertiary Industries for Industrial Restructuring: Truth and Myth*

**Li Gang (李钢), Liao Jianhui (廖建辉) and Xiang Yini (向奕霓)**

**Institute of Industrial Economics of Chinese Academy of Social Science, Beijing, China**

**Abstract**: By analyzing the efficiency, supply and demand of the three industries, and the foreign trade of developed countries, this paper argues: the ever-increasing proportion of the tertiary industry in developed countries has not yet proved that tertiary industry is the direction of industrial advance nor the tertiary industry is superior over the secondary industry. By estimating China's industrial structure with PPP-based industrial data, this paper argues that the proportion of China's secondary industry in its GDP is not as high as expected. China will still rely on its secondary industry for further growth because China's labor-intensive industries still possess the most comparative advantage and global competitiveness.

**Keywords**: industrial upgrading, industrial structure, competitiveness

## I. Introduction

According to a report made during China's 17th Party Congress in 2007, China's priority was to swiftly restructure its economy to sustain rapid growth. Among all the economic structures-supply structure (industrial structure), demand structure, and distribution structure-industrial structure adjustment is the most practical. Many scholars argue that industrial restructuring is based primarily on shifting from a manufacturing-based economy towards an economy driven by all the three industries. In particular there is an appeal for a higher proportion of the tertiary in-

---

* Corresponding author: gangli@ vip. sohu. net.

This paper is supported by the following programs: *Strategies to Change Industrial Competitiveness and the Evolution of Global Division of Labor* (2009&ZD035) under China's National Social Science Foundation; a national 973 project *Analysis on the Path and Peak of Green House Gases Emission and Cost-Effectiveness of Emission Reduction* (2010CB955205); the program *The Changing Landscape of Global Competitiveness and the Future of China's Industry* by Chinese Academy of Social Science (YZDA2010 – 03).

dustry in the national economy and a larger contribution from the modern service industry to economic growth.

The desirability of such an industrial structure, however, is not a deduction based on economic principles, but rather an induction rested upon the path of industrial restructuring followed by developed countries. For example, William Petty (1672) and Clarke (1940) found that a higher per capita GDP will result in labor transferring from the primary industry to the secondary industry and further to the tertiary industry. In addition, Simon Kuznets (1971) further proposed that industrial restructuring is subject to the changes of per capita income. Japanese scholars also pointed out the trend towards the softening of industrial structure, characterizing the production of service and information; and hence tertiary industry is referred to as "soft industry." Given that features of industrial structure in developed countries comply with the theories above, they are regarded as a guide to be followed by developing countries in their economic restructuring. Therefore, it is widely accepted that the path for China's industry development lied in increasing the proportion of the tertiary industry. They also argued that China should formulate relevant policies to encourage the service industry and to restrain secondary production particularly heavy industry. Nonetheless, disputes over China's industrial promotion are more than the priority of industries. Controversy has also arisen from the secondary industry regarding the direction of advancement. Some studies have suggested that China should accelerate its pace to evolve from labor-intensive industries to capital-and technology-intensive industries.

This paper starts with studying the level of tertiarization[①] in developed countries. The authors analyzed the fast growing proportion of the tertiary industry, then verified with new data whether China's secondary industry was oversized, and finally analyzed the direction for China's secondary industry enhancement.

## II. Rising Proportion of the Tertiary Industry in Developed Countries Does Not Suggest Its Superiority over the Secondary Industry

### (I) Labor Productivity of the Secondary Industry in Developed Countries Remains Higher than Other Industries

Developed countries possess a higher proportion of tertiary industry. For instance, in the U. S. tertiary industry employment contributed more than 78% of output in 2007 and 77.5% in 2008. In France and the UK, tertiary industries also contributed more than 75% output in 2008. However, the secondary industry in these developed countries displays higher labor productivity (in terms of per capita output) than the tertiary industry. Figure 1 exhibits the ratio of productivity of the secondary industry to that of the tertiary industry. It is evident from the figure that with the exception of France, the four countries listed displayed higher productivity in the secondary in-

① A shift from the primary and secondary sectors to the tertiary sector.

dustry.

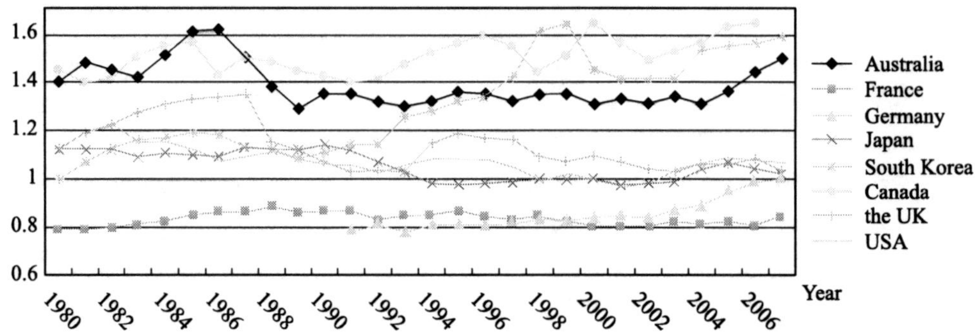


**Figure 1: Productivity between Secondary and Tertiary Industries in Main Developed Countries**

Source: *International Statistics Yearbook* (1995 – 2010).

(1) Prior to 1990, Japan's secondary industry maintained higher productivity than its tertiary industry. During the 1990s, productivity of Japan's tertiary industry began to equalize with that of the secondary industry and surpassed it in 1994. However, since 2004, the secondary industry has again experienced higher productivity than the tertiary industry.

(2) Since 1991, after reunification, Germany's economy was sluggish; in particular, the manufacturing industry in East Germany was in wreckage. With its gradual recovery, Germany's secondary industry began to register higher productivity than its tertiary industry.

(3) Other than in 1998, 2001 and 2003, the U. S. was unrivalled in modern service industries such as the financial sector and consultancy services consequently making the tertiary industry most dominant.

(4) France's tertiary industry has maintained higher productivity than its secondary industry. Since the 1980's the global competitiveness in the manufacturing industry and its status in the world economy have been in decline. France comprised 4. 97 of the world's total GDP in 1974, but dropped to 3. 81% in 2007.

### (II) Diminishing Demand Not the Major Cause for Decreasing Ratio of Secondary Industry

The proportion of the tertiary industry to GDP in developed countries has been growing since 1980 and exceeded 60% in 2007. Given that consumption is the sole end of production, is the changing industrial structure in developed countries a result of their changing consumption structure? Table 1 is the final consumption expenditures in the main developed countries, which shows that the proportion of secondary industry products in final consumption dropped less significantly than the secondary industry's proportion in the industrial structure.

**Table 1: Final Consumption Expenditure of Residents in Developed Countries (%)**

| | | 1992 | 1996 | 2000 | 2006 |
|---|---|---|---|---|---|
| Canada | Finished industrial products | 33. 3 | 33. 7 | 30. 2① | 29. 6② |
| | Service products | 31. 1 | 35. 2 | 34. 9① | 39. 3② |
| UK | Finished industrial products | 25. 9 | 26. 2 | 24. 5 | 25. 6 |
| | Service products | 28. 6 | 29. 5 | 39. 0 | 44. 8② |
| the U. S. | Finished industrial products | 24. 2 | 24. 0 | 22. 2① | 22. 3② |
| | Service products | 41. 3 | 43. 2 | 47. 1① | 49. 9 |
| France | Finished industrial products | 27. 7 | 29. 3 | 30. 1 | 30. 8 |
| | Service products | 33. 5 | 34. 0 | 37. 8 | 36. 9 |
| Holland | Finished industrial products | 25. 5 | 27. 5 | 28. 2① | 29. 5 |
| | Service products | 36. 6 | 35. 7 | 37. 2① | 34. 9 |
| Japan | Finished industrial products | 26. 3 | 28. 3 | 29. 7① | 28. 3② |
| | Service products | 31. 1 | 35. 2 | 34. 9① | 39. 3② |

Note: Industrial products refer to real estate, energy, furniture, home appliance, house maintenance cost, etc. Service products refer to medical and health service, transportation, communication, entertainment, culture, education, restaurant and hotels, etc. ① refers to the data in 1999 and ② refers to the data in 2005.

Source: original data from the *International Statistics Yearbook* (1995 – 2010), re-quoted from "The Mystery of Low Economic Growth of Big Economies in the Post-Industrial Age: A Prospective from Changing Economic Structure," written by Ji Ming and Liang Dongli, published in *Economic Management*, the 3rd issue of 2011.

Table 2 provides a detailed explanation for the discrepancy between the consumption structure and industrial structure. The table shows that from 1992 to 2006, the C value (see the note of Table 2) of the five developed countries were higher than 1, which indicates that the shrinking secondary industry and expanding tertiary industry in developed countries are not mainly caused by the changing structure of final demand. France is the exception; as shown in Table 2, France had a much larger C value than others in 2006. Also as Figure 1 shows, France's tertiary industry has always maintained higher productivity. In 2006, added value of France's tertiary industry was 3. 8 times that of the secondary industry. However, in final consumption, the service industry was only 1. 2 times that of the secondary industry.

**Table 2: Comparison of the Industrial Structure and Demand Structure among Key Developed Countries**

| | 1992 | | | 1996 | | | 2000 | | | 2006 | | |
|---|---|---|---|---|---|---|---|---|---|---|---|---|
| | A | B | C | A | B | C | A | B | C | A | B | C |
| France | 1. 21 | 2. 7 | 2. 2 | 1. 16 | 3. 1 | 2. 6 | 1. 26 | 3. 2 | 2. 6 | 1. 20 | 3. 8 | 3. 2 |
| Japan | 1. 18 | 1. 6 | 1. 3 | 1. 24 | 1. 9 | 1. 5 | 1. 18 | 2. 0 | 1. 7 | 1. 39 | 2. 3 | 1. 6 |
| Canada | 0. 93 | 2. 4 | 2. 6 | 1. 04 | 2. 1 | 2. 0 | 1. 16 | 1. 9 | 1. 7 | 1. 33 | 2. 1 | 1. 6 |

Continued

| | 1992 | | | 1996 | | | 2000 | | | 2006 | | |
|---|---|---|---|---|---|---|---|---|---|---|---|---|
| | A | B | C | A | B | C | A | B | C | A | B | C |
| UK | 1. 10 | 2. 2 | 2. 0 | 1. 13 | 2. 2 | 2. 0 | 1. 59 | 2. 6 | 1. 6 | 1. 75 | 3. 2 | 1. 8 |
| USA | 1. 71 | 2. 8 | 1. 6 | 1. 80 | 2. 8 | 1. 6 | 2. 12 | 3. 2 | 1. 5 | 2. 24 | 3. 5 | 1. 5 |

Note: A refers to the ratio between tertiary industry and secondary industry among demand structure; B refers to the proportion between tertiary and secondary industry in industrial structure; C equals B divided by A.

Source: Authors' calculation.

### (III) Higher Trade in Goods than Trade in Service Shrinks the Secondary Industry in Developed Countries

The disparity between the industrial structure and the demand structure in developed countries is a result of economic globalization and the fact that goods are more tradable than services. To date, trade in service only comprises 21. 1% of total world trade, far lower than trade in goods. Table 3 exhibits the exports and imports of the world's major traders, which show that the U. S. , U K, France, and some other countries registered net imports of goods. This further proves that the higher proportion of tertiary industry in developed countries is supported by the flourishing world trade in goods, rather than a change in the structure of final demand.

**Table 3: Trade Structure of Major Countries and World Average in 2009 (100 million USD)**

| | | China | USA | Japan | UK | France | Germany | The world's total |
|---|---|---|---|---|---|---|---|---|
| Import | Farm products | 766 | 1, 007 | 677 | 583 | 582 | 953 | 11, 688 |
| | Finished products | 6, 753 | 11, 215 | 2, 857 | 3, 377 | 4, 144 | 6, 737 | 83, 547 |
| | Raw material | 2, 505 | 3, 114 | 1, 875 | 631 | 840 | 1, 378 | 22, 629 |
| | Services | 1, 581 | 3, 343 | 1, 470 | 1, 575 | 1, 260 | 2, 525 | 31, 450 |
| Export | Farm products | 409 | 1, 196 | 79 | 260 | 638 | 773 | 11, 688 |
| | Finished products | 11, 248 | 8, 001 | 5, 079 | 2, 576 | 3, 831 | 530 | 83, 547 |
| | Raw material | 343 | 883 | 257 | 509 | 283 | 9, 645 | 22, 629 |
| | Services | 1, 286 | 4, 760 | 1, 259 | 2, 283 | 1, 420 | 2, 258 | 33, 500 |
| Net export | Farm products | -358 | 188 | -598 | -323 | 56 | -180 | |
| | Finished products | 4, 495 | -3, 214 | 2, 221 | -800 | -314 | -6, 207 | |
| | Raw material | -2, 162 | -2, 231 | -1, 618 | -122 | -558 | 8, 266 | |
| | Services | -295 | 1, 417 | -210 | 708 | 160 | -268 | |

Source: http: //www. wto. org/english/res_e/statis_e/statis_e. htm

### (IV) Over-priced Service Products Comprise the Industrial Structure in Developed Countries

Given that the physical quantity of various goods is impractical, value (quantity) is employed to measure the overall value of various goods. In computing industrial structure, comparative price fluctuation of products in each industry would have a huge impact on the composition. Xu (2010) pointed out that from 1995 to 2007, the proportion of South Korea's secondary industry in its GDP rose by 5.2 percentage points when calculated by constant price but decreased by 5.1 percentage points by current price; the proportion of Japan's secondary industry in its GDP from 1970 to 2005 was 3.8 percentage points higher by constant price but 16 percentage points lower by current price; and the proportion of France's secondary industry in its GDP from 1972 to 1990 was 3.7 percentage points higher by constant price but 10.7 percentage points lower by current price. Similar cases could also be found in other developed countries including the U.S. and Germany.

In the current international order, goods but not labor flow freely, which has reduced the total supply of service products of the developed countries. This further pushed up the price of tertiary industry products and lowered the price of secondary industry products, thus explaining why developed countries have a higher proportion of tertiary industry.

## III. Is China's Secondary Industry Disproportionately High?

### (I) China's Industrial Structure Differs from that of the Developed Countries

When it comes to the higher proportion of China's secondary industry, scholarly views could be divided into three groups. One maintains that China's industry is improperly structured with an out-of-proportion secondary industry. Ma (2011) argues that the proportion of China's secondary industry is too high while that of its tertiary industry is too low. To approach it from the perspective of growing from a middle-income country to a high-income one, China's tertiary industry should comprise at least 60% of GDP. Wang (2010) also believes that China's secondary industry is not proportionate and the financial crisis has provided an opportunity to curb China's booming secondary industry in favor of others. He also visualizes that in the 12th Five Year Period, if China's economic growth maintains its 9% rate while the primary, secondary and tertiary industries grow annually at approximately 5.5%, less than 9% and 9.5%, respectively, then the proportion of China's primary industry could be stabilized at 10%, the secondary industry less than 40% and the tertiary industry more than 45%.

A second school of thought maintains that the secondary industry's proportion is in line with the laws governing how industrial structure evolves. This group and the previous one agree that China's secondary industry has reached its maximum proportion and China should begin to witness a decreasing secondary industry and an enlarging tertiary industry.

A third faction believes China's manufacturing industry has room to grow. Li Gang and Jin Bei

(2009) consider that industry, especially the manufacturing industry, is the backbone of the national economy. Its fundamental role, to most developed and developing countries, is irreplaceable. At present, China has not yet been highly industrialized and the need exists to accelerate its secondary industry to comprise a higher proportion of GDP.

### (Ⅱ) Industrial Structure Computed Based on Purchasing Power Parity (PPP)

We will use PPP-based industrial data to estimate China's industrial structure. The PPP varies with products; for instance, the 2005 International Comparison Program (ICP) (released by the World Bank in February 2008) shows that China's PPP is 3.45 yuan against 1 dollar; the exchange rate by the PPP method for China's health and social security industry is 0.69, while at 8.97 for the equipment manufacturing industry. This equates that exchange rates for some industries are underestimated while for others they are overestimated.

This paper reassesses China's industrial structure by using added value data from *China Statistic Yearbook* 2006 and PPP by industry data from the World Bank's *China's Purchasing Power Parity and Expenditure* 2005. Given that these two sources have different classifications, we first list the parallel classifications (shown in Table 4). We begin with calculating PPP-based added value of each industry, and then calculate industrial structure. For the primary and the tertiary industry, it suffices to divide added value by the industry's PPP. For the secondary industry, as the only available data includes the added value of those enterprises of designed scale (annual sales revenue exceeds 5 million yuan), we need to divide PPP-based added value of those enterprises by their added value calculated by traditional methods and then to multiply the result by the total added value of the whole industry (Table 5). After all PPP-based added values by industry were collected, the PPP-based industrial structure in 2005 could be calculated. Similarly, industrial structure from 2000 to 2009 could also be computed as shown in Table 6, which also includes the industrial structure calculated by the traditional method.

**Table 4: PPP-based Added Value of the Primary, Tertiary, and Construction Industries (2005)**

| Industry by China's classification standard | Corresponding industry by the World Bank's classification | PPP (RMB/USD) | Added value by traditional method (RMB 100 million) | PPP - based added value (USD 100million) |
|---|---|---|---|---|
| Primary industry | Food and non - alcoholic drinks | 5.52 | 22,420.00 | 4,061.59 |
| Transportation, storage and mailing industry | Transportation | 5.98 | 10,835.67 | 1,811.99 |
| Information communication, PC service and software | Other goods and services | 4.13 | 4,768.00 | 1,154.48 |

Continued

| Industry by China's classification standard | Corresponding industry by the World Bank's classification | PPP (RMB/USD) | Added value by traditional method (RMB 100 million) | PPP - based added value (USD 100million) |
|---|---|---|---|---|
| Wholesale and retail | Other goods and services | 4. 13 | 13, 534. 54 | 3, 277. 13 |
| Hotel and restaurant | Hotel and restaurant | 6. 78 | 4, 193. 43 | 618. 50 |
| Finance | Other goods and services | 4. 13 | 6, 307. 23 | 1, 527. 18 |
| Real estate | Housing, water & electricity, other energies | 3. 37 | 8, 243. 84 | 2, 446. 24 |
| Leasing and business service | Other goods and services | 4. 13 | 2, 912. 43 | 705. 19 |
| Scientific research, technological service, geographic survey | Other goods and services | 4. 13 | 2, 050. 56 | 496. 50 |
| Water conservancy, environment and public facility management | Government's public expenditure | 1. 53 | 849. 93 | 555. 51 |
| Community service or other service | Other goods and services | 4. 13 | 3, 129. 43 | 757. 73 |
| Education | Education | 1. 02 | 5, 656. 32 | 5, 545. 41 |
| Health, social security and welfare | Health | 0. 69 | 2, 934. 49 | 4, 252. 89 |
| Culture, sports and entertainment | Culture and entertainment | 3. 47 | 1, 188. 23 | 342. 43 |
| Public management and social organization | Government's expenditure for community | 0. 83 | 6, 828. 75 | 8, 227. 42 |
| Sum for the tertiary industry | | | | 31, 718. 59 |
| Construction industry | Construction | 1. 93 | 10, 367. 31 | 5, 371. 67 |

Source: World Bank and the authors' classification.

**Table 5: PPP-based Added Value for Enterprises above Designed Scale (2005)**

| Industry | Corresponding industry | PPP (¥/$) | Added value by traditional method (RMB 100 million) | PPP - based added value (USD 100million) |
|---|---|---|---|---|
| Coal mining and washing | Other products | 4.43 | 2,888.25 | 651.98 |
| Oil and gas exploration | Other products | 4.43 | 4,813.96 | 1,086.67 |
| Metal mining | Other products | 4.43 | 426.50 | 96.28 |
| Non-ferrous metal mining | Other products | 4.43 | 427.60 | 96.52 |
| Non-metal mining | Other products | 4.43 | 280.51 | 63.32 |
| Other mining | Other products | 4.43 | 2.70 | 0.61 |
| The sum of the mining industry | | | | 1,995.38 |
| Agricultural food processing | Food and non-alcoholic drink | 5.52 | 2,745.96 | 497.46 |
| Food manufacturing | Food and non-alcoholic drink | 5.52 | 1,168.32 | 211.65 |
| Drink manufacturing | Food and non-alcoholic drink | 5.52 | 1,164.73 | 211.00 |
| Tobacco manufacturing | Alcoholic drink and tobacco | 5.75 | 2,059.99 | 358.26 |
| Textile | Clothes and shoes | 6.86 | 3,240.19 | 472.33 |
| Clothes, shoes and hat manufacturing | Clothes and shoes | 6.86 | 1,419.86 | 206.98 |
| Leather, fur and eiderdown manufacturing | Clothes and shoes | 6.86 | 944.38 | 137.66 |
| Wood processing and Wooden, bamboo, cane, palm and straw products | Other goods and services | 4.13 | 510.86 | 123.69 |
| Furniture | Furniture, home appliance and service | 5.27 | 384.87 | 73.03 |
| Paper-making | Other goods and services | 4.13 | 1,146.40 | 277.58 |
| Publishing and copying | Culture and entertainment | 3.47 | 463.06 | 133.45 |

Continued

| Industry | Corresponding industry | PPP (¥/$) | Added value by traditional method (RMB 100 million) | PPP - based added value (USD 100million) |
|---|---|---|---|---|
| Cultural and sports related products | Other goods and services | 4.13 | 379.71 | 91.94 |
| Petrochemical and nuclear industry | Water & gas & electricity, other energies | 3.37 | 1,981.64 | 588.02 |
| Chemistry | Other goods and services | 4.13 | 4,391.92 | 1,063.42 |
| Pharmacy | medical industry | 0.69 | 1,529.80 | 2,217.10 |
| Chemistry fiber product | Other goods and services | 4.13 | 485.31 | 117.51 |
| Rubber product | Other goods and services | 4.13 | 595.36 | 144.15 |
| Plastic product | Other goods and services | 4.13 | 1,272.05 | 308.00 |
| Non-metal mineral product | Other products | 4.43 | 2,807.92 | 633.84 |
| Ferrous metal smelting and rolling | Other products | 4.43 | 5,776.90 | 1,304.04 |
| Non-ferrous metal smelting and rolling | Other products | 4.43 | 1,929.65 | 435.59 |
| Metal product | Other products | 4.43 | 1,693.38 | 382.25 |
| General equipment manufacturing | Mechanics and equipment | 8.79 | 2,966.96 | 337.54 |
| Special equipment manufacturing | Mechanics and equipment | 8.79 | 1,681.56 | 191.30 |
| Transportation equipment manufacturing | Mechanics and equipment | 8.79 | 3,830.52 | 435.78 |
| Electric equipment manufacturing | Mechanics and equipment | 8.79 | 3,574.13 | 406.61 |
| Communication equipment, computer and other electronics manufacturing | Mechanics and equipment | 8.79 | 5,722.11 | 650.98 |
| Apparatus and stationary manufacturing | Mechanics and equipment | 8.79 | 733.19 | 83.41 |
| Handicraft making | Other goods and services | 4.13 | 570.83 | 138.22 |
| Recycling | Other goods and services | 4.13 | 59.93 | 14.51 |

Continued

| Industry | Corresponding industry | PPP ( ¥/ $ ) | Added value by traditional method (RMB 100 million) | PPP - based added value (USD 100million) |
|---|---|---|---|---|
| The sum of the manufacturing industry | | | | 12, 247. 32 |
| Electricity & heat production and provision | Water & gas & electricity, other energies | 3. 37 | 5, 719. 79 | 1, 697. 27 |
| Gas production and provision | Water & gas & electricity, other energies | 3. 37 | 134. 52 | 39. 92 |
| Water production and provision | Water & gas & electricity, other energies | 3. 37 | 261. 64 | 77. 64 |
| The sum of public utility industry | | | | 12, 247. 32 |

Source: authors' calculation.

**Table 6: PPP-based Industrial Structure: 2000 – 2009 (%)**

| Year | Primary industry | | Secondary industry | | Tertiary industry | |
|---|---|---|---|---|---|---|
| | Traditional approach | PPP approach | Traditional approach | PPP approach | Traditional approach | PPP approach |
| 2000 | 15. 06 | 10. 34 | 45. 92 | 46. 00 | 39. 02 | 43. 66 |
| 2001 | 14. 39 | 9. 98 | 45. 05 | 45. 62 | 40. 46 | 44. 40 |
| 2002 | 13. 74 | 9. 66 | 44. 79 | 45. 65 | 41. 47 | 44. 69 |
| 2003 | 12. 80 | 9. 26 | 45. 97 | 46. 51 | 41. 23 | 44. 23 |
| 2004 | 13. 39 | 7. 63 | 46. 23 | 37. 27 | 40. 38 | 55. 11 |
| 2005 | 12. 12 | 6. 96 | 47. 37 | 38. 69 | 40. 51 | 54. 35 |
| 2006 | 11. 11 | 6. 52 | 47. 95 | 39. 81 | 40. 94 | 53. 67 |
| 2007 | 10. 77 | 6. 44 | 47. 34 | 40. 15 | 41. 89 | 53. 41 |
| 2008 | 10. 73 | 6. 05 | 47. 45 | 37. 72 | 41. 82 | 56. 23 |
| 2009 | 10. 35 | 5. 04 | 46. 30 | 32. 53 | 43. 36 | 62. 43 |

Note: In 2008 and 2009, the added value by traditional method is the authors' estimation based on previous data.
Source: authors' calculation.

### (III) China's Secondary Industry Could Take Up a Higher Proportion

According to the above data, the proportion of China's secondary industry of GDP is not as high as assumed. From 2000 to 2009, its proportion on the whole was decreasing, down to 32.53% in 2009. According to Chen et al (2007). China is in the middle-late stage of industrialization when agriculture's proportion will decrease and the secondary industry's will increase. In addition, according to the report by the United Nations Industrial Development Organization, per capita output of China is still lower than the world's level. Similar conclusions could also be made from other comparisons. Observing Japan and Germany's industrial path, there is space for higher proportion of China's secondary industry. China's per capita GDP in 2010 stood at a mere USD 4, 254 (by the current exchange rate) and only USD 8, 000 when calculated by PPP, accounting for only 20% of Japan's per capita GDP in 2000 and 30% of Germany's per capita GDP in 2000. Japan's secondary industry took up 45.3% of its GDP in 1970, its highest proportion ever; and Germany's secondary industry in 1970 accounted for an even bigger 48.1%.

Considering the relationship between industrial structure and per capita GDP, the proportion of China's manufacturing in GDP is minuscule. China should now change focus toward the sustainability of growth in the real economy and ways to increase the global competitiveness of its secondary industry and primarily the manufacturing sector. The question remains of how to upgrade China's secondary industry.

## IV. Does China's Industrial Structure Reflect Its Comparative Advantage?

### (I) China's Comparative Advantage in Labor Will Continue

Despite a sharp increase in China's per capita capital inputs, its comparative advantage still lies in labor. Since 1949, China's savings rate has been high especially so after the pro market reforms of 1978. A curb in population growth and a booming economy have dramatically raised China's per capita capital. Based on other scholars' research, we estimated the changes in China's capital stock since 1978: its capital stock in 2008 is 28.25 times[①] that of 1978 (price changes considered). Since the population of China's labor market in 2008 was only 1.93 times that of 1978, the per capita capital in 2008 was 14.6 times that of 1978. According to OECD statistics, capital stock of the U.S. in 2007 was 2.1 times that of 1978 (price changes considered) and its per capita capital in 2007 was 1.4 times that of 1978. That is, China's per capita capital enjoyed faster growth than the U.S.'s by almost 10 times. Some scholars analyzed the changes in proportion of China's factors of production in the world. Table 7 shows that China's investment and R&D expenditure have increased enormously, but compared with other countries, labor remains the most abundant factor of production in China.

---

① The estimated figure though is subject to different scholars, is within the range of 20 – 30, and the little variation will not affect this paper's result. The estimation was based on the research done by He and Zhao in 2009.

**Table 7: The Proportion of China's Major Factors of Production in the World (%)**

| Year | Labor | Arable land and water | Oil and gas | Volume of investment | R&D expenditure |
|---|---|---|---|---|---|
| 1980 | 22 | 7 | 3 | 1 | 0.5 |
| 2004 | 22 | 7 | 3 | 8 | 3.5 |
| 2011 | 22 | 7 | 3 | 22 | 12.9 |

Source: data for 1980 and 2004 from *China's Economic Opening-Up and Expansion* 1980 – 2005, written by Jiang Xiaojuan etc, published by People's Publishing House; data for 2007 and 2011 from the authors' estimation; all R&D expenditure data from Battelle Memorial Institute.

The constant accumulation of China's per capita capital will surely change China's comparative advantage. Globally speaking, though China's labor-intensive industry still enjoys most comparative advantages, the advantages are diminishing while comparative advantage in the country's capital-intensive industry is on the rise. The Institute of Industrial Economics of China's Academy of Social Science began its research on the global competitiveness of China's industries. According to the latest findings, China is undergoing industrial upgrading, and its competitiveness is moving from labor-intensive to capital-intensive industry, but China is still most competitive in the labor-intensive industry which gives full play of its comparative advantage in labor.

It is worth mentioning that it is the capital stock, not capital flow (the yearly net investment), that plays the key role in social-economic development. In 2011, though China's per capita investment volume equaled that of the world average, its per capita capital stock would lag behind the world's average. We estimate that China's per capita capital stock in 2015 will be 2 – 2.5 times that of 2009, which will reduce China's comparative advantage in labor-intensive industries and increase its comparative advantage in capital-intensive industries. Yet as measured against other countries, China's comparative advantage will still lie in labor-intensive industries. Therefore, to upgrade China's industry will require making the best use of China's comparative advantage in labor-intensive areas.

### (II) China's Industrial Restructuring Should Follow the Law of Comparative Advantage

Whether China has followed the law of comparative advantage in the past 30 years depends on which industry developed faster, the labor-intensive or the capital-intensive. Thus, we re-defined the measurement of a country's labor intensity:

Labor intensity of one industry = 1/the proportion of this industry's output × per capita asset of this industry. The per capita asset of an industry was calculated based on data from China's 2008 economic census instead of the yearly data so as to remove the effect that per-capita assets usually appreciate during economic growth. To better compare yearly labor intensity, we indexed each year's labor intensity against 2009.

$$\text{Labor intensity index of a year} = \text{labor intensity of this year/labor intensity of year 2009} \times 100 \quad (1)$$

Traditionally, labor intensity was calculated after an industry was first categorized as labor-intensive or capital-intensive. The labor intensity index in this paper, compared with the traditional method, has the following two advantages:

First, this new method requires no classification of labor-intensive or capital-intensive, which used to be based on per capital fixed asset (Jiang, 2007) or per capita capital (Li, 2009). But the determination of the demarcation point suffers from subjectivity. The common practice is to use the industry's average for demarcation (Jin etc, 2011). Some scholars also proposed demarcation only when the data complies with some kinds of distribution, usually normal distribution (Li, 2009).

Second, this index can better reflect labor intensity changes. This new method will not only demonstrate the changes in the ratio of labor-intensity industry to capital-intensive industry, but could also reflect the changes within each industry. For example, presuming A and B both belong to the labor-intensive industry and A has smaller per capita capital than B (i. e. A is more labor-intensive). If the proportion of A and B combined stays the same while A's proportion increases and B's decreases during two years, the labor-intensity will remain unchanged by the old method while it will show decline by this index.

The rise and fall of the labor intensity index shows the correspondent increases/decreases of an industry's labor intensity. From Figure 2, it is evident that China's labor intensity has been in decline from 109 in 1986 to 100 in 2009. Regardless of possible inaccuracies caused by the data collected, this figure still reflects the general trend in China's labor-intensive industry evolution. Figure 2 shows that from 1986 to 2005, labor intensity was decreasing while from 2005 to 2009 it was increasing.

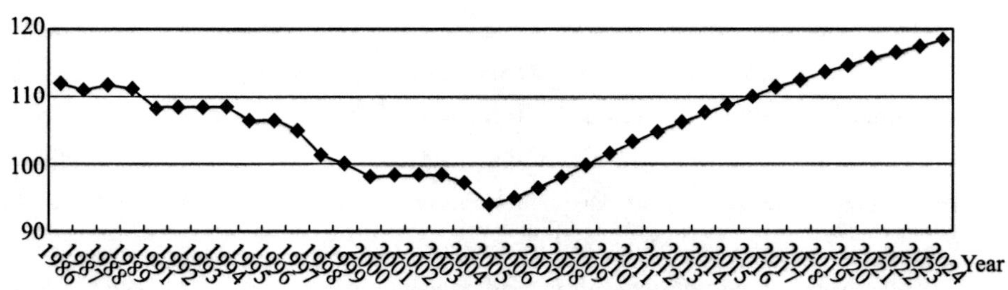


**Figure 2: The Industrial Labor Intensity Index of China from 1986 to 2014**

Note: data before 2009 were calculated by equation (1), data after 2009 were estimated.
Source: the authors' calculation

It is safe to say that China's decreasing labor-intensive industries before 2005 complied with economic theories, yet how is the decrease before 2005 explained? One justification may be that before 2005, China's capital market regulation restrained China's interest rate below the equilibrium level, which led capital-intensive industries to expand faster than labor-intensive industries. Since 2005, with accelerated marketization and World Trade Organization entry, China's industrial restructuring has followed the law of comparative advantage more closely and labor-intensive industries grew more rapidly than capital-intensive industries.

### (III) China's Economy Will Continue to Follow the Law of Comparative Advantage

Since 2005, it is justifiable to say that China has followed the law of comparative advantage; but will China continue this course? In August 2010, the research team for this paper distributed questionnaires to 1, 338 enterprises covering different industries in various regions. Based on data from the survey, we used the Markov matrix to predict China's future industrial structure. Resource-intensive industries are declining while labor-intensive industries are increasing. We calculated China's labor intensity from 2010 to 2024 (Figure 2). This upward trend is in line with the above prediction that China's comparative advantage will continue to be positioned in labor-intensive industries.

## V. Conclusions and Policy Recommendations

As each country faces its own unique conditions, it is unwise to formulate industrial policy based on the experience of other developed countries. The following observations are presented:

(1) Though the tertiary industry in developed countries enjoy higher added value than the secondary industry, its productivity normally is lower than that of the secondary industry. When the economy slows, the productivity of the secondary industry will drop faster than that of the tertiary industry. In economic growth periods, the productivity of the secondary industry will increase faster than that of the tertiary industry. Therefore, lower productivity within the secondary industry is generally a sign preceding an economic downturn.

(2) A higher proportion of the tertiary industry in developed countries neither signals the direction of industrial improvements nor proves the superiority of the tertiary industry over the secondary industry. Even though developed countries maintain greater tertiary industries, their final consumption of secondary industry products have not shown noticeable reductions. Larger tertiary industries are built upon prosperous world trade and the booming secondary industries in developing countries. Accordingly, with the current technologic and economic development, the world will not be able to sustain a meaningfully larger tertiary industry. Given that the tertiary industry in developed countries expanded at the cost of distorted prices between secondary industry and tertiary industry products, if the secondary industry products are priced much higher, the secondary industry will take up a much bigger proportion.

(3) China's industrial structure, which is newly calculated based on PPP, shows that the proportion of China's secondary industry stands at a modest 32. 53%. We argue that China's secondary industry has ample room to grow and should continue to be developed. Xu Zhaoyuan (2010) pointed out that the proportion of China's service industry as a proportion of its GDP from 1990 to 2005 jumped 8. 5 percentage points calculated by current price but decreased 5 percentage points by constant price; the proportion of China's secondary industry during the same period increased by 5. 5

percentage points by current price while decreasing by 25.2 percentage points by current price. This paper shows that the proportion of China's secondary industry will be smaller when calculated by PPP. These seemingly contradictory results advise that the industrial structure differs when calculated by different price systems. The PPP-based method in nature used The U. S.'s 2005 price system which equals China's would-be 2040 price system; while the Xu's research employed China's 1990 price system. The Institute of Industrial Economics recently predicted China's industrial structure based on CGS model. The result shows that the proportion of China's tertiary industry in 2050 will stand at 54% when the constant price in 2005 is adopted, but the figure will reach 73% when the price factor is considered. That is to say that the higher tertiary industry is not a result of faster growth but from price changes. Consequently, China will still rely on its secondary industry for economic growth.

(4) China witnessed much higher per capita capital stock, changing quantity of factors of endowment, diminishing comparative advantage in labor-intensive industries and increasing comparative advantage in capital-intensive industries. However, China's factors of endowment have not changed in quality and China will lag behind the world in per capita capital. It is predicted that in the 12th Five Year Period (2011 – 2015), China's labor-intensive industries will hold the largest comparative advantage and the greatest global competitiveness. Based on data collected and the Markov matrix, it is predicted that by 2025, China's economic development will be in line with the law of comparative advantage and China's labor-intensive industries will experience even faster growth.

## References

1. Jin, Bei, Tie Lu, and Xiaohua Li. 2010. "On Some Problems Concerning Industrial Restructuring." *Economic Perspectives*, (8).

2. Lv, Tie. 2007. "China's Industrial Technology Innovation and Korean Experience." *Journal of the Party School of the Central Committee of the C. P. C.* (9).

3. Li, Ping, and Hongguang Sui. 2008. "Three Kinds of Capacity for Indigenous Innovation and Technology Progress." *Journal of World Economy*, (2).

4. Li, Gang. 2009. "China's Path Towards Industrial Upgrading within the Dual Sector Model." Economic Restructuring (5).

5. Li, Gang, Bei Jin, and Minjie Dong. 2009. "The Basic Judgment of China's Manufacturing Industry." *Review of Economic Research*, (41).

6. Li, Gang, and Yongmei Liang. 2010. "What is the Change of Economic Development Model." *Economic & Trade Herald*, (4).

7. Li, Gang, and Jianhui Liao. 2011. "Study on the Clustering of Provincial Industries and its Evolving in Time and Space." *Economic Management*, (7).

8. Ma, Xiaohe. 2011. "Furthering the Development of China's Service Industry." *China Development Observation*, (6).

9. Huang, Zhigang. 2008. "Industrial Restructuring, Economic Restructuring and the Chan-

ges of Economic Development Model." *Economic Affairs*, (6).

10. The Project on Economics undertaken by China's Academy of Social Science. 2007. China's Entry into the Other Phase of Industrialization: Comments and Analysis on China's Industrialization from 1995 to 2005, *China's Academy of Social Science Journal* (9).

11. Xu, Zhaoyuan. 2010. *Factors Affecting China's Industrial Restructuring and International Experiences*. Beijing: The Development Center of China's State Council.

# Chapter 18

# Technology Gaps, Resource Allocation and Economic Growth of Large Late-starting Countries*

**Ouyang Yao (欧阳峣), Yi Xianzhong (易先忠) and Sheng Yanchao (生延超)**

**Research Center for Large Country Economies, Hunan University of Commerce, Changsha, China**

**Abstract**: In the evolution of economic growth drivers, technology gaps are a key variable that determines the efficiency of resource allocation. Analysis of an optimal resource allocation path based on an extended endogenous growth model reveals that economic growth drivers evolve from productive investment to R&D investment and a shift from imitation to innovation. Empirical analysis based on China's provincial-level panel data suggests that the effect of productive investment and R&D investment, as well as innovation and imitation, on economic growth and technological progress varies greatly among regions of disparate technology levels. As a late-starting country, China should properly allocate resources between productive investment and R&D investment, and between imitational investment and innovative investment while advancing the transformation of economic growth patterns on a differentiated basis in light of regional technology disparities.

**Keywords**: Economic growth, technology gaps, indigenous innovation, late-starting country

## I. Introduction

Since adopting the strategy of building an "innovation-oriented country" in 2005, China has made great headway in both R&D investment and output and expedited the transition from "investment-driven" to "innovation-driven" economic growth. However, most of China's technological progress still relies on the acquisition of foreign technologies and productive investment remains the

* Corresponding author: Ouyangyao008@163.com.

main driver of economic growth (Zhang, Liu 2007). This reality forces us to further think about the relationship between imitation and innovation as two basic options of technological progress, together with the relationship between productive investment and R&D investment.

Actually, most enterprises in developing countries do not have R&D departments, as they feel pressured to devote already limited resources to productive activities. Indeed, a proper balance has to be struck between R&D investment and productive investment for late-starting countries (Zhang *et al.*, 2006). This raises the issue of the relationship between innovation and imitation. On the one hand, the positive effect of technology acquisition and imitation has been recognized by the theory of "late starter's advantage". For developing countries with limited R&D resources, their gaps of economic development with developed countries can be narrowed by acquisition and imitation of advanced foreign technologies alone (Grossman and Helpman, 1990; Helpman and Hoffmaister, 1997; Keller, 2004). On the other hand, developed countries are taking advantage of international IPR protection protocols and high-tech export restrictions, and these technology barriers prevent developing countries from realizing their late starter's advantage (Yang and Maskus, 2011). Moreover, international experience also suggests that most developing countries failed to achieve "economic catch-up" predicted by new growth theory through "late starter's advantage", and that technology imitation alone cannot help achieve such catch-up (Yi and Zhang, 2007). The key to transforming economic growth pattern is the transition from technology acquisition and imitation to indigenous innovation (Zhang, 2003). As for how to achieve such a transition, Currie *et al.* (1999) made preliminary discussions on the transition of late starting countries from imitation to innovation and believe that the pattern of technological progress and its evolving trend are subject to the level of difficulty for imitation, as well as knowledge capital stock per person. However, there is no mention about the limitation of R&D resources and the impact of technology gaps on the pattern of technological progress. According to the research of Lai *et al.* (2009), Yi (2010), and Ji and Zhu (2011), technology gaps are an important factor affecting the acquisition and imitation of foreign technologies and thus technology catch-up. Rachel (1996) believes that differences in technological capabilities and opportunities deriving from technology gaps are also important factors affecting the transition from imitation to innovation. Therefore, investments in innovation and imitation should be balanced in light of technology gaps.

Both the technology gap theory represented by Fagerberg (1987) and the South-North technology dispersion model represented by Barro and Sala-i-Martin (1997) and Grossman and Helpman (1990) failed to explore whether the technological progress of late-starting countries under different technology levels and factors mainly derives from the imitation of foreign technologies or indigenous innovation. Most studies have neglected the innovation capabilities of late-starting countries and have not discussed the relationship between indigenous innovation and technology imitation and the distribution of resources between them. In the depiction of technological progress, existing studies tend to examine the positive effect of a single factor (such as human capital) on technological progress, and yet technological progress entails not only human capital but material capital as well. This requires that sufficient consideration be given to both the allocation of R&D resources between innovation and imitation and the allocation of limited financial resources between productive investment and R&D investment. Given the inadequacies of existing studies, this paper adopts an R&D-based endogenous growth model with indigenous innovation and imitation of foreign technologies as endogenous factors. It extends the single factor of technology function in a conventional South-North technology dispersion model to the technology production function with dual factor input of material capital and human capital for the analysis of optimal allocation of financial resources between productive investment and R&D investment, together with the optimal allocation of R&D resources between indigenous innovation and foreign imitation. These analyses will provide additional inputs to the theory of economic growth transformation.

## II. Theoretical Analysis

Assuming that the production function of final product sector of a late-starting country is in Cobb-Douglas format with fixed return to scale: $Y = A(uH)^{\alpha}K^{1-\alpha}(0<\alpha<1)$. Where, $Y$ is total product and production inputs are material capital$K$ and human capital $H$, and$A$ denotes technology factor for the evaluation of a country's technology level; $u$ is the share of aggregate human capital employed for the production of final products. In this model, we categorize R&D departments into ($I$) innovation sector and (c) imitation sector, with $R_I$ and $R_C$ respectively denoting material capital invested in these two departments; $H_I$ and $H_C$ respectively denoting the human capital invested in these two departments. The following is the equation for the accumulation of material capital:

$$\dot{K} = Y - C - R_I - R_C - \delta K \tag{1}$$

Equation for human capital accumulation:

$$\dot{H} = B\left[(1-u)H - H_I - H_C\right] \tag{2}$$

Where, $B$ is positive efficiency parameter, $\delta$ is capital depreciation rate, and $0<\delta<1$, without taking into account human capital depreciation. Technology production no longer uses single-factor (human capital) as depicted by Romer (1990), Grossman and Helpman (1990) and Fidel Perez-Sebastian (2000) but two factors of material and human capital. In this paper, the word "imitation" means imitative innovation through such means as "reverse engineering", which requires the input of material capital and human capital all the same. $A^*$ is assumed to be foreign technology factor, whose growth rate $g_{A^*}=b$ is given endogenously and foreign countries are assumed to possess superior technologies against technology gaps existing between late-starting countries and advanced countries, $A<A^*$. Dynamic equation of technological progress in late-starting countries can be expressed as:

$$\dot{A} = \mu A^{\phi}\left[R_I^{\lambda}H_I^{\omega} + \left(\frac{\eta A^*}{A}\right)^{\beta} R_C^{\lambda}H_C^{\omega}\right] \tag{3}$$

Where, $\beta>0$, $0<\lambda+\omega<1$, $0<\phi<1$; $0<\eta<1$. $0<\phi<1$ indicates the existence of cross-phase knowledge spillover and diminishing technology opportunities; $0<\eta<1$ denotes that some foreign technologies are so complicated that imitation is prohibited by cost or difficult; $\frac{\eta A^*}{A}$ measures effective technology gaps, which are assumed to be $\frac{\eta A^*}{A} > 1$. The front part to the right of bracket in equation (3) $R_I^{\lambda} H_I^{\omega}$ denotes the technology production of innovative sectors and the rear part denotes the technology production of imitative sectors. Profitability of imitation is in direct proportion to technology gaps, i. e. the greater that technology gaps are, the more technologies there are available for imitation, and the less costly and more efficient for the imitation. With increasing technology levels of late-starting countries, fewer and fewer technologies there are available to be imitated and the profitability of imitation declines. Under the condition that $\frac{\eta A^*}{A} > 1$ and with the same level of R&D investment, imitation leads to the creation of a higher number of technologies than does innovation, resulting in the late starting advantage. Consequently, the rate of technological progress is higher in late starting countries compared to advanced countries, $g_{A^*} < g_A$.

With $C$ defined as the consumption level of representative consumers, the problem for central planners is to maximize the lifelong utility level for representative consumers through selection of optimal paths of $C(t)$, $R_I(t)$, $R_C(t)$, $H_I(t)$, $H_C(t)$ and $u$, so that problem can be described as:

$$\max_{\{C,R_I,R_C,H_I,H_C,u\}} \int_0^{\infty} \frac{C^{1-\sigma} - 1}{1 - \sigma} e^{-\rho t} dt$$

$$\begin{aligned} s.t. \quad & Y = A(uH)^{\alpha} K^{1-\alpha} \\ & \dot{K} = Y - C - R_I - R_C - \delta K \\ & \dot{H} = B[(1-u)H - H_I - H_C] \\ & \dot{A} = \mu A^{\phi}\left[R_I^{\lambda} H_I^{\omega} + \left(\frac{\eta A^*}{A}\right)^{\beta} R_C^{\lambda} H_C^{\omega}\right] \\ & \frac{\dot{A}^*}{A^*} = b \end{aligned}$$

Where, $\sigma$ is the cross-phase constant elasticity of substitution, and $\rho$ is discount rate, $0 < \rho < 1$. In addition, the model's variables should meet the constraint of inequality $H_I + H_C < (1 - u) H$. The problem of optimality includes three state variables of $K(t)$, $A(t)$, $H(t)$ and six control variables of $C$, $R_I$, $R_C$, $H_I$, $H_C$, $u$. The present value Hamilton function is defined according to preconfigured model to calculate optimal conditions and the Eula equation. Based on an equivalent marginal output of material capital and human capital in innovation and imitation, the optimal ratio of material capital and human capital allocation between the two types of R&D activity-innovation and imitation-can be calculated:

$$\frac{H_I}{H_C} = \frac{R_I}{R_C} = \left(\frac{\eta A^*}{A}\right)^{\frac{\beta}{(\lambda+\omega-1)}} \tag{4}$$

It can be seen from equation (4) that the optimal ratio of R&D resources allocation between innovation and imitation is subject to the technology gaps between late-starting countries and countries with superior technologies, i. e. $T\left(T = \frac{\eta A^*}{A}\right)$. Considering that $0 < \lambda + \omega < 1$ and $\beta > 0$, the greater technology gaps ($T$), the smaller ratio of resource allocation between innovation and imitation; the smaller technology gaps ($T$), the higher this ratio appears. The reason is that when there are significant technology disparities between late-starting countries and foreign countries, late-starting countries will face more opportunities of imitation with relatively high efficiency, so that allocation of resources to imitation sectors will yield a higher rate of technological progress. As technology gaps narrow, late-starting countries will gradually have fewer opportunities of imitation, making imitation more costly and less efficient. In this case, innovation then becomes more efficient, which justifies the higher proportion of capital to innovation sectors and lower proportion of capital to imitation sectors.

Assume $R = R_I + R_C$, which indicates aggregate material capital investment for R&D; and that $H_0 = H_I + H_C$, which denotes aggregate human capital investment for R&D.

$$\dot{A} = \mu A^{\phi} R^{\lambda} H_0^{\omega} \left(1 + T^{\frac{\beta}{(1-\lambda-\omega)}}\right)^{1-(\lambda+\omega)} \tag{5}$$

Equation (5) is employed to create a new Hamilton function. According to optimal conditions, the dynamic path of material capital invested in R&D under optimal conditions can be calculated:

$$\frac{\dot{R}}{R} = r - \lambda \frac{Y\dot{A}}{RA} - \frac{\dot{A}}{A}\left(\phi - \beta + \frac{\beta}{1 + T^{\frac{\beta}{(1-\lambda-\omega)}}}\right) + \frac{\frac{\mathrm{d}\dot{A}}{\mathrm{d}t}}{\dot{A}} \tag{6}$$

It can be known from Equation (6) that there is a negative correlation between material capital invested in R&D and technology gaps. With the marginal productivity of human capital in final product sectors defined as $\varepsilon$ and substituting $\varepsilon$ into production function gives us $\varepsilon = \alpha A u^{\alpha} H^{\alpha-1} K^{1-\alpha}$. Dynamic path of human capital invested in R&D under optimal conditions can be arrived at according to the optimal conditions of the Hamilton function:

$$\frac{\dot{H}_0}{H_0} = \varepsilon \frac{\lambda B H_0}{\omega R} - r + \frac{\dot{R}}{R} + B(1-u) \tag{7}$$

It can be known from Equation (7) that there is a negative correlation between human capital invested in R&D and technology gaps. Given that the growth rates of variables are all constants under equilibrium, it can be known from equation (1) that under an equilibrium growth path: $g_K^* = g_C^* = g_Y^* = g_R^* = g_{R_I}^* = g_{R_C}^*$; equation (2) derives $g_H^* = g_{H_I}^* = g_{H_C}^* = g_{H_0}^*$; and equation (5) derives $g_A^* = g_{A^*}^*$, where $T*$ is a constant. The growth rate under equilibrium conditions can be calculated to be:

$$g_K^* = g_C^* = g_Y^* = g_R^* = g_{R_I}^* = g_{R_C}^* = \frac{\left(\frac{\omega}{\alpha} - \phi + 1\right)b}{(\lambda + \omega)} \tag{8}$$

$$g_H^* = g_{H_I}^* = g_{H_C}^* = g_{H_0}^* = \frac{\left(-\frac{\lambda}{\alpha} - \phi + 1\right)b}{(\lambda + \omega)} \tag{9}$$

Share of total material capital invested in R&D sectors under equilibrium conditions:

$$S_R^* = \left(\frac{R}{Y}\right)^* = \frac{\lambda b}{\rho + \frac{\beta b T^{*\frac{B}{(1-\lambda-w)}}}{1 + T^{*\frac{B}{(1-\lambda-w)}}} + \frac{b}{\lambda+\omega}\left[(\sigma-1)\frac{\omega}{\alpha} + (\sigma+\lambda+\omega-1)(1-\phi)\right]} \tag{10}$$

Under equilibrium, the optimal share of total human capital invested in sectors of final product manufacturing $u^*$ is:

$$u^* = \frac{(B - g_H^*)\lambda\alpha}{B\omega S_R^*\left(B + \frac{\lambda\alpha}{\omega S_R^*}\right)} \quad (11)$$

Under equilibrium, the optimal share of total human capital invested in R&D sector $v^*$ is:

$$v^* = \frac{(B - g_H^*)\omega S_R^*}{(\omega S_R^* B + \lambda\alpha)} \quad (12)$$

Where, $S_R^*$ is given by equation (10) and $g_H^*$ is given by equation (9). In addition, equation (10) has $\frac{dS_R^*}{dT^*} < 0$, i. e. the share of material capital invested in R&D is a decreasing function of technology gaps, which is consistent with the empirical conclusions of Zhang Yabin *et al.* (2006). According to equations (10) and (12), $\frac{dv^*}{dT^*} < 0$. On the other hand, $\frac{du^*}{dT^*} = -\frac{dv^*}{dT^*} > 0$, i. e. the share of human capital invested in the manufacturing of final products under equilibrium conditions is an increasing function, while human capital invested in R&D is a decreasing function of technology gaps. In other words, under equilibrium conditions, technology gaps and the share of total resources invested in R&D sectors are in a negative relationship. The reason is that under significant technology gaps, productive investment has a higher contribution to economic growth compared with R&D investment. With the above calculations, we arrived at Proposition 1.

Proposition 1: optimal economic growth and technological progress can only be achieved by balancing productive investment with R&D investment and balancing imitative R&D investment with innovative R&D investment according to the level of technology disparities. R&D resources (including material capital and human capital) allocated by late-starting countries to R&D activities (including imitation and indigenous innovation) are in inverse proportion to technology gaps. With increasing levels of technology, drivers of economic growth tend to shift from productive investment to R&D investment and from imitation to innovation.

Shifting drivers of economic growth also suggest changing patterns of economic growth. According to Proposition 1, as international frontier technology gaps narrow, the growth drivers of late-starting countries will transition from productive investment to R&D investment and from imitation to innovation. Therefore, the priorities of economic growth policies should reflect such a tendency subject to the technology level. When technology gaps increase, the economic policy focus should reflect how limited resources must be employed in productive investment and imitational investment. When technology gaps narrow, indigenous innovation and R&D efficiency should top the policy agenda.

In the final analysis, technology policy exerts its impact on technological progress and economic growth through change of resource allocation. R&D policies (such as R&D allowances, tax and credit preferences, etc.) expedite the reallocation of resources from productive activities to R&D activities, while innovation policies divert R&D resources from imitational activities to innovational activities. It is assumed that the economy can swiftly respond to policies without any time lag. If the government takes vigorous policies to encourage R&D that lead to cost reductions, the expected profitability of R&D activities will increase and more resources will be diverted from productive activities to R&D activities. It can be deduced from technology growth equation $g_A = \mu A^{\phi - 1} R^{\lambda} H_0 \left(1 + T^{\frac{\beta}{(1-\lambda-\omega)}}\right)^{1-\lambda-\omega}$ that the technology growth rate will increase. In the short term, policy impact will not affect the technology growth rate under a long-term economic equilibrium or the growth rates of other economic variables. However, increasing the contribution of technological progress to output in the process of catch-up will reduce technology gaps under equilibrium conditions. Namely, R&D incentive policies will not generate a long-term growth effect and will only generate a leveling effect.

The process of economic adjustment can be described by changes in the contribution of technological progress to output and technology gaps. Given that in the process of economic catch-up of late-starting countries, $g_A > g_{A^*}$ and $\frac{\dot{T}}{T} = g_{A^*} - g_A < 0$, it can be known that technology gaps have a diminishing tendency in the dynamic process of transition and $\frac{dg_A}{dT} > 0$. Therefore, $g_A$ will keep decreasing until equilibrium $g_A^* = g_{A^*}^*$. After reaching equilibrium, the technology growth rate will remain constant and so will technology gaps. Economic movement from disequilibrium (time point 0) to equilibrium (time point $t*$) can be indicated by Figure 1 and Figure 2.

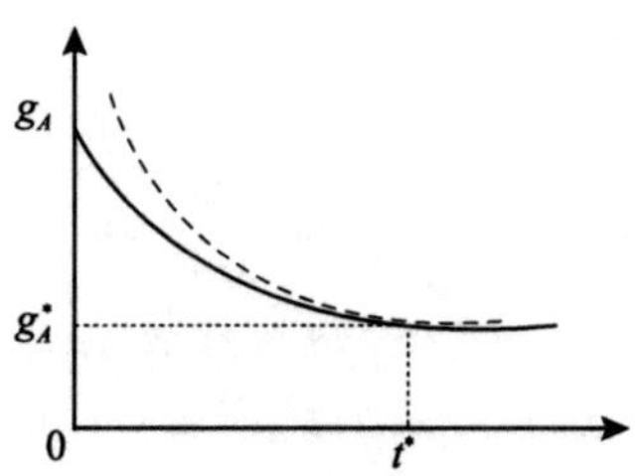


**Figure 1: Changes in Technology Growth Rate**

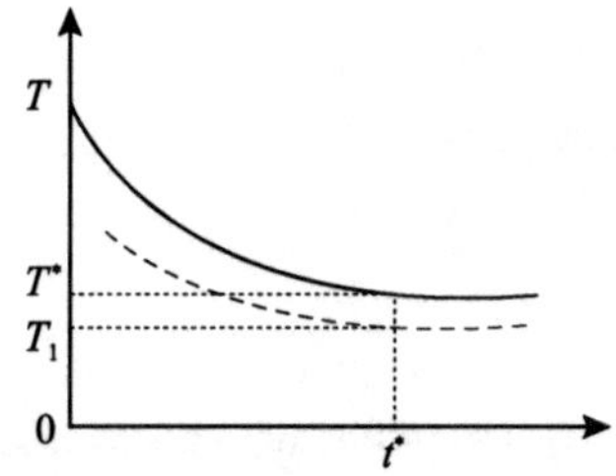


**Figure 2: Changes in Technology Gaps**

R&D incentive policies result in an increasing flow of economic resources to R&D sectors, so that the contribution of technological progress to output increases after the implementation of R&D policies, and converges at the point of equilibrium contribution of technological progress to output (represented by dotted lines of Figure 1). Technology gaps are no smaller at the inception of policy implementation than before the policy implementation. When the contribution of technological progress to output reaches equilibrium, technology gaps reduce to the level of $T_1$ (indicated by dotted lines of Figure 2). Therefore, from a long-term perspective, pro-R&D policies only have a leveling effect and will not affect the growth rate under economic equilibrium, i. e. no growth effect. Although the pro-R&D policies of late-starting countries have failed to increase the contribution of technological progress to output under equilibrium, they have narrowed the technology gaps with advanced countries.

The effect of deviations in the proportion of R&D resource allocation between imitation and innovation from optimal level is further examined. With initial status defined as $\frac{R_I}{R_C}=F_1$, $\frac{H_I}{H_C}=F_2$ and considering that $R=R_I+R_C$ and $H_0=H_I+H_C$, technology accumulation equation (3) can be converted into:

$$g_A=\mu A^{\phi-1}R^{\lambda}H_0^{w}(1+F_1)^{-\lambda}(1+F_2)^{-\omega}(F_1F_2^{w}+F^{*\lambda+w-1}) \quad (13)$$

For simplicity considerations, assuming that $F_2=F^*=T^{\frac{\beta}{(\lambda+\omega-1)}}$ is under optimal allocation status, we first examined the impact of $F_1$ as non-optimal allocation status on technological progress:

$$\frac{\partial g_A}{\partial F_1}=\lambda\mu A^{\phi-1}R^{\lambda}H_0^{w}(1+F_1)^{-\lambda}(1+F^*)^{-\omega}\frac{[(F_1^{\lambda-1}-F^{*\lambda-1})F^{*w}]}{(1+F_1)} \quad (14)$$

Given that $\lambda-1<0$, $sign\left(\frac{dg_A}{dF}\right)=sign\ (F_1^{\lambda-1}-F^{*\lambda-1})\ =sign\ (F^*-F_1)$, if initially $F_1>F^*$, then $\frac{\partial g_A}{\partial F}<0$; if initially, $F_1<F^*$, then $\frac{\partial g_A}{\partial F}>0$, and only when $F_1=F^*=T^{\frac{\beta}{(\lambda+\omega-1)}}$, i. e. allocation of material capital between imitation and innovation reaches the optimal proportion, the contribution of technological progress to output will be the highest. By the same token, similar conclusions can be drawn from the allocation of human capital. Only when $F_1=F_2=F^*$ will the contribution of technological progress to output become optimal. Deviations from optimal proportion of R&D resources allocation between imitation and innovation will result in decreased contribution of technological progress to output. Even within R&D sectors, any technological policies that lead to such deviations from optimal allocation proportion ($F*$) will inevitably diminish technological progress rate and thus widen technology gaps under equilibrium. With the above analysis, we have come up with Proposition 2.

Proposition 2: although pro-R&D policies adopted by late-starting countries have failed to increase the contribution of technological progress to output under equilibrium, they can reduce technology gaps with advanced countries. Any policies that result in deviations of R&D resources allocation between foreign imitation and indigenous innovation from optimal level (F *) will diminish technological progress rate and thus widen technology gaps under equilibrium.

Proposition 2 has the following strategic significance to the economic development of late-starting countries: in the short term, appropriate government incentives of R&D will contribute to economic catch-up. However, once incompatible with factor structure and the technology level, encouraging innovative investment increases the opportunity cost of exercising the late starter advantage, thereby slowing economic convergence.

## III. Empirical Analysis on China

The above theoretical analysis has led to the following key conclusions: the only way for late-starting countries to achieve optimal technological progress and economic growth is to strike a proper balance between productive investment and R&D investment, as well as between imitational R&D investment and innovative R&D investment. For late-starting countries, their economic growth drivers will shift from productive investment to R&D investment and from imitation to innovation. China is a large late-starting country with tremendous differences in regional factor endowment and technology disparities. According to the conclusions of theoretical analysis, there should be different drivers behind economic growth across regions with disparate technology levels. In order to verify this theoretical hypothesis, this part mainly conducts an empirical analysis on the impact of material capital allocation across Chinese regions with disparate technology levels on economic growth and technological progress.

Following the methodologies of Fagerberg (1994), Chen and Puttitanun (2005) and with an overall technology level represented by per capita GDP, overall regional technology disparities are represented by the ratios between actual per capita GDP across Chinese regions and the US actual per capita GDP. According to the level of technology, the 30 Chinese regions can be divided into two categories, and about 5% of the regions fall into the category of high-tech regions based on the ratio between actual per capita GDP of these regions and the US actual per capita GDP. These include nine municipalities/provinces of Beijing, Tianjin, Liaoning, Shanghai, Jiangsu, Zhejiang, Shandong, Fujian and Guangdong; and the remaining are low-technology regions. In order to take into account the different impact of productive investment and R&D investment across regions with varying technology levels on economic growth, we have constructed the following dynamic panel data model based on our theoretical analyses:

$$Lrjgdp_{i,t} = C + a_1 Lrjgdp_{i,(t-1)} + a_2 Lkjjfei_{i,t} + a_3 Lkjjfei_{i,(t-1)} + a_4 Ltuzi_{i,t} + a_5 Ltuzi_{i,(t-1)} + a_6 Ltrade_{i,t} + u_{i,t} \tag{15}$$

Where, *rjgdp* stands for economic growth with per capita GDP as substitute indicator. In order to exclude the impact of other factors on economic growth, we have included $rjgdp_{i,(t-1)}$ as per capita GDP during inception stage; *kjjfei* denotes total R&D material capital input with internal expenditure of technology funding as substitute indicator; *tuzi* denotes productive investment with fixed asset investment as substitute indicator. In order to examine the lagging effect of material capital investment and productive investment on economic growth, the lag phases of two variables are introduced. *trade* denotes trade openness, measured by the ratio between total import/export value and GDP. Given that trade openness is considered as an important means to promote economic growth of late-starting countries, it is included as a control variable.

In order to take into account the disparate impact of indigenous innovation and foreign imitation on technological progress across regions with different levels of technology, the following technological progress econometric model is configured based on theoretical analysis:

$$Lshchl_{i,t} = C + b_1 Lrd_{i,t} + b_2\ Lhh_{i,t} *\ Lim_{i,t} + b_3\ Lhh_{i,t} * Lfdi_{i,t} + u_{i,t} \qquad (16)$$

Where, *shchl* denotes technological progress with total labor productivity as substitute indicator, and total labor productivity is calculated by dividing actual GDP deflated with the base year of 2000 by the number of employees①; *rd* denotes indigenous innovation, measured by R&D expenditure②; *hh* denotes human capital with the number of scientists and engineers as substitute indicator; *hh * im* denotes the imitation of foreign technology through import of high-tech products and is represented by the interaction term between high-tech import and human capital; *hh * fdi* is the interaction term between human capital and *FDI* and indicates *FDI*'s technology spillover effect; $\mu_{i,,t}$ is error term; and *C* denotes intercept. Natural logarithms are calculated for variables and the interaction term is the product after calculating the logarithms.

Sample data are sourced from *China Technological Statistical Yearbook*, *China Statistical Yearbook* and *China Regional Economic Statistics Yearbook* for various years and China technology statistics website http: //www. sts. org. cn. The sample range is the data of 30 provincial-level regions of China between 2000 and 2007. In order to offset the impact of price factor, per capita GDP has been deflated using provincial GDP deflator; fixed asset investment, internal expenditure of technology funding, R&D expenditure, high-tech import and *FDI* are deflated using provincial fixed-asset investment indicators, with constant prices of 2000.

All data processing and model-based calculations in this paper are conducted using econometric software Stata10. 0. Before panel data analysis, the existence of level equation's fixed effect is verified through the Hausman test. Please refer to Table 1 for the regression results of the econometric model of economic growth. The fact that the Sargan statistic remains insignificant indicates that the selection of instrument variable is effective and that AR (1) test rejects original assumption while AR (2) test accepts original assumption (original assumption is the non-existence of serial correlation), which suggests non-correlation between residual series of original equation. Results of economic growth estimation suggest that technology gaps are indeed an important factor affecting the allocation of limited resources between R&D and productive activities.

According to Table 1, results of both approaches suggest disparate levels of effect on economic growth deriving from productive material capital investment and R&D material investment across regions of different technology levels. On a nationwide basis, the estimation results of both approaches all suggest that productive investment (*Ltuzi*) with fixed asset-investment as substitute indicator has

① Estimation of *TFP* varies greatly depending on the data employed and estimation methodology, and thus we did not include this indicator.

② It is difficult to find an indicator that fully captures technological innovation. Previous literature usually used R&D expenditure and new product output as indicators for the evaluation of technological innovation, yet these indicators are all subject to a certain extent of limitations. There are two problems for new product output to be technological innovation evaluation indicator: first, there is no strict definition of new products and some of new products cannot reflect technological innovation; second, technological innovation also includes process innovation, which cannot be reflected in new products. Therefore, we follow Ji Yahui *et al.* (2011)'s approach of using R&D expenditure to measure indigenous innovation.

a significant positive effect on economic growth, while technology funding that represents R&D material capital investment (*Lkjjfei*) has a positive yet insignificant effect in the GMM system estimation, while the elasticity coefficient of productive investment (*Ltuzi*) is higher than that of technology funding (*Lkjjfei*). This indicates that generally speaking, China's economic growth mainly relies on the increase of productive investments, which is consistent with the reality of China's current economic growth pattern. In high-tech regions, productive investment (*Ltuzi*) and current-phase R&D material capital investment (*Lkjjfei*) can have a significantly positive effect on economic growth. Increasing R&D investments in high-tech regions can drive technological progress and thereby promote economic growth. The implication is that in the technologically advanced regions of China, with the increase of capital stock per person and under the effect of "marginal diminishing return to capital investment" as demonstrated in neoclassical growth theories, the positive effect of long-term productive investment on economic growth will diminish, and economic growth drivers will evolve from the quantitative increase of factors to the efficiency gains stemming from technological progress. In low-tech regions, however, current-phase and one-phase-lag R&D investment has an insignificant effect on economic growth while productive investment has a significantly positive effect on economic growth with an obvious lagging effect. The message is that in low-tech regions, allocation of limited resources to productive activities has a more positive effect on economic growth. Still, in the early stages of economic upsurge and industrialization, China's low-tech regions are far from developing a sophisticated factor structure and advanced technologies. However, in these low-tech regions, capital intensification has a significantly positive effect on economic growth, which still relies on increase of the input of conventional factors, particularly increase of the input of productive material capital. As a matter of fact, R&D investment is inconsistent with the factor structure characteristics of China's low-tech regions. In these low-tech regions, massive R&D investments regardless of the reality of factor mix may not be conducive to optimal allocation of resources and would actually impede economic growth.

**Table 1: Results of Economic Growth Regression**

| *Lrjgdp* | The whole country | | Hi – tech regions | | Low – tech regions | |
|---|---|---|---|---|---|---|
| | FE | One – step GMM | FE | One – step GMM | FE | One – step GMM |
| *Lrjgdp* (*t* – 1) | 0.809*** (10.19) | 0.732*** (5.82) | 0.419** (3.30) | 0.327* (2.74) | 0.950*** (5.21) | 0.913*** (5.17) |
| *Lkjjfei* | 0.057* (2.37) | 0.008 (0.16) | 0.089* (2.19) | 0.013** (3.27) | 0.042 (1.30) | –0.040 (–1.16) |
| *Lkjjfei* (*t* – 1) | 0.017 (0.91) | –0.010 (–0.32) | 0.021 (0.56) | –0.018 (–0.39) | 0.012 (0.49) | 0.012 (0.31) |
| *Ltuzi* | 0.039*** (3.55) | 0.068** (2.40) | 0.161*** (4.21) | 0.092* (2.39) | 0.0216 (1.51) | 0.034* (2.68) |

Continued

| *Lrjgdp* | The whole country | | Hi - tech regions | | Low - tech regions | |
|---|---|---|---|---|---|---|
| | FE | One - step GMM | FE | One - step GMM | FE | One - step GMM |
| *Ltuzi* (*t* - 1) | 0.044** (3.25) | 0.020*** (3.73) | 0.035 (0.85) | 0.034 (0.60) | 0.028** (2.70) | 0.034*** (6.17) |
| *Ltrade* | 0.005 (0.74) | 0.002 (0.12) | 0.029 (1.93) | 0.043* (1.87) | 0.001 (0.12) | 0.025** (3.16) |
| *C* | -0.770*** (-3.50) | - | -1.846*** (-4.16) | - | -0.433* (-2.43) | - |
| *Adjust* - $R^2$ | 0.945 | 0.844 | 0.456 | 0.397 | 0.909 | 0.748 |
| F test | 854.18 [0.000] | 811.01 [0.000] | 562.46 [0.000] | 896.54 [0.000] | 345.82 [0.000] | 278.09 [0.000] |
| Arellano - Bond AR (1) | - | -1.89 [0.059] | - | -1.99 [0.046] | - | -2.48 [0.013] |
| Arellano - Bond AR (2) | - | 0.13 [0.898] | - | 0.30 [0.767] | - | 0.08 [0.935] |
| Sargan test | - | 19.71 [0.539] | - | 11.32 [0.333] | - | 13.11 [0.665] |

Note: number in the round bracket indicates t value of Heteroskedasticity robustness standard error; ***, ** and * respectively denote significance levels at 1%, 5% and 10%, and number in square bracket [ ] is p value.

In order to further illustrate the impact of technology gaps on innovation and imitation, we have estimated the econometric model (16) of technological progress, with results shown in Table 2. *Davidson-MacKinnon* test indicates that the variable of indigenous innovation (*Lrd*) measured by R&D expenditure indeed has the problem of endogeny, i. e. indigenous R&D investments are high in high-tech regions. The insignificance of the Sargan statistic indicates that using the lag phase of *Lrd* as instrument variable is valid and that estimated panel data model provides a roughly accurate revelation that in regions of different technology levels, indigenous innovation and foreign imitation have different levels of contribution to technological progress.

**Table 2: Results of Technological Progress Regression**

| *Lshchl* | The whole country | | Hi-tech regions | | Low-tech regions | |
|---|---|---|---|---|---|---|
| | FE | FE_IV | FE | FE_IV | FE | FE_IV |
| *Lrd* | 0.058 (1.04) | 0.083 (0.70) | 0.338*** (7.58) | 0.385*** (7.62) | 0.053 (1.00) | 0.042 (1.09) |
| *Lhh*Lim* | 0.087*** (6.03) | 0.069** (2.70) | 0.040*** (4.09) | 0.014 (0.91) | 0.070*** (3.97) | 0.072*** (2.46) |
| *Lhh*Lfdi* | 0.001 (0.21) | 0.006 (0.93) | -0.018** (-3.52) | -0.010 (-1.29) | 0.008 (0.80) | 0.010 (1.36) |
| *C* | -0.263* (-2.37) | — | 0.041 (0.26) | — | -0.288* (-2.17) | — |
| *Adjust-$R^2$* | 0.481 | 0.436 | 0.204 | 0.327 | 0.453 | 0.376 |
| *Hausman test* | 48.37 [0.000] | — | 11.1 [0.011] | — | 10.50 [0.015] | — |
| *F test* | 60.66 [0.000] | 12.62 [0.000] | 81.15 [0.000] | 47.72 [0.000] | 44.76 [0.000] | 55.49 [0.001] |
| *Davidson – MacKinnon test* | — | 4.505 [0.037] | — | 5.660 [0.032] | — | 11.21 [0.012] |
| *Sargan test* | — | 0.386 [0.824] | — | 2.258 [0.323] | — | 5.334 [0.149] |

Note: number in the round bracket indicates t value of Heteroskedasticity robustness standard error; ***, ** and * respectively denote significance levels at 1%, 5% and 10%, and number in square bracket [ ] is p value.

On a nationwide basis, indigenous innovation (*Lrd*) does not have a significant effect on technological progress, which mainly relies on the imitation of foreign technologies through high-tech imports (*Lhh* * *Lim*). This suggests that technology upgrade and acquisitions remain the primary means of technological progress in China. However, in the test by regions we have identified great discrepancies in the positive effect of indigenous innovation on technological progress. In high-tech regions, indigenous innovation has a significantly positive effect on technological progress, whereas in low-tech regions indigenous innovation plays an insignificant role to technological progress but the imitation of foreign technologies (*Lhh* * *Lim*) contributes to technological progress in low-tech regions. This is consistent with the research conclusions of Vandenbussche *et al.* (2006) and Acemoglu *et al.* (2006), i. e. "in the initial stages of economic development with great technology gaps with high-tech countries, a country benefits from policy incentives to encourage technology imitation and acquisition". The reason for this is that greater technology gaps mean more opportunities for imitation and greater efficiency in such imitation compared with indigenous innovation, and more potential for technologically backward enterprises to learn from existing technologies and achieve technology catch-up (Glass and Saggi, 1998).

In short, this paper can reach a basic conclusion through empirical analysis: generally speaking, China's economic growth and technological progress mainly rely on productive investment and imitation of foreign technologies. However, in high-tech regions, indigenous innovation and R&D investments can significantly promote technological progress and economic growth; whereas in low-tech regions, technological progress and economic growth mainly derive from the imitation of foreign technologies and productive investment. This indicates that with the improvement of technology, economic growth drivers have a tendency to evolve from productive investment to R&D and from imitation to innovation.

## IV. Concluding Remarks and Suggestions

Using an extended R&D-based endogenous growth model, this paper depicts the technological progress of late-starting countries as deriving from two sources of indigenous innovation and foreign imitation and under the joint effect of material capital and human capital inputs. With a dynamic optimality approach, this paper has analyzed the optimal allocation of resources between productive investment and R&D investment and between indigenous innovation and foreign imitation, together with the impact of technology policies on technological progress. In the final analysis, this paper has identified the tendency that, under technology improvement, economic growth drivers of late-starting countries evolve from productive investment to R&D investment and from imitation to innovation; and encouragement of innovative investments regardless of unsophisticated factor structure and technology level will slow down economic convergence. Empirical analysis based on China's provincial-level panel data suggests that economic growth drivers have the tendency to shift from productive investment to R&D investment and from imitation to innovation. This conclusion has great policy implications for China's transformation of its economic growth pattern.

### (I) Productive and R&D investments should be balanced according to the level of technology gaps

It remains true that the transition towards innovation-driven growth through R&D investment is China's policy orientation. However, for China as a large late-starting country that has great gaps with international frontier technologies, there is still great potential for the acquisition and imitation of foreign technologies and capital intensification to derive further economic growth. Therefore, China should pay closer attention to the positive effect of productive investment towards China's economic growth. Meanwhile, China's capital stock is relatively limited and capital factor is insufficient. Considering such a factor structure, China should give sufficient consideration to the quantity and performance of R&D investment. In fact, capital-intensive R&D activities may not be consistent with the reality of China's factor endowment and technology level. Given China's current stage of economic development, a more realistic choice remains to increase conventional factor input and technology acquisition through productive investment. Over recent years, China has increased technology investments by multiple times, yet these investments failed to deliver satisfactory results and R&D

yield remains limited. This coincides with the theoretical expectation of this paper: under insufficient capital stock and a limited level of technology, it is premature for China to encourage innovative R&D investments on a massive nationwide scale. In the current stage, most Chinese enterprises are not innovative and the reason is that conventional factor input still plays a greater role in national economic growth. Technology acquisition, imitation, and low-cost competition are sufficient to ensure the survival of Chinese firms (Zhang Ping, Liu Xiahui, 2007). Given the current factor structure and technology level, vigorous encouragement of innovative R&D investment on a nationwide basis is inconsistent with China's comparative advantage and will divert production factors that may otherwise be more efficiently employed in productive activities to inefficient R&D activities, which will slow down economic convergence and cause substantial pressures on employment.

### (II) China should establish a dominant technological progress model in light of the level of technology gaps, and its technology policies should be constantly updated with the evolving patterns of technological progress.

First, it is undeniable that China has great gaps with technologically advanced countries in terms of technological capabilities and R&D resources, and that imitation of foreign technologies will remain a major source of China's technological progress in the long-term. Due to limited capabilities of the indigenous innovation of China's large and medium-sized industrial enterprises, technology upgrade and acquisition are still major sources of technological progress① (Jin Bei, 2004). This requires the creation of micro-level mechanisms to realize a late-starter advantage for Chinese companies to integrate into a global innovation network, and learn from the R&D experience of multinational firms through such methods as "reverse engineering". Meanwhile, uneven development of China's industries and regions requires differentiated approaches of technological progress. Technology policies, therefore, should accommodate these disparities between industries and regions. For high-tech industries and regions, incentives should be offered to promote human capital, indigenous innovation, and protection of intellectual property rights; for low-tech industries and regions, creative imitation through "reverse engineering" should be encouraged. Finally, China should develop a roadmap for the development stages from imitation to innovation. South Korea and Japan, for example, went through the three stages of acquisition, imitation, and innovation. Correspondingly, the focus of policy incentives constantly evolved from patent acquisition to utility model that encourages imitation, and then industrial design and strategies of innovation and promotion of intellectual property. To make the most of its limited R&D resources, China should draw on these evolving policy priorities to keep abreast of the changes of frontier technology.

### (III) For a large late-starting country with uneven regional economic development, China should differentiate its economic development strategies for various regions.

China remains a late-starting country, and its central and western regions are still underdevel-

① The Ministry of Science and Technology: *Research Report on China's Scientific and Technological Capabilities*, November 2007.

oped and in the stage of extensive growth that relies on additional factor input as a driver of economic growth. Less developed regions of China should take advantage of efficient productive investments and late-starting advantage, and apply appropriate technologies and creative imitation. On the other hand, China's prosperous coastal regions have experienced a significant marginal diminishing return on factors, and sustained economic growth increasingly relies on technological progress. With superior R&D resources and advanced technologies, the coastal regions in the east should adopt an innovation-oriented catch-up strategy. In light of regional advantages, the limited resources should be properly allocated for transformation of the economic growth pattern through differentiated approaches across specific industries and regions.

## References

1. Acemoglu, D., Aghion, P, and Zilibotti, F. 2006. "Distance to Frontier, Selection, and Economic Growth." *Journal of the European Economic Association*, 4 (1): 37 – 74.

2. Barro R, and Sala-i-Martin X. 1997. "Technological Diffusion, Convergence, and Growth." *Journal of Economic Growth*, 2: 1 – 27.

3. Coe, D. T and Helpman, E. 1995. "International R&D Spillover." *European Economic Review*, 39 (5): 859 – 887.

4. Currie, David, Paul L. Levine, Joseph Pearlman, and Michael Chui. 1999. "Phases of Imitation and Innovation in a North-South Endogenous Growth Model." *Oxford Economic Papers*, 51: 60 – 88.

5. Chen, Yongmin, and Thitima Puttitanun. 2005. "Intellectual Property Rights and Innovation in Developing Countries." *Journal of Development Economics*, 78: 474 – 493.

6. Fagerberg, Jan. 1987. "A Technology Gap Approach to Why Growth Rates Differ." *Research Policy*, 16 (2 – 4): 87 – 99.

7. Fagerberg, Jan. 1994. "Technology and International Differences in Growth Rates." *Journal of Economic Literature*, 32: 1147 – 1175.

8. Perez-Sebastian, Fidel. 2000. "Transitional Dynamics in an R&D-based Growth Model with Imitation: Comparing its Predictions to the Data." *Journal of Monetary Economics*, 45: 437 – 461.

9. Grossman, Geme M., and Helpman, Elhanam. 1990. "Comparative Advantage and Long-run Growth." *American Economic Review*, 80: 796 – 815.

10. Helpman, Elhanan and Hoffmaister, Alexander W. 1997. "North-South R&D spillover." *The Economic Journal*, 1107: 134 – 149.

11. Ji, Yahui, and Fengwen Zhu. 2011. "Technology Gap, National Separation of Learning by Doing and the Technical Progress in Developing Countries." *The Journal of Quantitative & Technical Economics*, 4: 49 – 63.

12. Jin, Bei. 2004. "Technology innovation in China's Industry." *China Industrial Economy*, 5 (194): 5 – 14.

13. Keller, W. 2004. "International Technology Diffusion." *Journal of Economic Literature*,

42: 752 – 782.

14. Kim, Linsu. 1997. *Imitation to Innovation: The Dynamics of Korea's Technological Learning*. Boston, Massachusetts: Harvard Business School Press, 13 – 14.

15. Ouyang, Yao. 2011. *The Comprehensive Advantages of Big Country*. Shanghai: Shanghai Sanlian Press.

16. Romer, P. 1990. "Endogenous Technological Change." *Journal of Political Economy*, 98 (1): S71 – S102.

17. Rachel, van Elkan. 1996. "Catching Up and Slowing Down: Learning and Growth Patterns in an Open Economy." *Journal of International Economics*, 3 (41): 95 – 11.

18. Vandenbussche, Aghion, and Meghir Costas. 2006. "Growth, Distance to Frontier and Composition of Human Capital." *Journal of Economic Growth*, 11: 97 – 127.

19. Yang, G., and Maskus, K. E. 2001. "Intellectual Property Rights, Licensing, and Innovation in an Endogenous Product Cycle Model." *Journal of International Economics*, 53: 169 – 187.

20. Yi, Xianzhong, and Yabin Zhang. 2008. "Technology Progress Models under Constraint of Technology Gap and Human Capital." *Journal of Management Science in China*, 11 (6): 51 – 59.

21. Zhang, Jingan. 2003. "Strategic Thinking on Transit from Technology Import to Independent Innovation." *China Soft Science*. 11: 1 – 5.

22. Zhang, Yabin, Zheng Zen, and Kaijun Chen. 2006. "The Trade-off between R&D Investment and Production Investment." *Journal of World Economy*, 6: 34 – 46.

23. Zhang, Pin, and Xiahui Liu. 2007. *Frontier Theories of China Economic Growth*. Beijing: Chinese Social Science Press.

This book is the result of a co-publication agreement between Economic Science Press (China) and Paths International Ltd (UK).

---------------------------------------------------

**Title: China's Economy Amid New Challenges: Exploration of Chinese Economists**

**Editors in Chief: Prof. Jin Bei, Prof. Li Gang**

**ISBN: 978-1-84464-472-8**
**Ebook ISBN: 978-1-84464-473-5**



**Paths International Ltd**

**Published in the United Kingdom**
**www.pathsinternational.com**

CPSIA information can be obtained at www.ICGtesting.com
Printed in the USA
LVOW09*0815220916

505571LV00012B/33/P

9 781844 644728